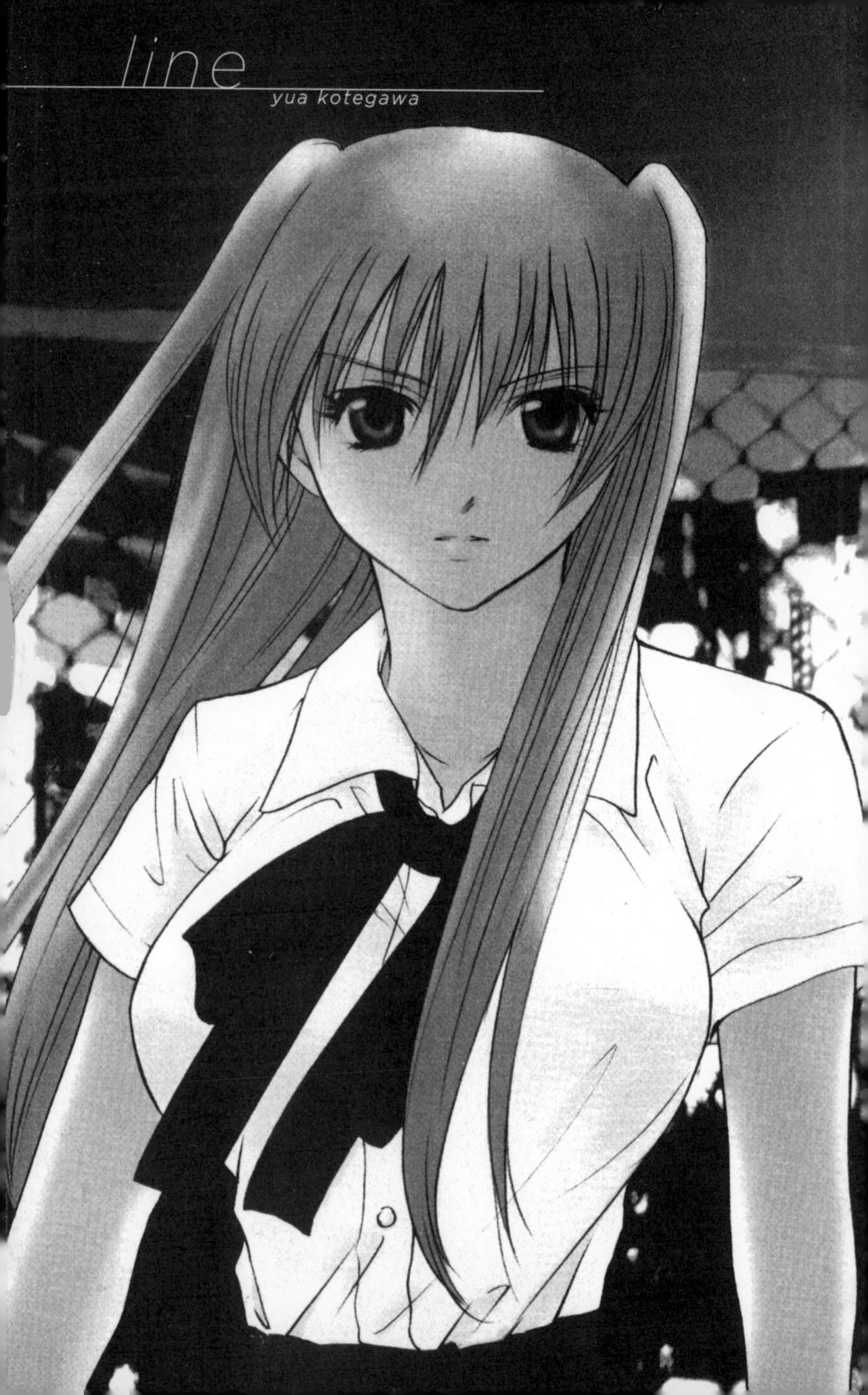
line
yua kotegawa

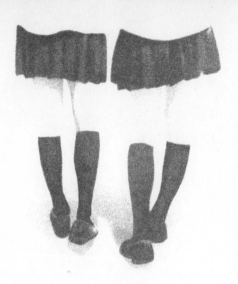

C O N T E N T S

First Quarter Line   001

Second Quarter Line   051

Third Quarter Line   087

Final Quarter Line   123

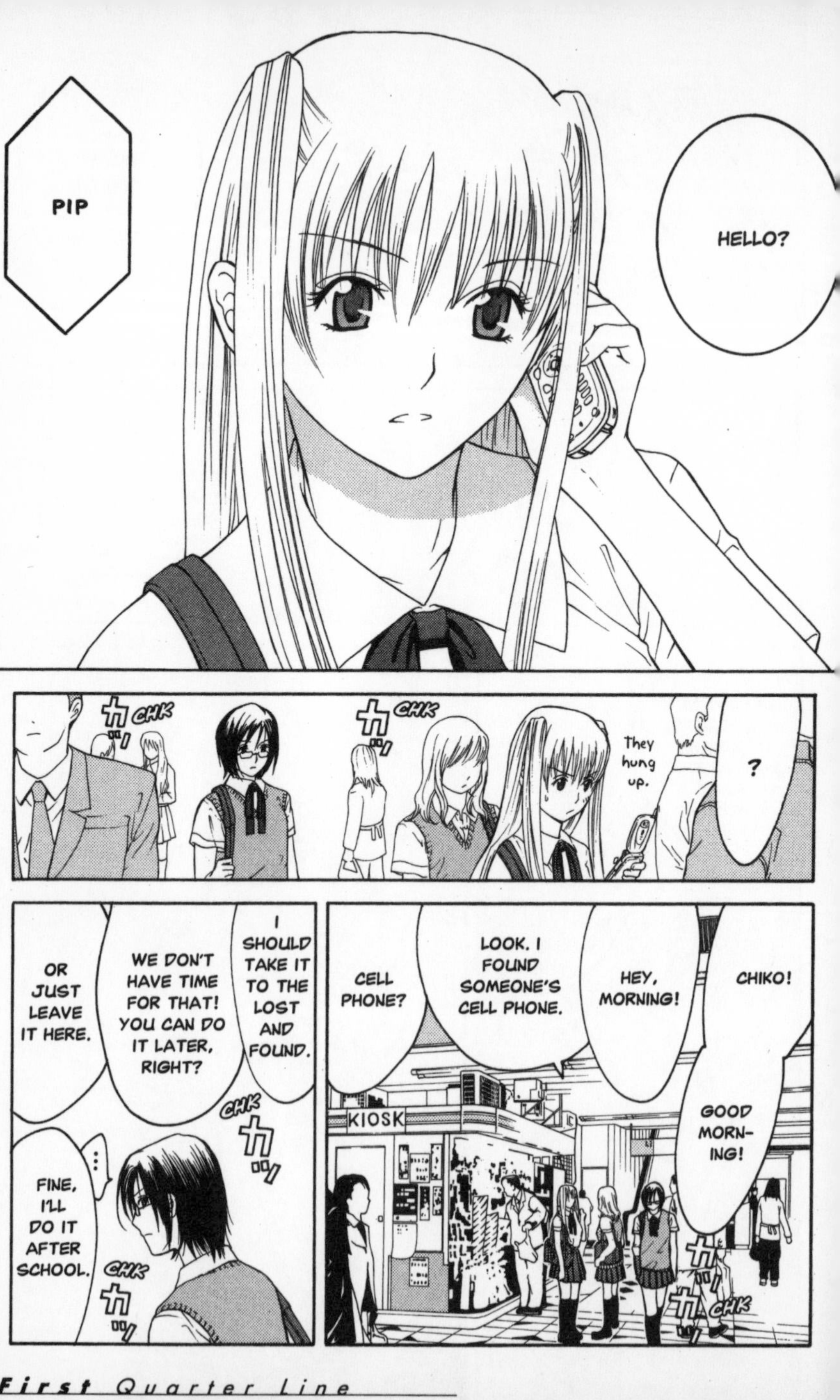
HELLO?
PIP
?
They hung up.
CHK
CHK
CHIKO!
HEY, MORNING!
LOOK. I FOUND SOMEONE'S CELL PHONE.
CELL PHONE?
GOOD MORN-ING!
KIOSK
CHK
I SHOULD TAKE IT TO THE LOST AND FOUND.
WE DON'T HAVE TIME FOR THAT! YOU CAN DO IT LATER, RIGHT?
OR JUST LEAVE IT HERE.
CHK
...
FINE, I'LL DO IT AFTER SCHOOL.
CHK

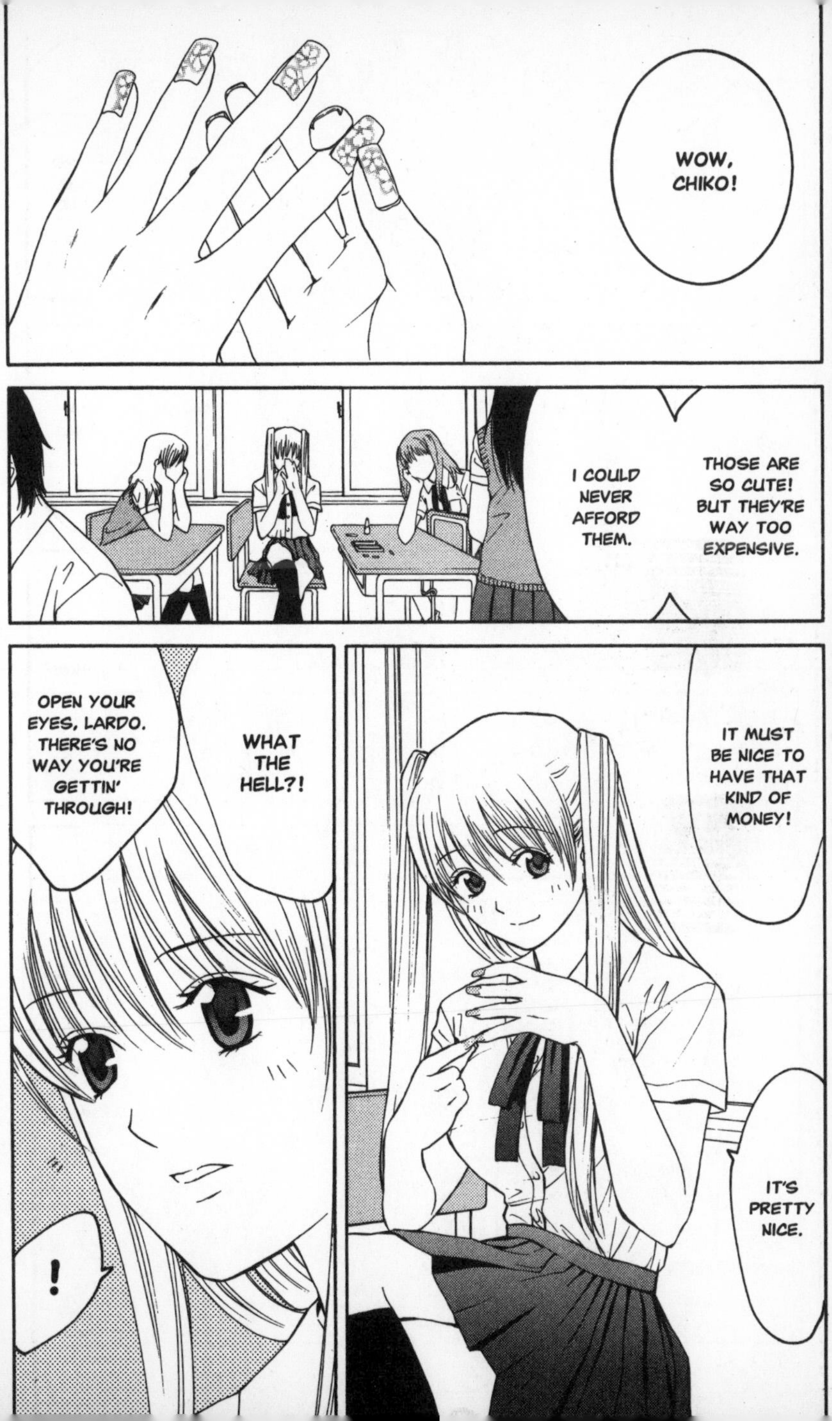
WOW, CHIKO!
THOSE ARE SO CUTE! BUT THEY'RE WAY TOO EXPENSIVE.
I COULD NEVER AFFORD THEM.
IT MUST BE NICE TO HAVE THAT KIND OF MONEY!
IT'S PRETTY NICE.
WHAT THE HELL?!
OPEN YOUR EYES, LARDO. THERE'S NO WAY YOU'RE GETTIN' THROUGH!
!

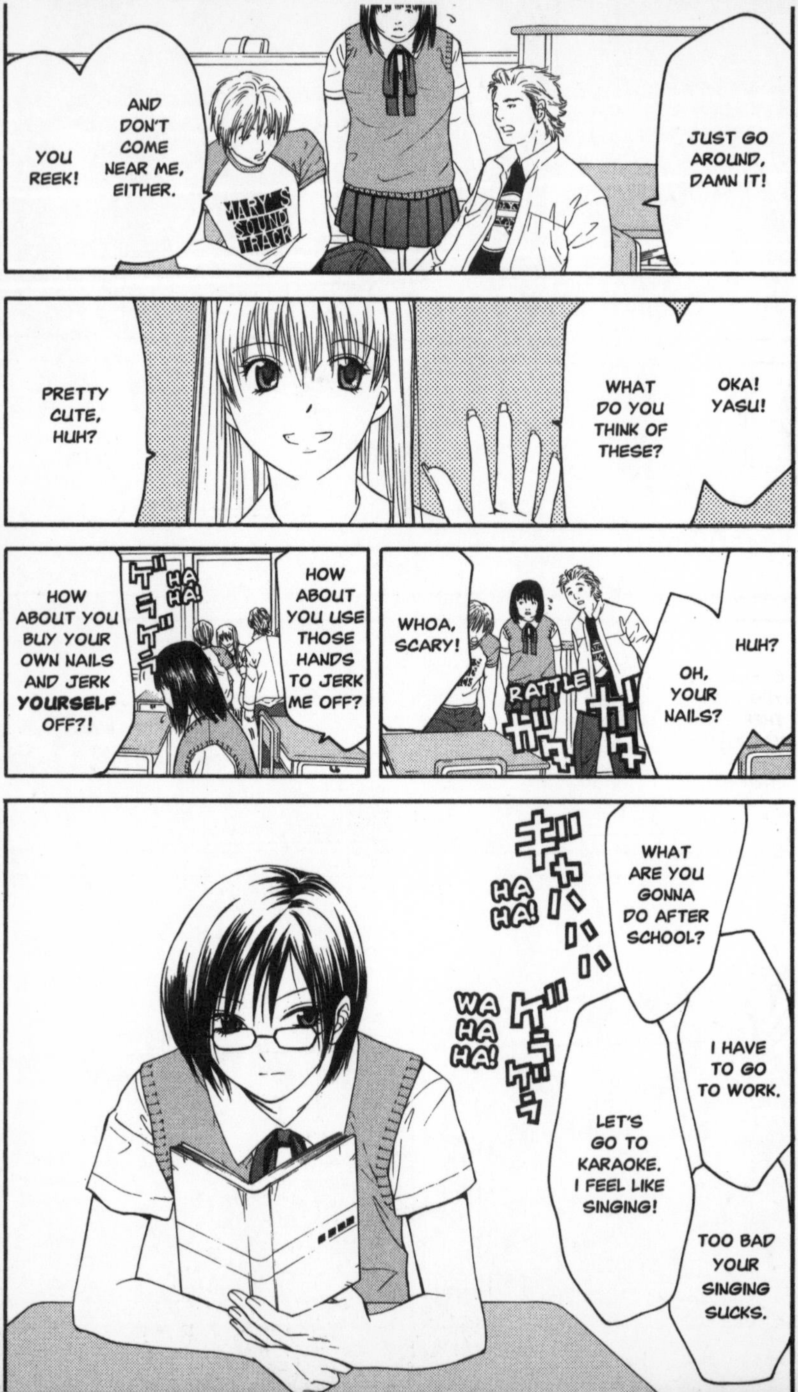
JUST GO AROUND, DAMN IT!
AND DON'T COME NEAR ME, EITHER.
YOU REEK!
OKA! YASU!
WHAT DO YOU THINK OF THESE?
PRETTY CUTE, HUH?
HUH?
OH, YOUR NAILS?
RATTLE
WHOA, SCARY!
HOW ABOUT YOU USE THOSE HANDS TO JERK ME OFF?
HA HA!
HOW ABOUT YOU BUY YOUR OWN NAILS AND JERK **YOURSELF** OFF?!
WHAT ARE YOU GONNA DO AFTER SCHOOL?
HA HA!
I HAVE TO GO TO WORK.
WA HA HA!
LET'S GO TO KARAOKE. I FEEL LIKE SINGING!
TOO BAD YOUR SINGING SUCKS.

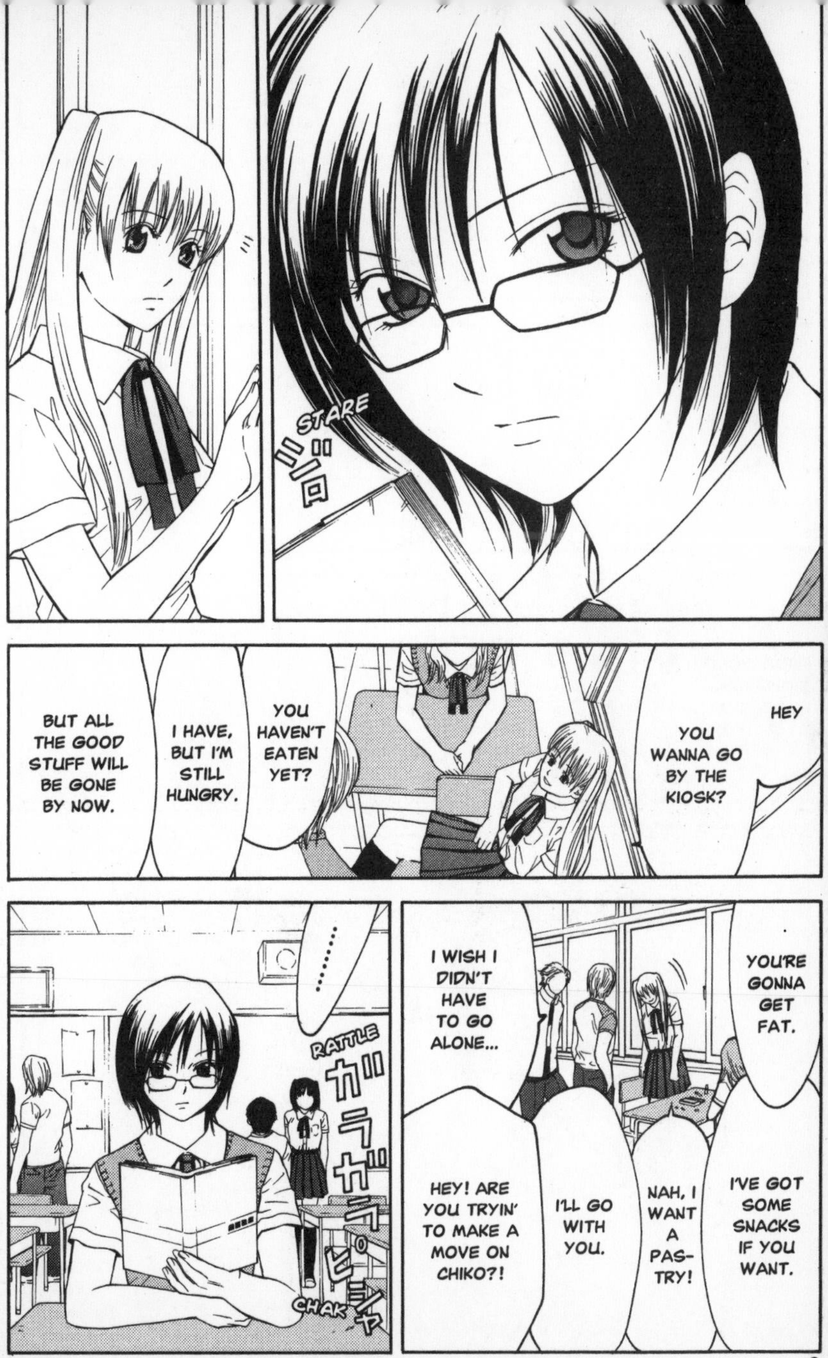
STARE
ジロ
HEY
YOU WANNA GO BY THE KIOSK?
YOU HAVEN'T EATEN YET?
I HAVE, BUT I'M STILL HUNGRY.
BUT ALL THE GOOD STUFF WILL BE GONE BY NOW.
YOU'RE GONNA GET FAT.
I WISH I DIDN'T HAVE TO GO ALONE...
I'VE GOT SOME SNACKS IF YOU WANT.
NAH, I WANT A PASTRY!
I'LL GO WITH YOU.
HEY! ARE YOU TRYIN' TO MAKE A MOVE ON CHIKO?!
......
RATTLE
カラガラ
CHAK
ピシャ

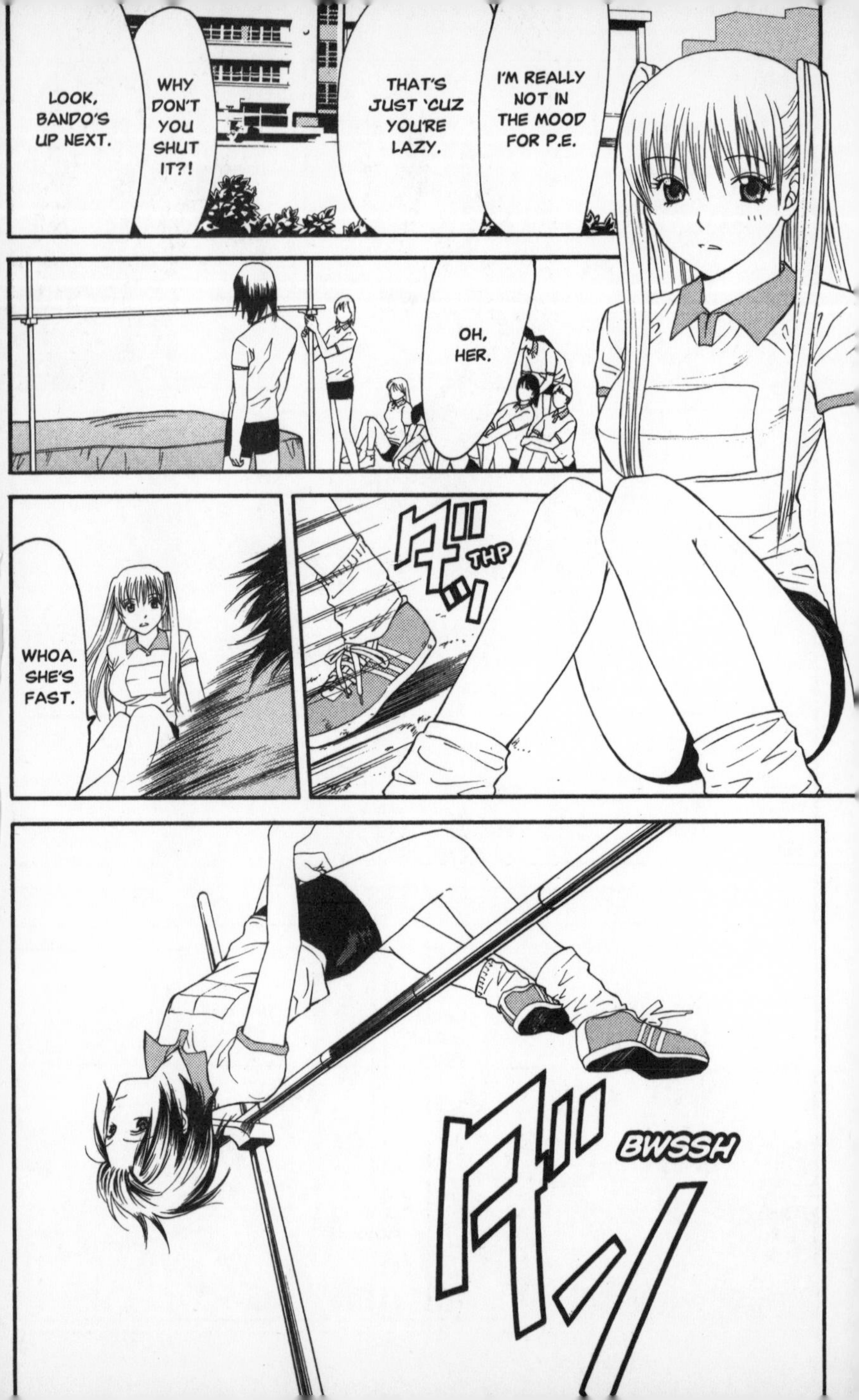
I'M REALLY NOT IN THE MOOD FOR P.E.
THAT'S JUST 'CUZ YOU'RE LAZY.
WHY DON'T YOU SHUT IT?!
LOOK, BANDO'S UP NEXT.
OH, HER.
THP
WHOA. SHE'S FAST.
BWSSH

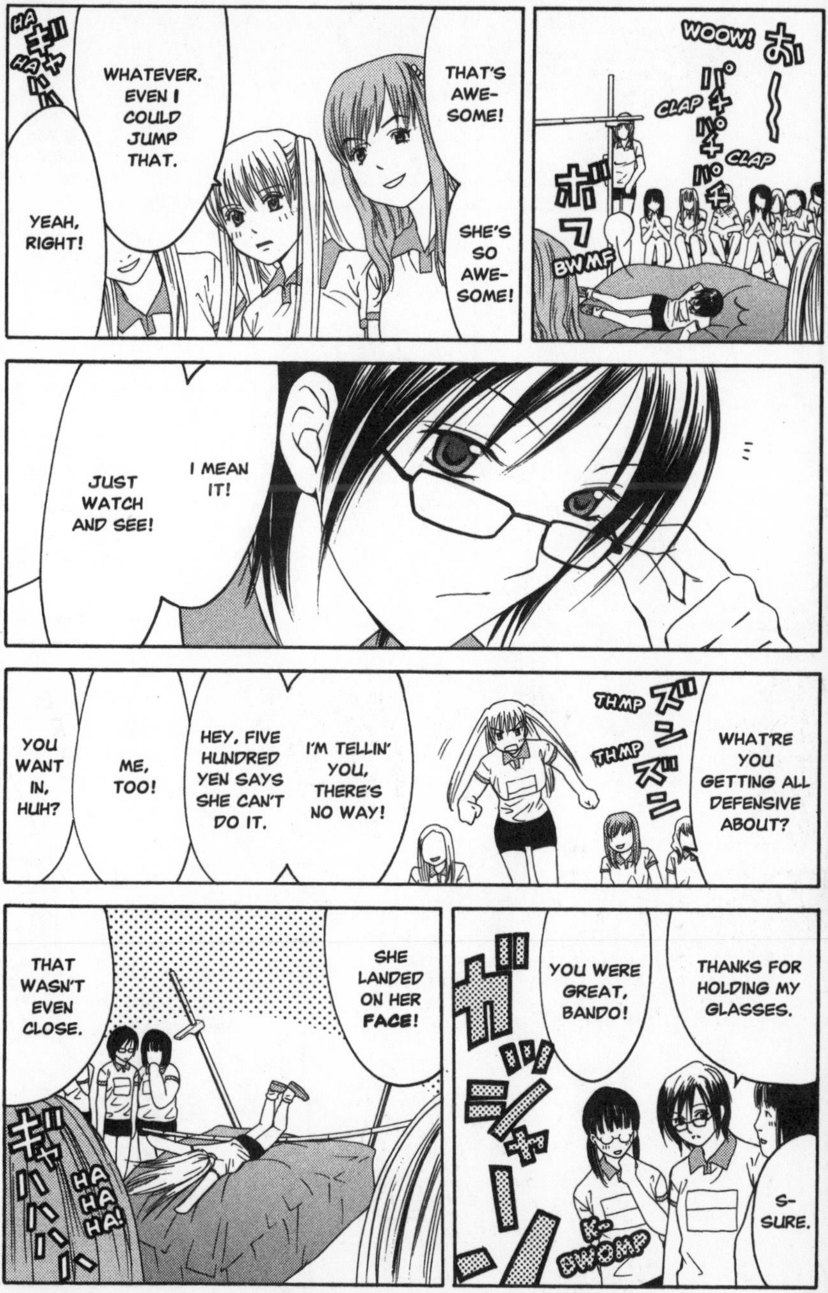
WOOW! おー
CLAP パチパチ CLAP
ボフ BWMF
THAT'S AWE-SOME!
SHE'S SO AWE-SOME!
WHATEVER. EVEN I COULD JUMP THAT.
YEAH, RIGHT!
HA HA ギャハハ
I MEAN IT!
JUST WATCH AND SEE!
WHAT'RE YOU GETTING ALL DEFENSIVE ABOUT?
THMP THMP ズンズン
I'M TELLIN' YOU, THERE'S NO WAY!
HEY, FIVE HUNDRED YEN SAYS SHE CAN'T DO IT.
ME, TOO!
YOU WANT IN, HUH?
THANKS FOR HOLDING MY GLASSES.
YOU WERE GREAT, BANDO!
S-SURE.
K-BWOMP
SHE LANDED ON HER FACE!
THAT WASN'T EVEN CLOSE.
HA HA HA! ギャハハハ

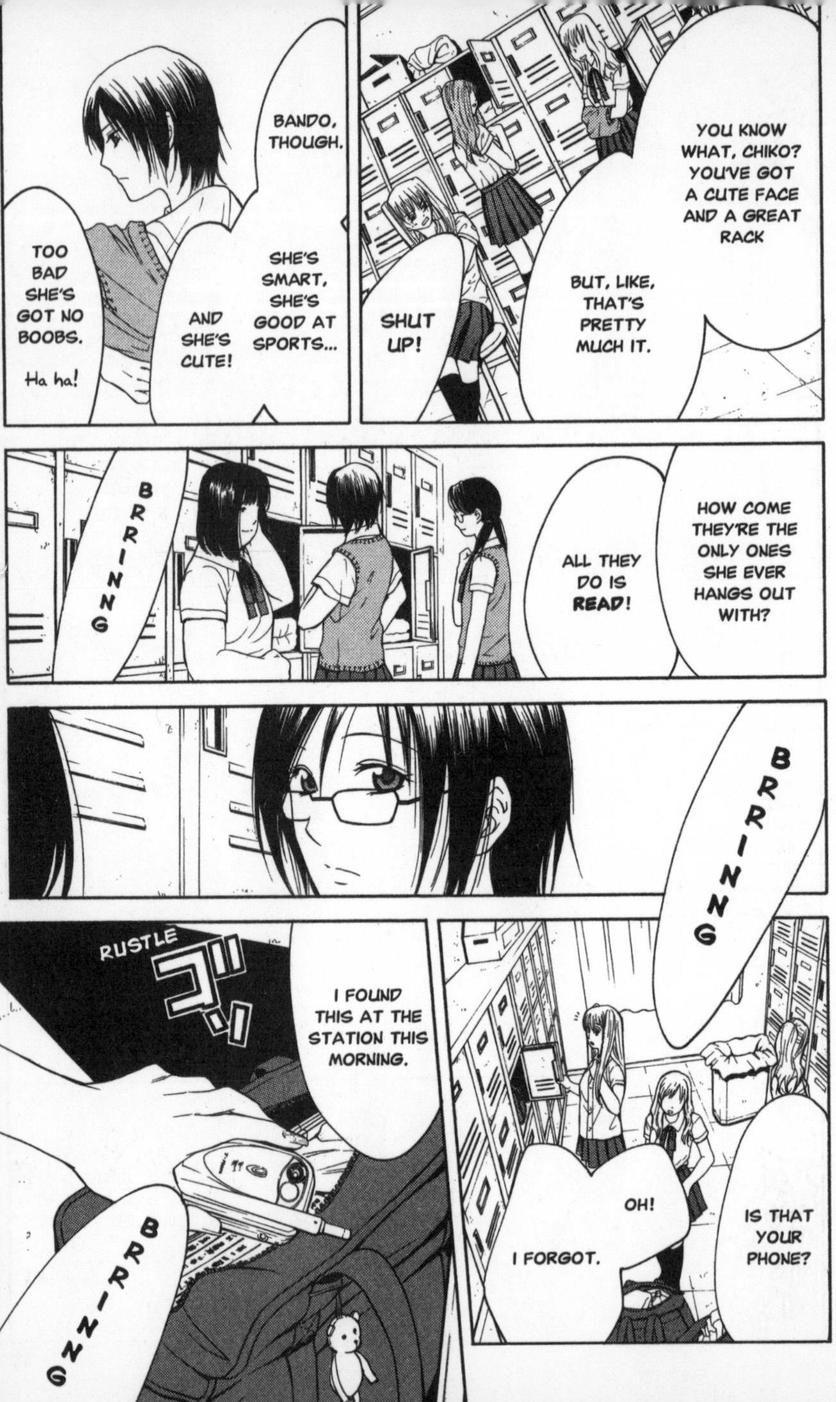
YOU KNOW WHAT, CHIKO? YOU'VE GOT A CUTE FACE AND A GREAT RACK
BUT, LIKE, THAT'S PRETTY MUCH IT.
SHUT UP!
BANDO, THOUGH.
SHE'S SMART, SHE'S GOOD AT SPORTS...
AND SHE'S CUTE!
TOO BAD SHE'S GOT NO BOOBS.
Ha ha!
HOW COME THEY'RE THE ONLY ONES SHE EVER HANGS OUT WITH?
ALL THEY DO IS **READ**!
BRRINNG
BRRINNG
IS THAT YOUR PHONE?
OH!
I FORGOT.
I FOUND THIS AT THE STATION THIS MORNING.
RUSTLE
BRRINNG

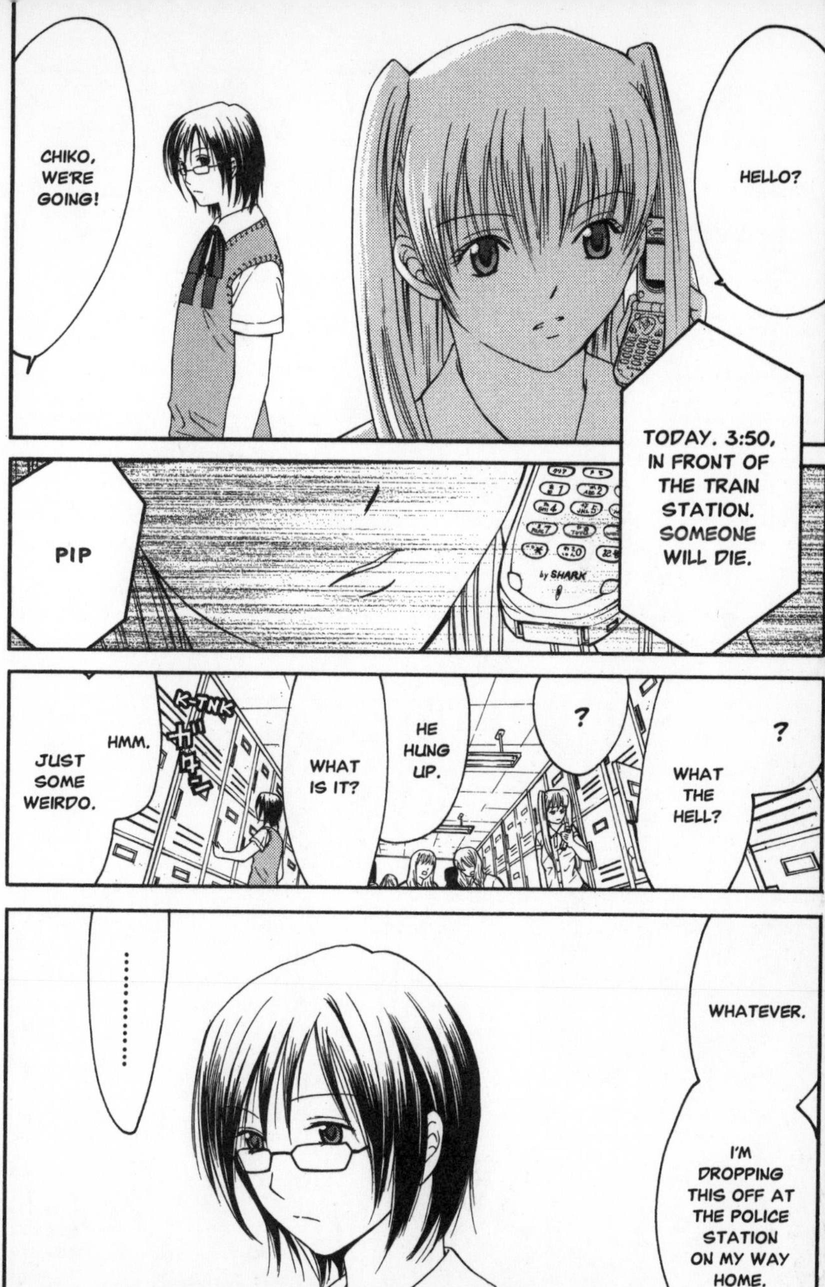
HELLO?
TODAY. 3:50, IN FRONT OF THE TRAIN STATION. SOMEONE WILL DIE.
CHIKO, WE'RE GOING!
PIP
?
WHAT THE HELL?
?
HE HUNG UP.
WHAT IS IT?
K-TNK
HMM.
JUST SOME WEIRDO.
WHATEVER.
I'M DROPPING THIS OFF AT THE POLICE STATION ON MY WAY HOME.
....

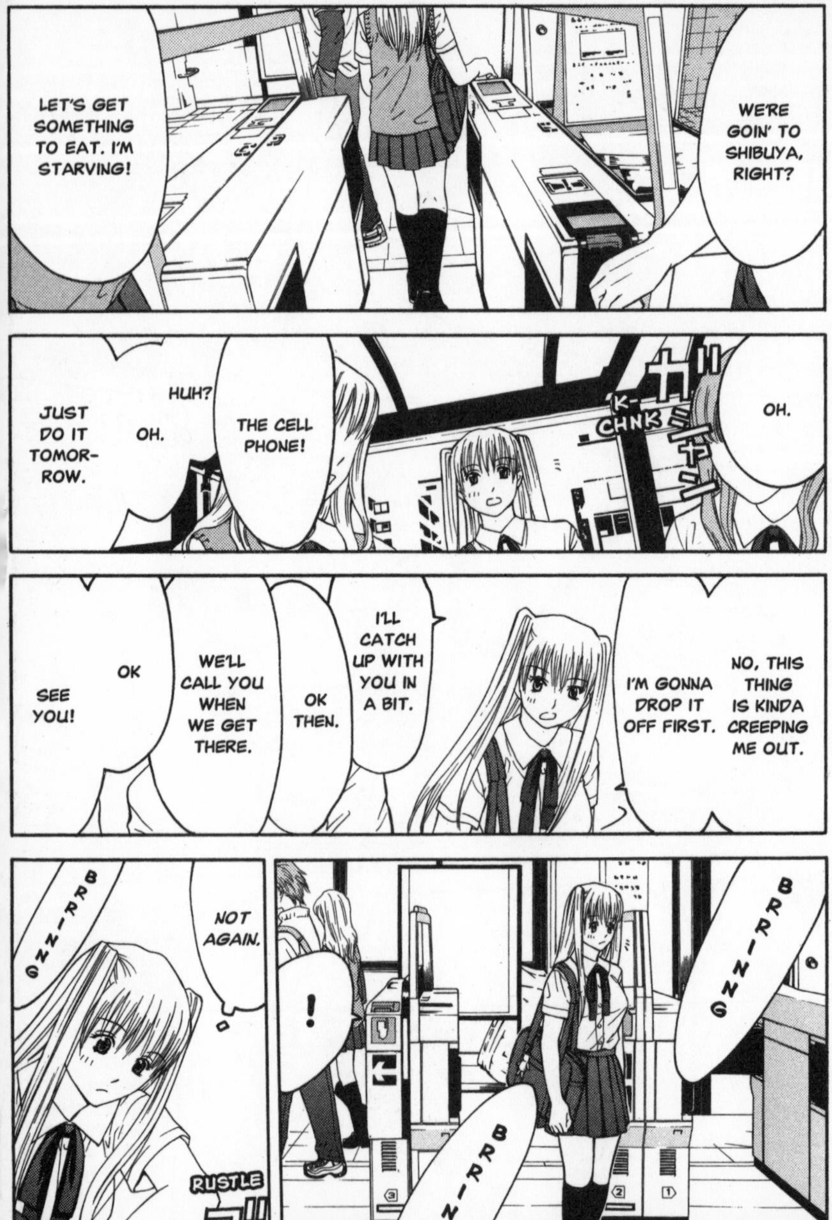
WE'RE GOIN' TO SHIBUYA, RIGHT?
LET'S GET SOMETHING TO EAT. I'M STARVING!
OH.
K-CHNK
THE CELL PHONE!
HUH?
OH.
JUST DO IT TOMORROW.
NO, THIS THING IS KINDA CREEPING ME OUT.
I'M GONNA DROP IT OFF FIRST.
I'LL CATCH UP WITH YOU IN A BIT.
OK THEN.
WE'LL CALL YOU WHEN WE GET THERE.
OK
SEE YOU!
BRRRINNNG
BRRRINNNG
!
NOT AGAIN.
BRRRINNNG
RUSTLE

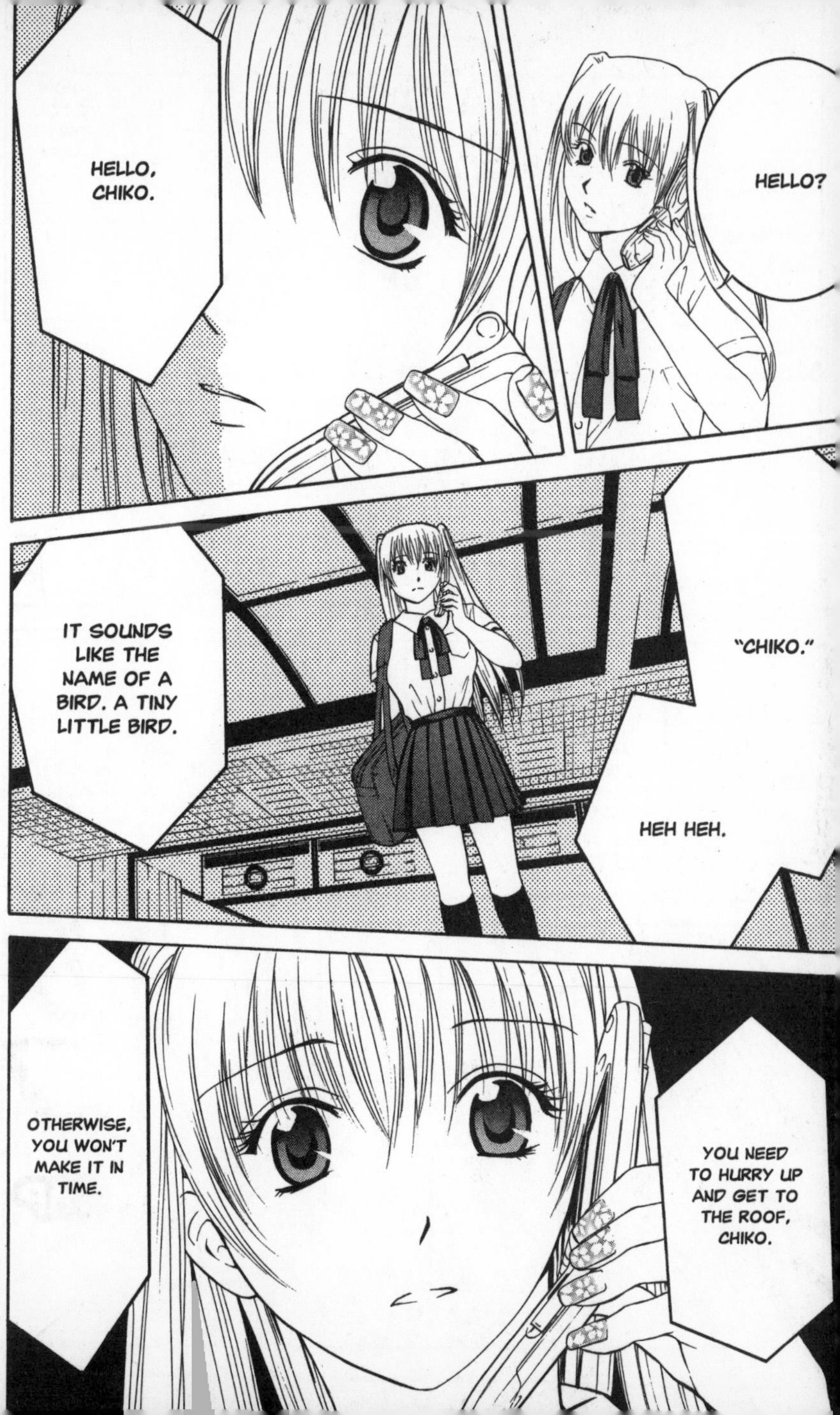
HELLO?
HELLO, CHIKO.
"CHIKO."
HEH HEH.
IT SOUNDS LIKE THE NAME OF A BIRD. A TINY LITTLE BIRD.
YOU NEED TO HURRY UP AND GET TO THE ROOF, CHIKO.
OTHERWISE, YOU WON'T MAKE IT IN TIME.

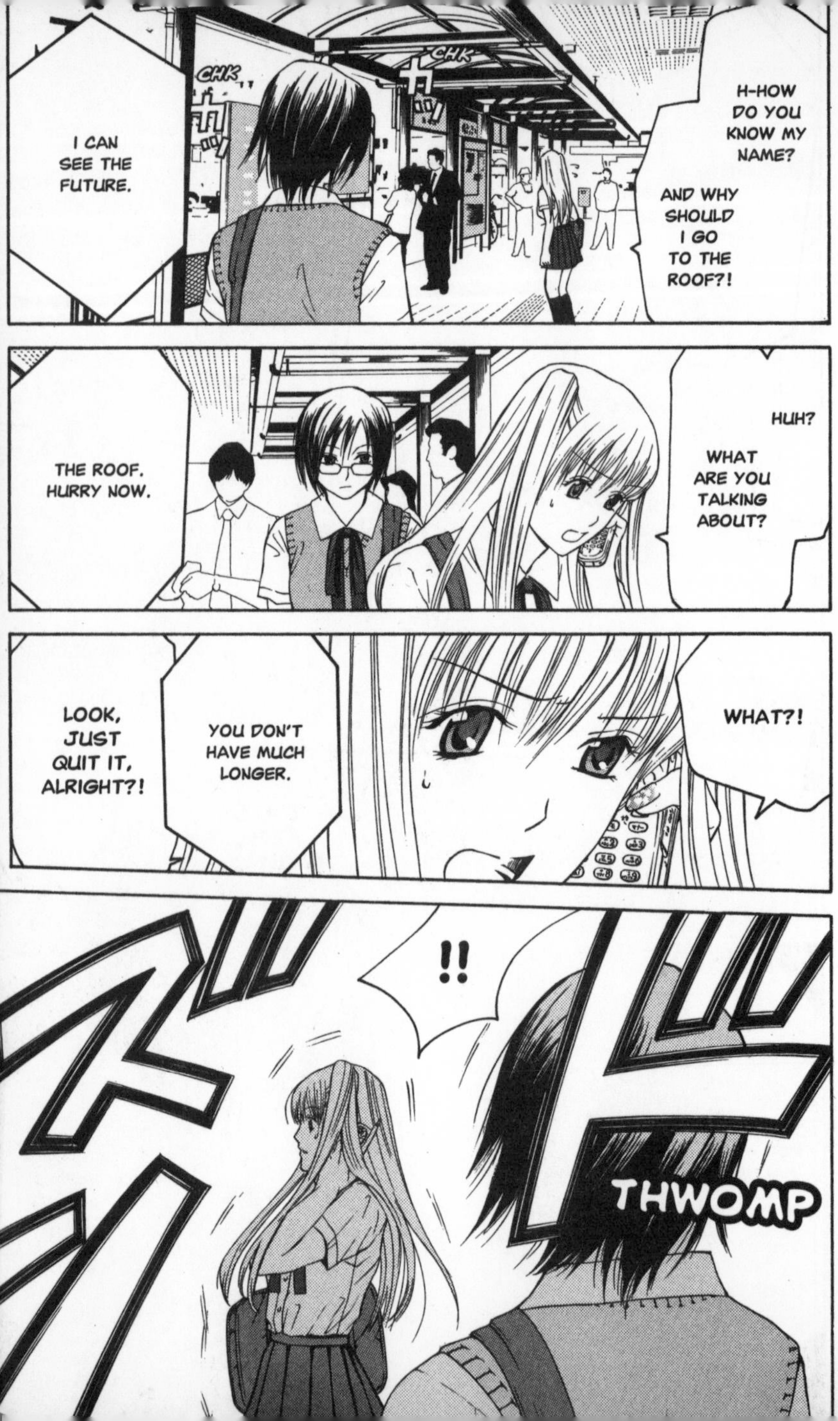
CHK
CHK
H-HOW DO YOU KNOW MY NAME?
AND WHY SHOULD I GO TO THE ROOF?!
I CAN SEE THE FUTURE.
HUH?
WHAT ARE YOU TALKING ABOUT?
THE ROOF. HURRY NOW.
WHAT?!
YOU DON'T HAVE MUCH LONGER.
LOOK, JUST QUIT IT, ALRIGHT?!
!!
THWOMP

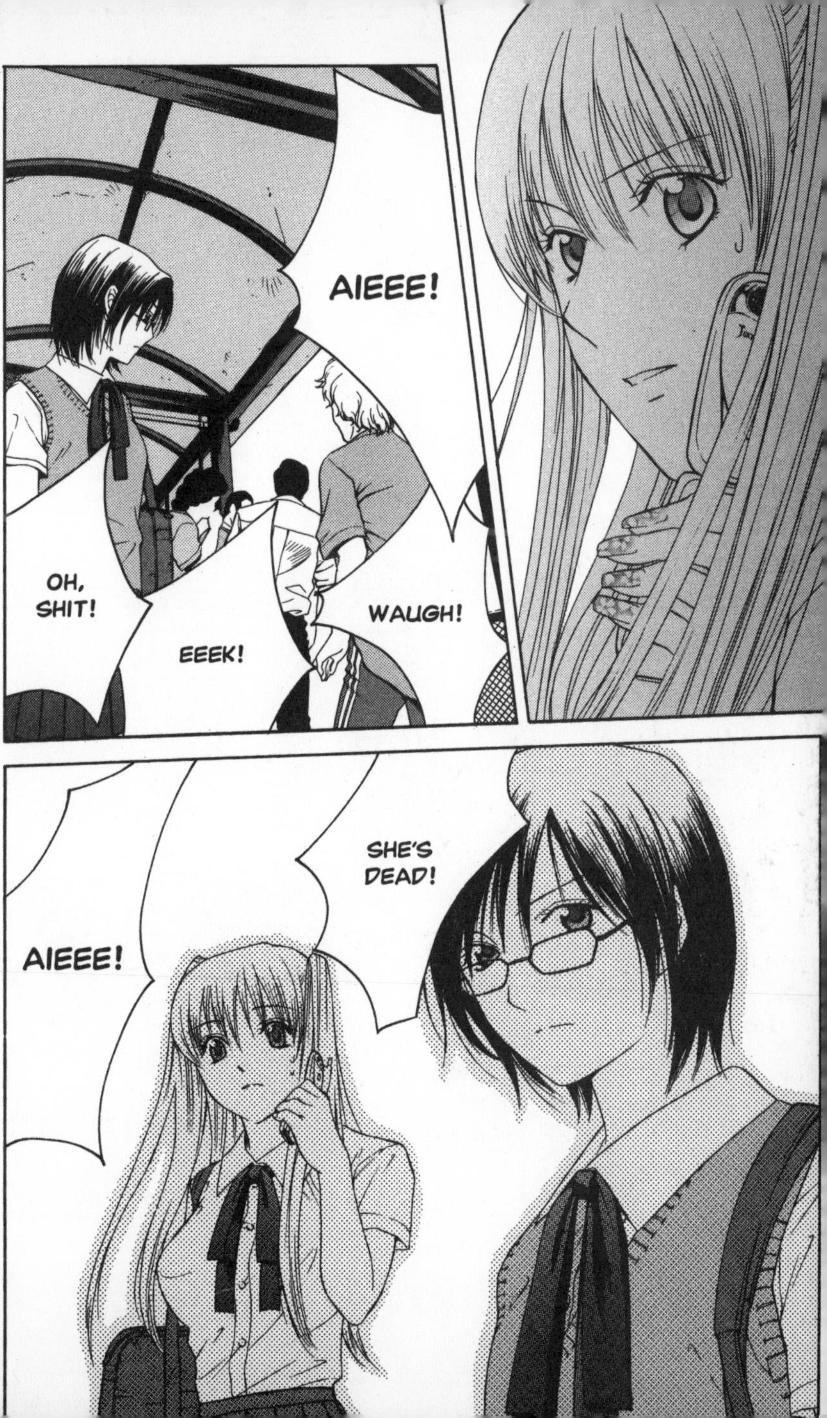
AIEEE!
WAUGH!
EEEK!
OH, SHIT!
SHE'S DEAD!
AIEEE!

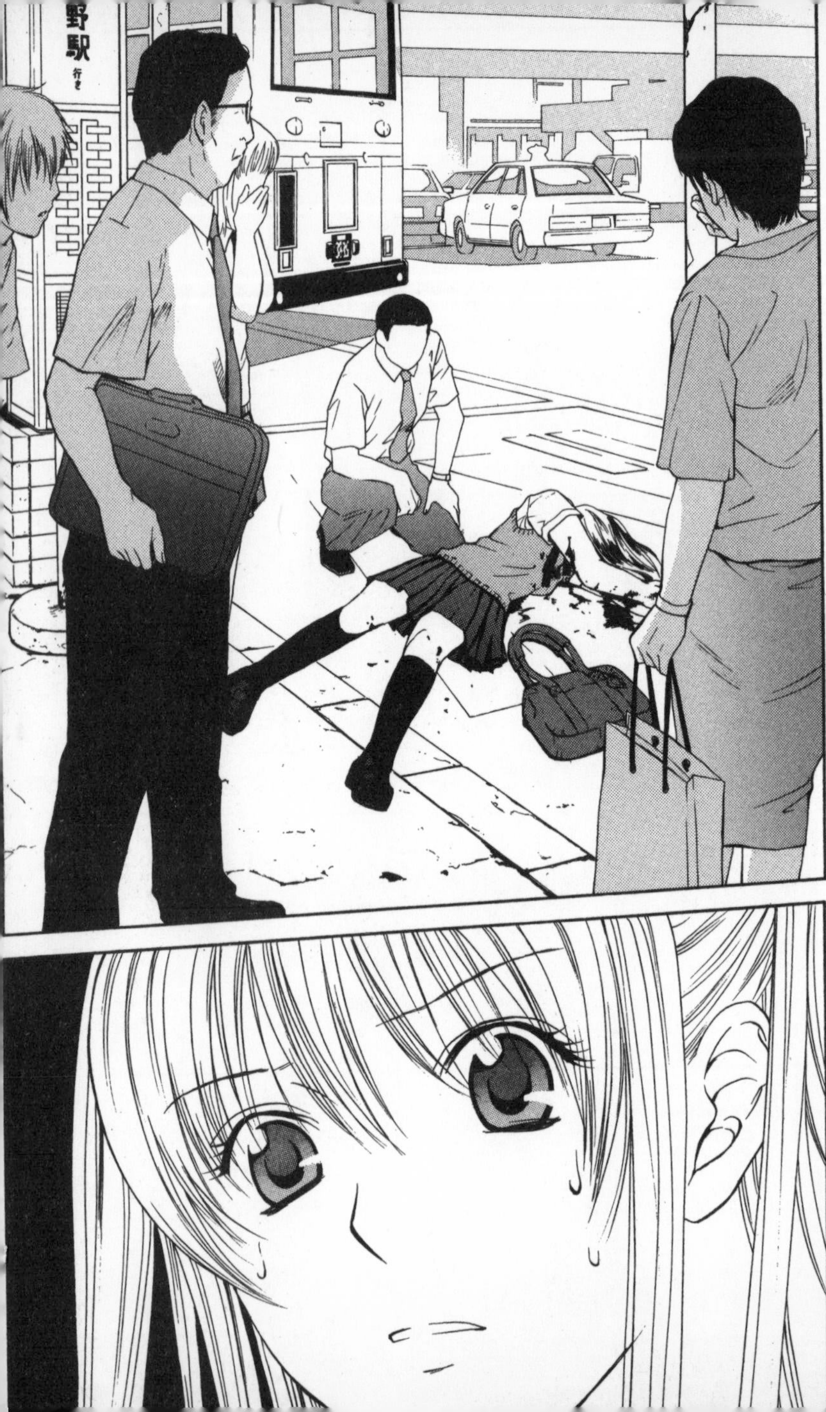
野駅
行き

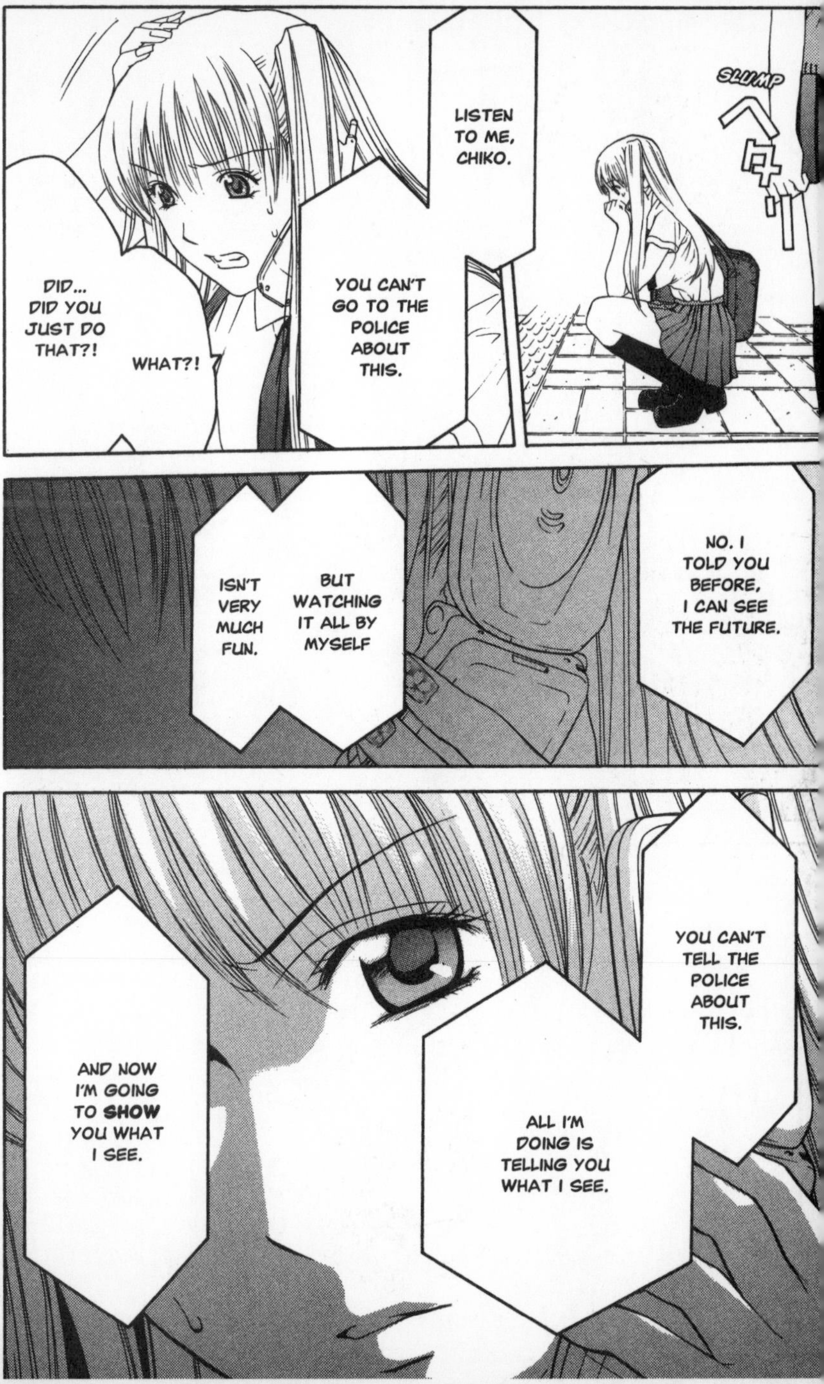
SLUMP
LISTEN TO ME, CHIKO.
YOU CAN'T GO TO THE POLICE ABOUT THIS.
WHAT?!
DID... DID YOU JUST DO THAT?!
NO. I TOLD YOU BEFORE, I CAN SEE THE FUTURE.
BUT WATCHING IT ALL BY MYSELF
ISN'T VERY MUCH FUN.
YOU CAN'T TELL THE POLICE ABOUT THIS.
ALL I'M DOING IS TELLING YOU WHAT I SEE.
AND NOW I'M GOING TO **SHOW** YOU WHAT I SEE.

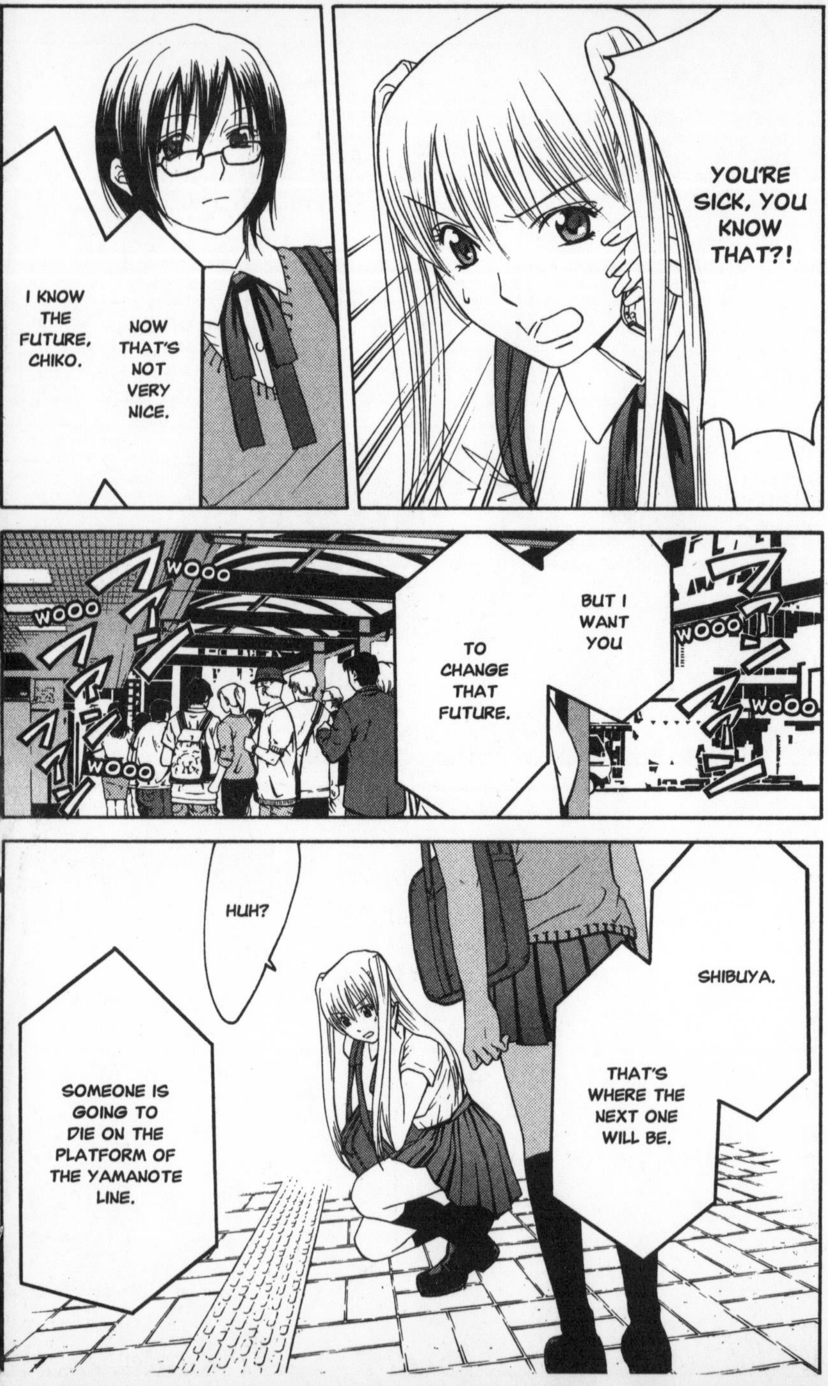

YOU'RE SICK, YOU KNOW THAT?!
NOW THAT'S NOT VERY NICE.
I KNOW THE FUTURE, CHIKO.
WOOO
WOOO
BUT I WANT YOU
TO CHANGE THAT FUTURE.
WOOO
WOOO
WOOO
SHIBUYA.
THAT'S WHERE THE NEXT ONE WILL BE.
HUH?
SOMEONE IS GOING TO DIE ON THE PLATFORM OF THE YAMANOTE LINE.

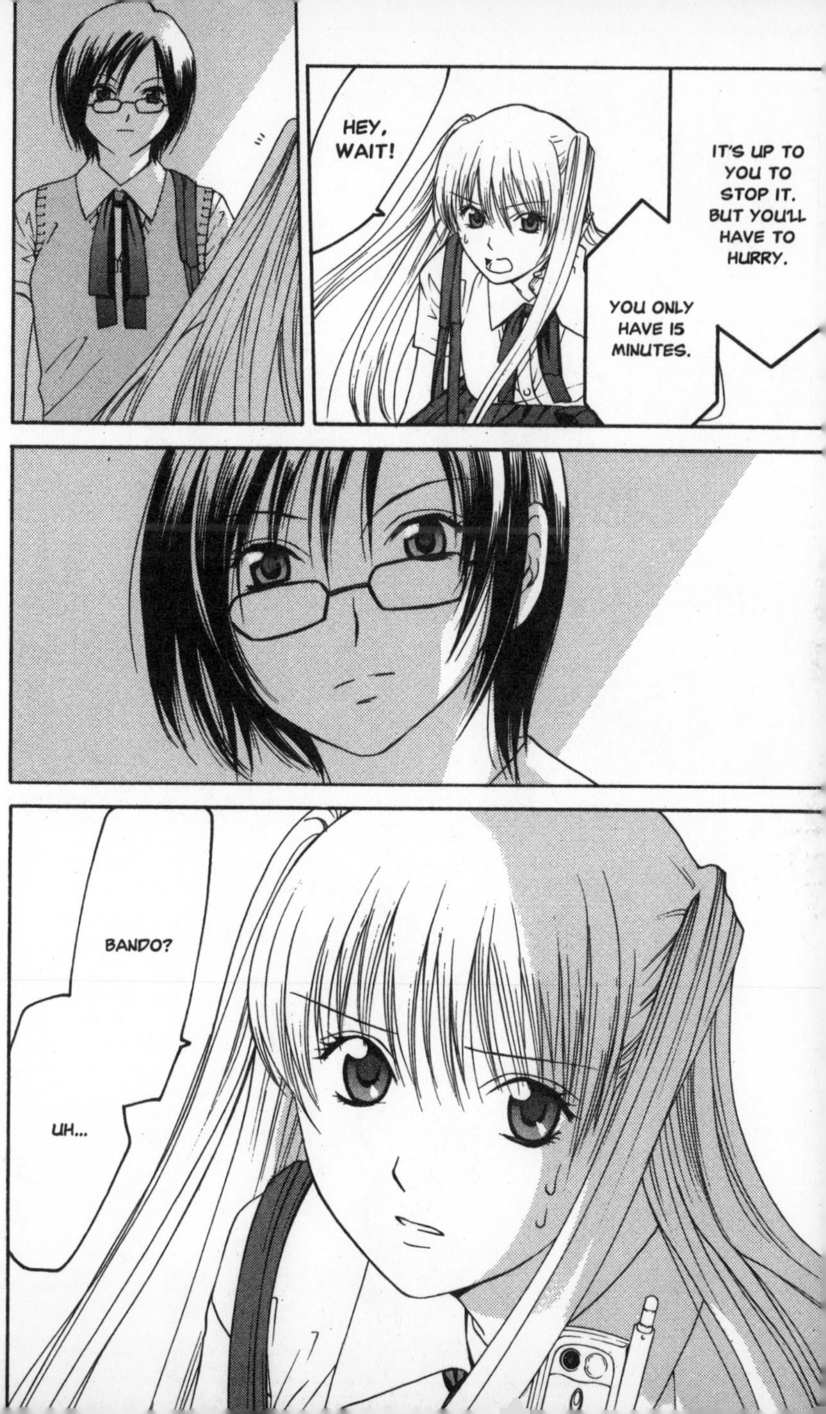
IT'S UP TO YOU TO STOP IT. BUT YOU'LL HAVE TO HURRY.
YOU ONLY HAVE 15 MINUTES.
HEY, WAIT!
BANDO?
UH...

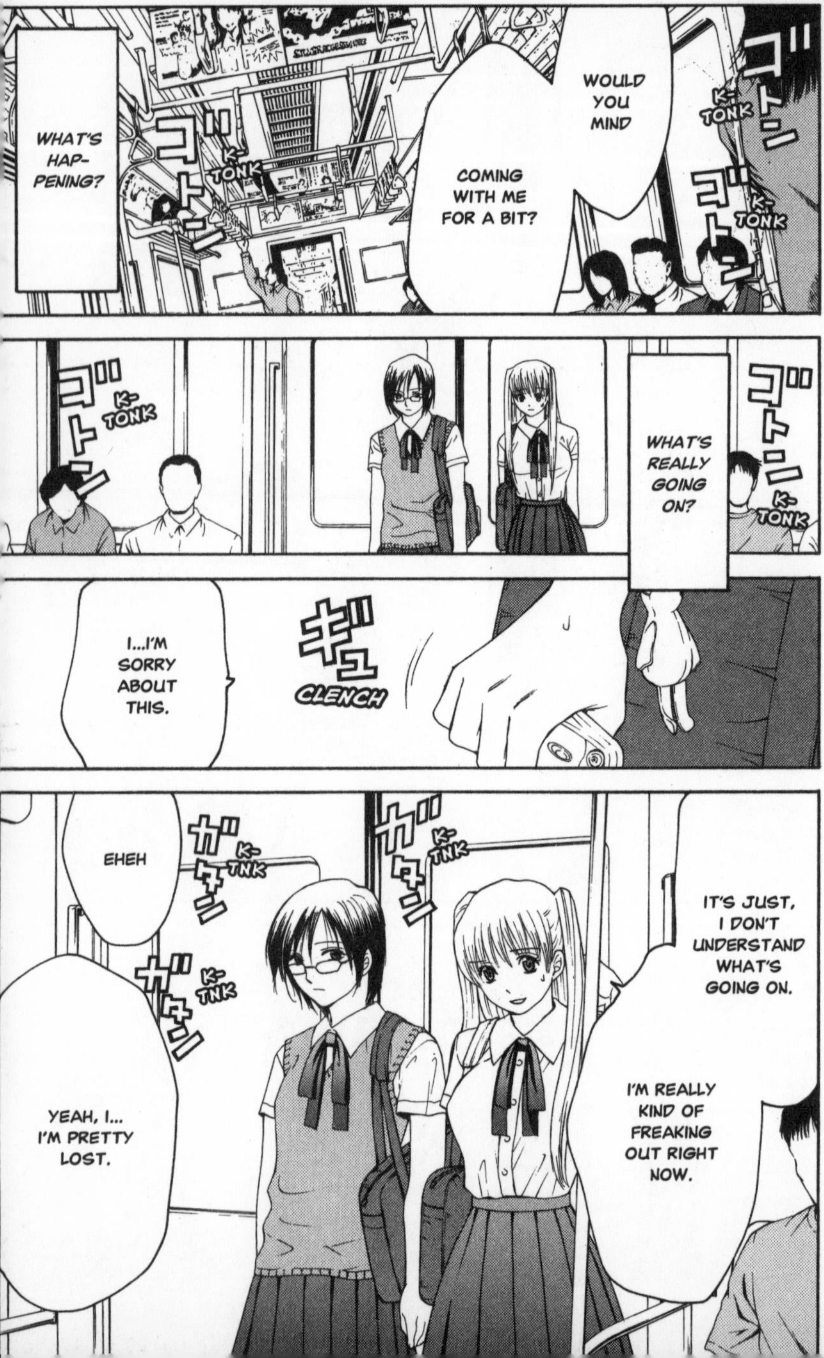
ゴトン
K-TONK
ゴトン
K-TONK
WOULD YOU MIND
COMING WITH ME FOR A BIT?
ゴトン
K-TONK
WHAT'S HAP-PENING?
ゴトン
K-TONK
WHAT'S REALLY GOING ON?
ゴトン
K-TONK
ギュ
CLENCH
I...I'M SORRY ABOUT THIS.
IT'S JUST, I DON'T UNDERSTAND WHAT'S GOING ON.
I'M REALLY KIND OF FREAKING OUT RIGHT NOW.
ガタン
K-TNK
ガタン
K-TNK
EHEH
ガタン
K-TNK
YEAH, I... I'M PRETTY LOST.

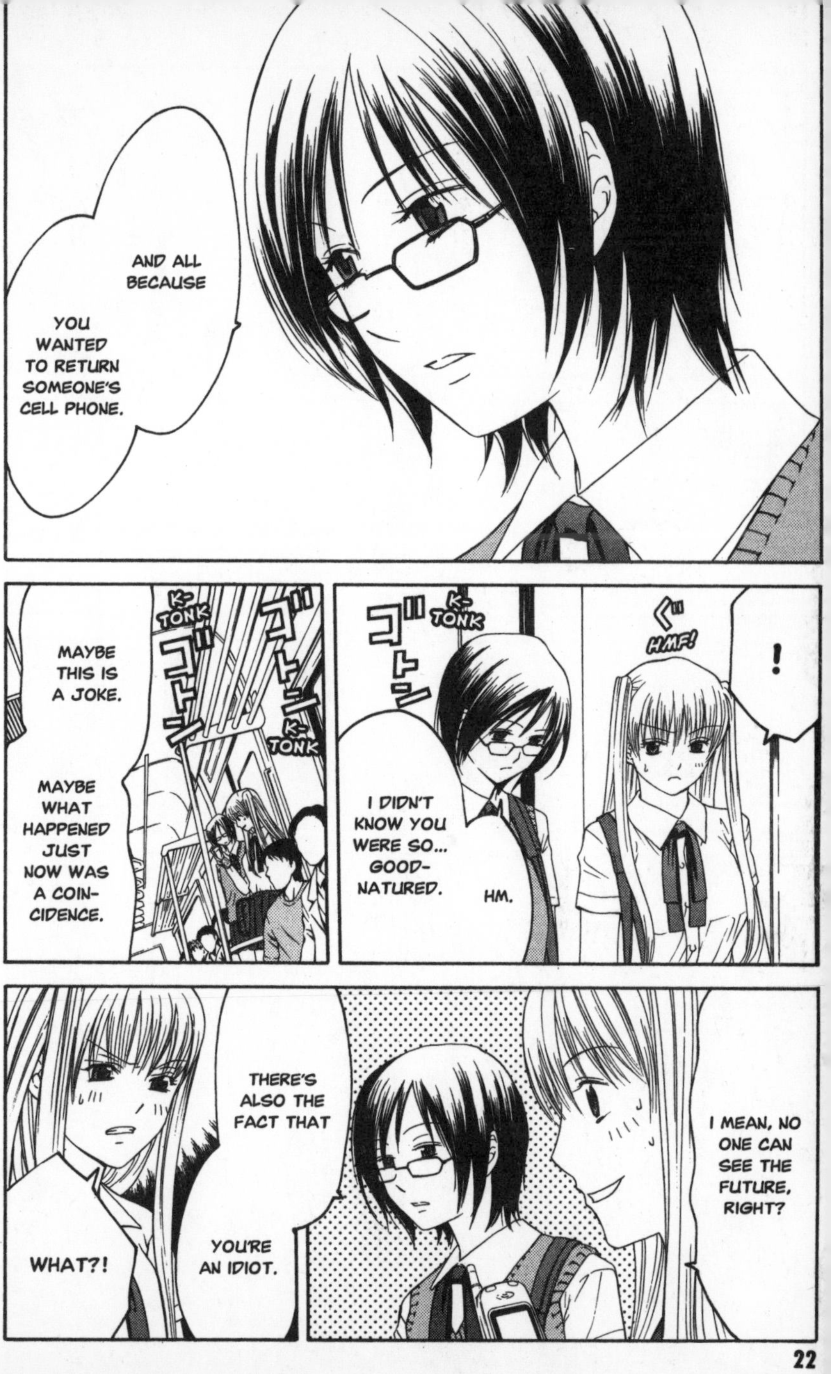
AND ALL BECAUSE
YOU WANTED TO RETURN SOMEONE'S CELL PHONE.
!
ぐ
HMF!
ゴトン
K-TONK
I DIDN'T KNOW YOU WERE SO... GOOD-NATURED.
HM.
K-TONK
K-TONK
MAYBE THIS IS A JOKE.
MAYBE WHAT HAPPENED JUST NOW WAS A COIN-CIDENCE.
I MEAN, NO ONE CAN SEE THE FUTURE, RIGHT?
THERE'S ALSO THE FACT THAT
YOU'RE AN IDIOT.
WHAT?!

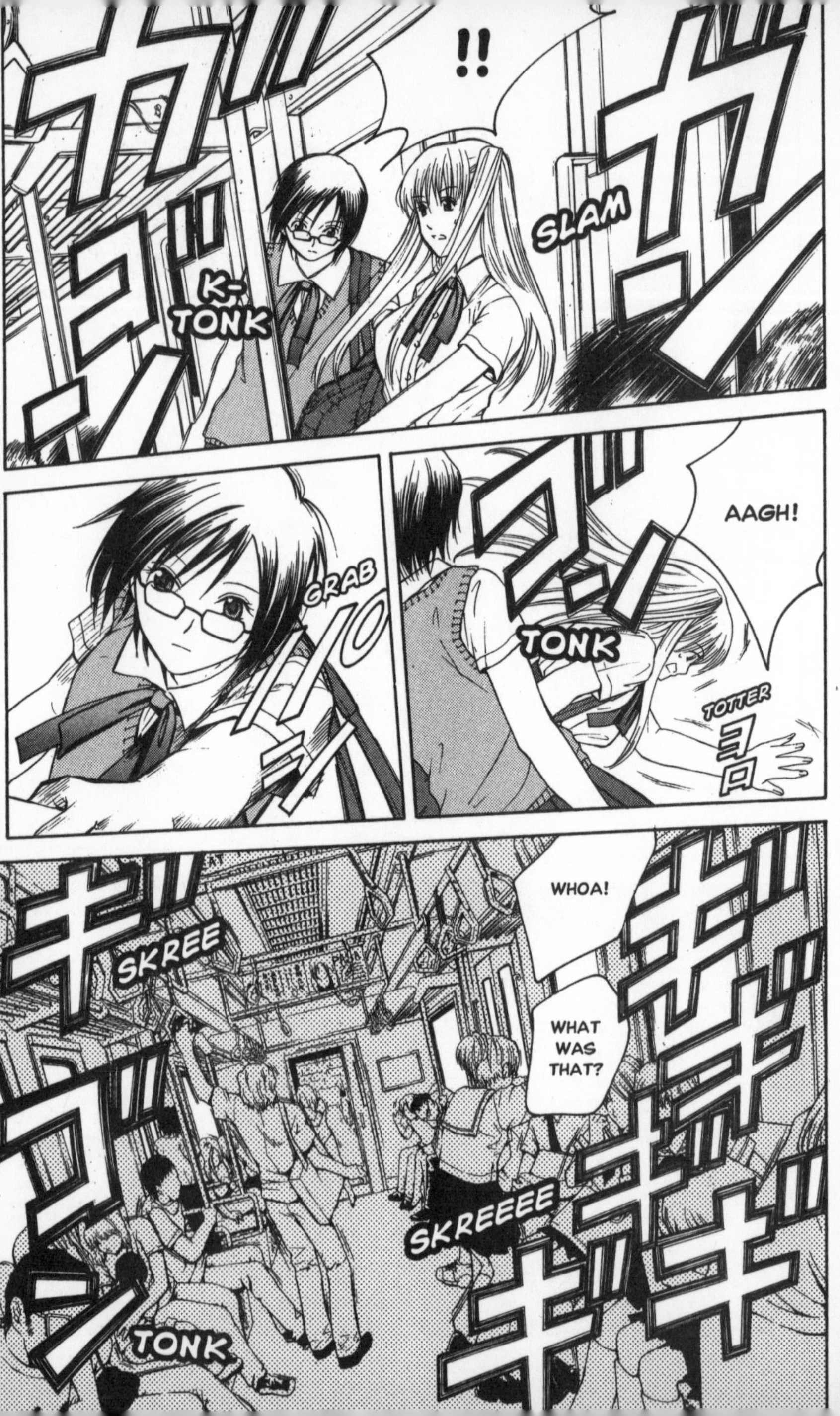
!!
SLAM
K-TONK
AAGH!
TONK
TOTTER
ヨロ
GRAB
WHOA!
SKREE
WHAT WAS THAT?
SKREEEE
TONK

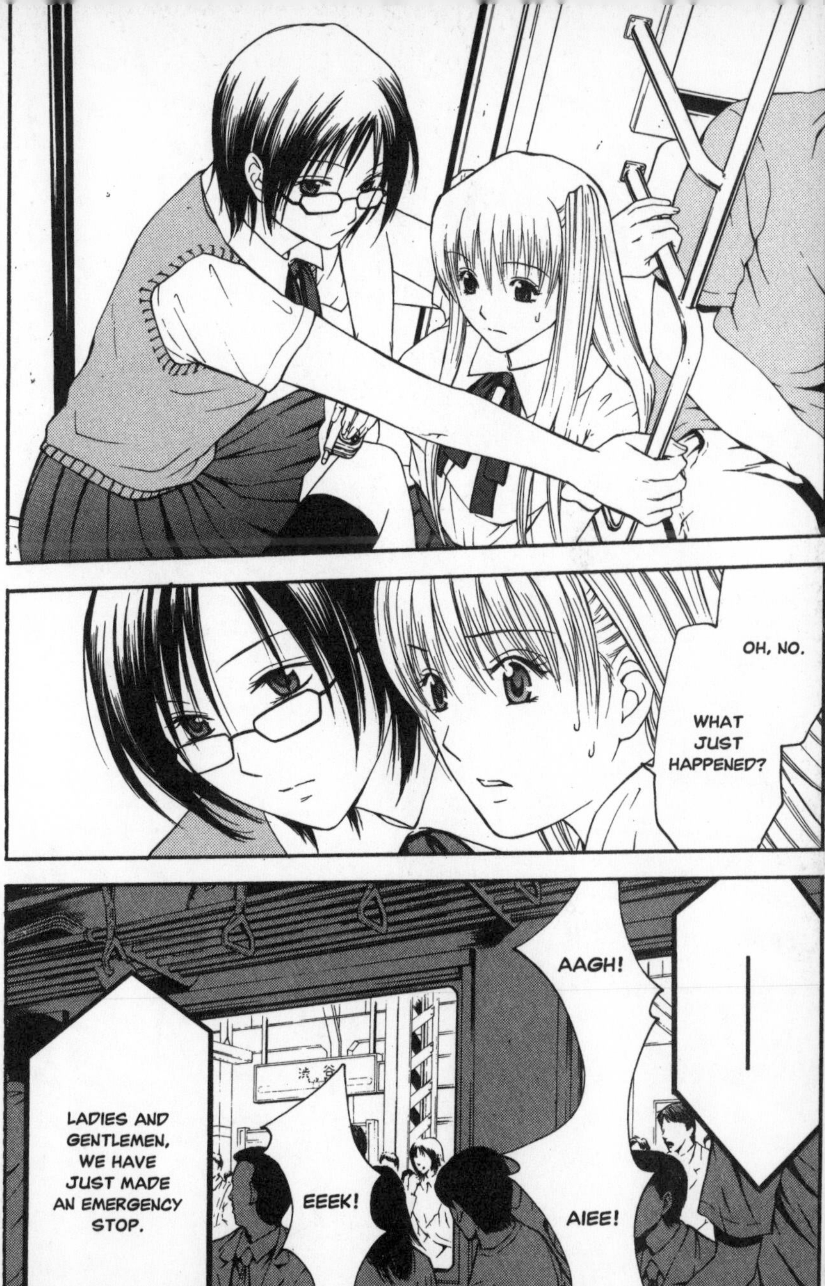
OH, NO.
WHAT JUST HAPPENED?
AAGH!
AIEE!
EEEK!
LADIES AND GENTLEMEN, WE HAVE JUST MADE AN EMERGENCY STOP.

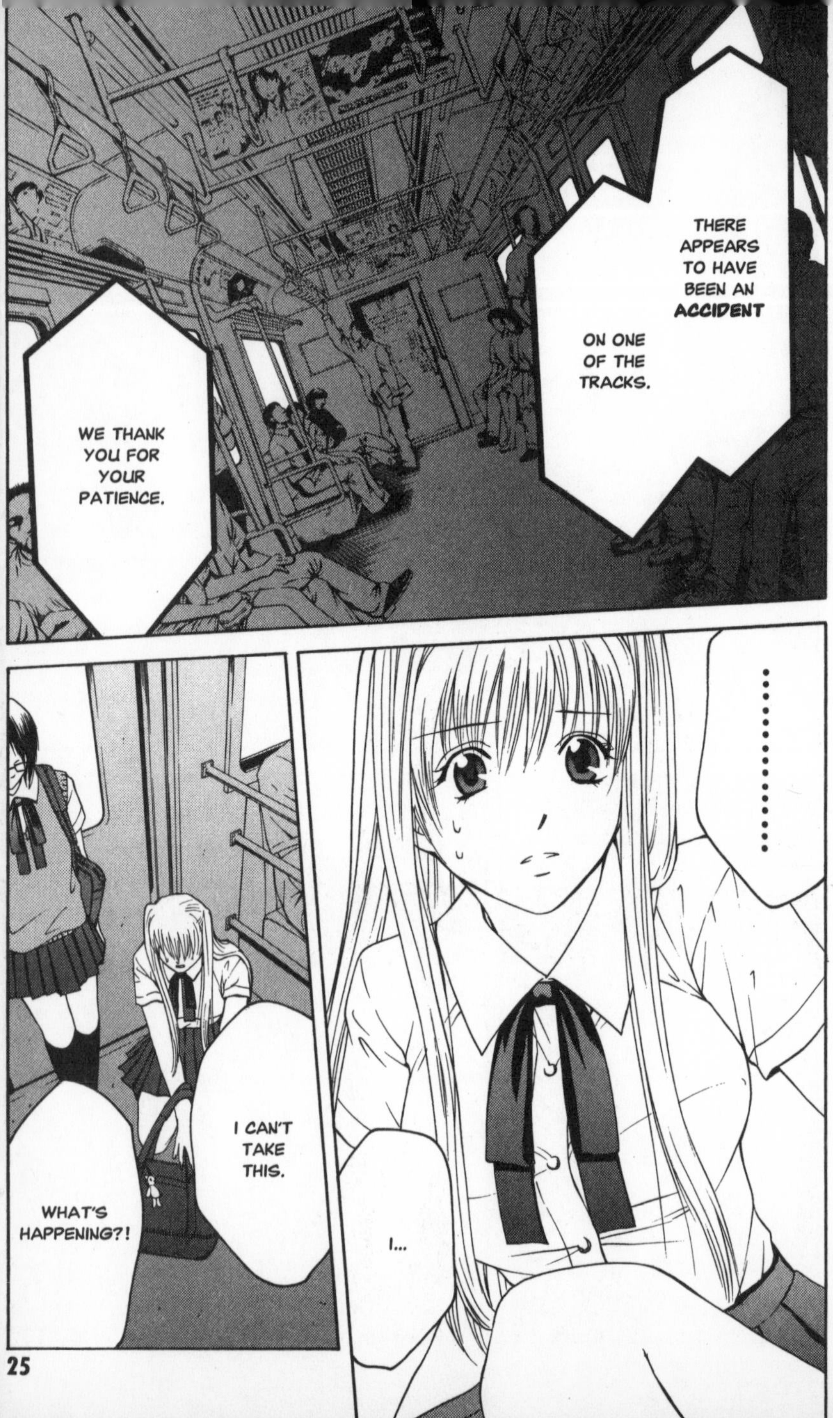
THERE APPEARS TO HAVE BEEN AN ACCIDENT
ON ONE OF THE TRACKS.
WE THANK YOU FOR YOUR PATIENCE.
......
I...
I CAN'T TAKE THIS.
WHAT'S HAPPENING?!

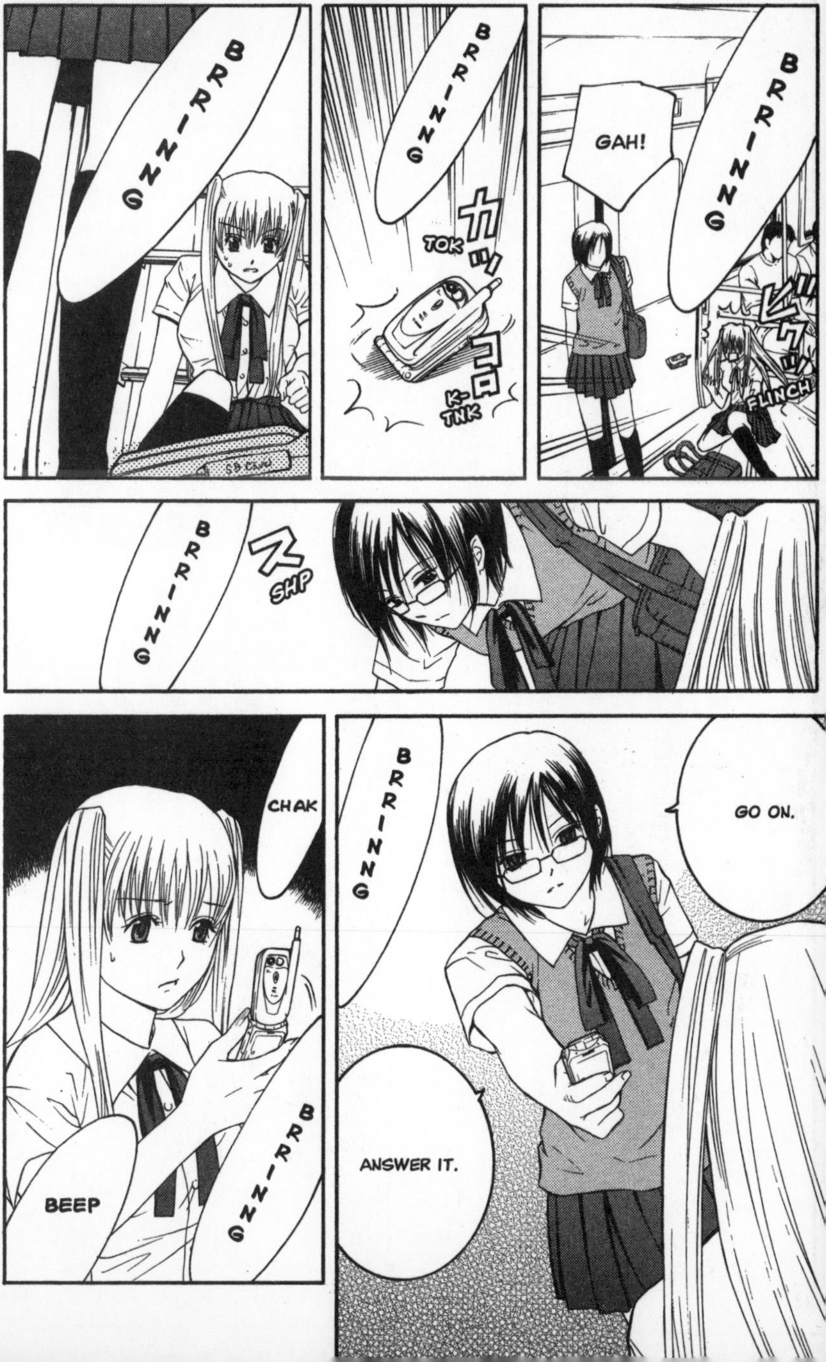
BRRINNG
GAH!
FLINCH
BRRINNG
TOK
K-TNK
BRRINNG
BRRINNG
SHP
GO ON.
BRRINNG
ANSWER IT.
CHAK
BRRINNG
BEEP

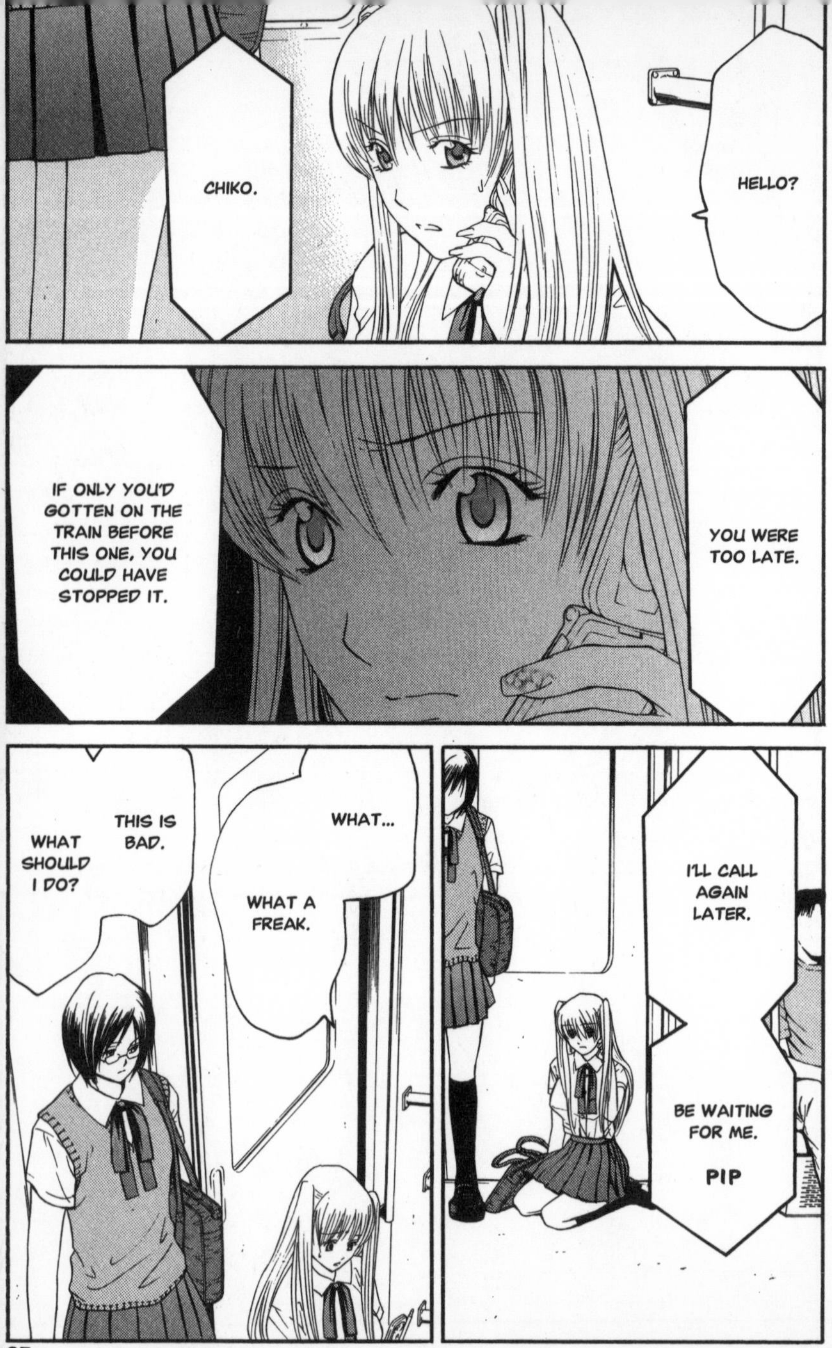
HELLO?
CHIKO.
YOU WERE TOO LATE.
IF ONLY YOU'D GOTTEN ON THE TRAIN BEFORE THIS ONE, YOU COULD HAVE STOPPED IT.
I'LL CALL AGAIN LATER.
BE WAITING FOR ME.
PIP
WHAT...
WHAT A FREAK.
THIS IS BAD.
WHAT SHOULD I DO?

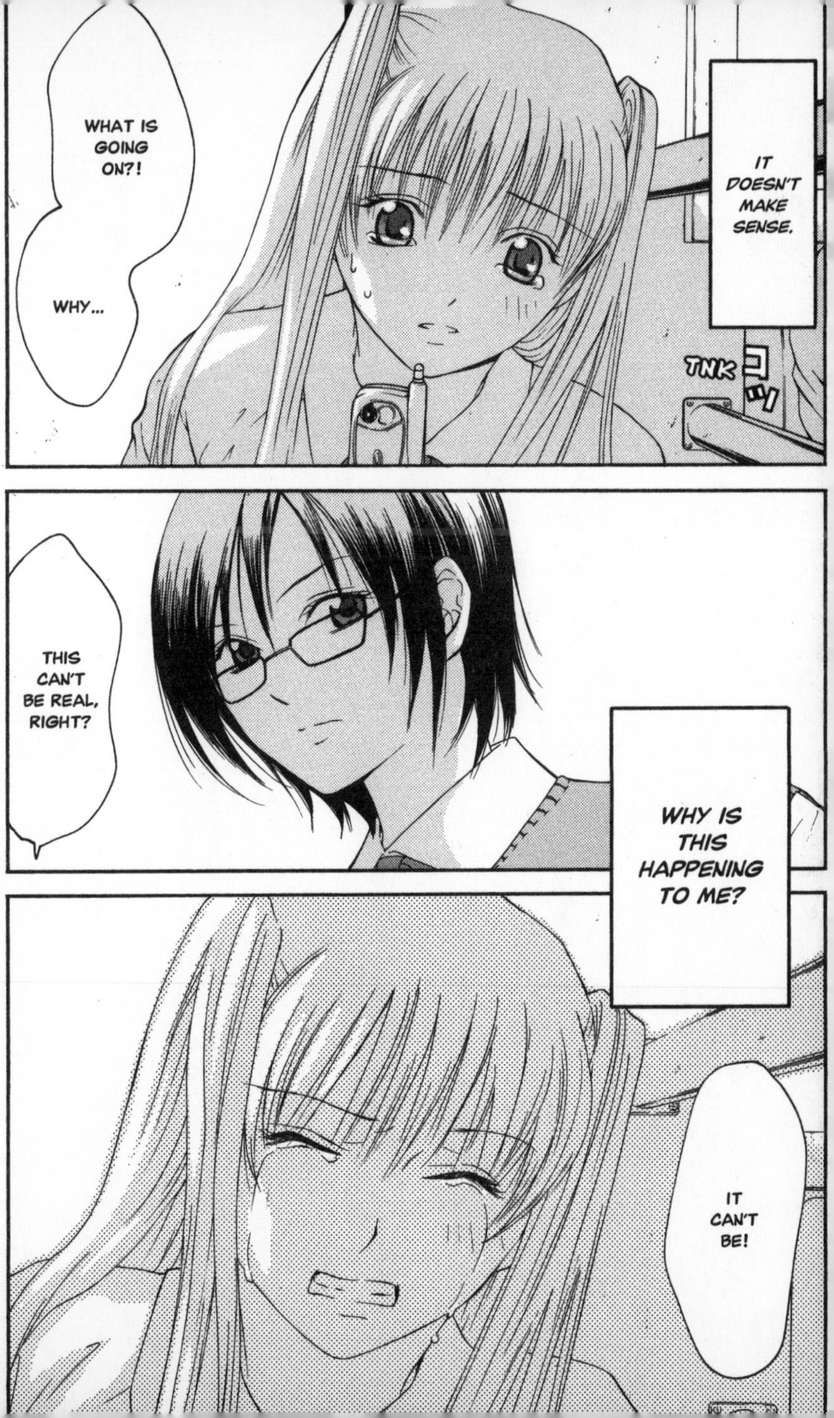
IT DOESN'T MAKE SENSE.
TNK
コッ
WHAT IS GOING ON?!
WHY...
WHY IS THIS HAPPENING TO ME?
THIS CAN'T BE REAL, RIGHT?
IT CAN'T BE!

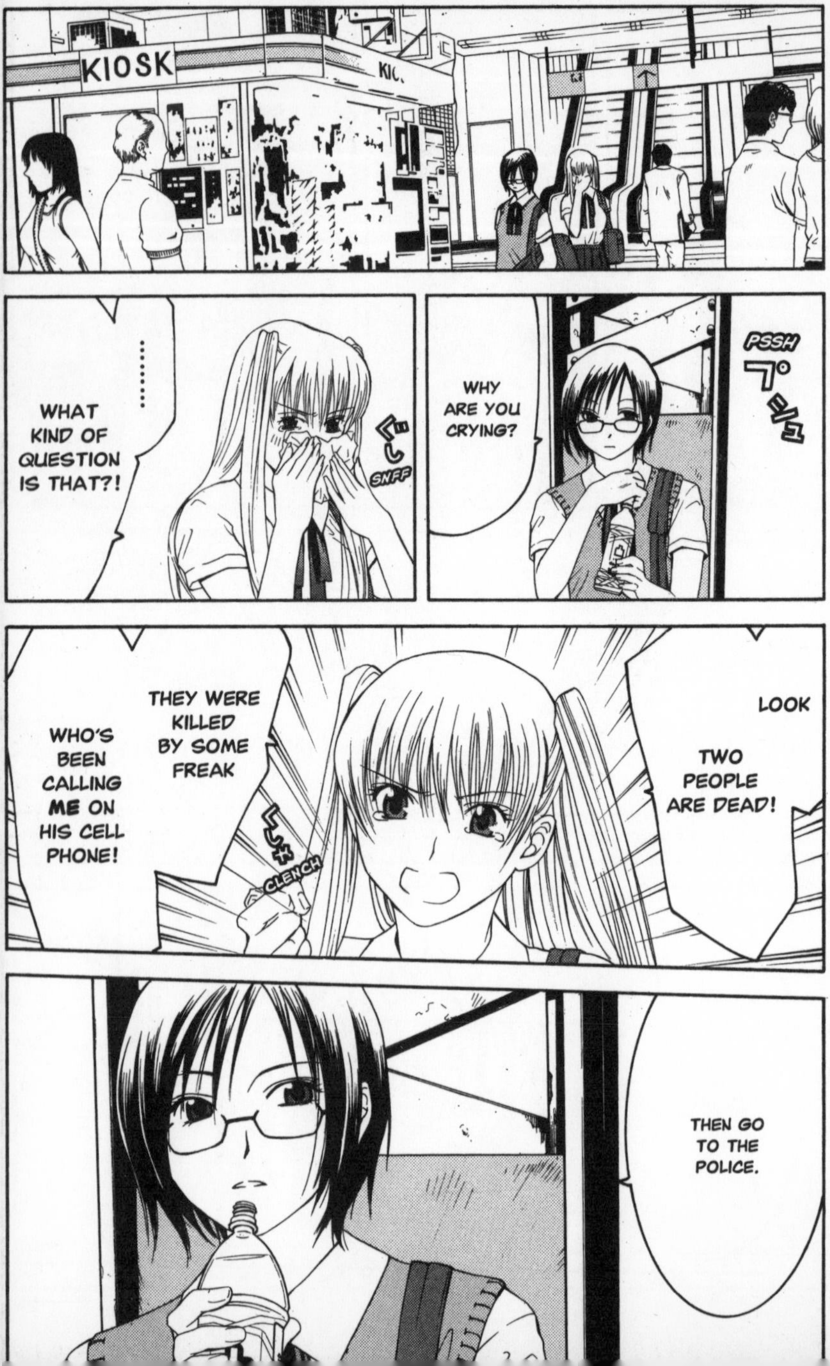
KIOSK
PSSH
WHY ARE YOU CRYING?
....
WHAT KIND OF QUESTION IS THAT?!
SNFF
LOOK
TWO PEOPLE ARE DEAD!
THEY WERE KILLED BY SOME FREAK
CLENCH
WHO'S BEEN CALLING **ME** ON HIS CELL PHONE!
THEN GO TO THE POLICE.

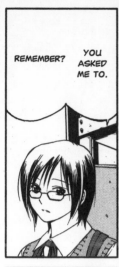

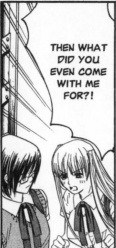

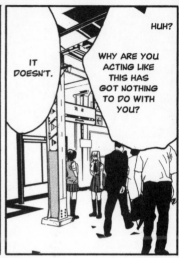

HUH?
WHY ARE YOU ACTING LIKE THIS HAS GOT NOTHING TO DO WITH YOU?
IT DOESN'T.
THEN WHAT DID YOU EVEN COME WITH ME FOR?!
YOU ASKED ME TO.
REMEMBER?
DON'T YOU FEEL ANYTHING?! THOSE PEOPLE ARE DEAD
AND THAT BASTARD IS PLAYING GAMES WITH US!
I THINK IT'S INTERESTING.

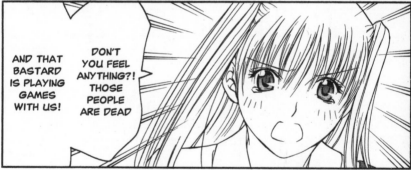

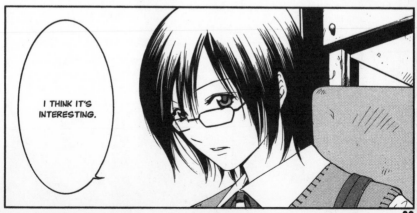

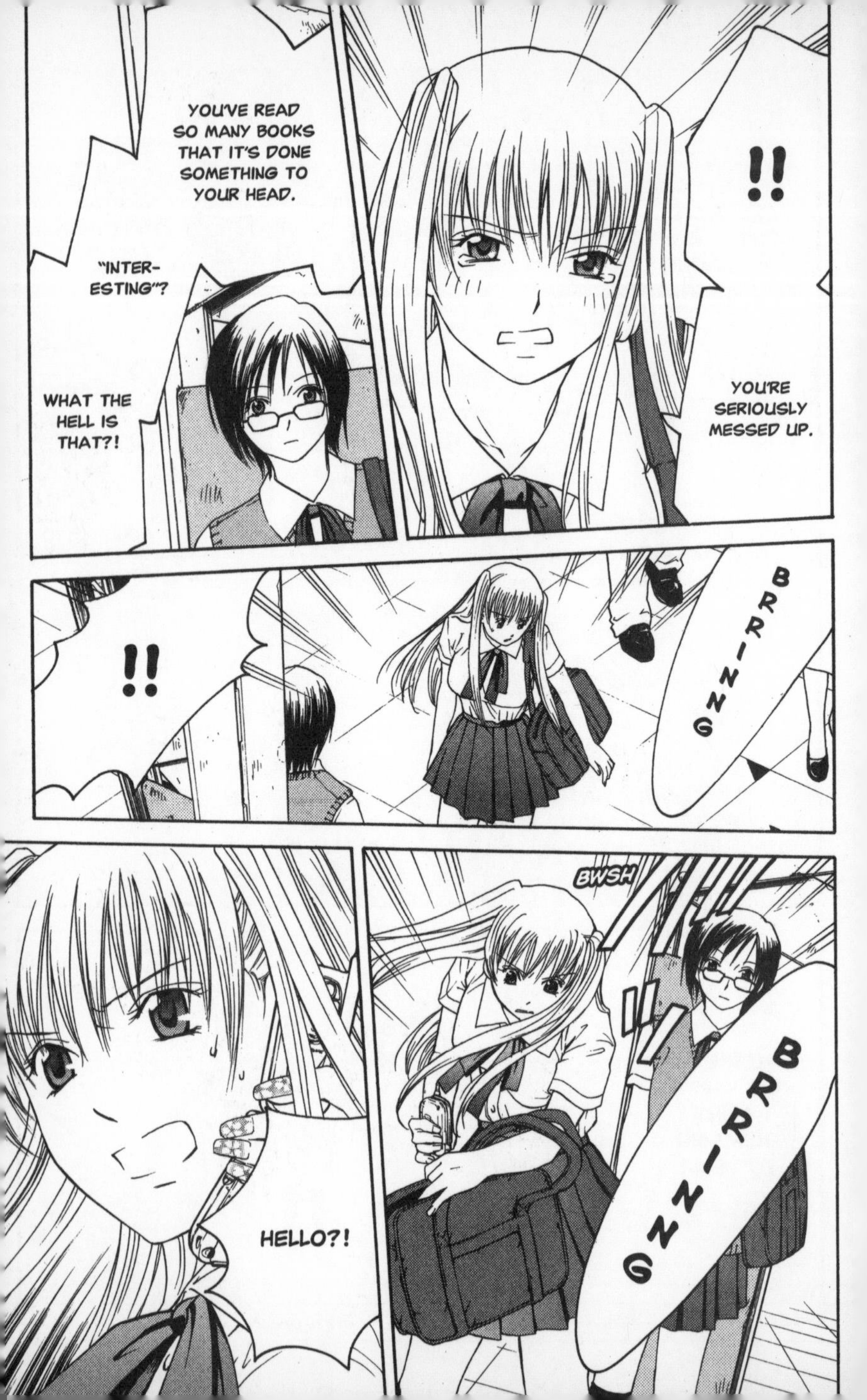
!!
YOU'RE SERIOUSLY MESSED UP.
YOU'VE READ SO MANY BOOKS THAT IT'S DONE SOMETHING TO YOUR HEAD.
"INTER-ESTING"?
WHAT THE HELL IS THAT?!
BRRING
!!
BWSH
BRRING
HELLO?!

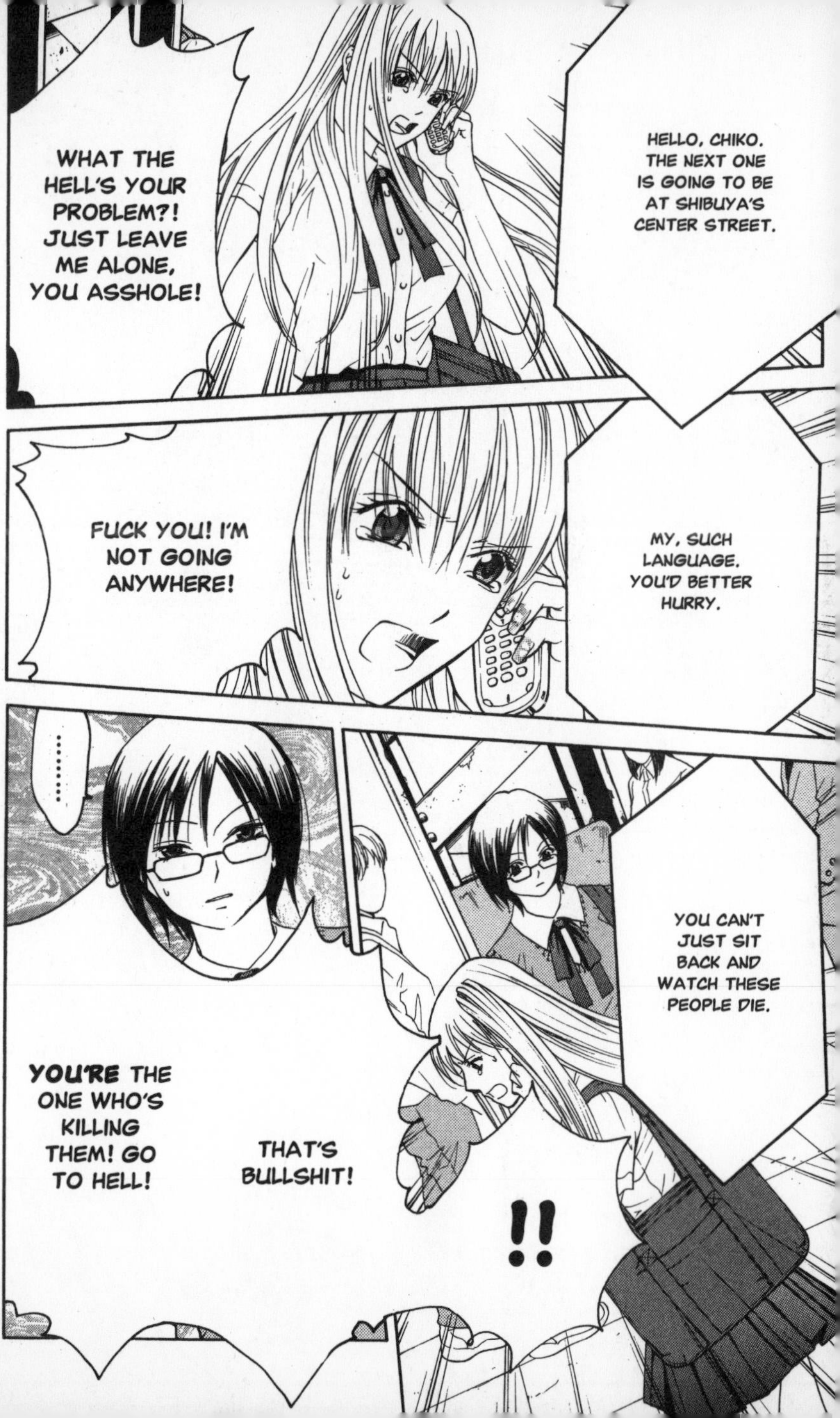
HELLO, CHIKO. THE NEXT ONE IS GOING TO BE AT SHIBUYA'S CENTER STREET.
WHAT THE HELL'S YOUR PROBLEM?! JUST LEAVE ME ALONE, YOU ASSHOLE!
MY, SUCH LANGUAGE. YOU'D BETTER HURRY.
FUCK YOU! I'M NOT GOING ANYWHERE!
YOU CAN'T JUST SIT BACK AND WATCH THESE PEOPLE DIE.
!!
THAT'S BULLSHIT!
YOU'RE THE ONE WHO'S KILLING THEM! GO TO HELL!
......

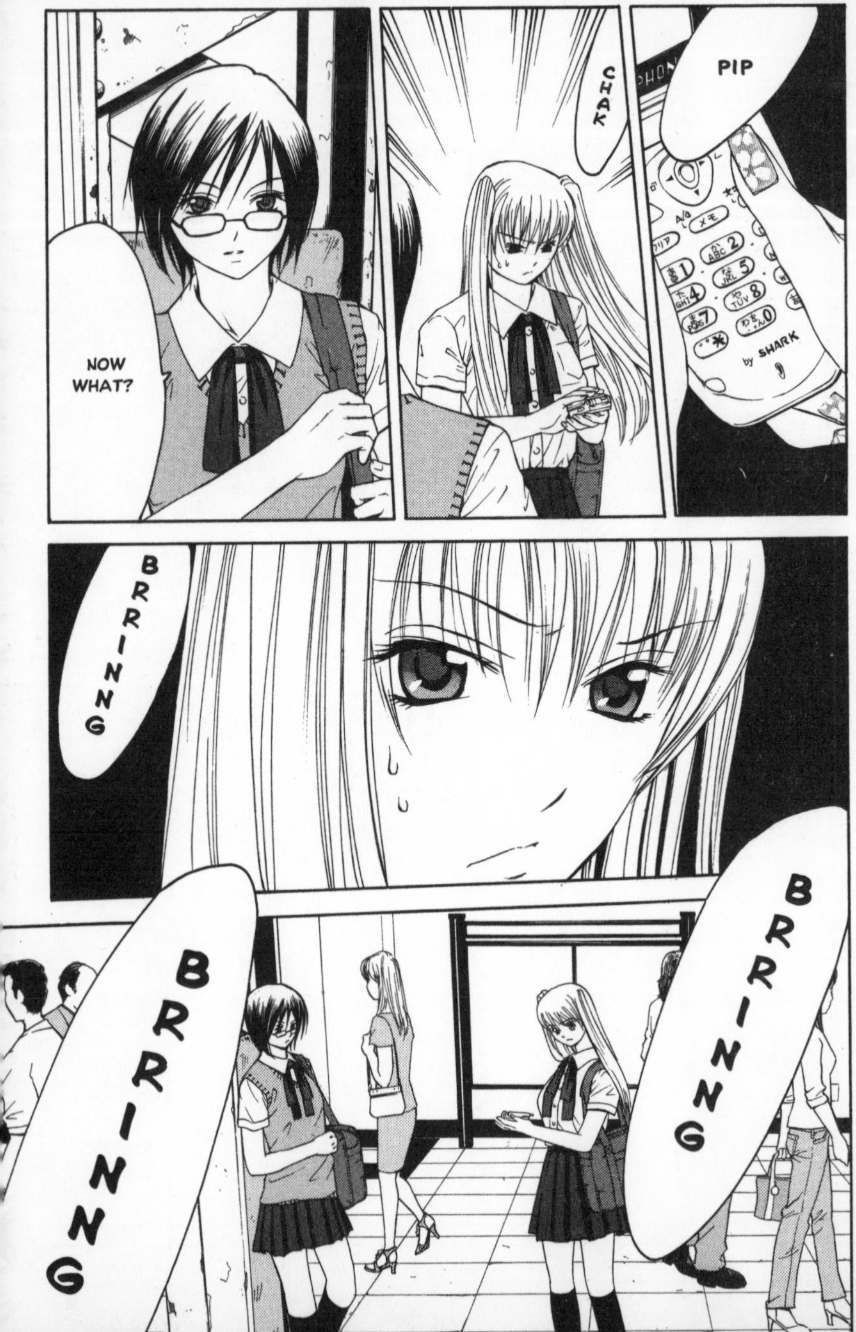
PIP
by SHARK
CHAK
NOW WHAT?
BRRINNG
BRRINNG
BRRINNG

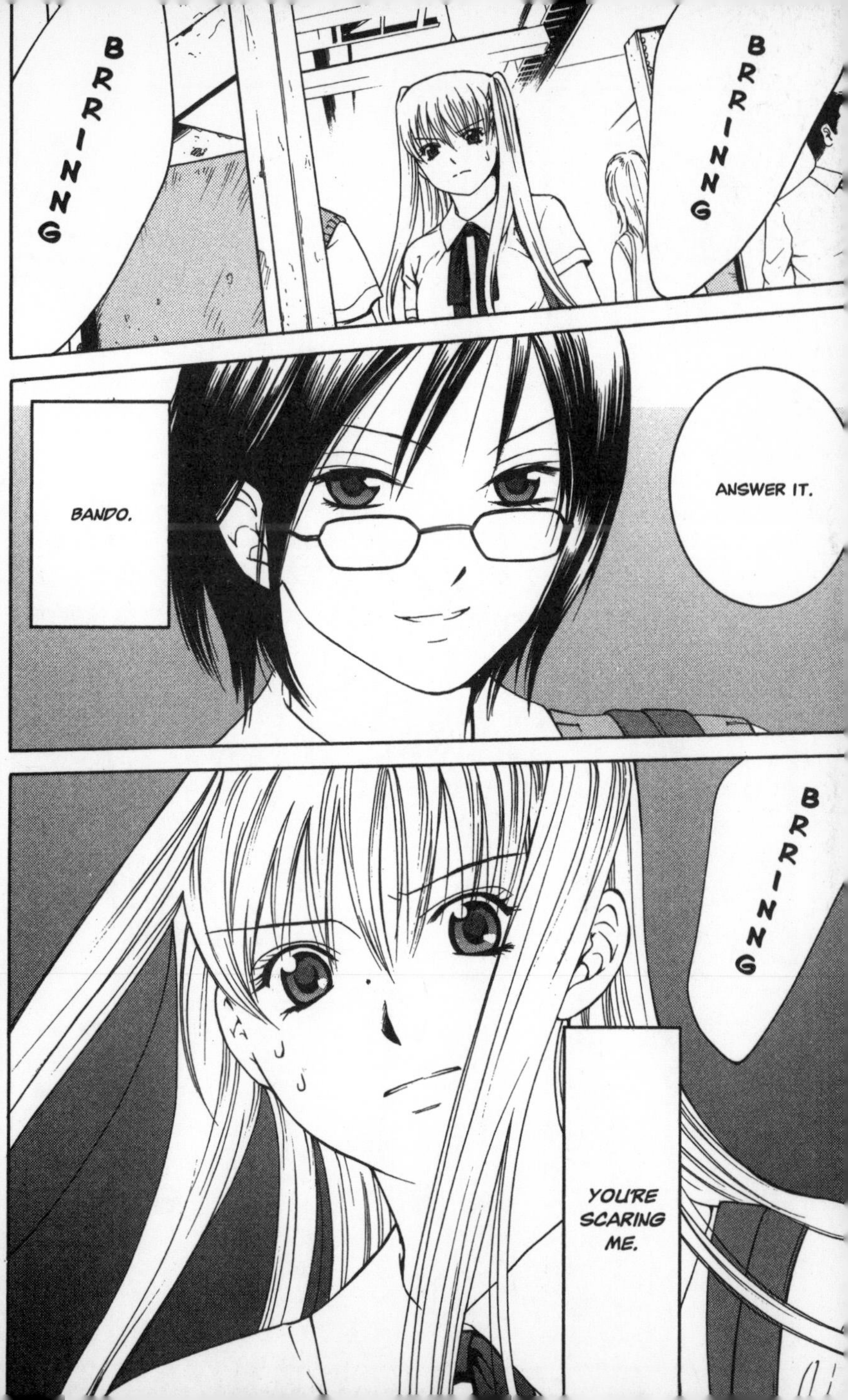
BRRINNG
BRRINNG
ANSWER IT.
BANDO.
BRRINNG
YOU'RE SCARING ME.

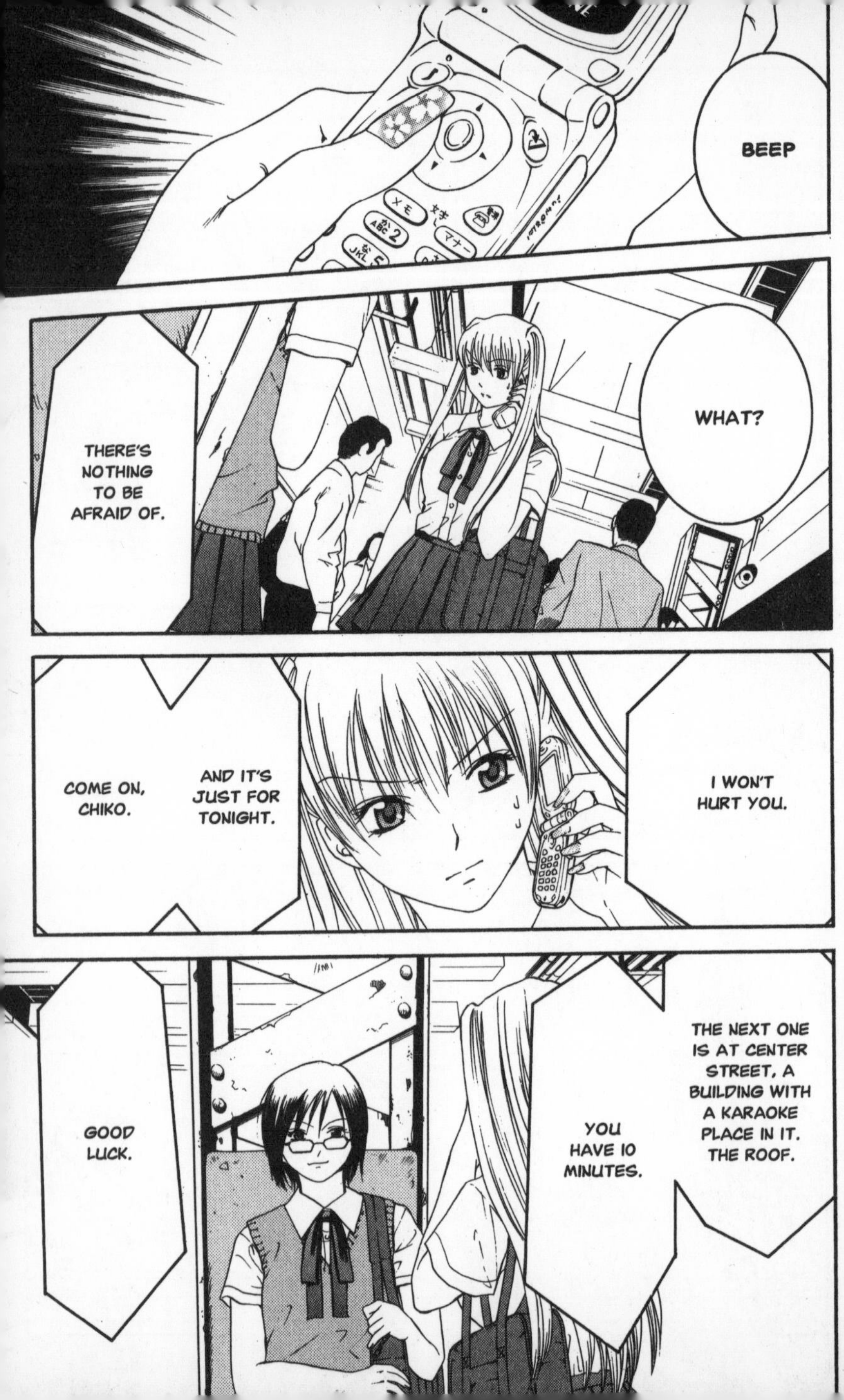
BEEP
WHAT?
THERE'S NOTHING TO BE AFRAID OF.
I WON'T HURT YOU.
AND IT'S JUST FOR TONIGHT.
COME ON, CHIKO.
THE NEXT ONE IS AT CENTER STREET, A BUILDING WITH A KARAOKE PLACE IN IT. THE ROOF.
YOU HAVE 10 MINUTES.
GOOD LUCK.

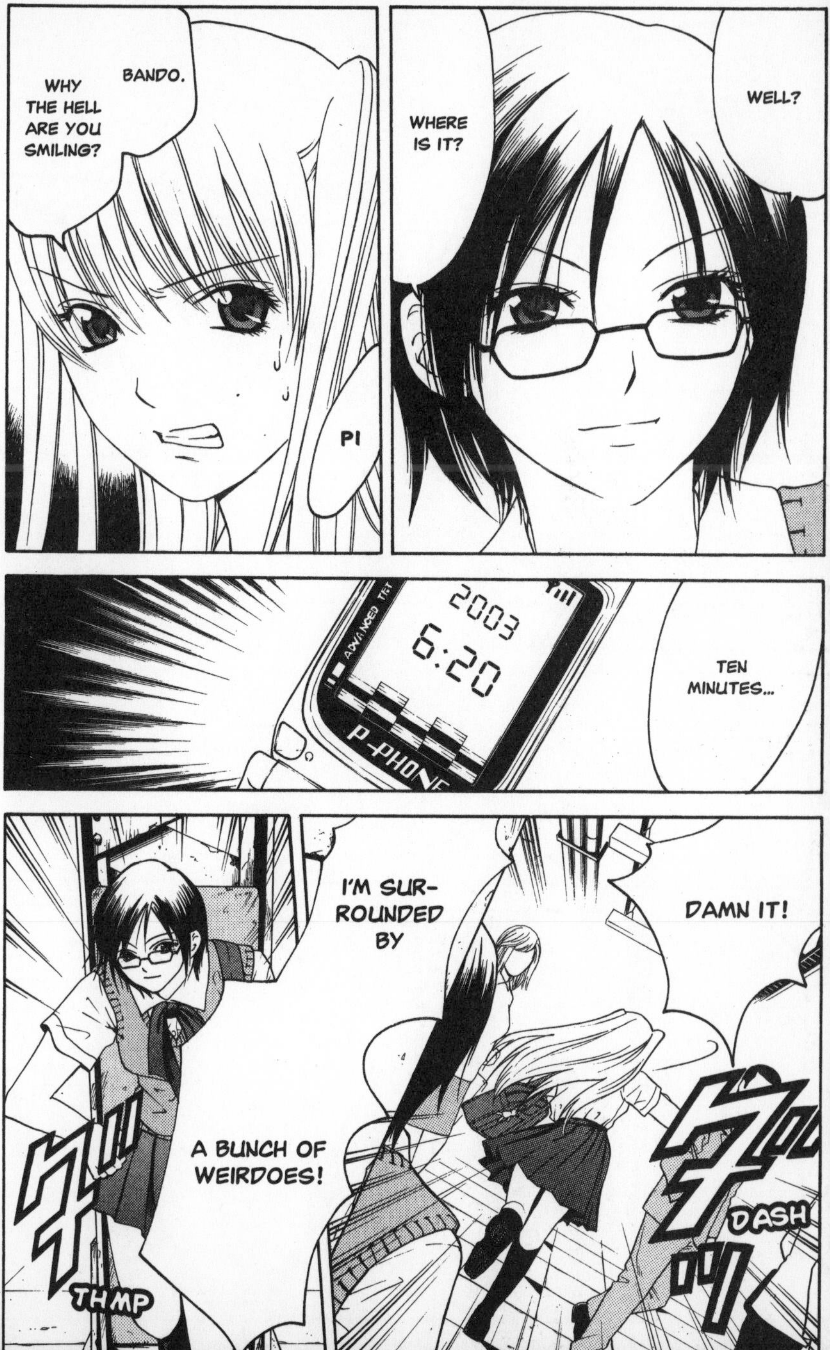
WELL?
WHERE IS IT?
BANDO.
WHY THE HELL ARE YOU SMILING?
PI
TEN MINUTES...
2003
6:20
DAMN IT!
I'M SUR-ROUNDED BY
A BUNCH OF WEIRDOES!
DASH
THMP

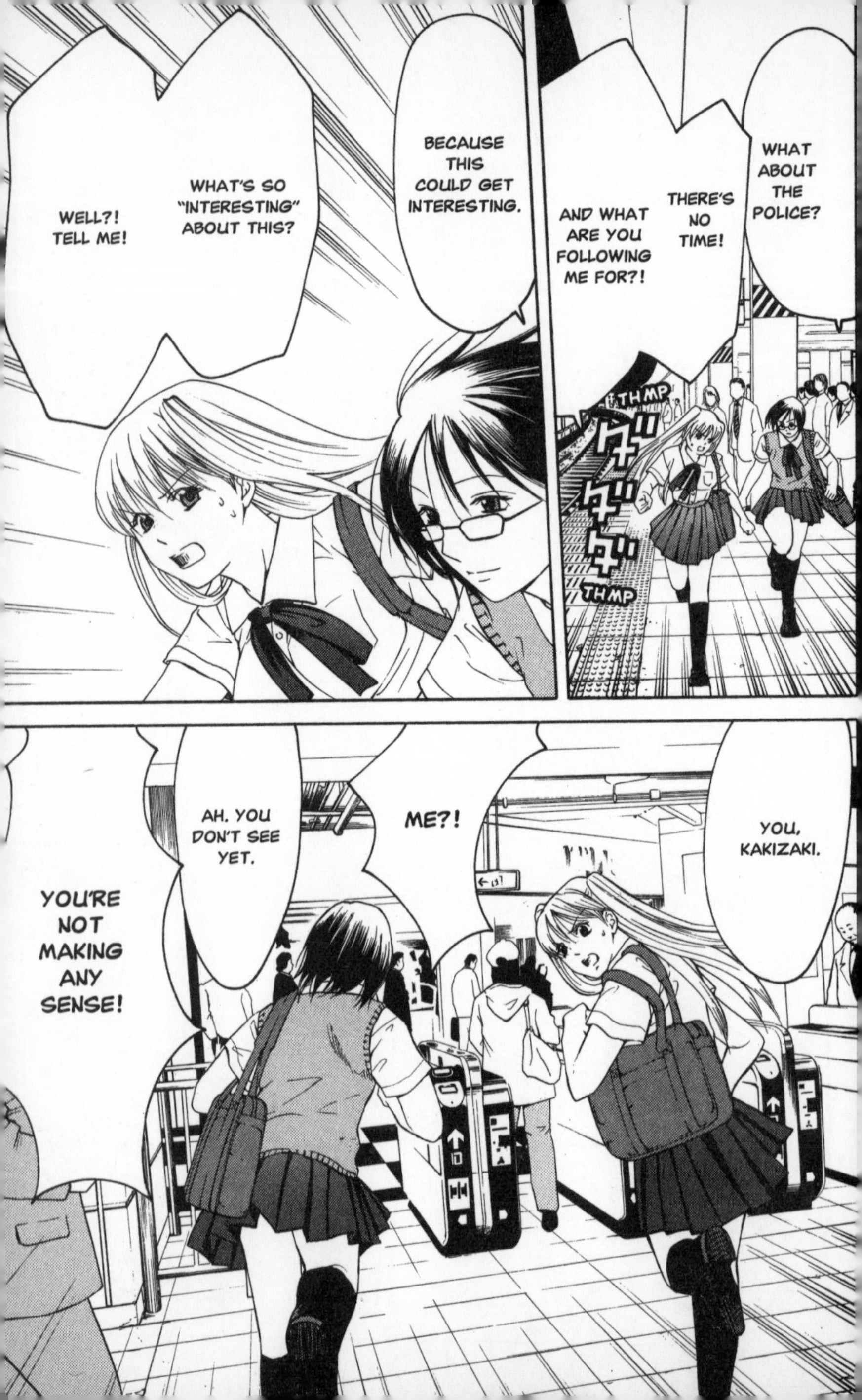
WHAT ABOUT THE POLICE?
THERE'S NO TIME!
AND WHAT ARE YOU FOLLOWING ME FOR?!
THMP
THMP
BECAUSE THIS COULD GET INTERESTING.
WHAT'S SO "INTERESTING" ABOUT THIS?
WELL?! TELL ME!
YOU, KAKIZAKI.
ME?!
AH. YOU DON'T SEE YET.
YOU'RE NOT MAKING ANY SENSE!

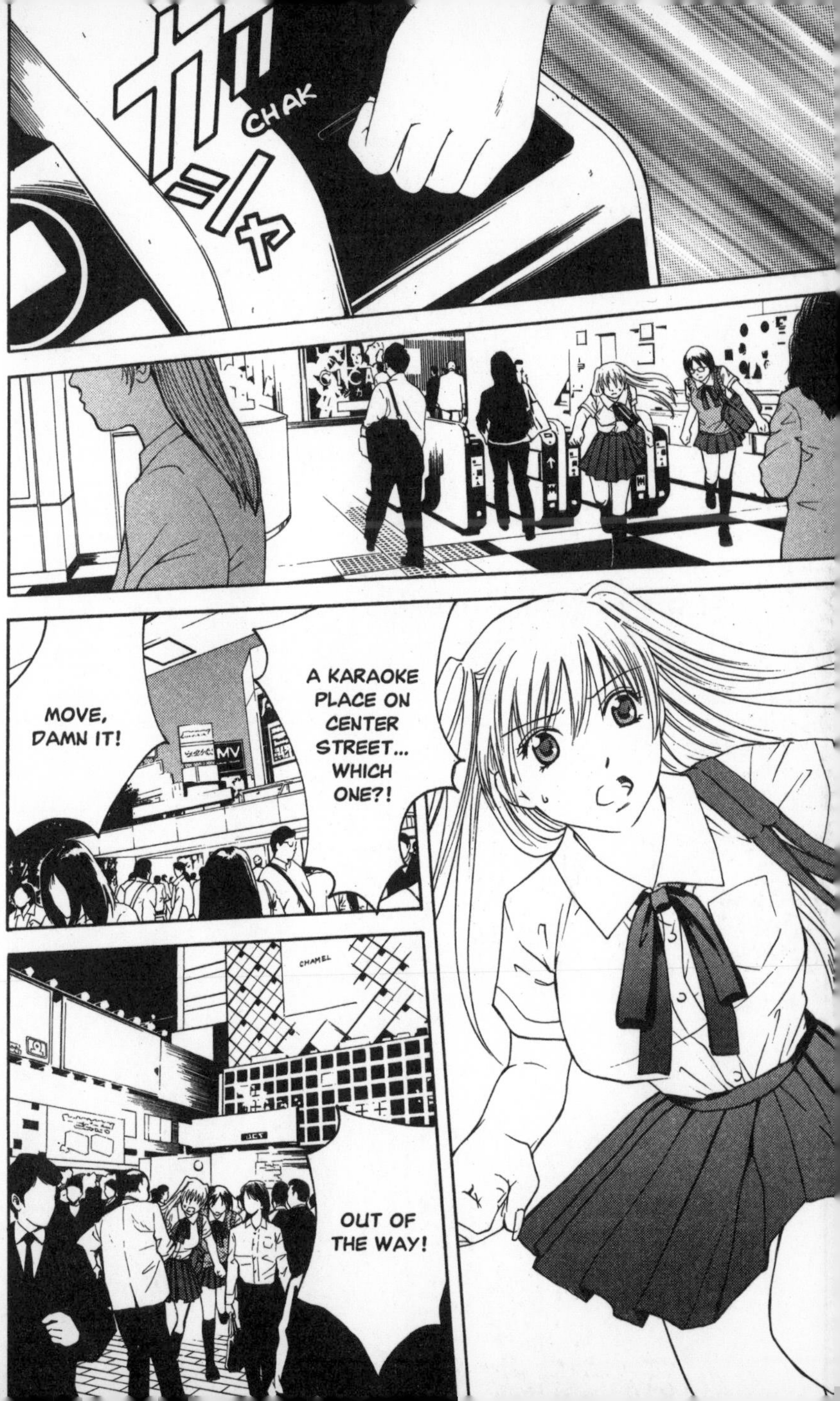
カシャ
CHAK
A KARAOKE PLACE ON CENTER STREET... WHICH ONE?!
MOVE, DAMN IT!
OUT OF THE WAY!

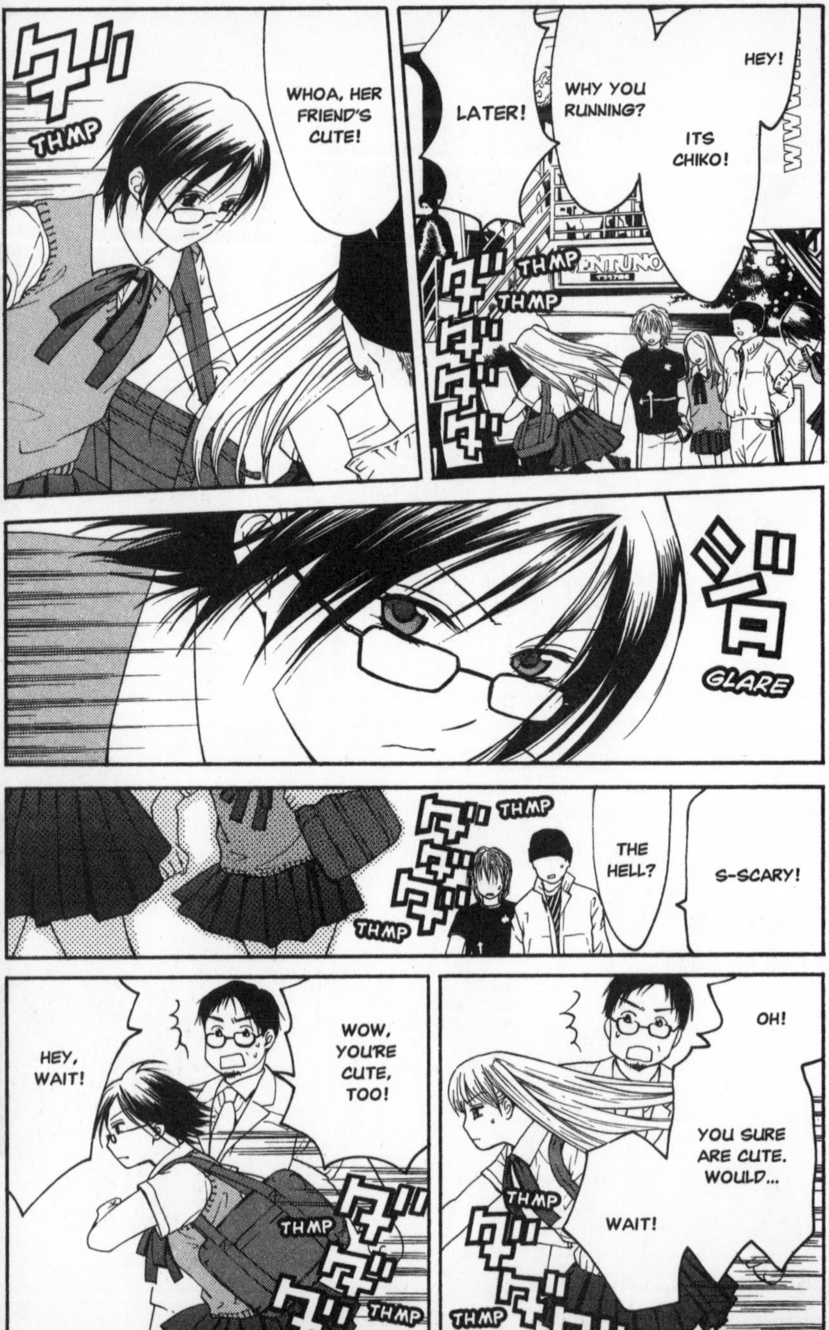
HEY!
ITS CHIKO!
WHY YOU RUNNING?
LATER!
THMP
THMP
WHOA, HER FRIEND'S CUTE!
THMP
GLARE
S-SCARY!
THE HELL?
THMP
THMP
OH!
YOU SURE ARE CUTE. WOULD...
WAIT!
THMP
THMP
WOW, YOU'RE CUTE, TOO!
HEY, WAIT!
THMP
THMP

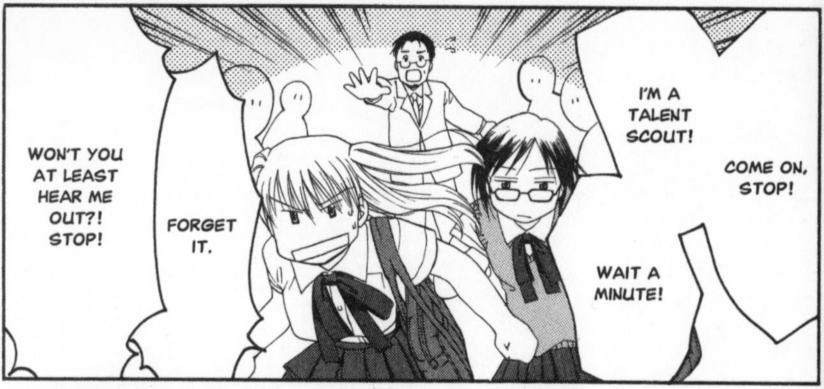
COME ON, STOP!
I'M A TALENT SCOUT!
WAIT A MINUTE!
FORGET IT.
WON'T YOU AT LEAST HEAR ME OUT?! STOP!

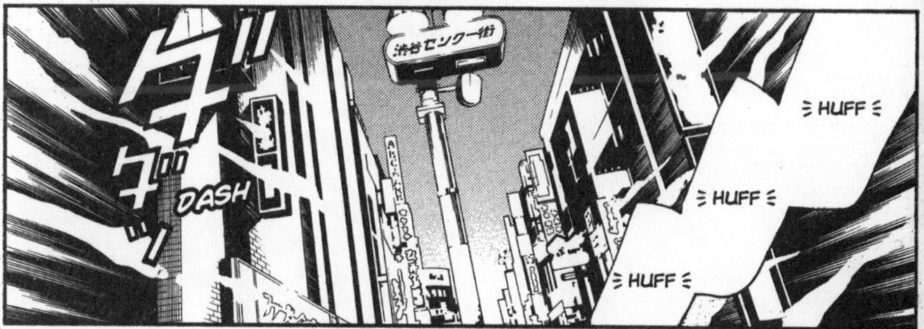
HUFF
HUFF
HUFF
DASH

*ON SIGN: "SHIBUYA CENTER STREET."

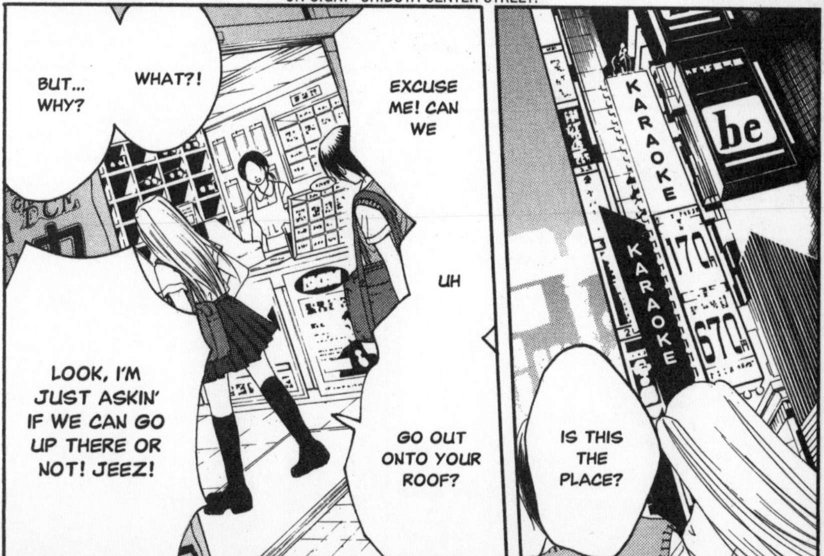
KARAOKE
be
KARAOKE
IS THIS THE PLACE?
EXCUSE ME! CAN WE
GO OUT ONTO YOUR ROOF?
UH
WHAT?!
BUT... WHY?
LOOK, I'M JUST ASKIN' IF WE CAN GO UP THERE OR NOT! JEEZ!

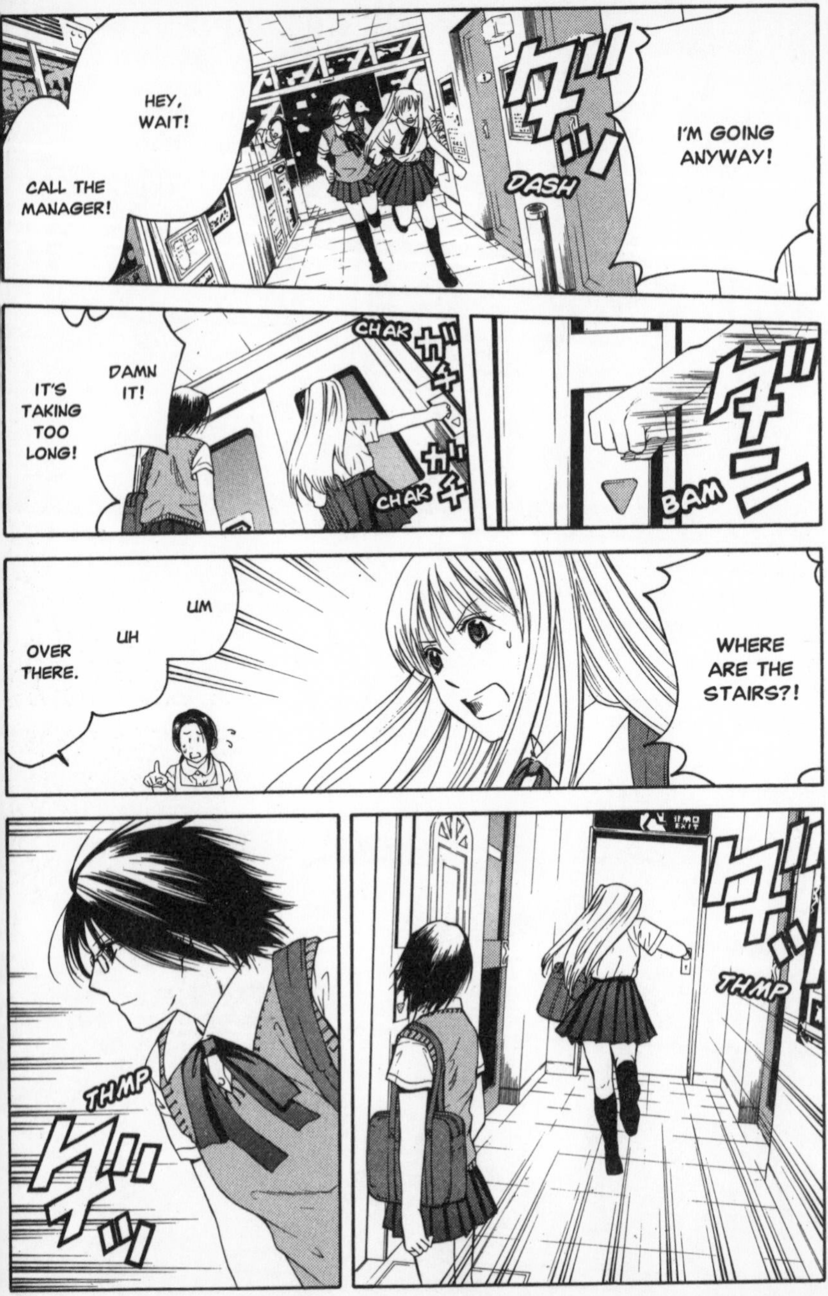
ダッ
DASH
I'M GOING ANYWAY!
HEY, WAIT!
CALL THE MANAGER!
ダン
BAM
ガチ
CHAK
ガチ
CHAK
DAMN IT!
IT'S TAKING TOO LONG!
WHERE ARE THE STAIRS?!
UM
UH
OVER THERE.
ダッ
THMP
ダッ
THMP

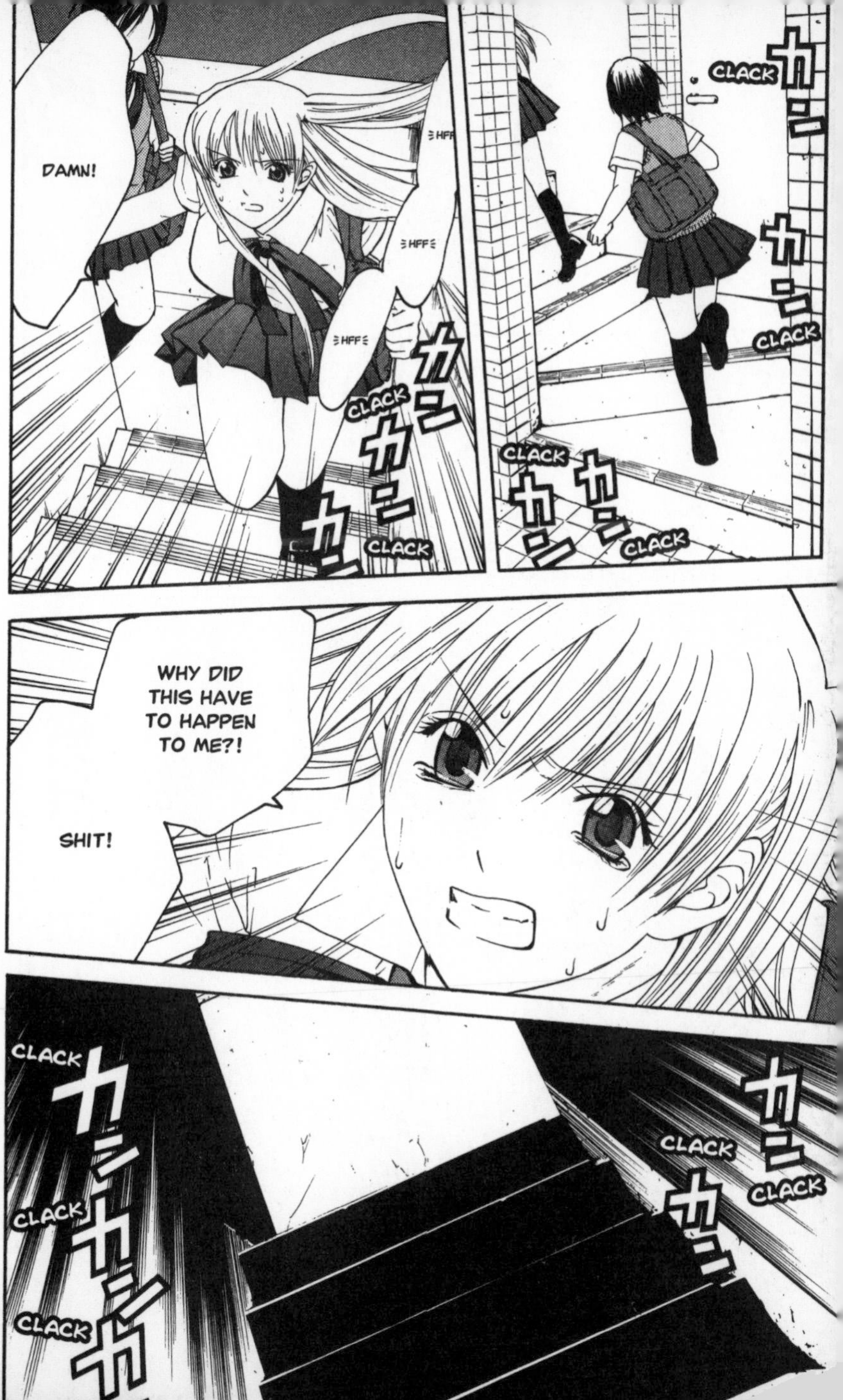
CLACK
CLACK
CLACK
CLACK
DAMN!
HFF
HFF
HFF
CLACK
CLACK
WHY DID THIS HAVE TO HAPPEN TO ME?!
SHIT!
CLACK
CLACK
CLACK
CLACK
CLACK
CLACK

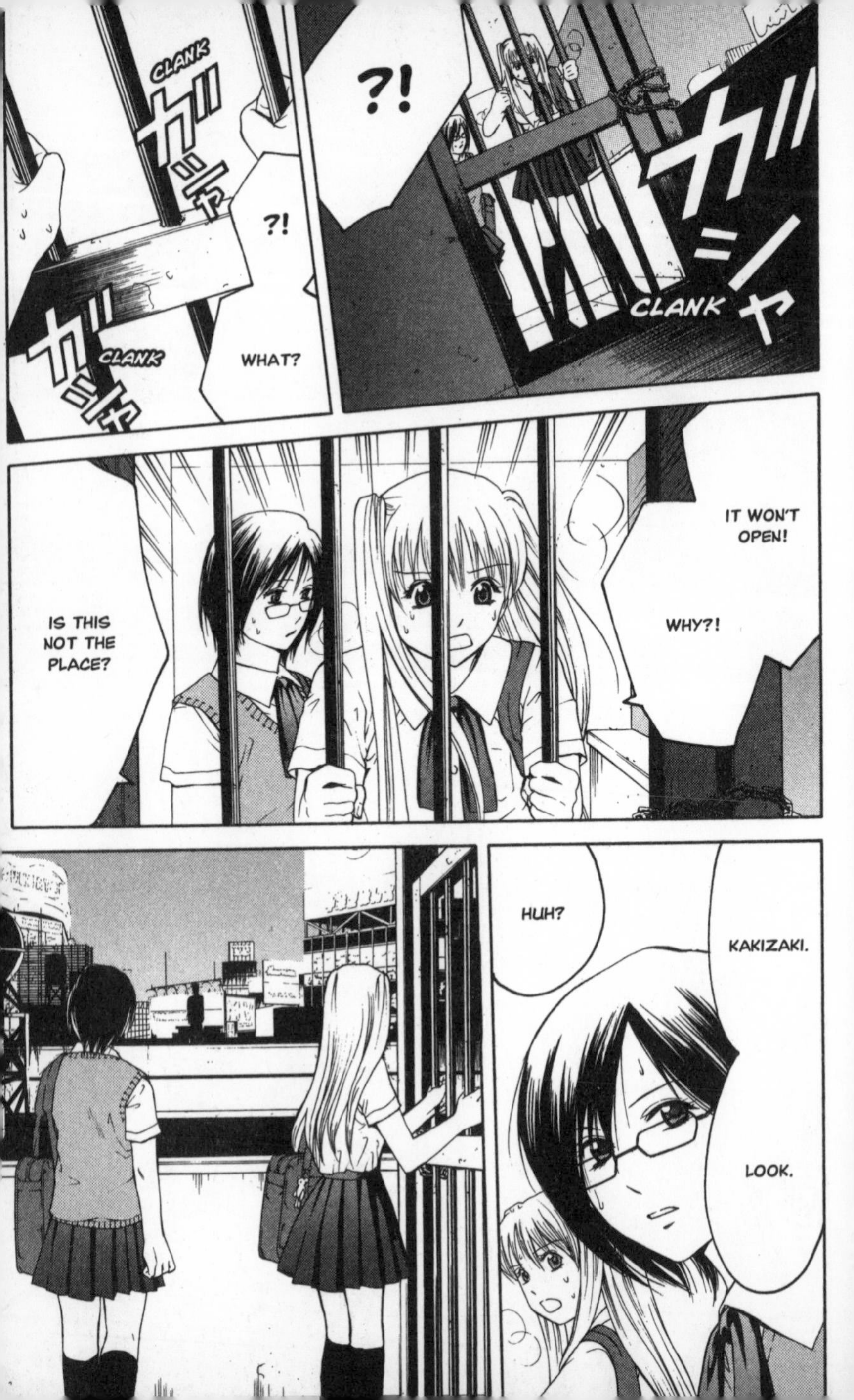

ガシャ
CLANK
?!
CLANK
ガシャ
?!
WHAT?
ガシャ
CLANK
IT WON'T OPEN!
WHY?!
IS THIS NOT THE PLACE?
KAKIZAKI.
LOOK.
HUH?

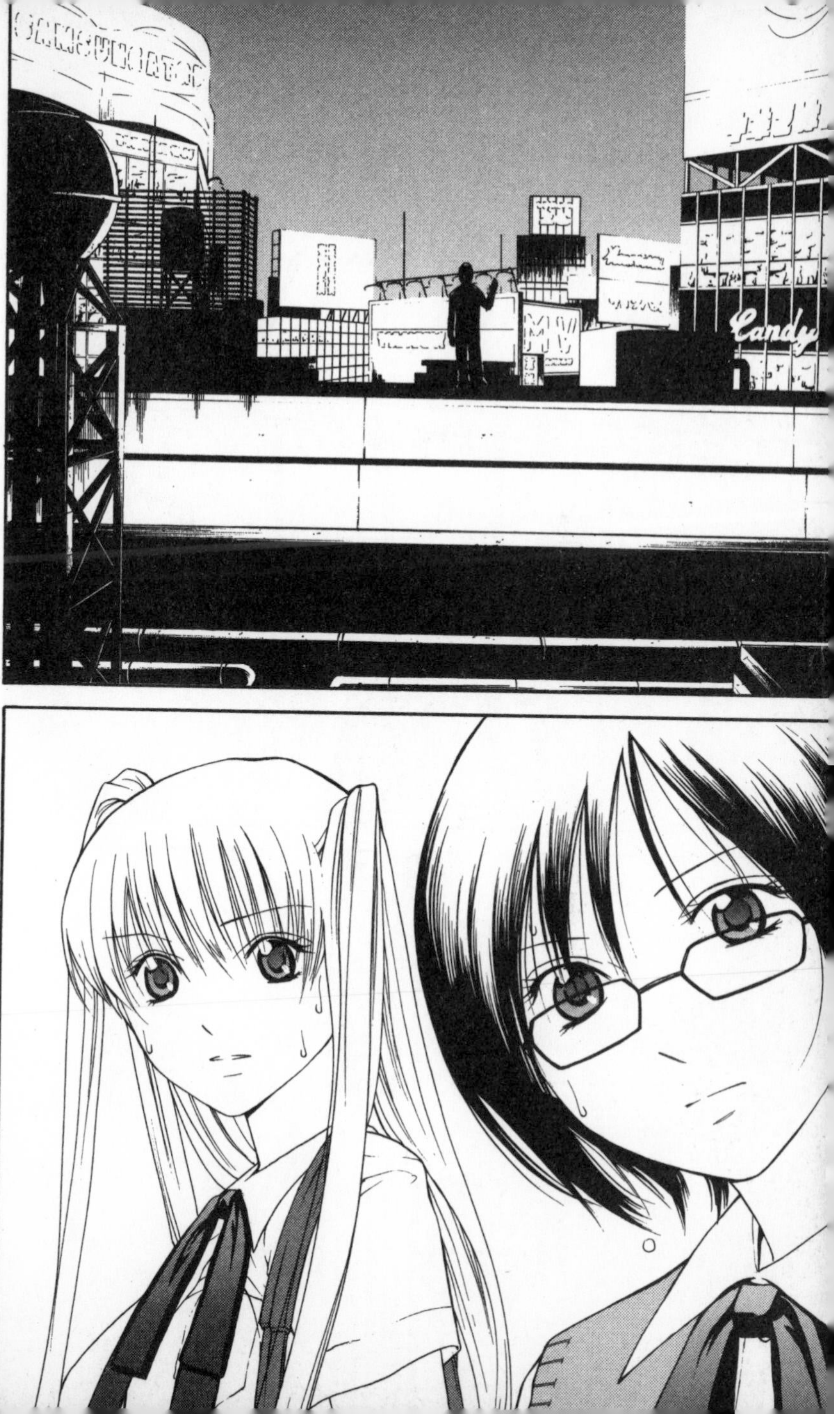
Candy

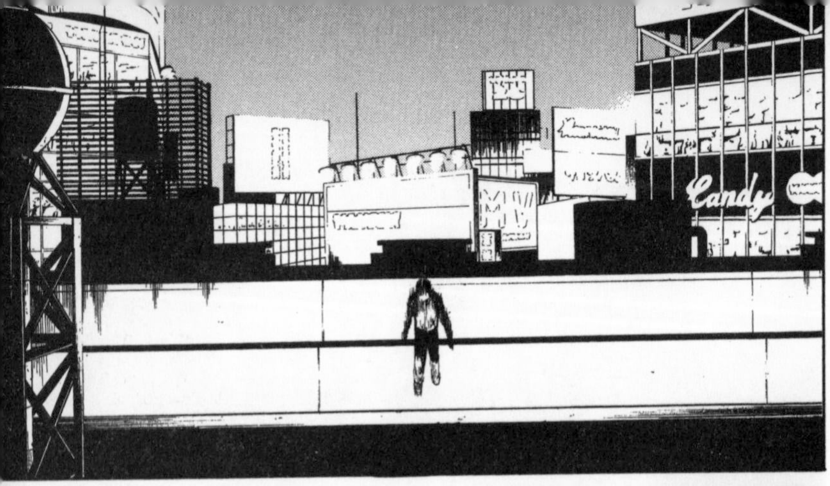
Candy
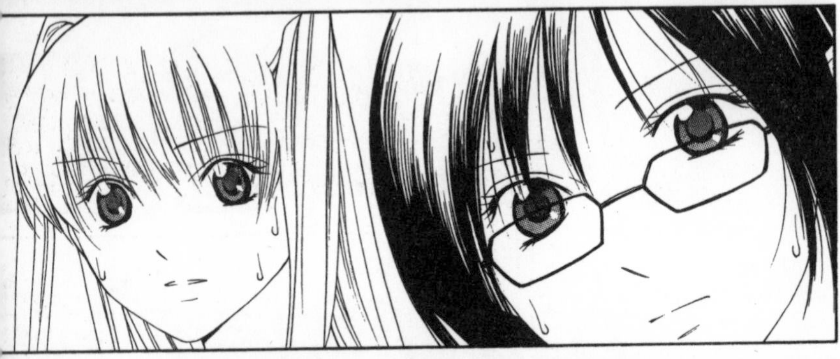
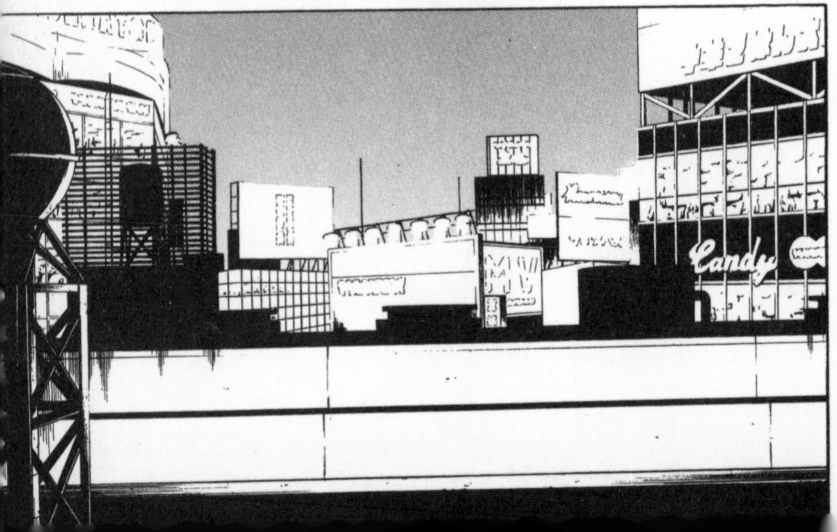
Candy

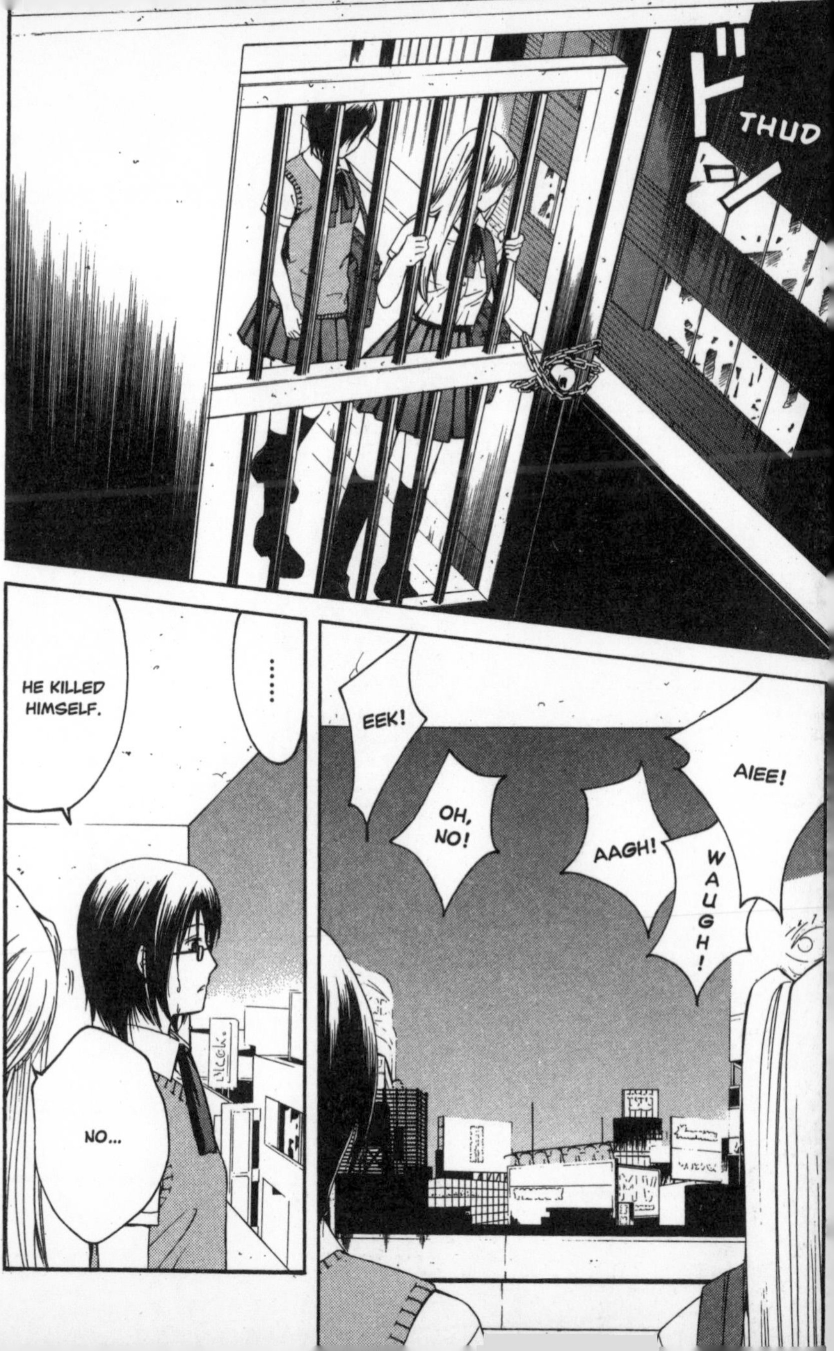
THUD
AIEE!
EEK!
WAUGH!
AAGH!
OH, NO!
......
HE KILLED HIMSELF.
NO...

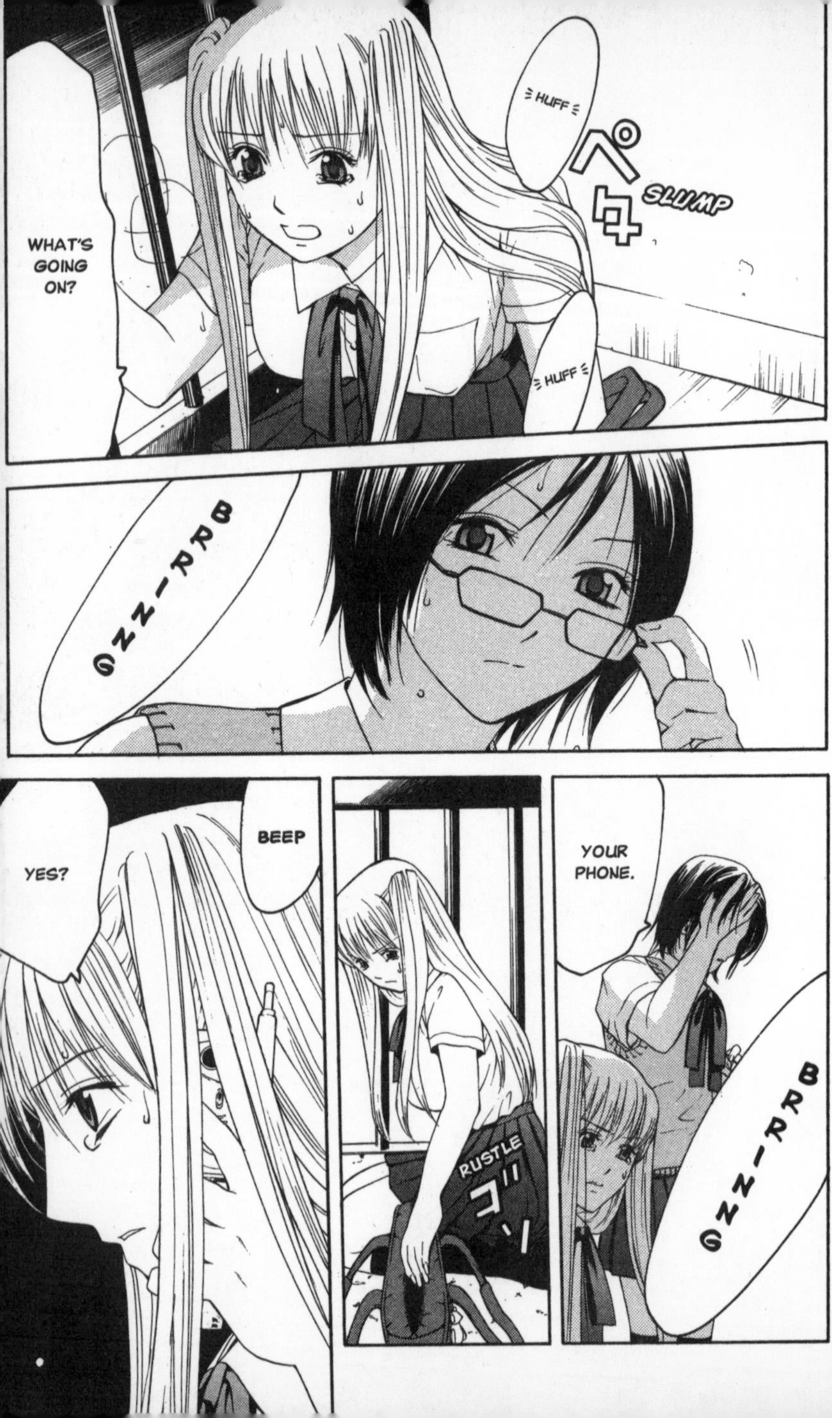
HUFF
SLUMP
HUFF
WHAT'S GOING ON?
BRRINNG
YOUR PHONE.
BRRINNG
RUSTLE
BEEP
YES?

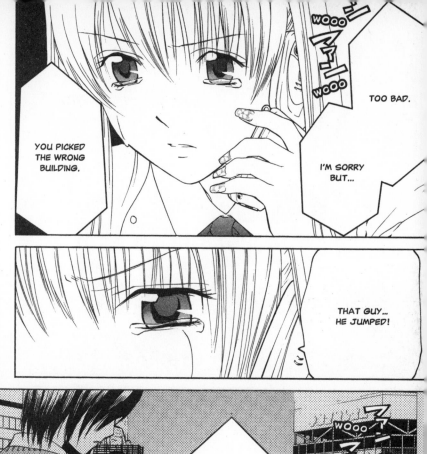

TOO BAD.

YOU PICKED THE WRONG BUILDING.

I'M SORRY BUT...

THAT GUY... HE JUMPED!

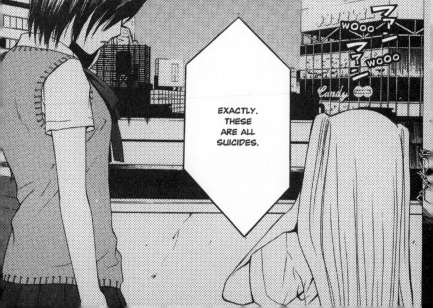

EXACTLY. THESE ARE ALL SUICIDES.

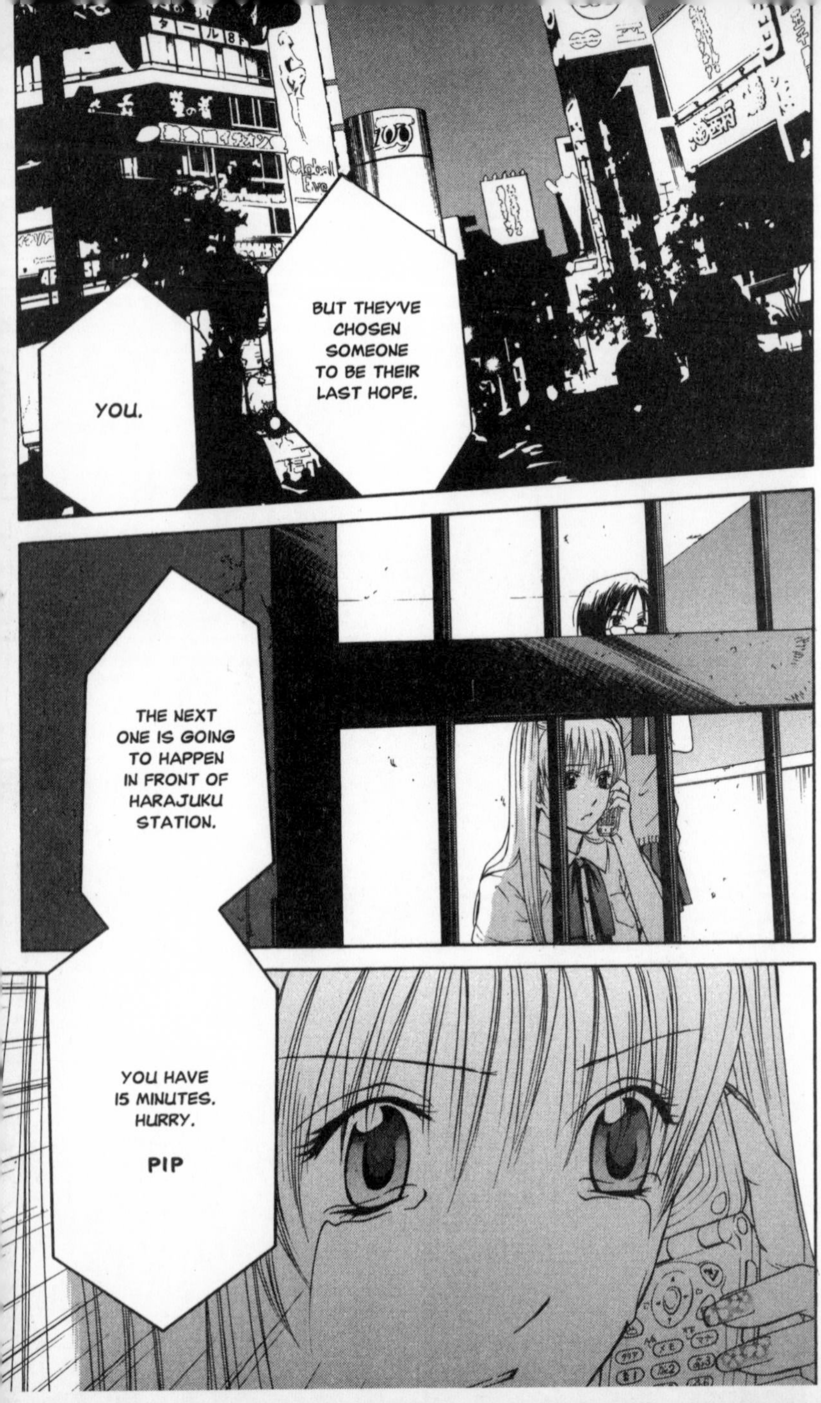
BUT THEY'VE CHOSEN SOMEONE TO BE THEIR LAST HOPE.
YOU.
THE NEXT ONE IS GOING TO HAPPEN IN FRONT OF HARAJUKU STATION.
YOU HAVE 15 MINUTES. HURRY.
PIP

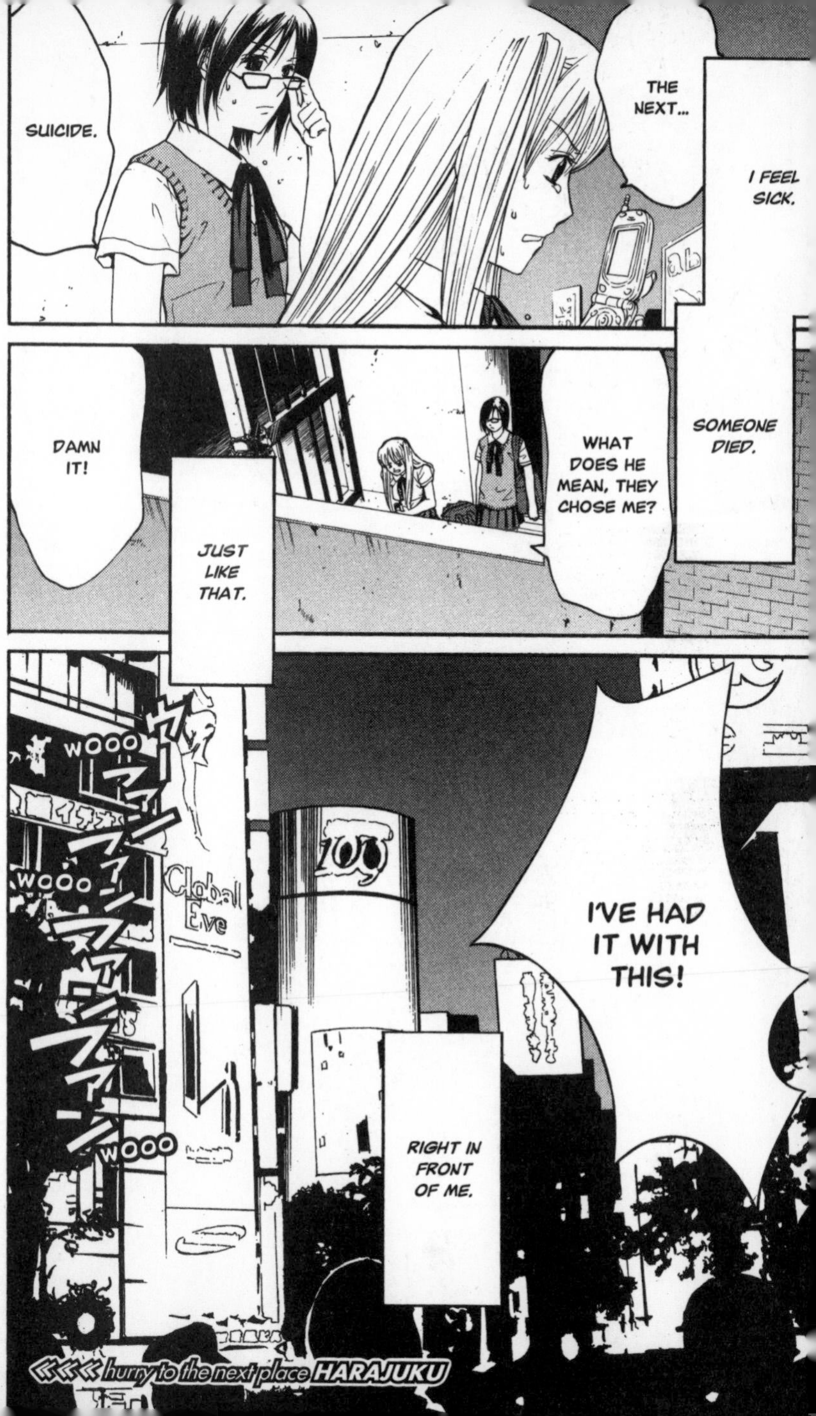
I FEEL SICK.
THE NEXT...
SUICIDE.
SOMEONE DIED.
WHAT DOES HE MEAN, THEY CHOSE ME?
JUST LIKE THAT.
DAMN IT!
I'VE HAD IT WITH THIS!
RIGHT IN FRONT OF ME.
WOOO
WOOO
WOOO
hurry to the next place HARAJUKU

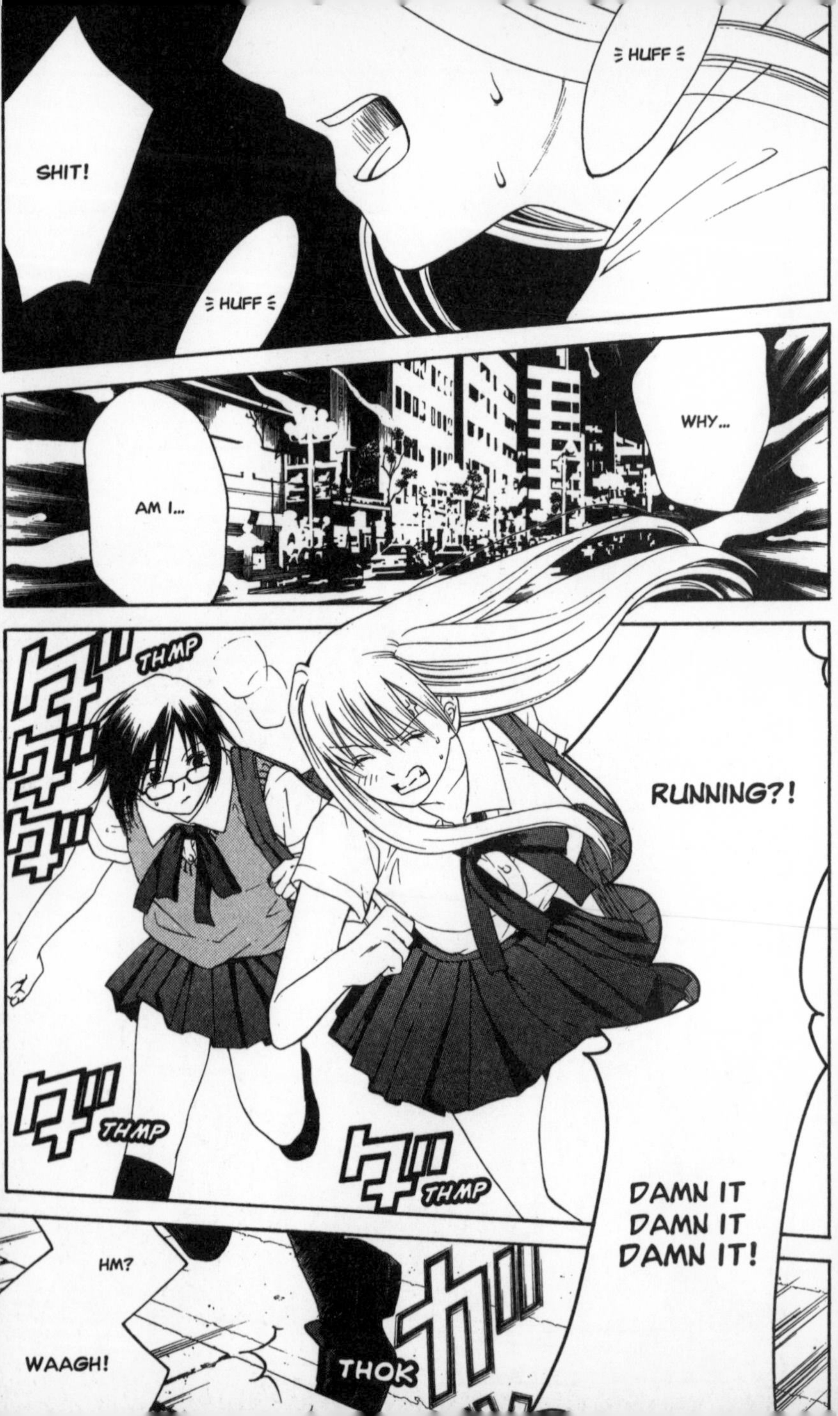

≡ HUFF ≡
SHIT!
≡ HUFF ≡
WHY...
AM I...
RUNNING?!
DAMN IT
DAMN IT
DAMN IT!
THMP
THMP
THMP
THOK
HM?
WAAGH!

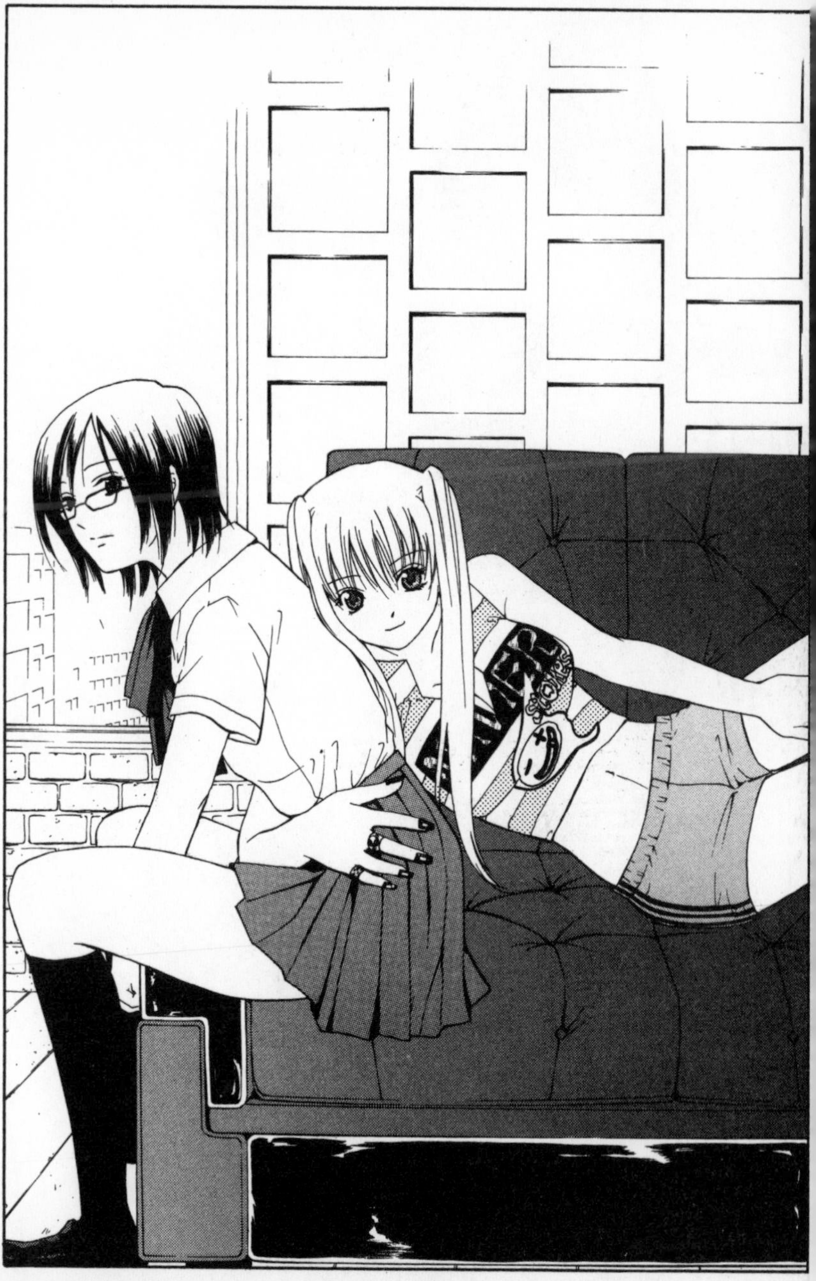

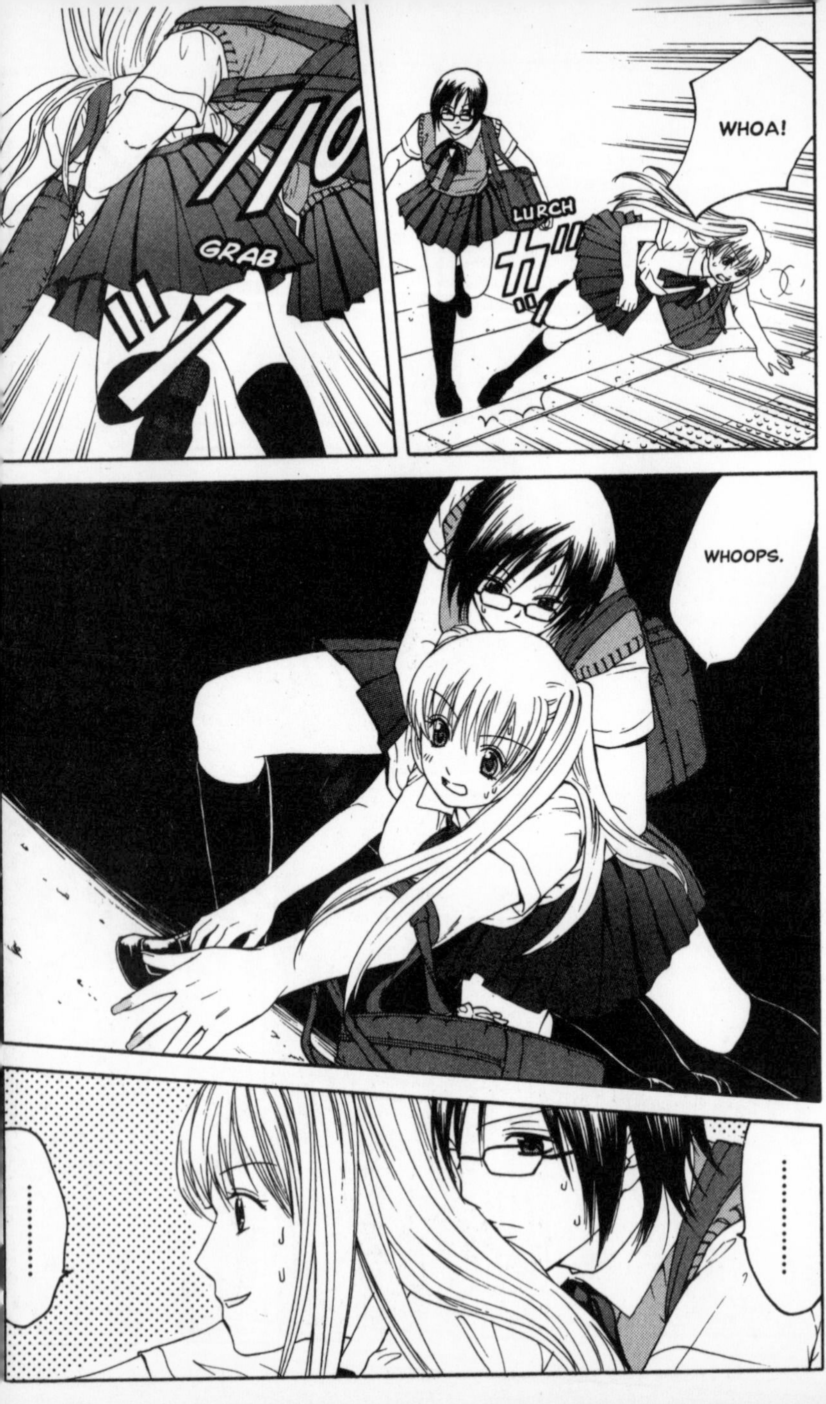
WHOA!
LURCH
GRAB
WHOOPS.
......
......

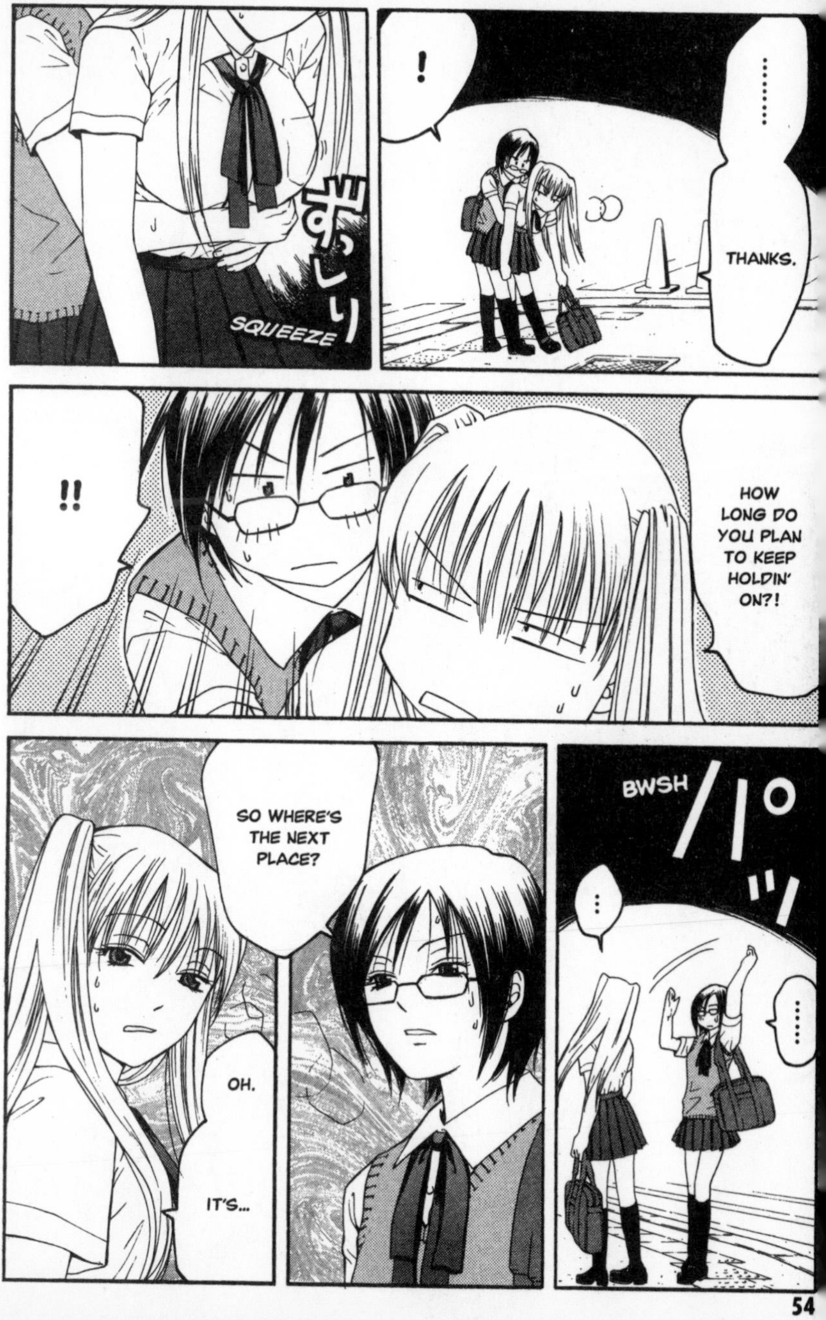

……
THANKS.
!
ずっしり
SQUEEZE
HOW LONG DO YOU PLAN TO KEEP HOLDIN' ON?!
!!
BWSH
パッ
……
…
SO WHERE'S THE NEXT PLACE?
OH.
IT'S...

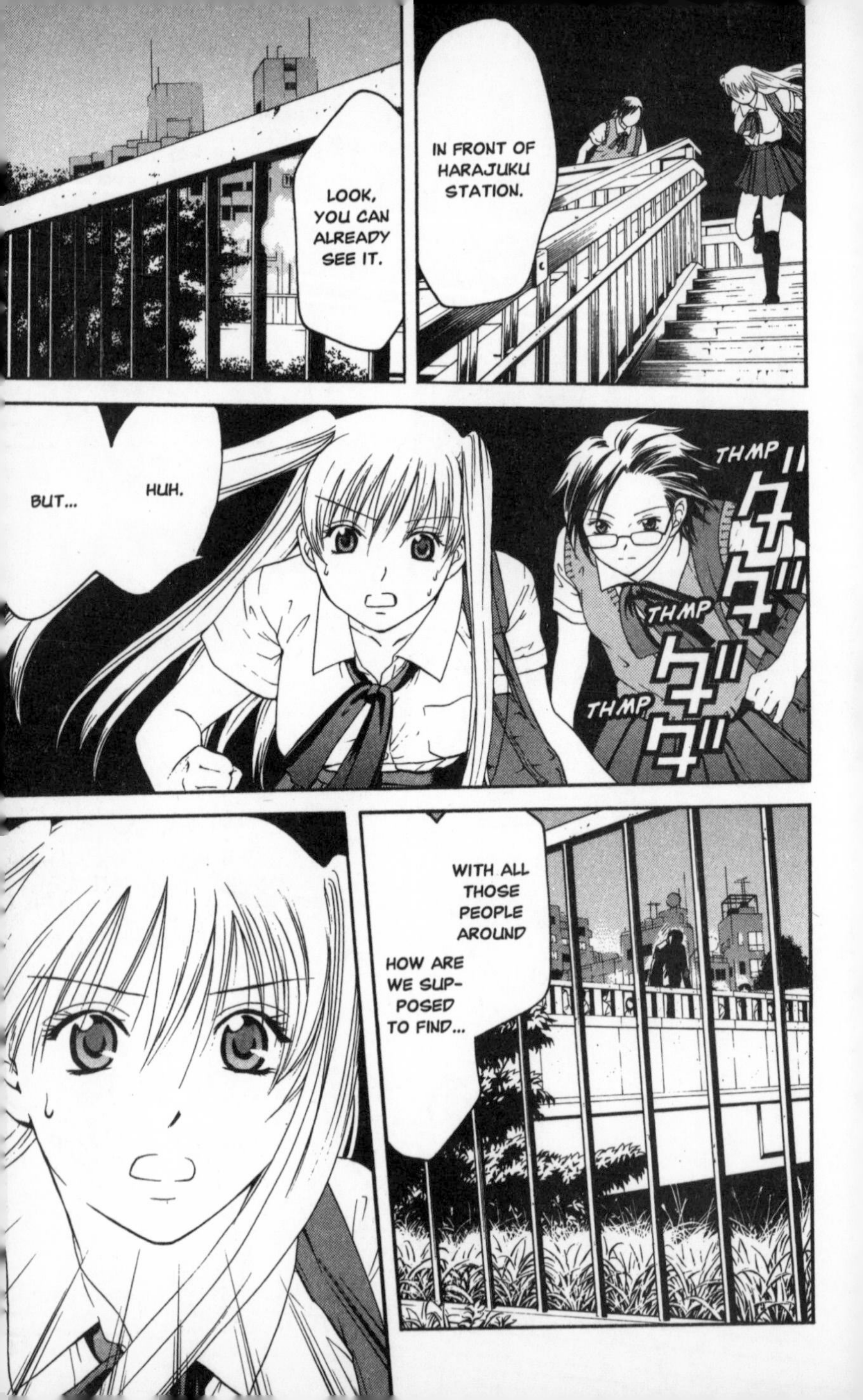
IN FRONT OF HARAJUKU STATION.
LOOK, YOU CAN ALREADY SEE IT.
THMP
THMP
THMP
BUT...
HUH.
WITH ALL THOSE PEOPLE AROUND
HOW ARE WE SUP-POSED TO FIND...

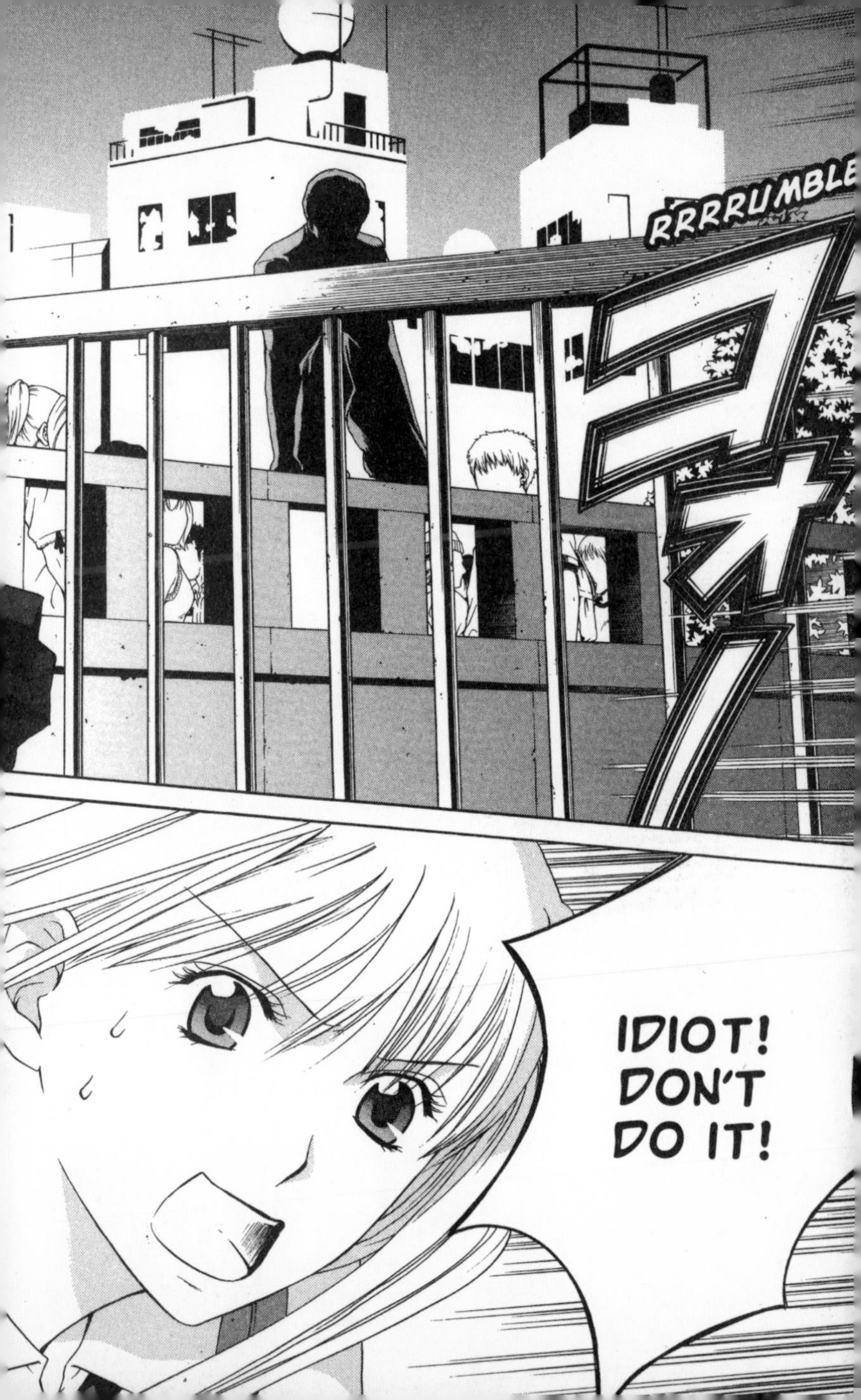
RRRRUMBLE
IDIOT! DON'T DO IT!

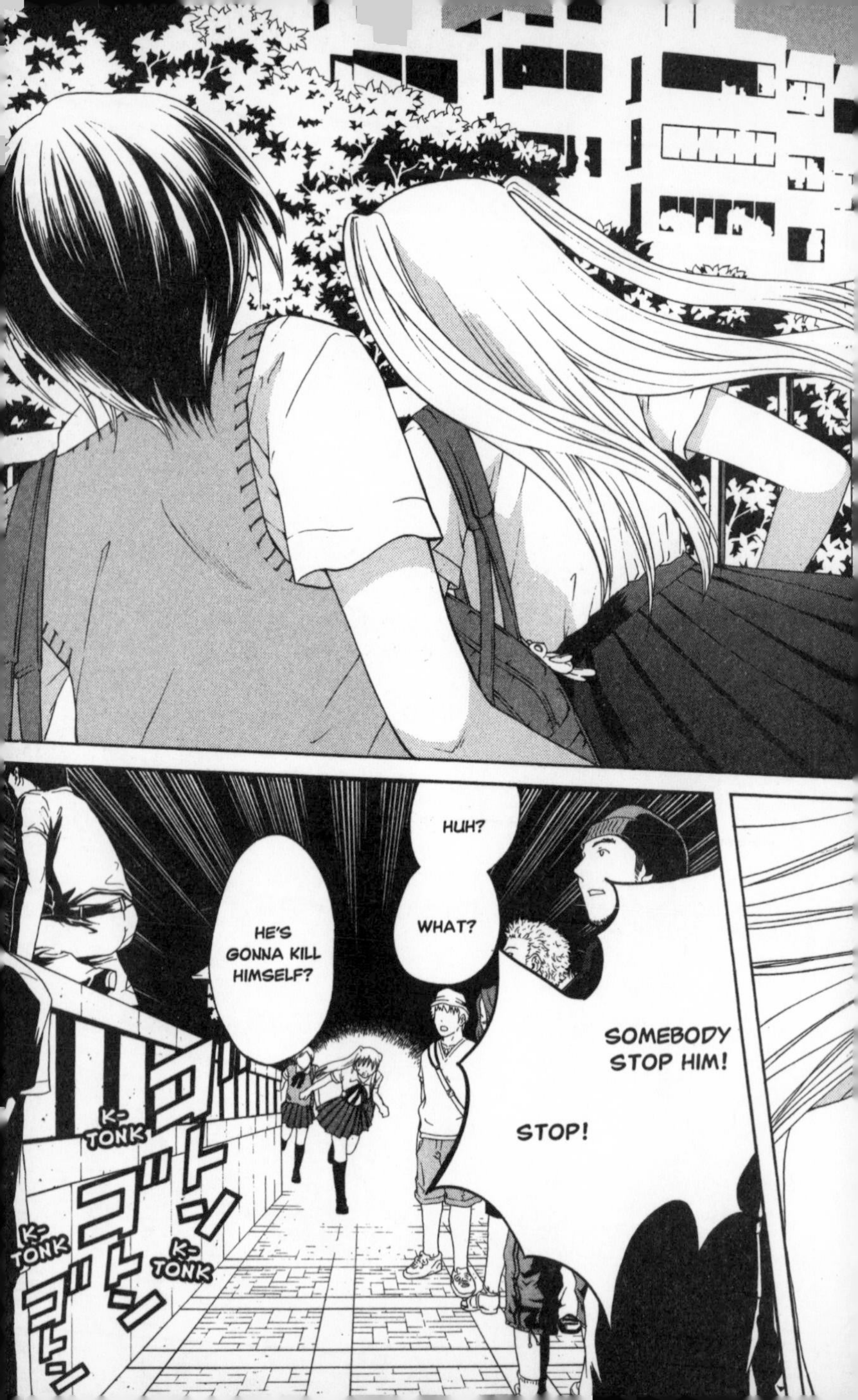
HUH?
WHAT?
SOMEBODY STOP HIM!
STOP!
HE'S GONNA KILL HIMSELF?
K-TONK
K-TONK
K-TONK

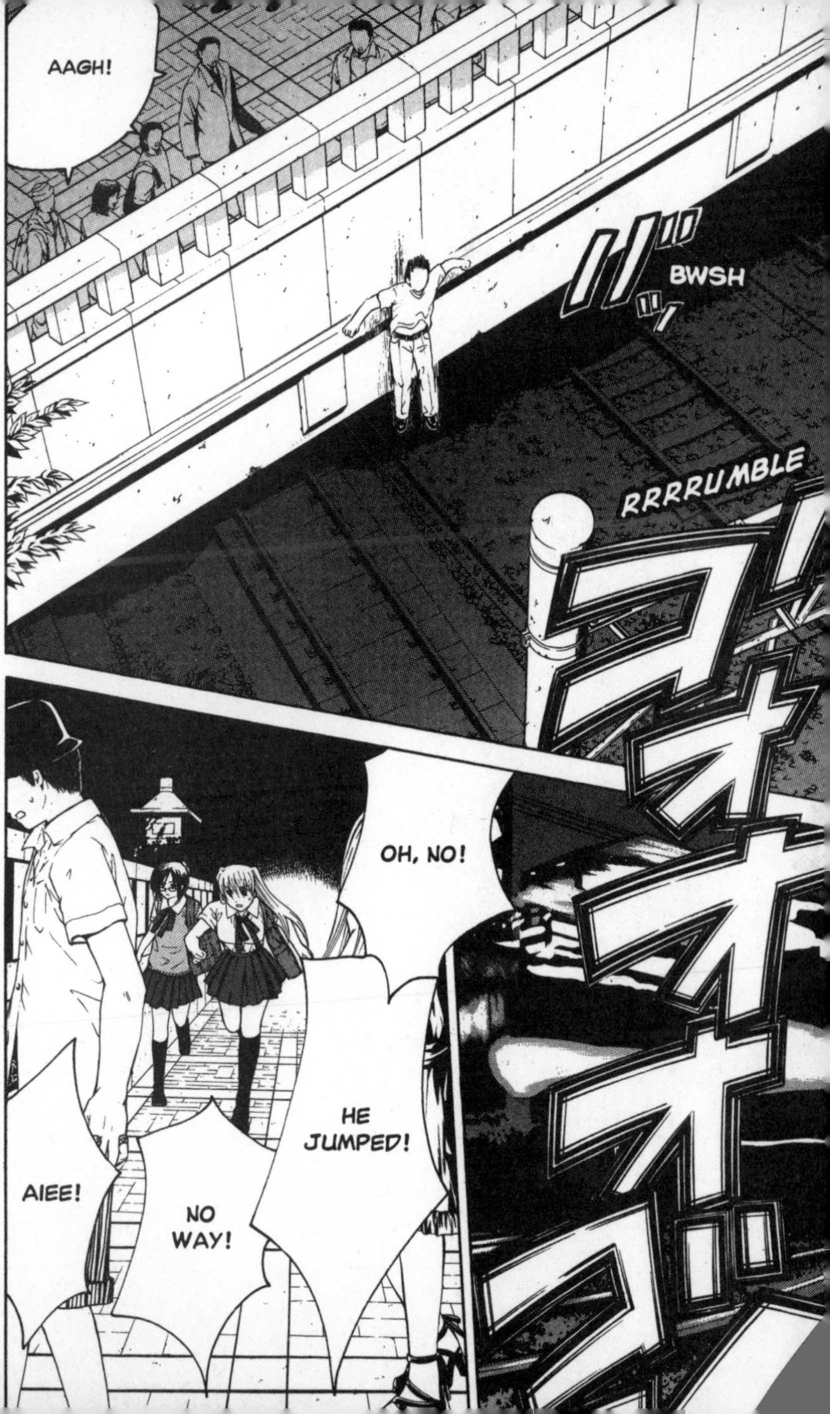
AAGH!
BWSH
RRRRUMBLE
OH, NO!
HE JUMPED!
NO WAY!
AIEE!

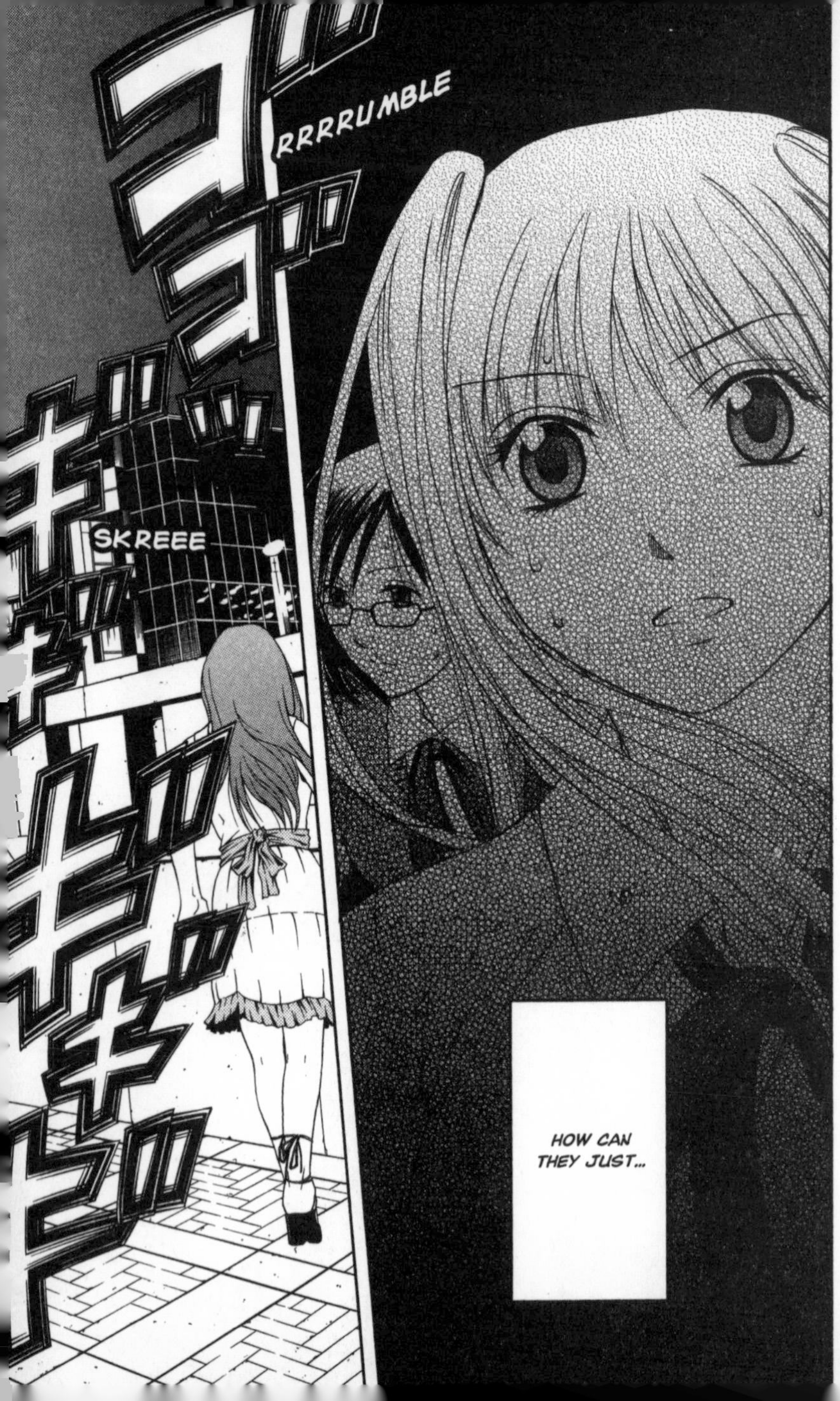
RRRRUMBLE
SKREEE
HOW CAN THEY JUST...

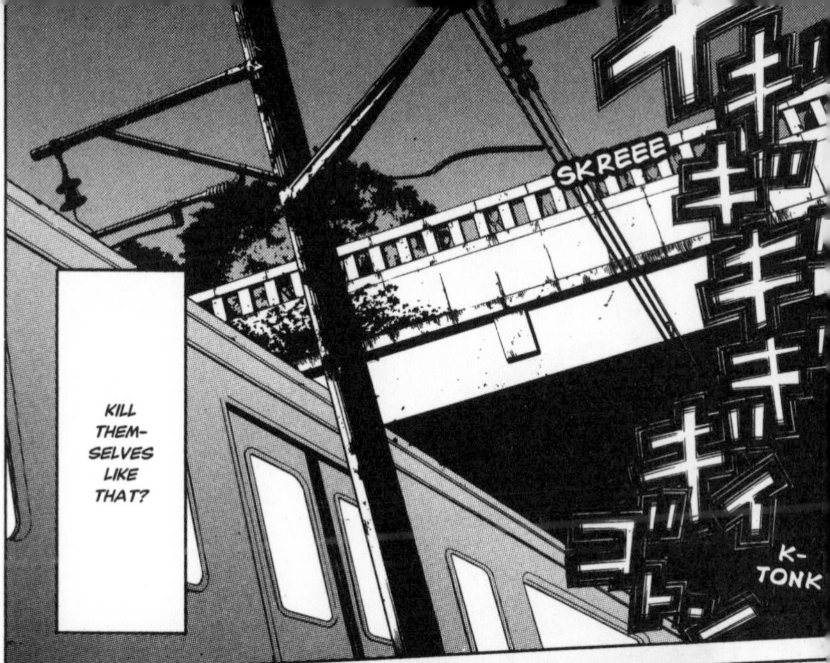
SKREEE
K-TONK
KILL THEM-SELVES LIKE THAT?
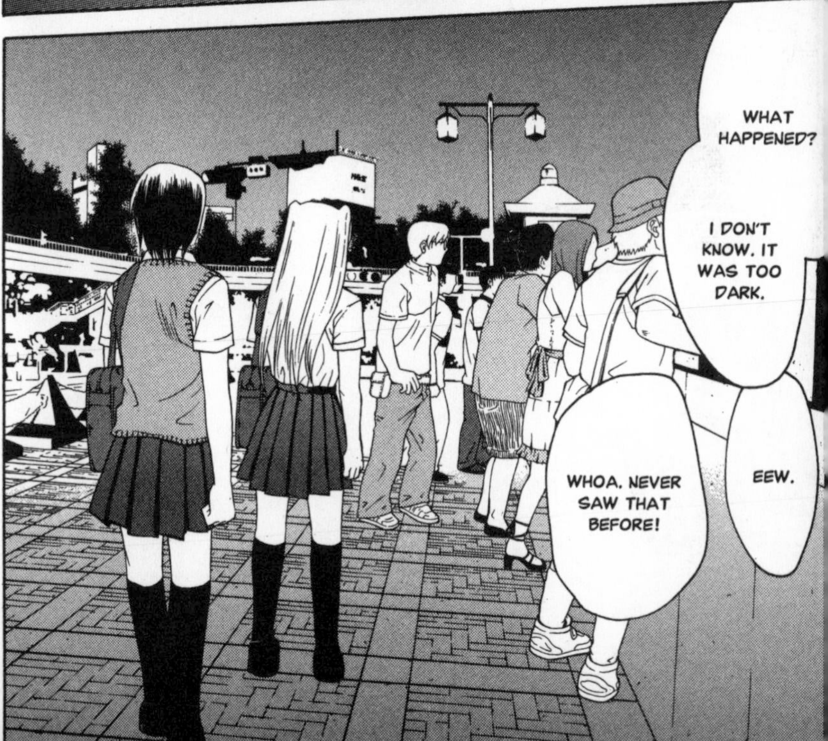
WHAT HAPPENED?
I DON'T KNOW. IT WAS TOO DARK.
EEW.
WHOA. NEVER SAW THAT BEFORE!

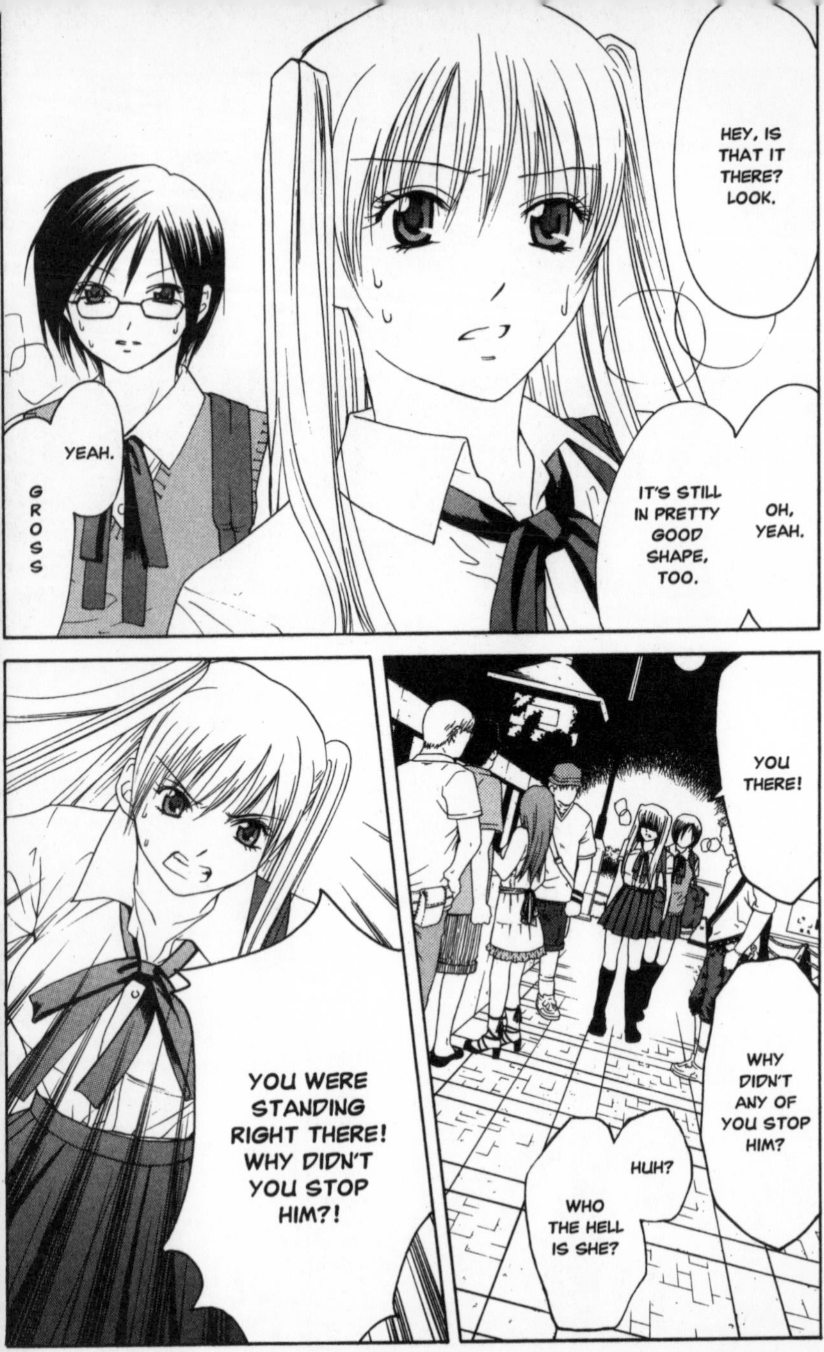
HEY, IS THAT IT THERE? LOOK.
OH, YEAH.
IT'S STILL IN PRETTY GOOD SHAPE, TOO.
YEAH.
GROSS
YOU THERE!
WHY DIDN'T ANY OF YOU STOP HIM?
HUH?
WHO THE HELL IS SHE?
YOU WERE STANDING RIGHT THERE! WHY DIDN'T YOU STOP HIM?!

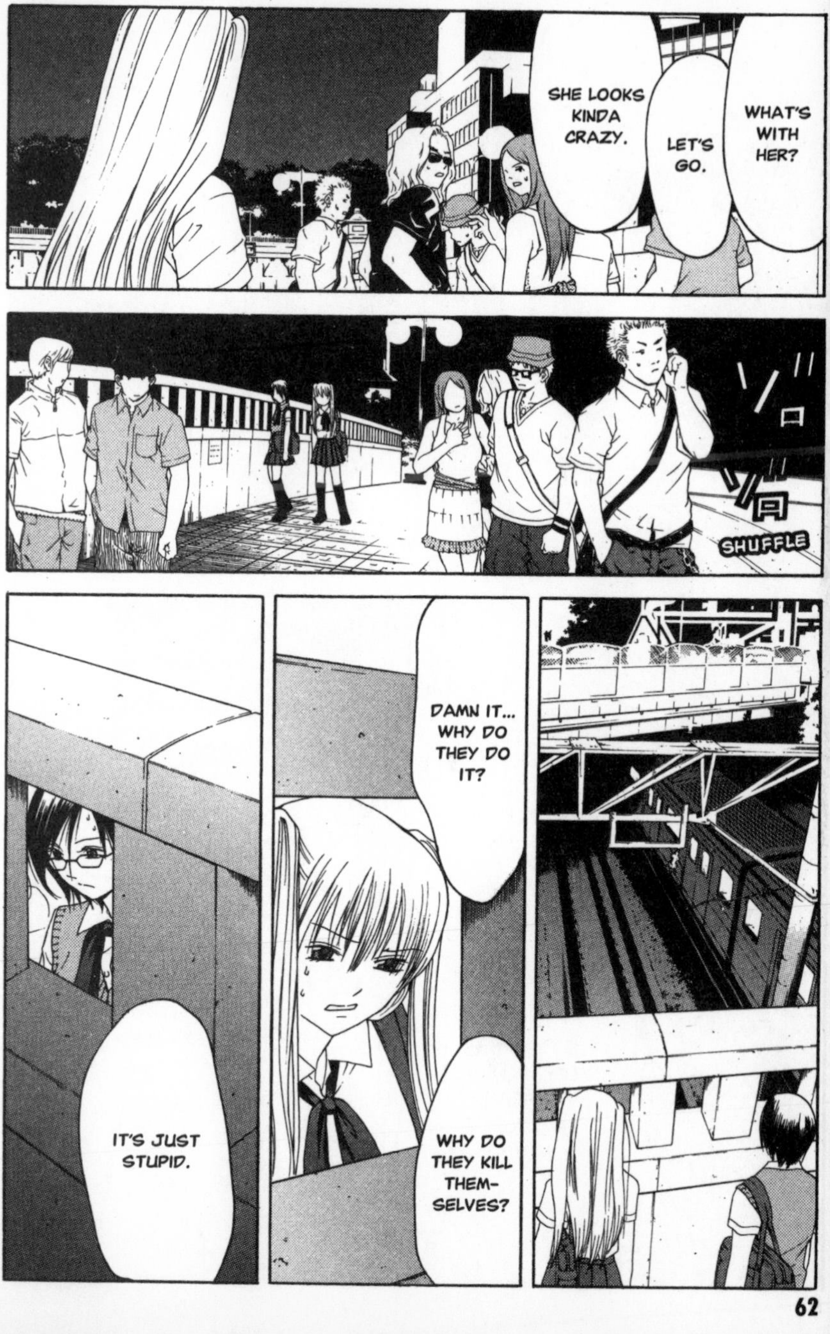
WHAT'S WITH HER?
LET'S GO.
SHE LOOKS KINDA CRAZY.
SHUFFLE
DAMN IT... WHY DO THEY DO IT?
WHY DO THEY KILL THEM-SELVES?
IT'S JUST STUPID.

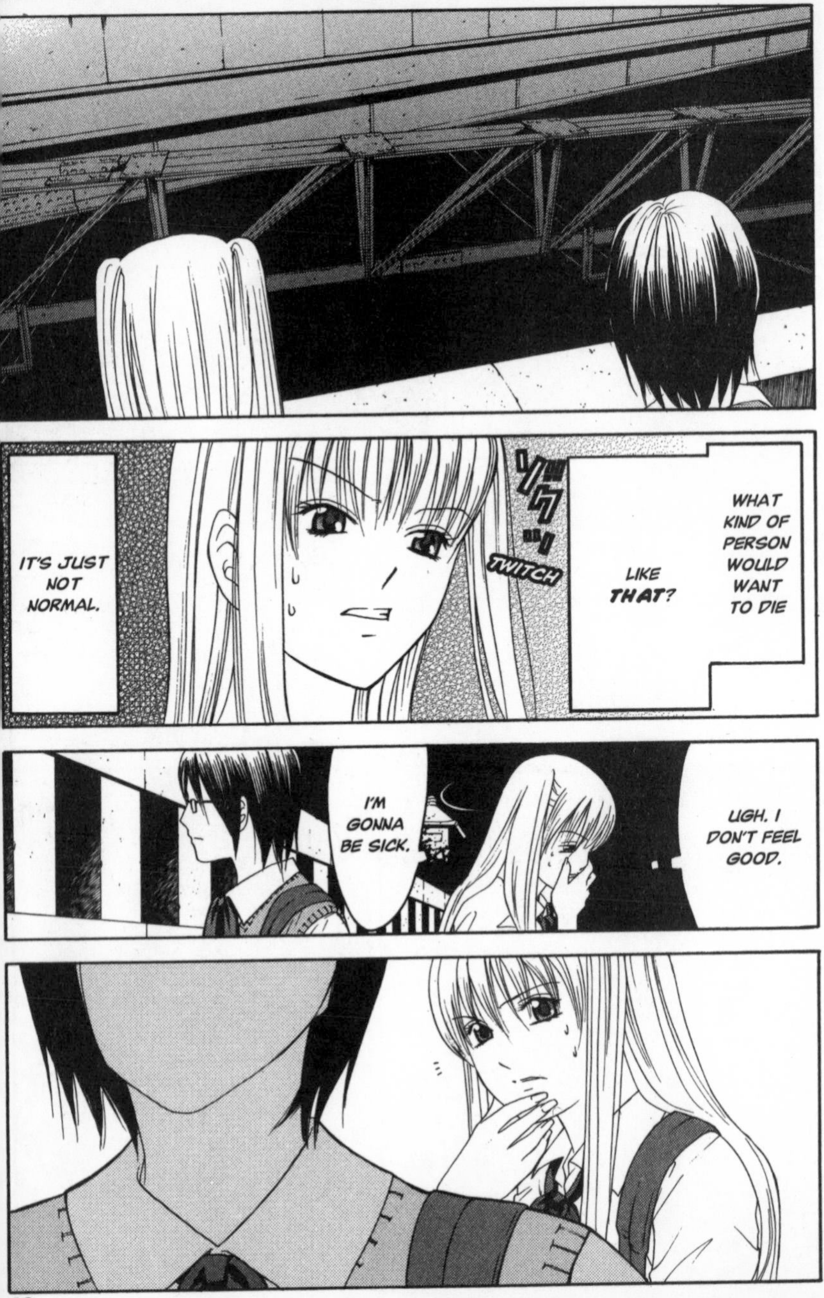
WHAT KIND OF PERSON WOULD WANT TO DIE
LIKE **THAT**?
TWITCH
IT'S JUST NOT NORMAL.
UGH. I DON'T FEEL GOOD.
I'M GONNA BE SICK.

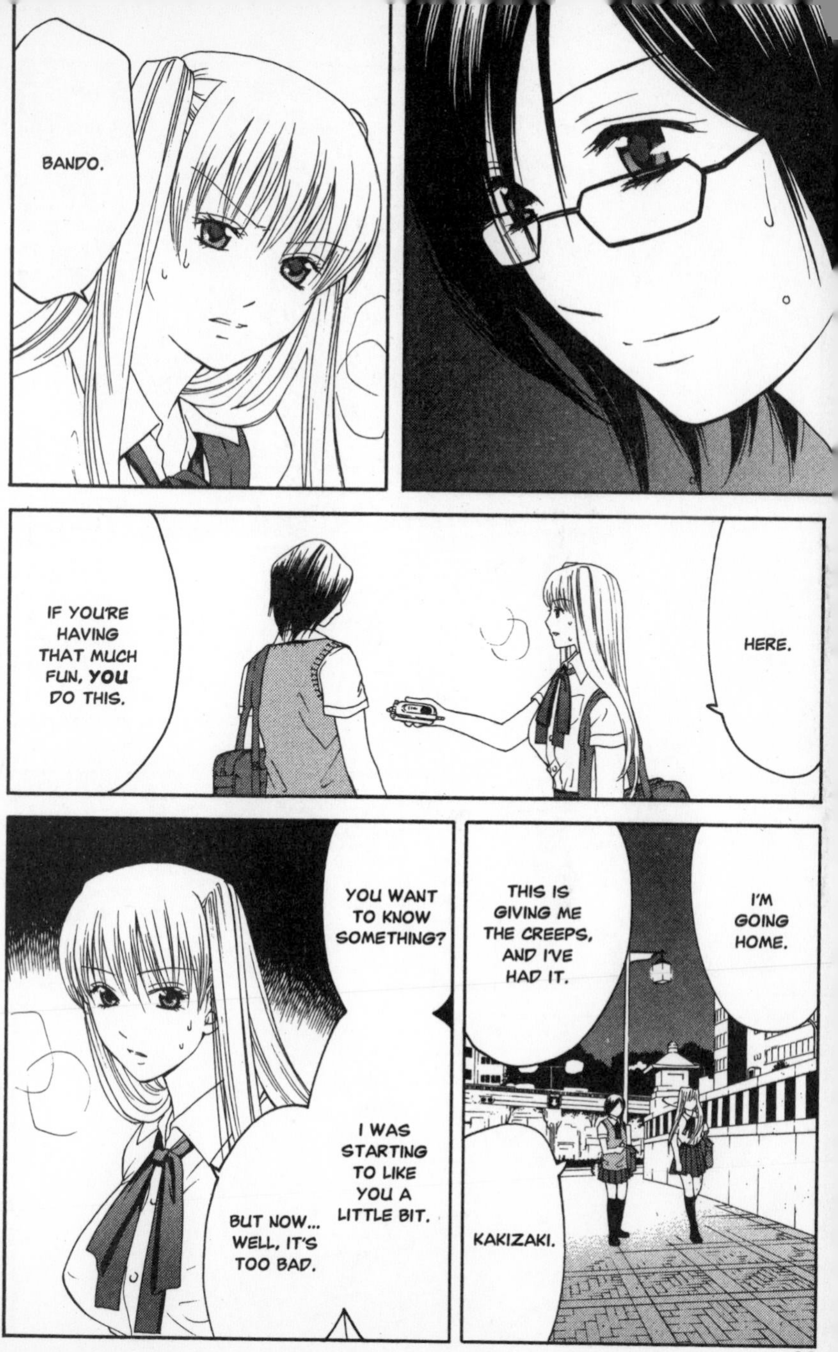
BANDO.
HERE.
IF YOU'RE HAVING THAT MUCH FUN, **YOU** DO THIS.
I'M GOING HOME.
THIS IS GIVING ME THE CREEPS, AND I'VE HAD IT.
KAKIZAKI.
YOU WANT TO KNOW SOMETHING?
I WAS STARTING TO LIKE YOU A LITTLE BIT.
BUT NOW... WELL, IT'S TOO BAD.

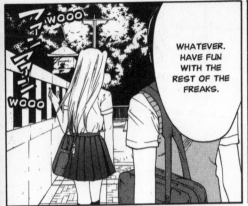

WOOO
WOOO
WOOO
WOOO
WHATEVER. HAVE FUN WITH THE REST OF THE FREAKS.
WOOO
SEE YA.
WOOO
KARAOKE
WHAT'S UP?
YAAAAY!
CHIKO! WE'VE BEEN WAITIN' FOR YOU, GIRL!
JEEZ, TOOK YOU LONG ENOUGH!

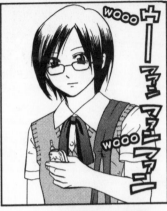

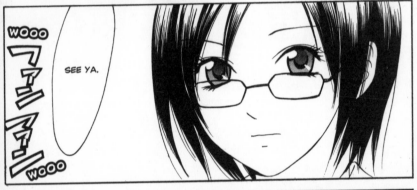

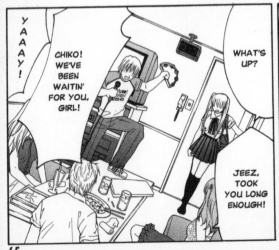

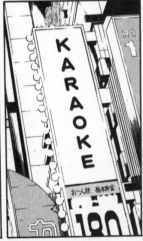

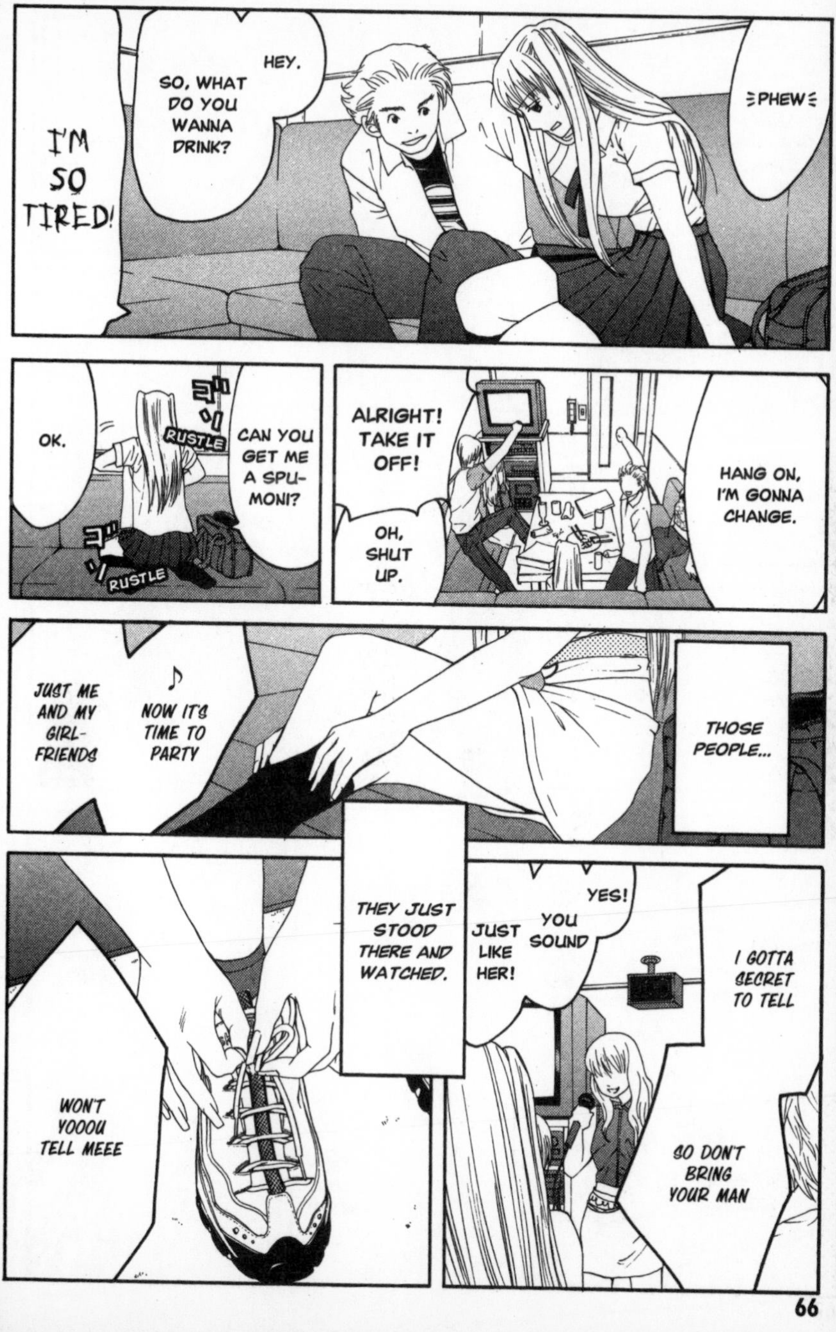
PHEW
HEY. SO, WHAT DO YOU WANNA DRINK?
I'M SO TIRED!
HANG ON, I'M GONNA CHANGE.
ALRIGHT! TAKE IT OFF!
OH, SHUT UP.
CAN YOU GET ME A SPU-MONI?
RUSTLE
OK.
RUSTLE
THOSE PEOPLE...
♪ NOW IT'S TIME TO PARTY
JUST ME AND MY GIRL-FRIENDS
I GOTTA SECRET TO TELL
YES! YOU SOUND JUST LIKE HER!
THEY JUST STOOD THERE AND WATCHED.
SO DON'T BRING YOUR MAN
WON'T YOOOU TELL MEEE

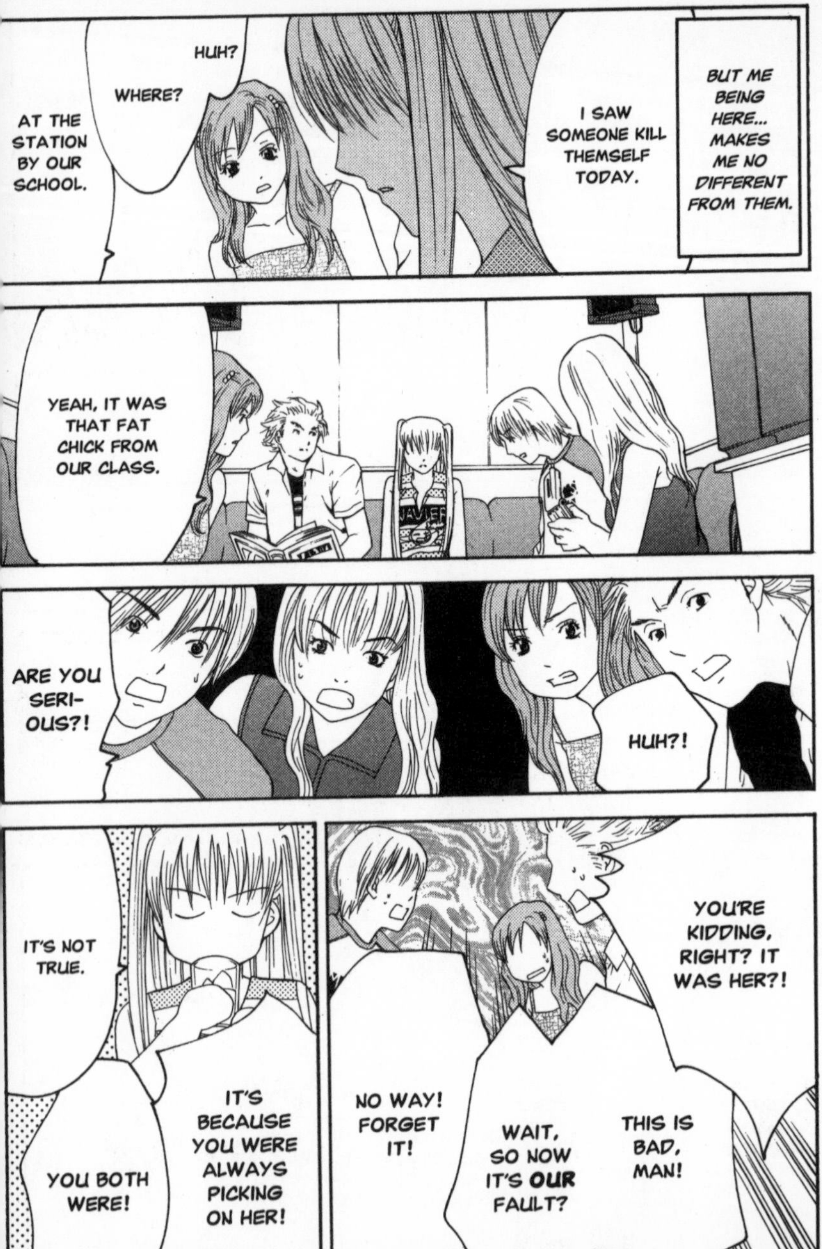

BUT ME BEING HERE... MAKES ME NO DIFFERENT FROM THEM.
I SAW SOMEONE KILL THEMSELF TODAY.
HUH?
WHERE?
AT THE STATION BY OUR SCHOOL.
YEAH, IT WAS THAT FAT CHICK FROM OUR CLASS.
HUH?!
ARE YOU SERI- OUS?!
YOU'RE KIDDING, RIGHT? IT WAS HER?!
THIS IS BAD, MAN!
WAIT, SO NOW IT'S **OUR** FAULT?
NO WAY! FORGET IT!
IT'S NOT TRUE.
IT'S BECAUSE YOU WERE ALWAYS PICKING ON HER!
YOU BOTH WERE!

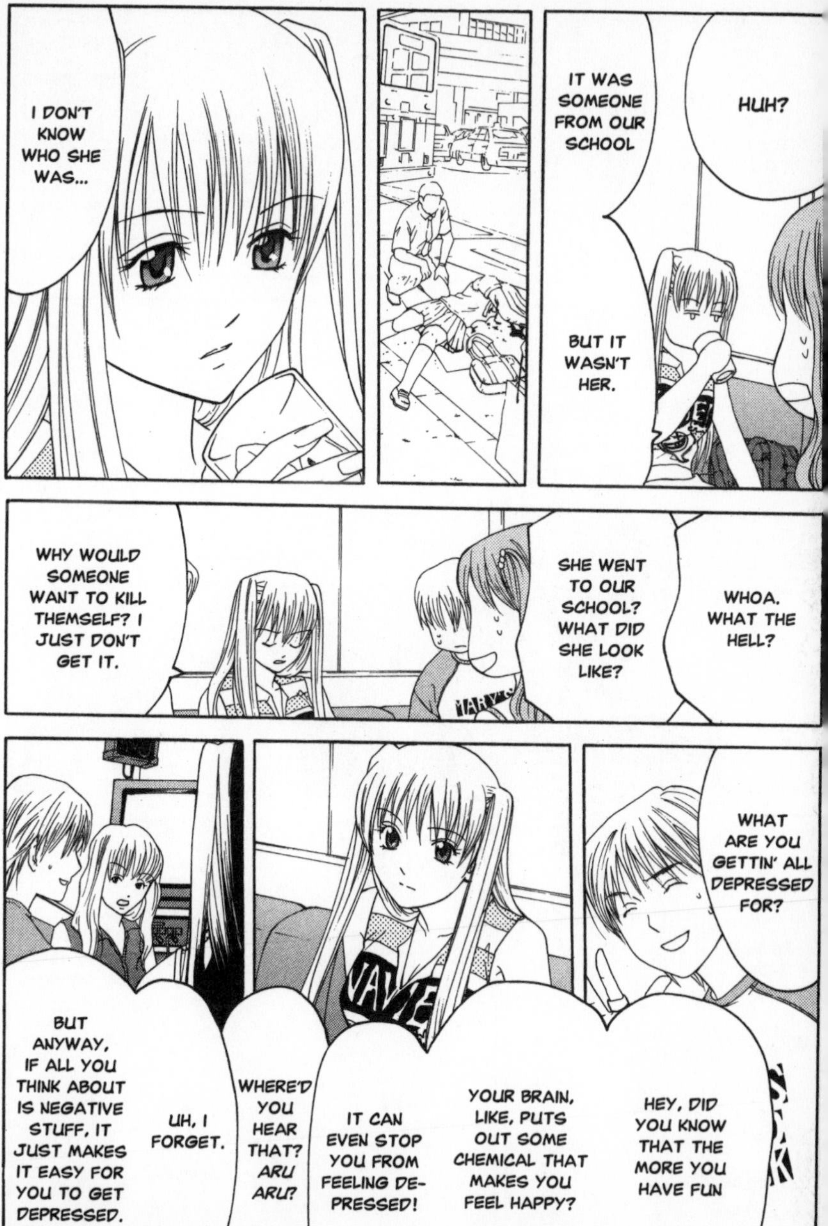
HUH?
IT WAS SOMEONE FROM OUR SCHOOL
BUT IT WASN'T HER.
I DON'T KNOW WHO SHE WAS...
WHOA. WHAT THE HELL?
SHE WENT TO OUR SCHOOL? WHAT DID SHE LOOK LIKE?
WHY WOULD SOMEONE WANT TO KILL THEMSELF? I JUST DON'T GET IT.
WHAT ARE YOU GETTIN' ALL DEPRESSED FOR?
HEY, DID YOU KNOW THAT THE MORE YOU HAVE FUN
YOUR BRAIN, LIKE, PUTS OUT SOME CHEMICAL THAT MAKES YOU FEEL HAPPY?
IT CAN EVEN STOP YOU FROM FEELING DE-PRESSED!
WHERE'D YOU HEAR THAT? ARU ARU?
UH, I FORGET.
BUT ANYWAY, IF ALL YOU THINK ABOUT IS NEGATIVE STUFF, IT JUST MAKES IT EASY FOR YOU TO GET DEPRESSED.

**HAKKUTSU! ARU ARU DAIJITEN*: A TV SHOW THAT FOCUSES ON FOOD AND HEALTH.

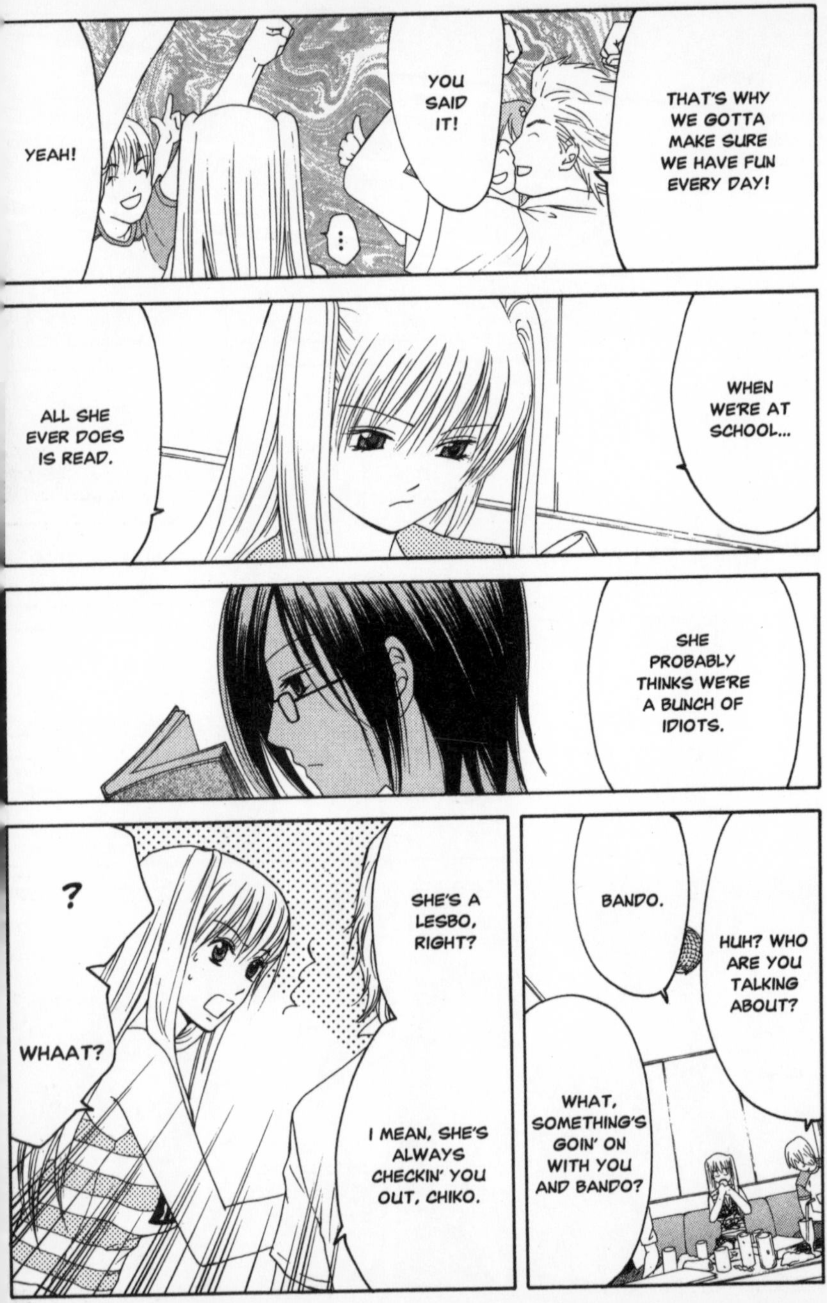
THAT'S WHY WE GOTTA MAKE SURE WE HAVE FUN EVERY DAY!
YOU SAID IT!
...
YEAH!
WHEN WE'RE AT SCHOOL...
ALL SHE EVER DOES IS READ.
SHE PROBABLY THINKS WE'RE A BUNCH OF IDIOTS.
BANDO.
HUH? WHO ARE YOU TALKING ABOUT?
WHAT, SOMETHING'S GOIN' ON WITH YOU AND BANDO?
SHE'S A LESBO, RIGHT?
I MEAN, SHE'S ALWAYS CHECKIN' YOU OUT, CHIKO.
?
WHAAT?

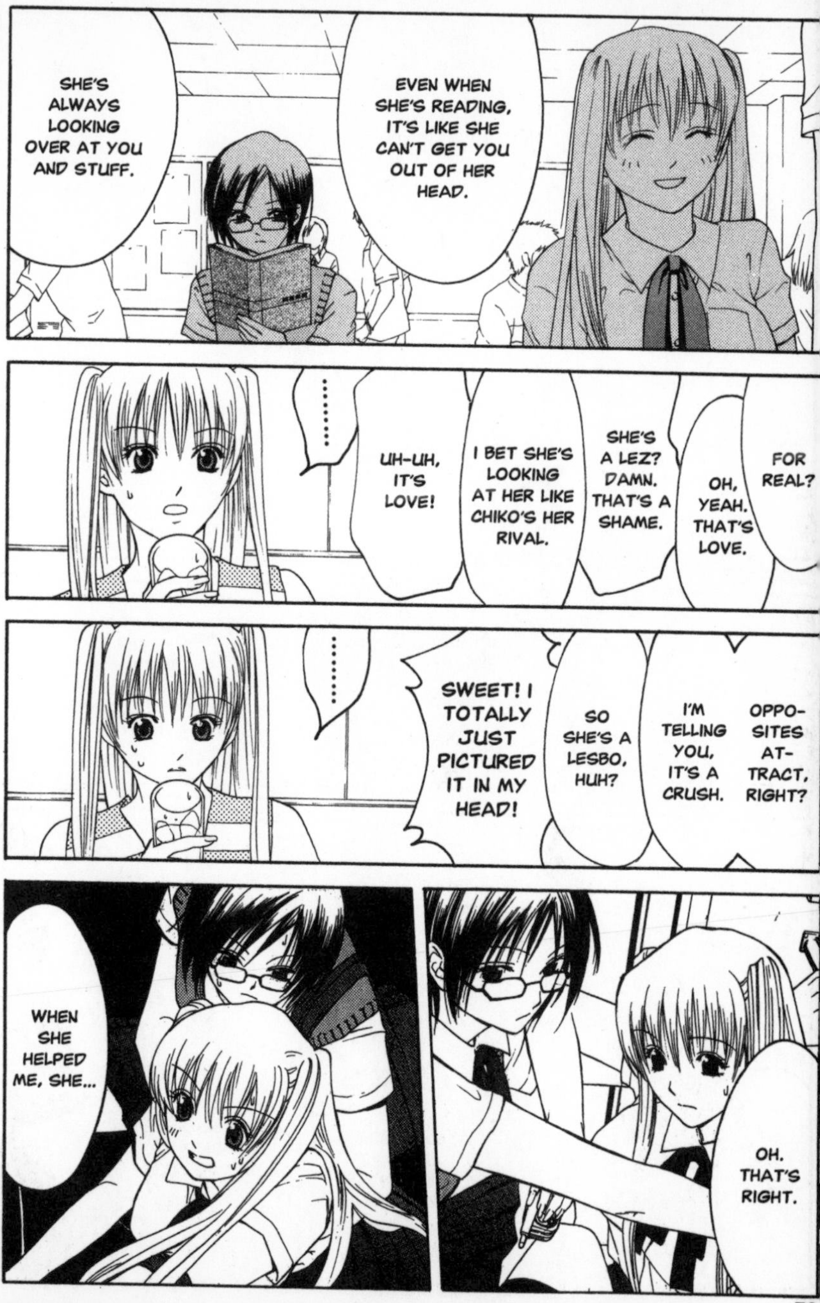
EVEN WHEN SHE'S READING, IT'S LIKE SHE CAN'T GET YOU OUT OF HER HEAD.
SHE'S ALWAYS LOOKING OVER AT YOU AND STUFF.
FOR REAL?
OH, YEAH. THAT'S LOVE.
SHE'S A LEZ? DAMN. THAT'S A SHAME.
I BET SHE'S LOOKING AT HER LIKE CHIKO'S HER RIVAL.
UH-UH, IT'S LOVE!
......
OPPO-SITES AT-TRACT, RIGHT?
I'M TELLING YOU, IT'S A CRUSH.
SO SHE'S A LESBO, HUH?
SWEET! I TOTALLY JUST PICTURED IT IN MY HEAD!
......
OH. THAT'S RIGHT.
WHEN SHE HELPED ME, SHE...

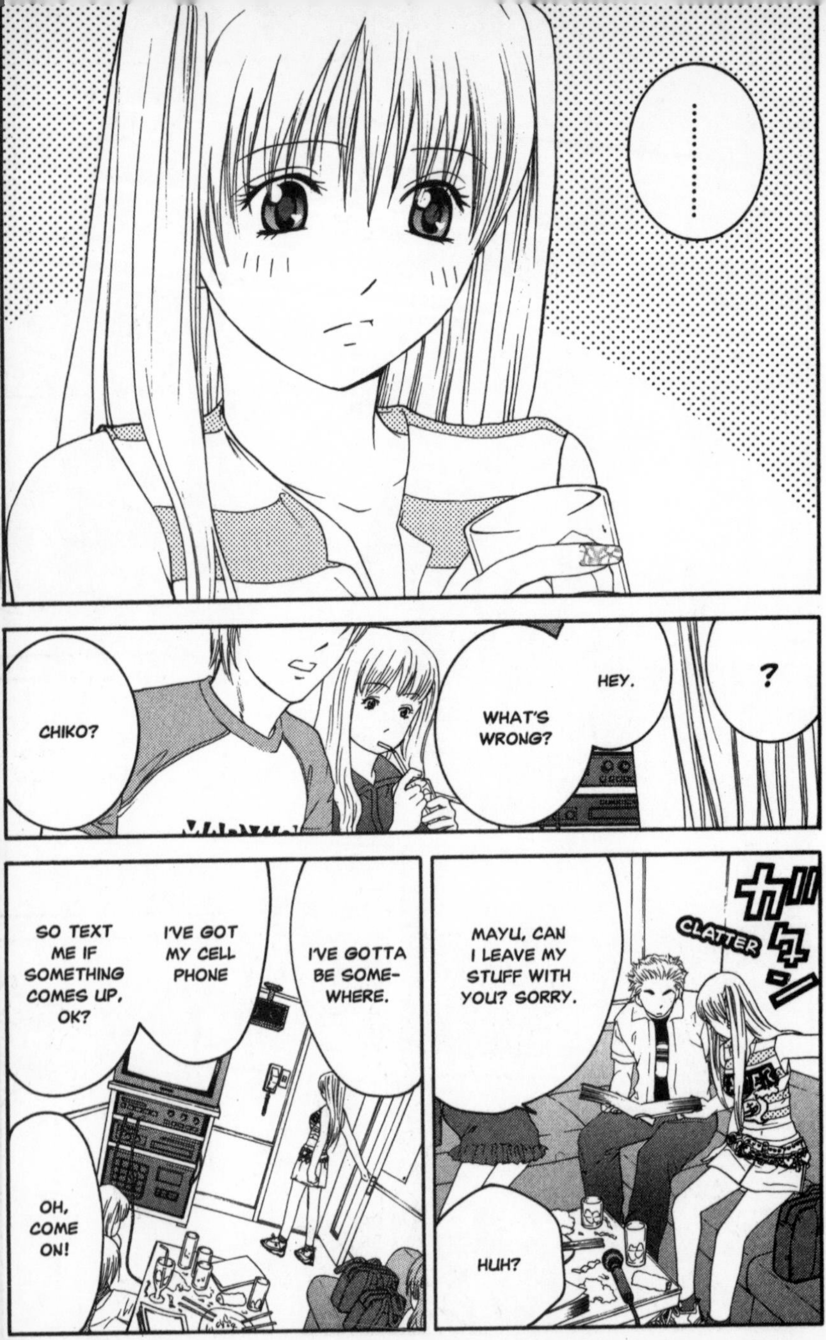
......
?
HEY. WHAT'S WRONG?
CHIKO?
CLATTER
MAYU, CAN I LEAVE MY STUFF WITH YOU? SORRY.
HUH?
I'VE GOTTA BE SOME-WHERE.
I'VE GOT MY CELL PHONE
SO TEXT ME IF SOMETHING COMES UP, OK?
OH, COME ON!

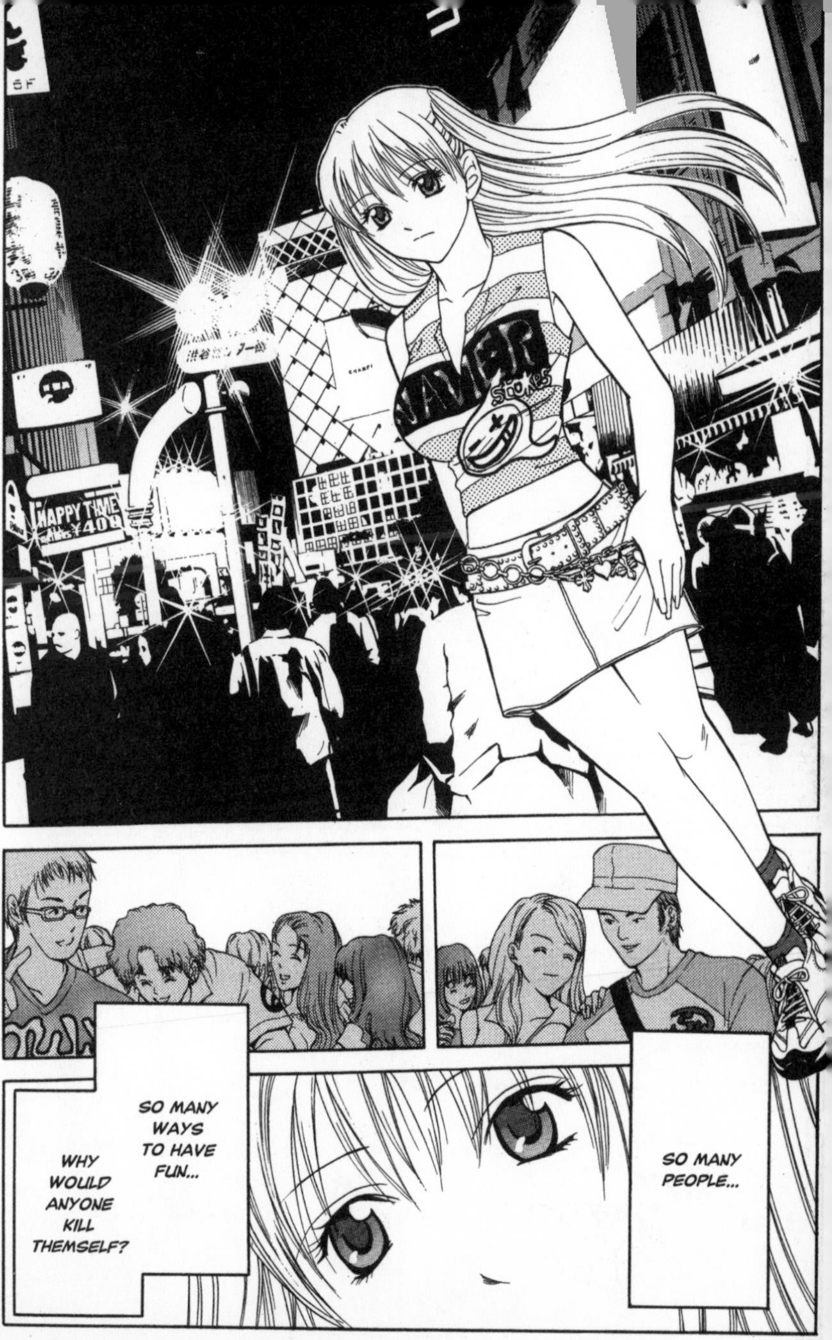
5F
HAPPY TIME
¥400
SO MANY PEOPLE...
SO MANY WAYS TO HAVE FUN...
WHY WOULD ANYONE KILL THEMSELF?

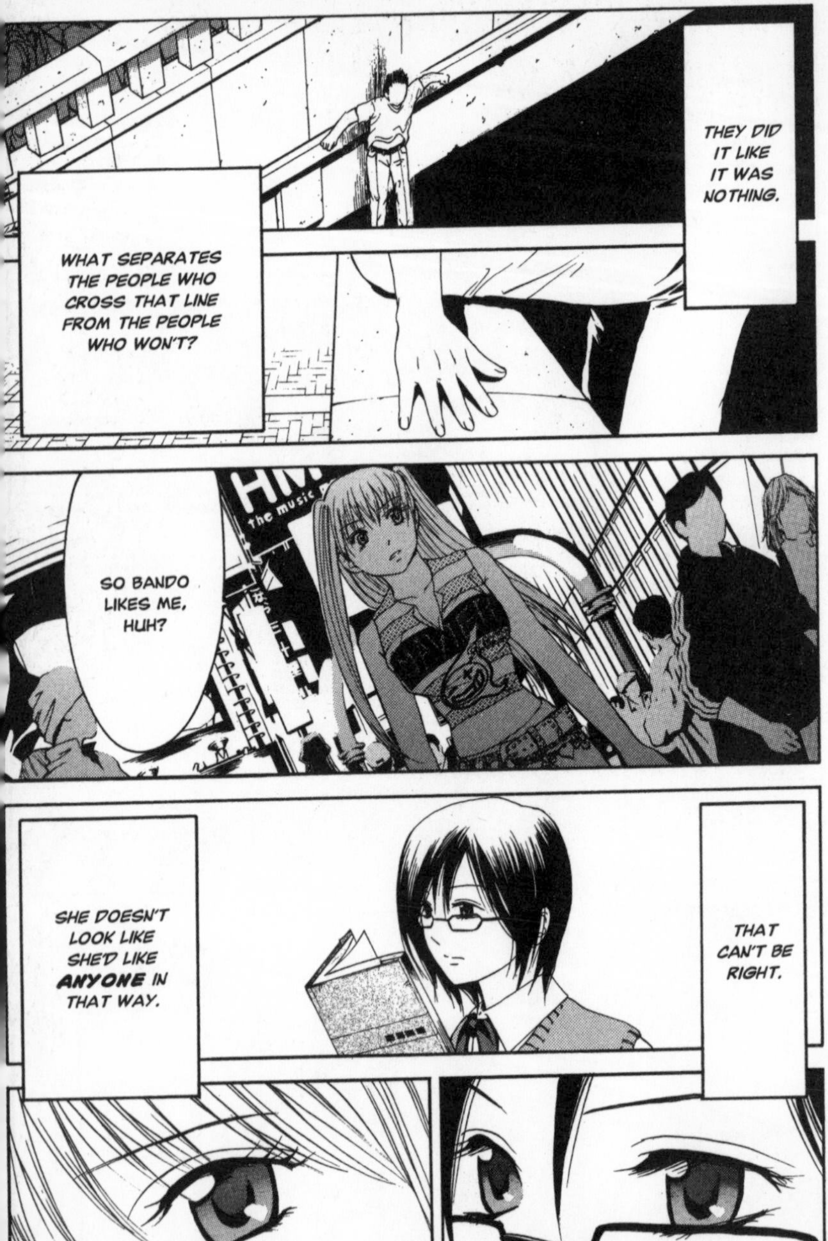
THEY DID IT LIKE IT WAS NOTHING.
WHAT SEPARATES THE PEOPLE WHO CROSS THAT LINE FROM THE PEOPLE WHO WON'T?
SO BANDO LIKES ME, HUH?
THAT CAN'T BE RIGHT.
SHE DOESN'T LOOK LIKE SHE'D LIKE **ANYONE** IN THAT WAY.

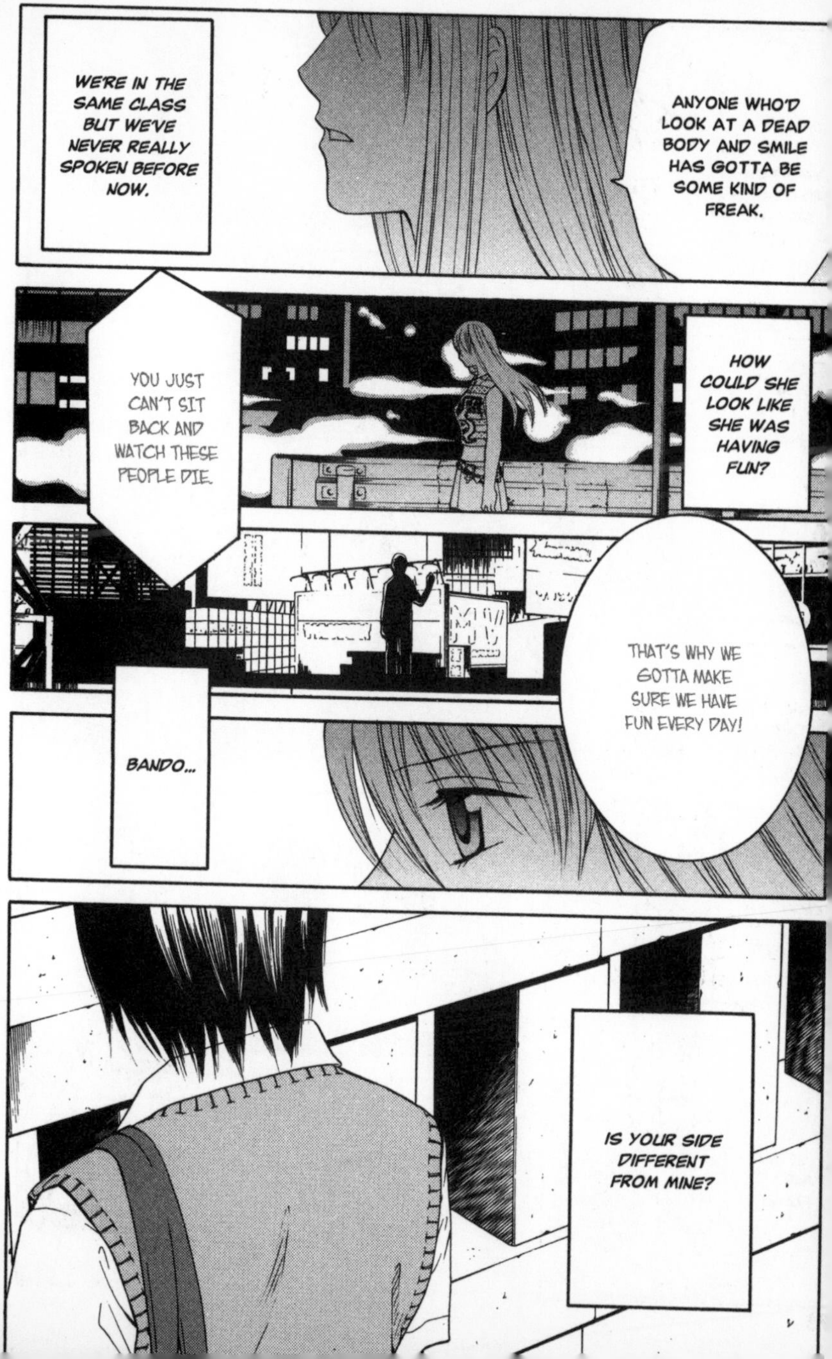
ANYONE WHO'D LOOK AT A DEAD BODY AND SMILE HAS GOTTA BE SOME KIND OF FREAK.
WE'RE IN THE SAME CLASS BUT WE'VE NEVER REALLY SPOKEN BEFORE NOW.
HOW COULD SHE LOOK LIKE SHE WAS HAVING FUN?
YOU JUST CAN'T SIT BACK AND WATCH THESE PEOPLE DIE.
THAT'S WHY WE GOTTA MAKE SURE WE HAVE FUN EVERY DAY!
BANDO...
IS YOUR SIDE DIFFERENT FROM MINE?

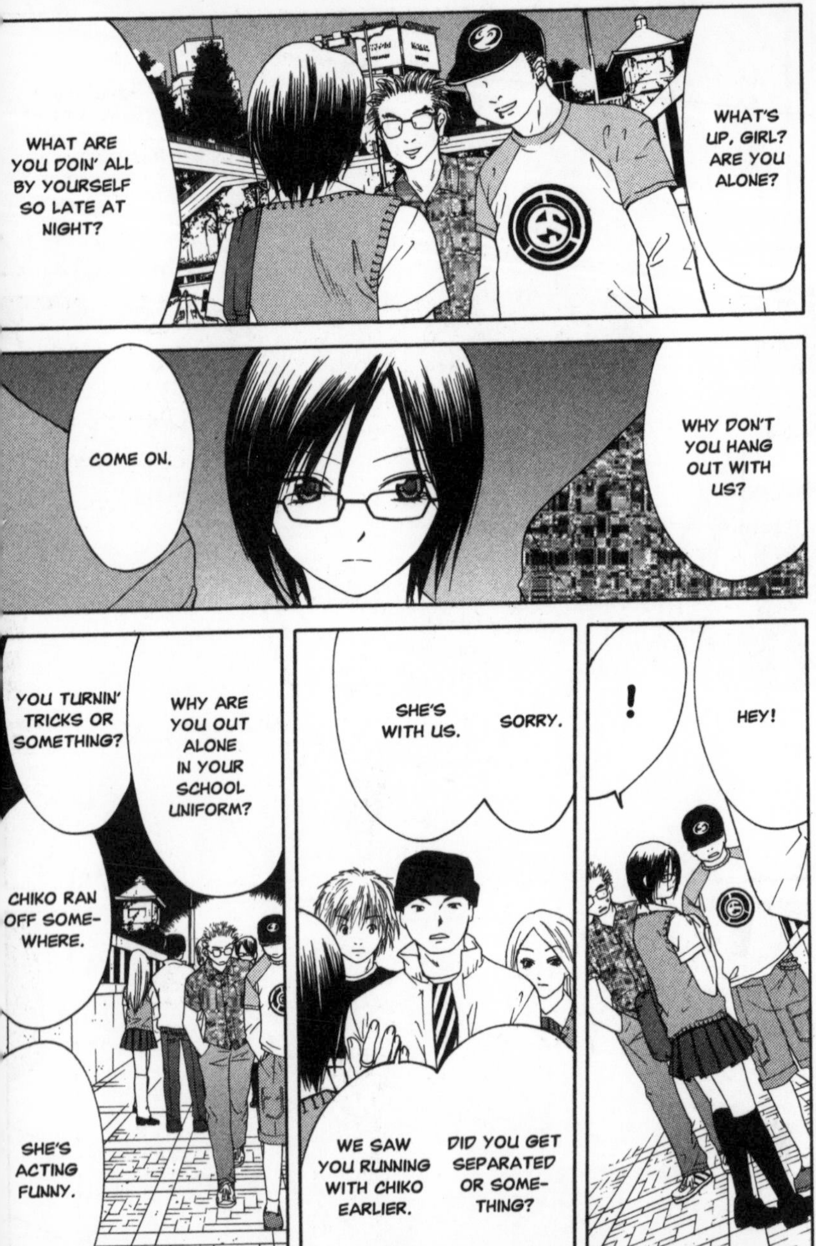
WHAT'S UP, GIRL? ARE YOU ALONE?
WHAT ARE YOU DOIN' ALL BY YOURSELF SO LATE AT NIGHT?
WHY DON'T YOU HANG OUT WITH US?
COME ON.
HEY!
!
SORRY.
SHE'S WITH US.
DID YOU GET SEPARATED OR SOME-THING?
WE SAW YOU RUNNING WITH CHIKO EARLIER.
WHY ARE YOU OUT ALONE IN YOUR SCHOOL UNIFORM?
YOU TURNIN' TRICKS OR SOMETHING?
CHIKO RAN OFF SOME-WHERE.
SHE'S ACTING FUNNY.

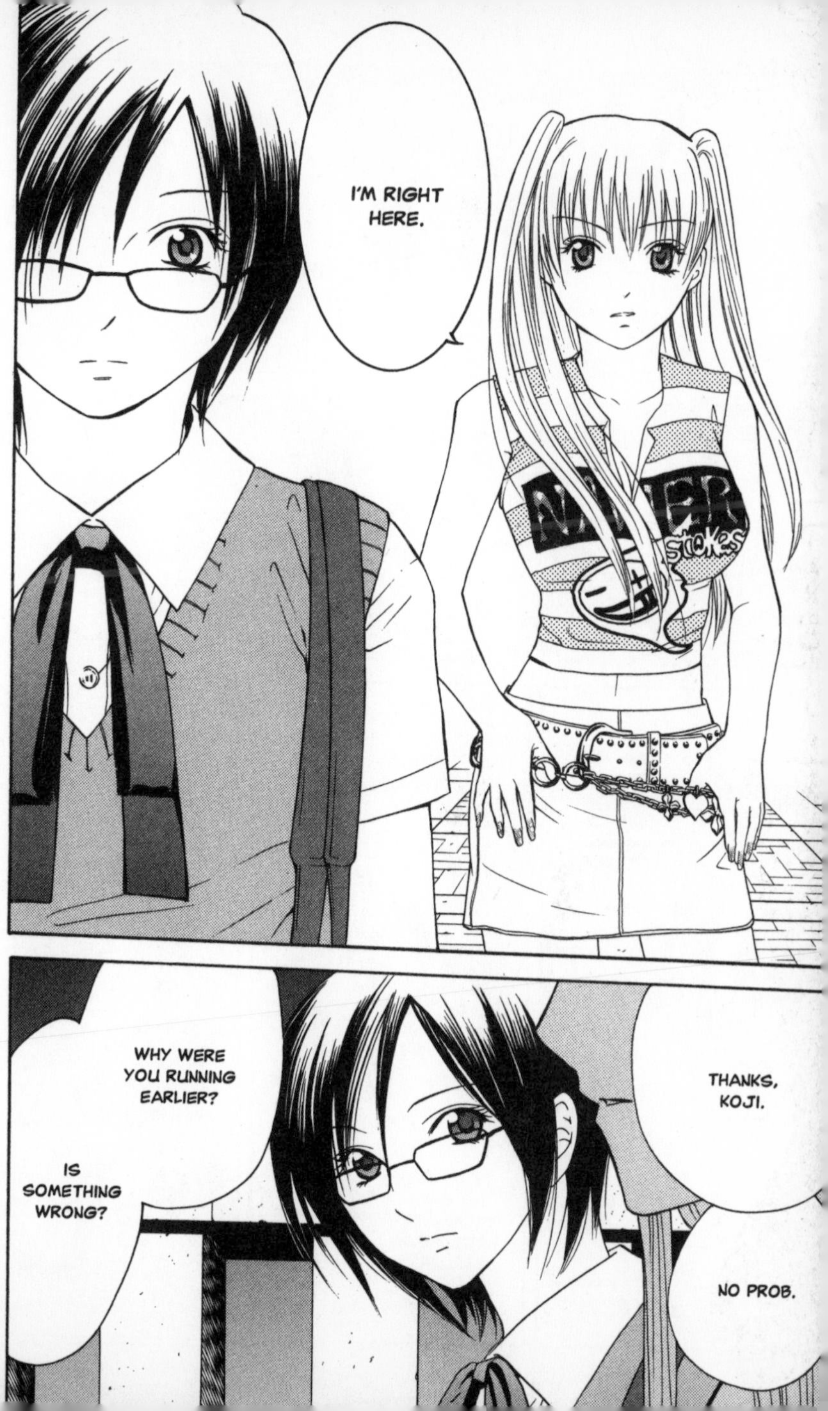
I'M RIGHT HERE.
THANKS, KOJI.
NO PROB.
WHY WERE YOU RUNNING EARLIER?
IS SOMETHING WRONG?

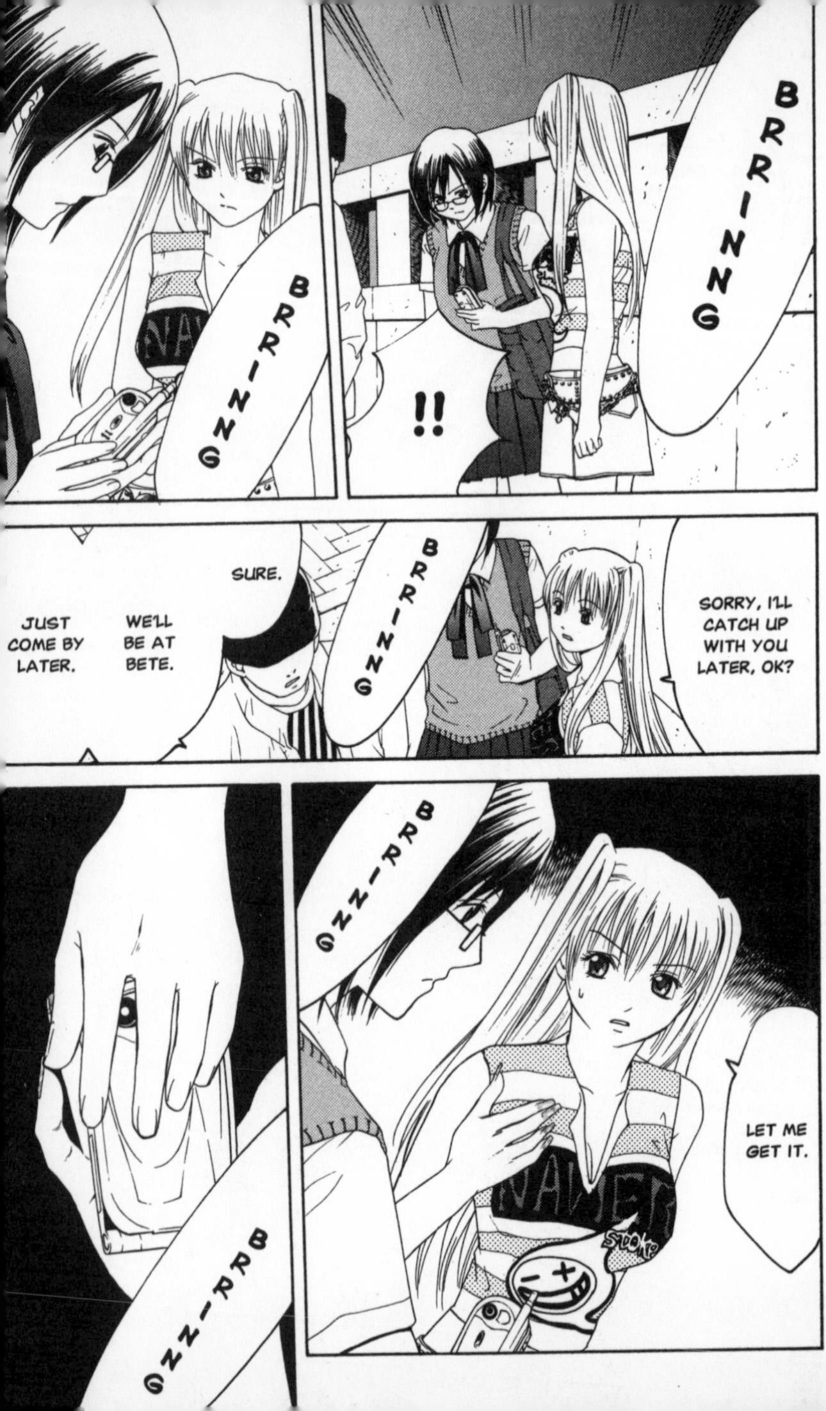
BRRINNG
!!
BRRINNG
SORRY, I'LL CATCH UP WITH YOU LATER, OK?
BRRINNG
SURE.
WE'LL BE AT BETE.
JUST COME BY LATER.
LET ME GET IT.
BRRINNG
BRRINNG

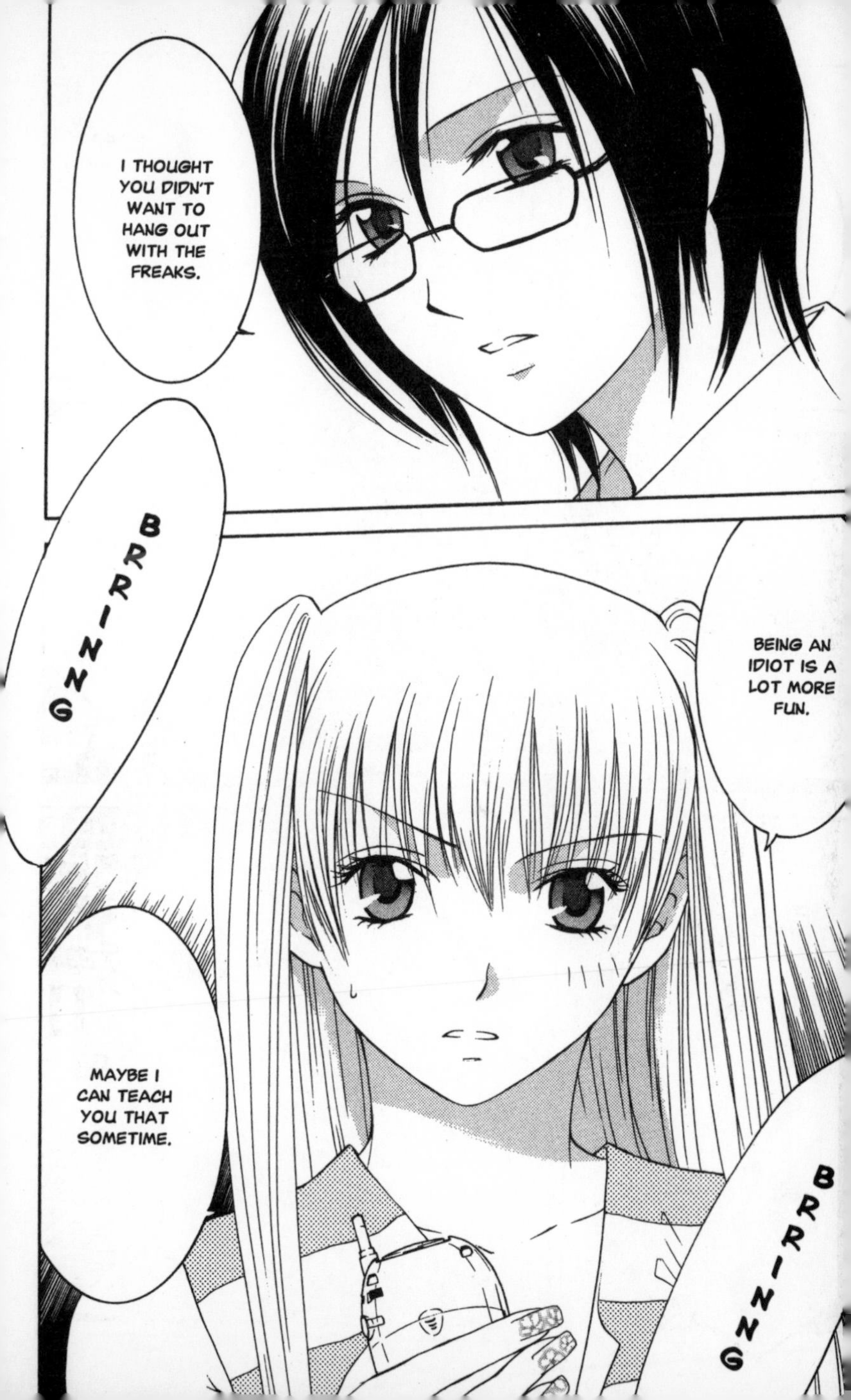
I THOUGHT YOU DIDN'T WANT TO HANG OUT WITH THE FREAKS.
BEING AN IDIOT IS A LOT MORE FUN.
BRRINNG
BRRINNG
MAYBE I CAN TEACH YOU THAT SOMETIME.

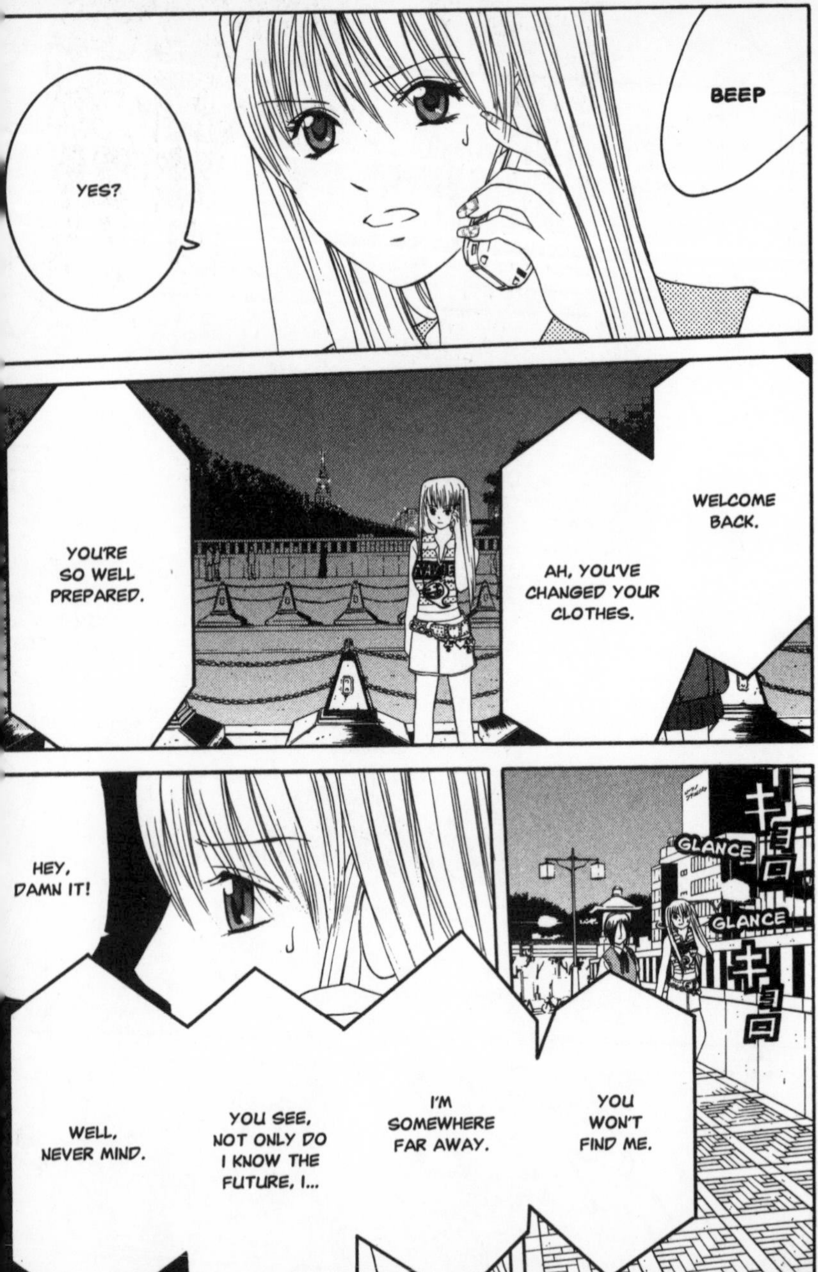
BEEP
YES?
WELCOME BACK.
AH, YOU'VE CHANGED YOUR CLOTHES.
YOU'RE SO WELL PREPARED.
キョロ
GLANCE
GLANCE
キョロ
YOU WON'T FIND ME.
I'M SOMEWHERE FAR AWAY.
HEY, DAMN IT!
YOU SEE, NOT ONLY DO I KNOW THE FUTURE, I...
WELL, NEVER MIND.

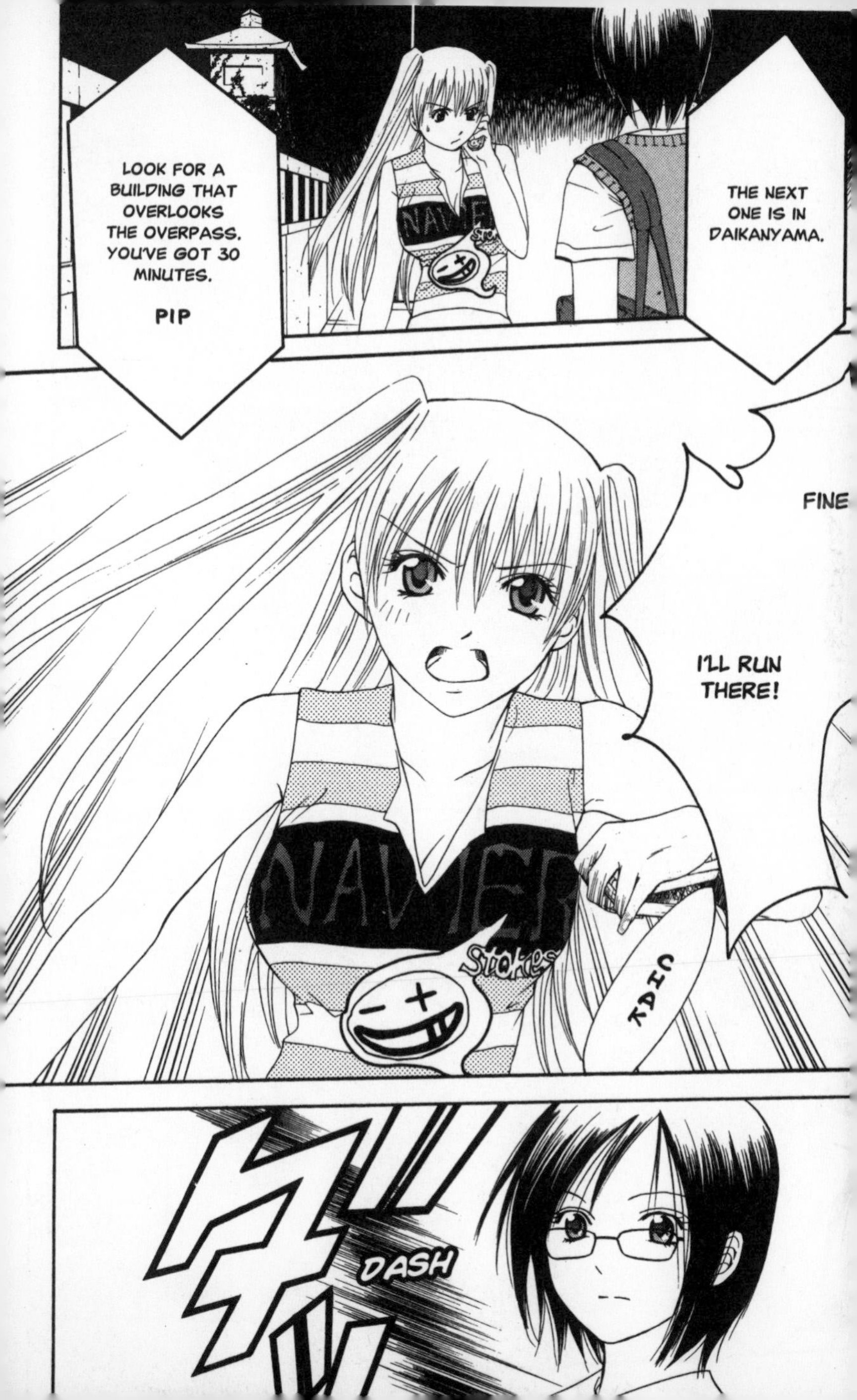
THE NEXT ONE IS IN DAIKANYAMA.
LOOK FOR A BUILDING THAT OVERLOOKS THE OVERPASS. YOU'VE GOT 30 MINUTES.
PIP
FINE
I'LL RUN THERE!
DASH

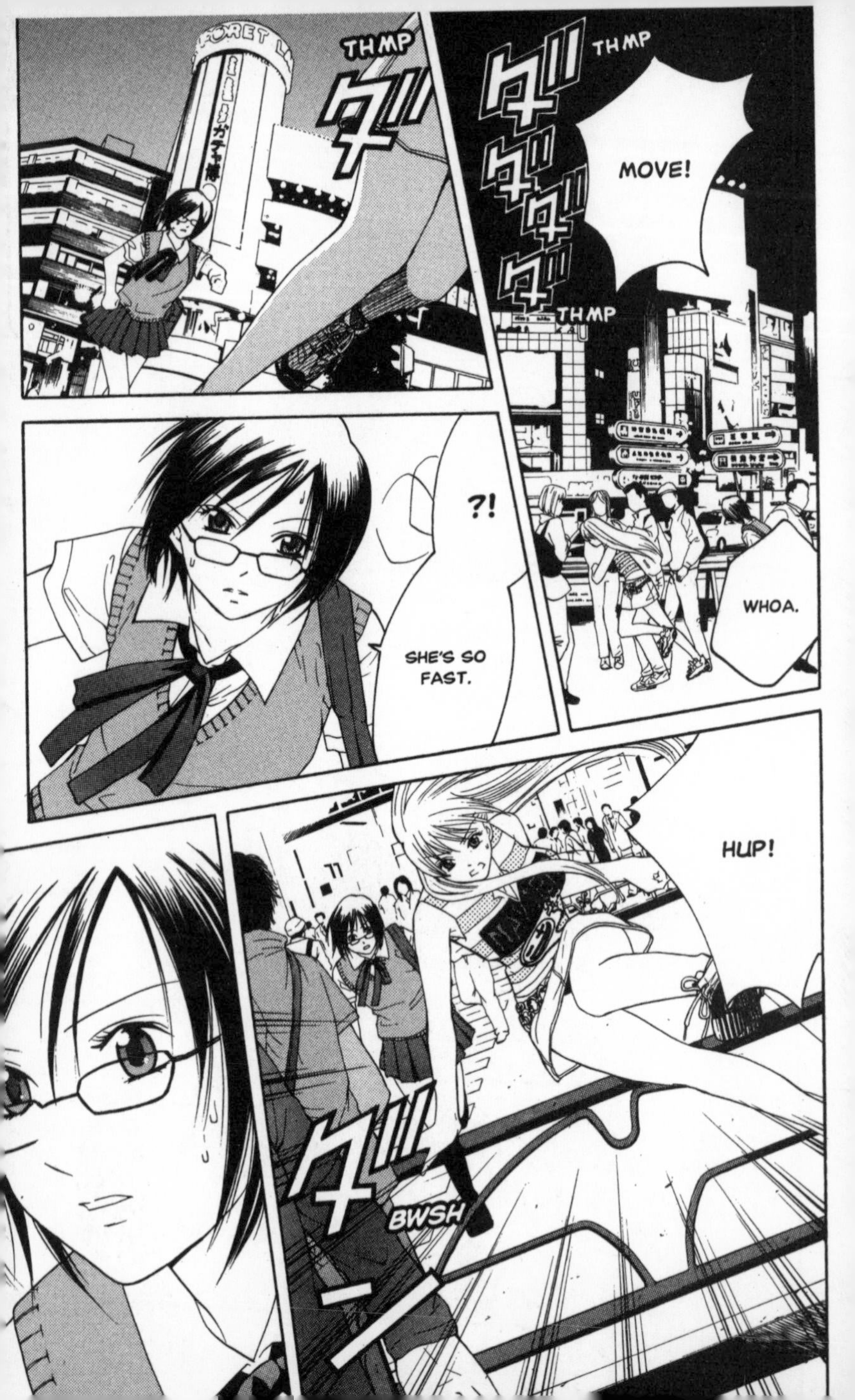
THMP
MOVE!
THMP
WHOA.
THMP
?!
SHE'S SO FAST.
HUP!
BWSH

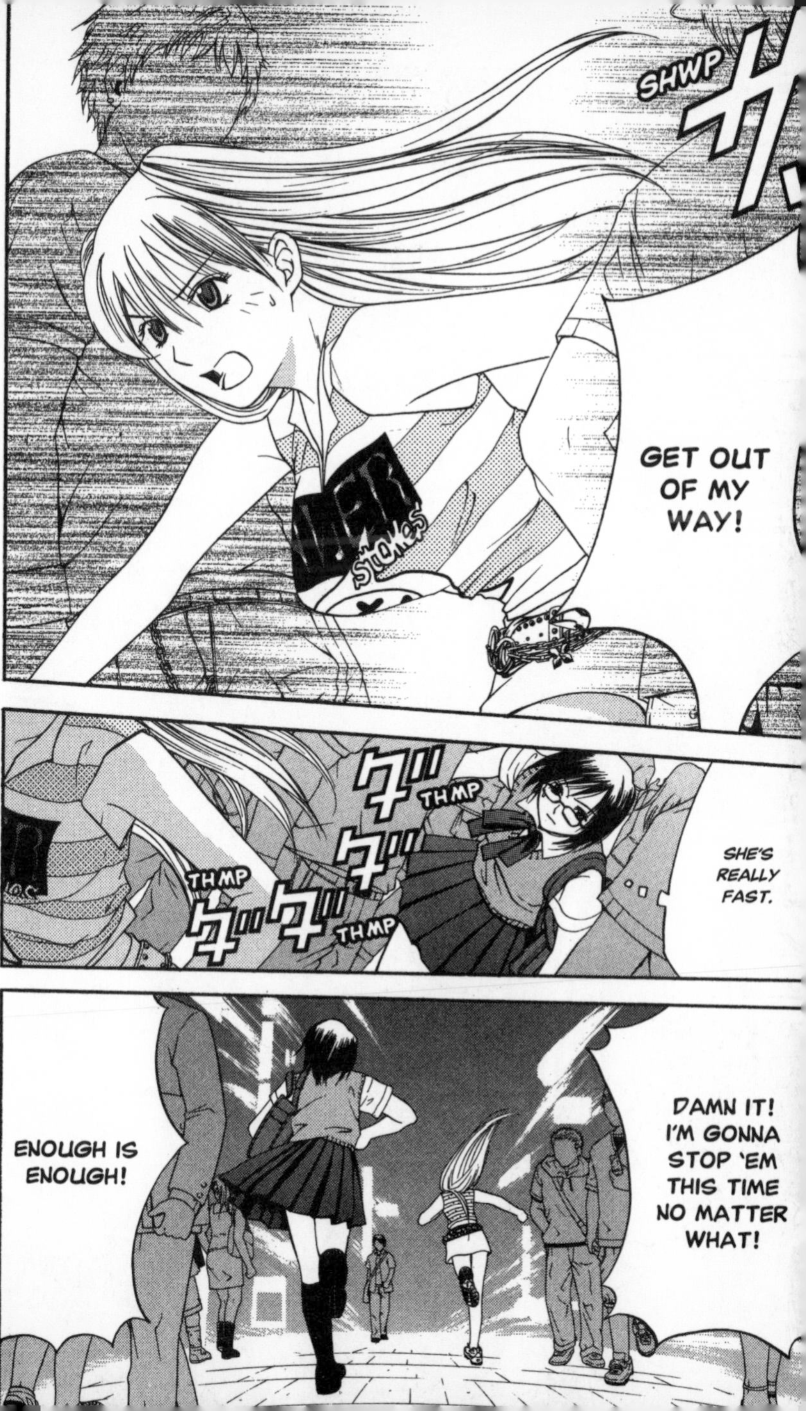
SHWP
GET OUT OF MY WAY!
SHE'S REALLY FAST.
THMP
THMP
THMP
DAMN IT! I'M GONNA STOP 'EM THIS TIME NO MATTER WHAT!
ENOUGH IS ENOUGH!

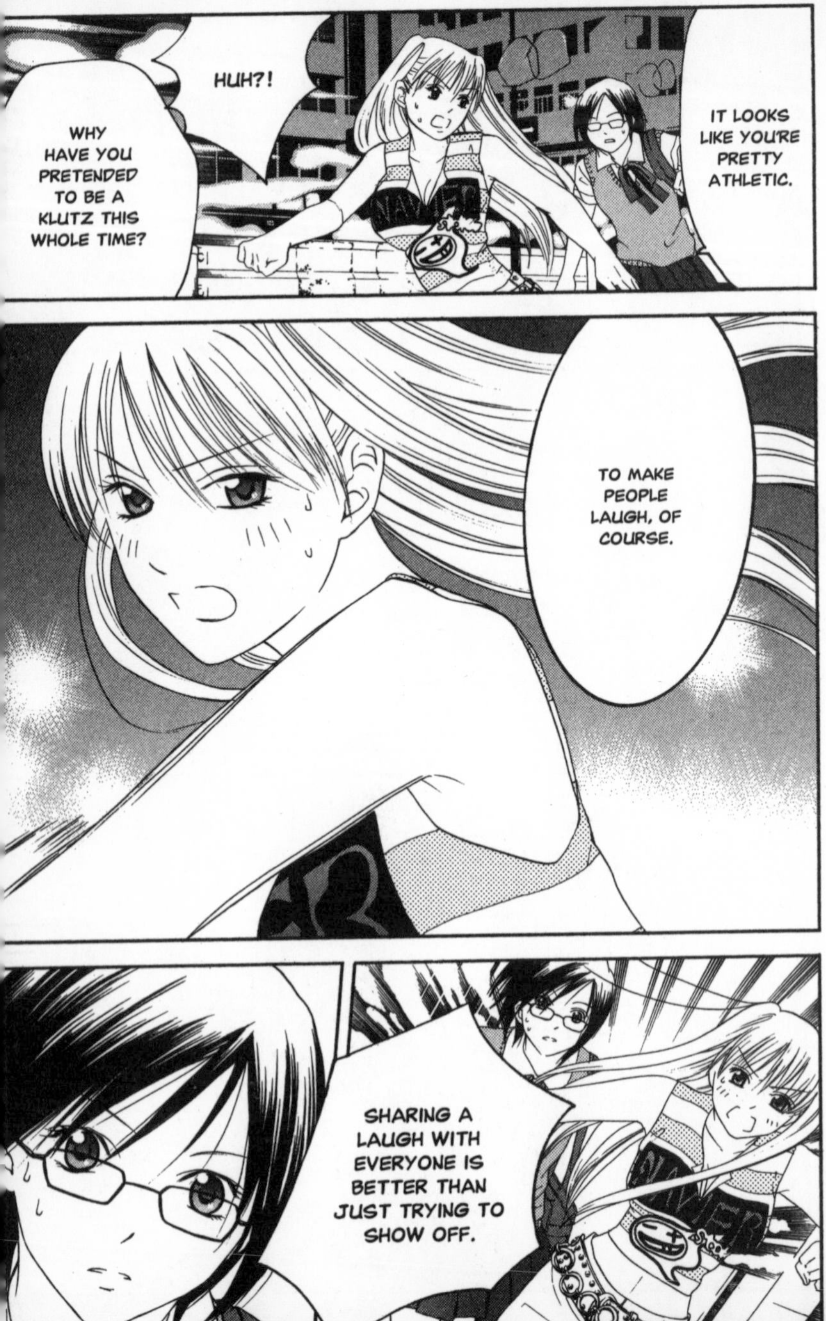
IT LOOKS LIKE YOU'RE PRETTY ATHLETIC.
HUH?!
WHY HAVE YOU PRETENDED TO BE A KLUTZ THIS WHOLE TIME?
TO MAKE PEOPLE LAUGH, OF COURSE.
SHARING A LAUGH WITH EVERYONE IS BETTER THAN JUST TRYING TO SHOW OFF.

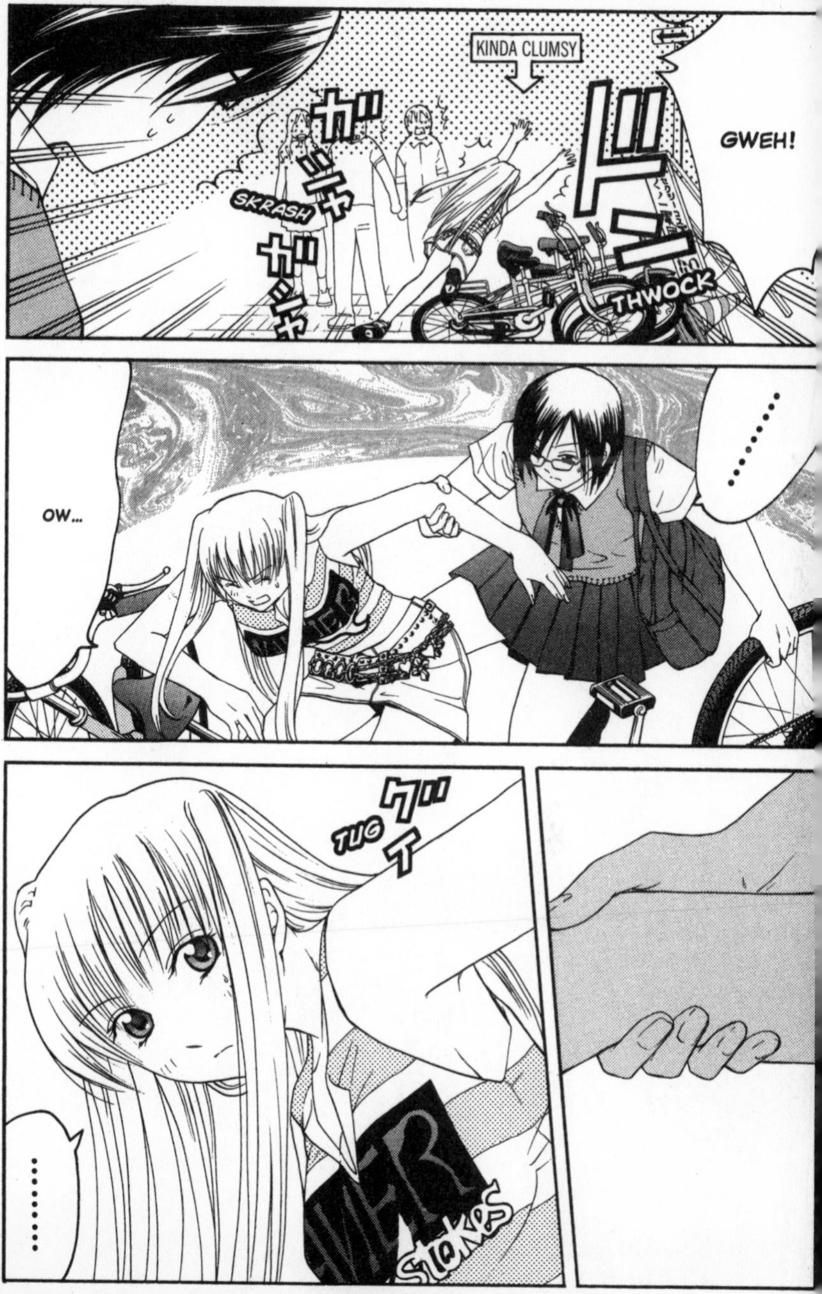
KINDA CLUMSY
GWEH!
THWOCK
SKRASH
......
OW...
TUG
......

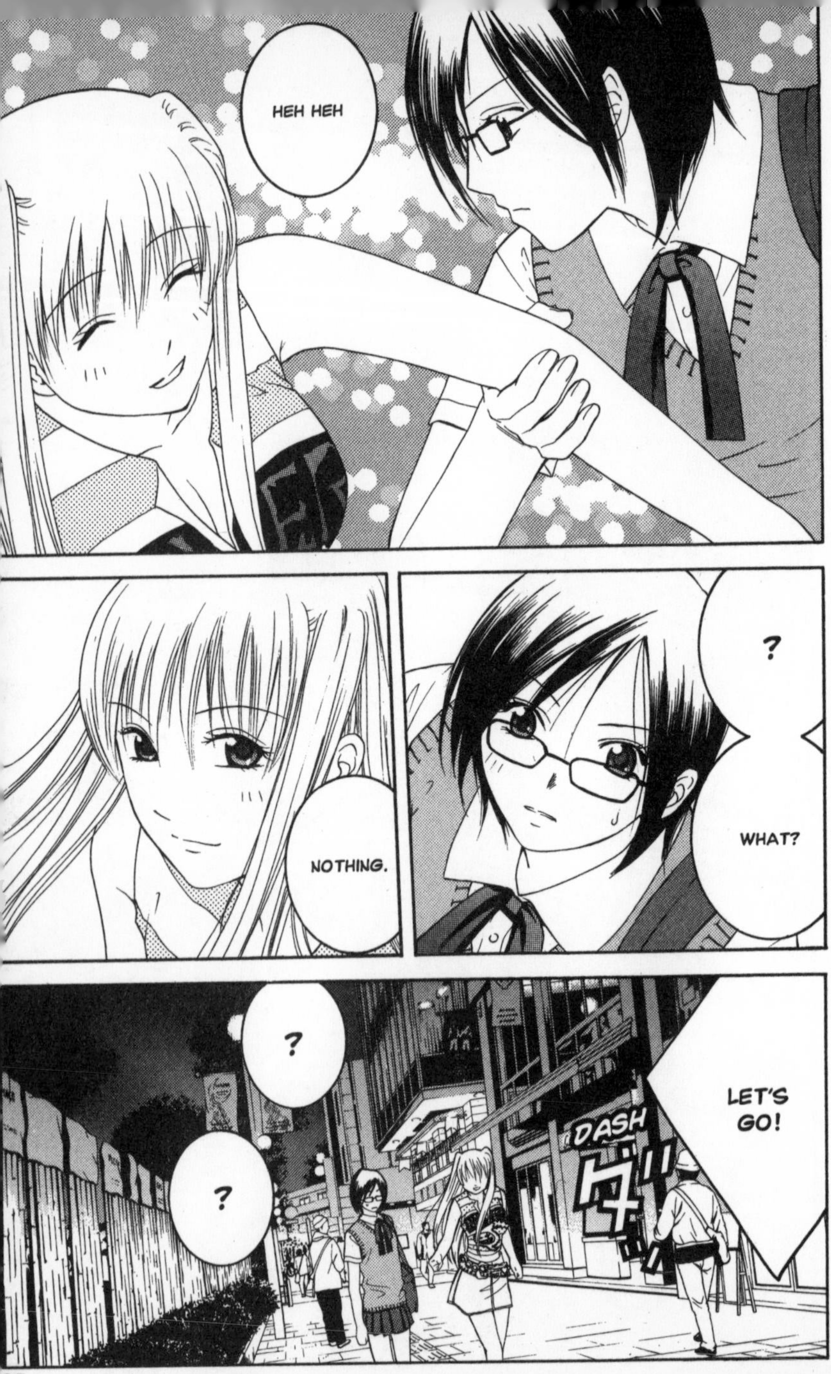
HEH HEH
?
WHAT?
NOTHING.
LET'S GO!
DASH
?
?

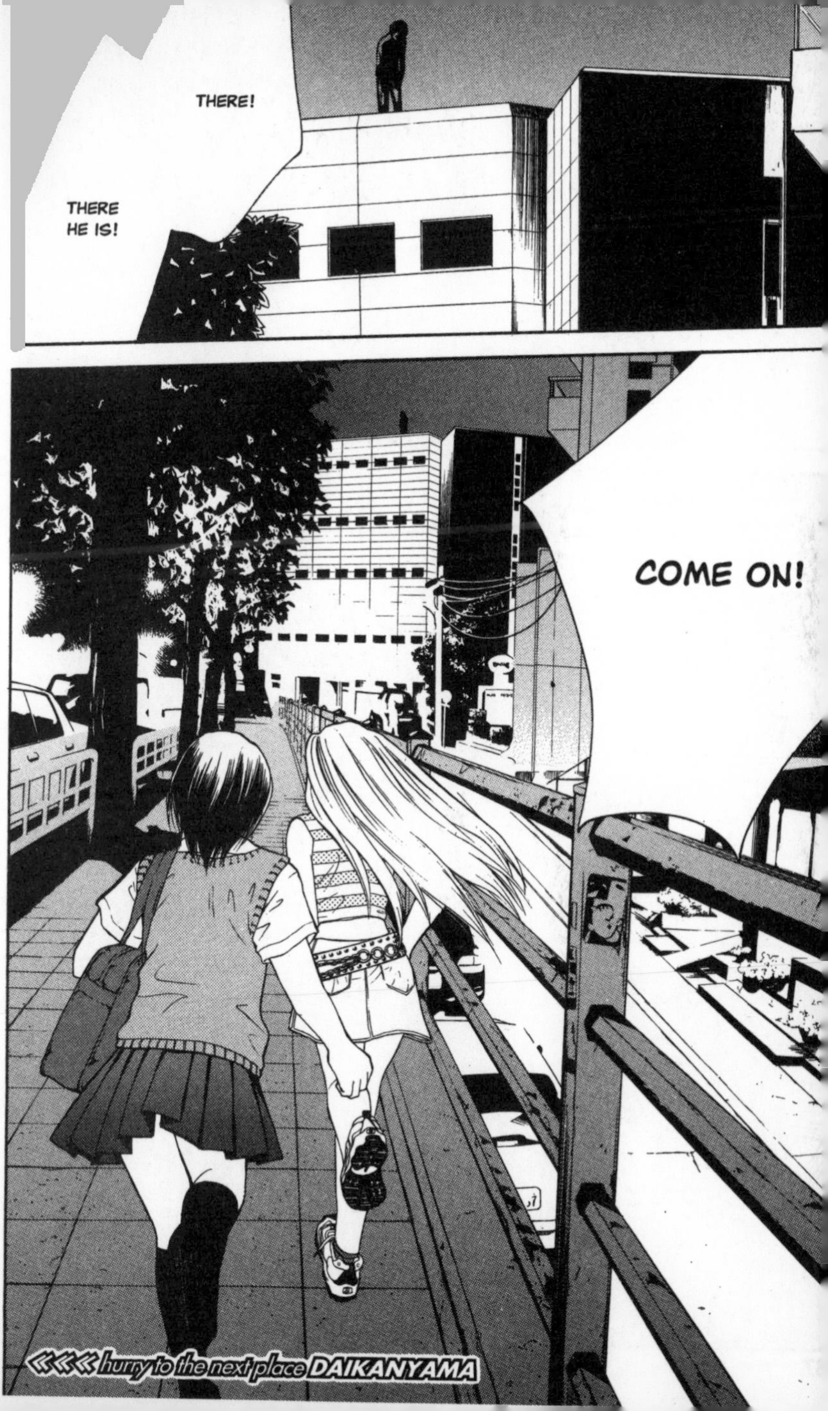
THERE!
THERE HE IS!
COME ON!
hurry to the next place DAIKANYAMA

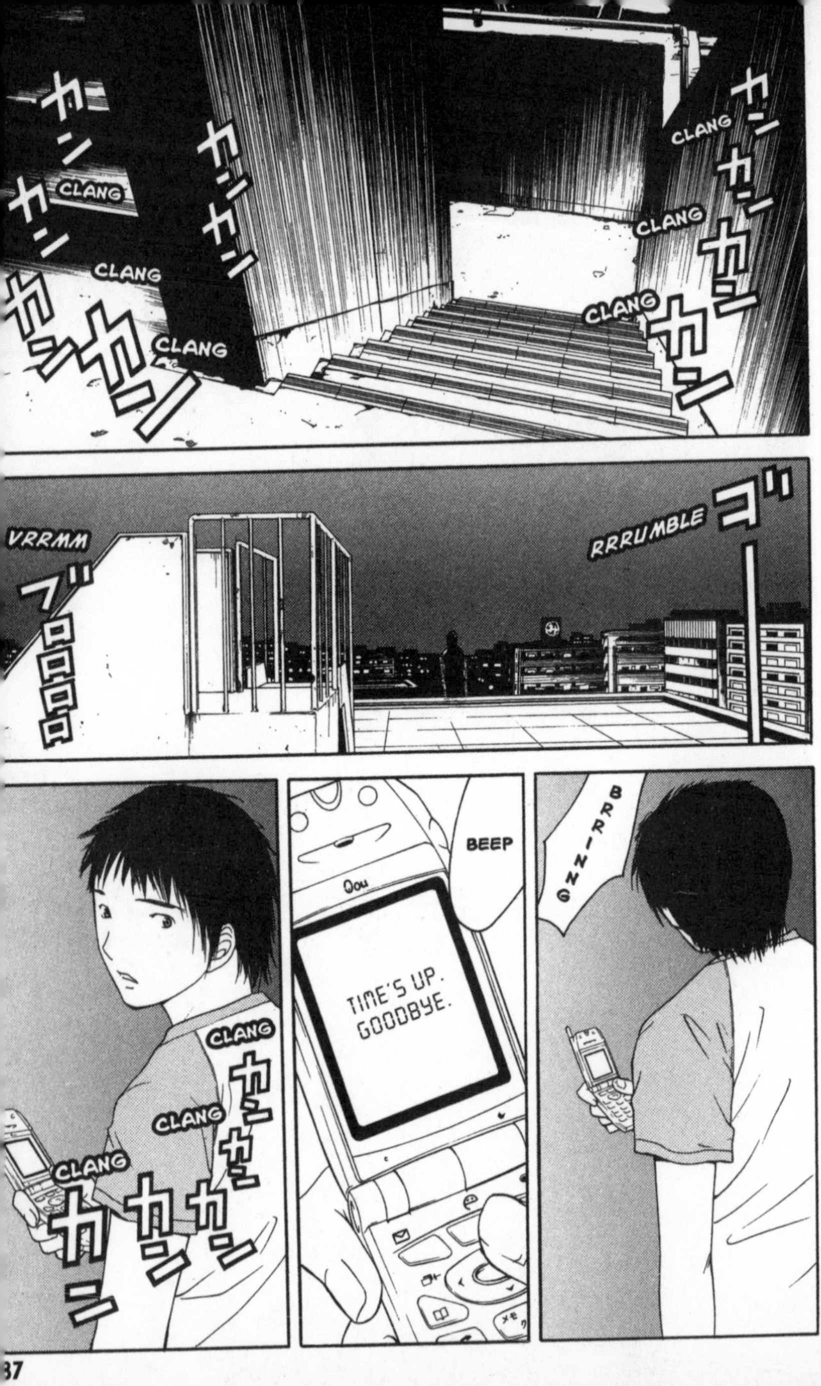
CLANG
CLANG
CLANG
CLANG
CLANG
CLANG
CLANG
RRRUMBLE
VRRMM
BRRRINNG
BEEP
TIME'S UP. GOODBYE.
CLANG
CLANG
CLANG

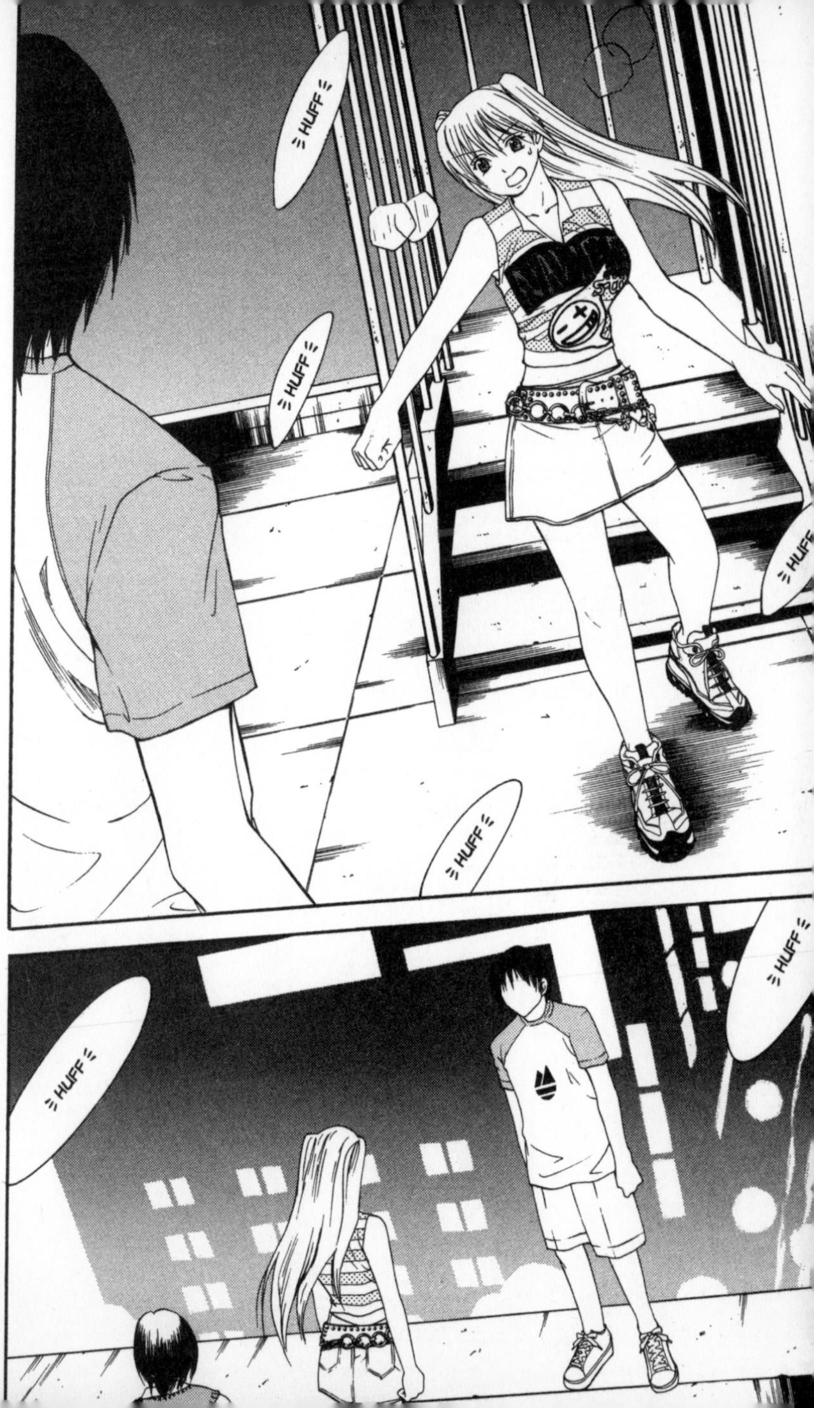
HUFF
HUFF
HUFF
HUFF
HUFF
HUFF

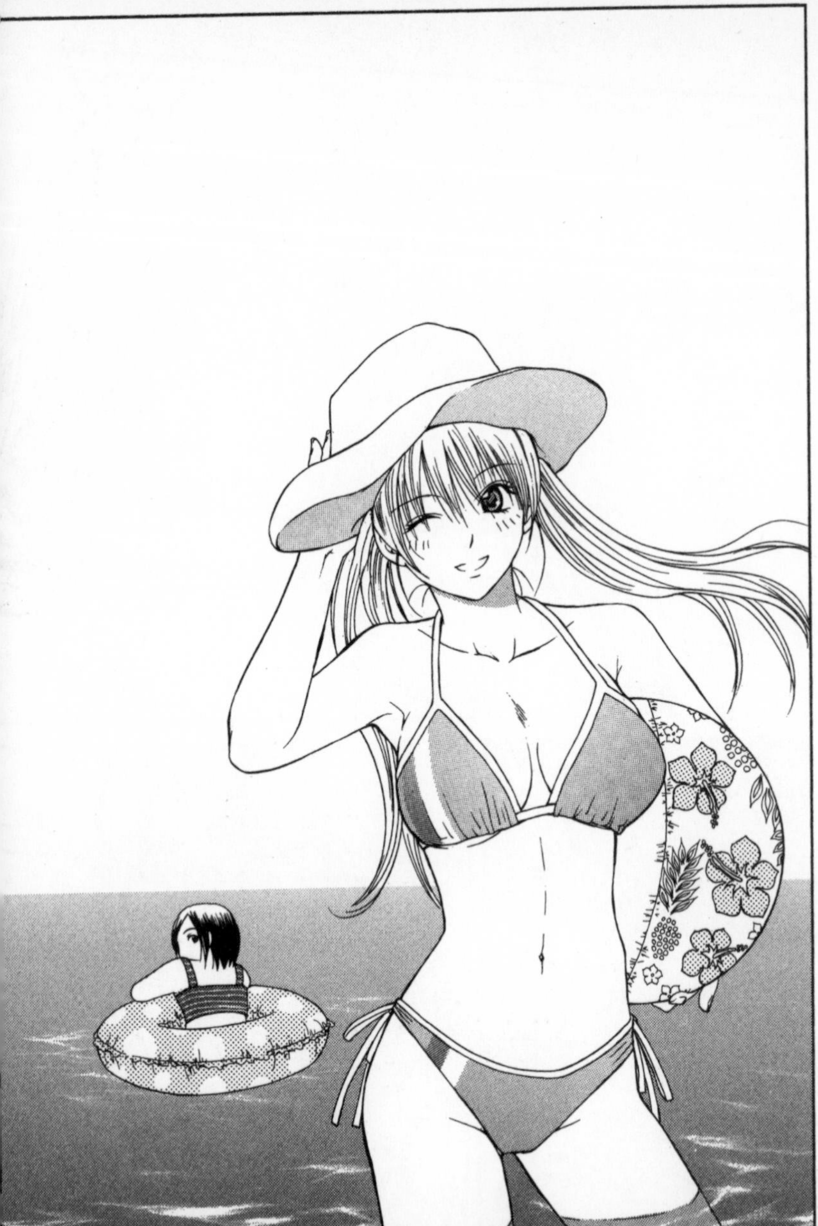

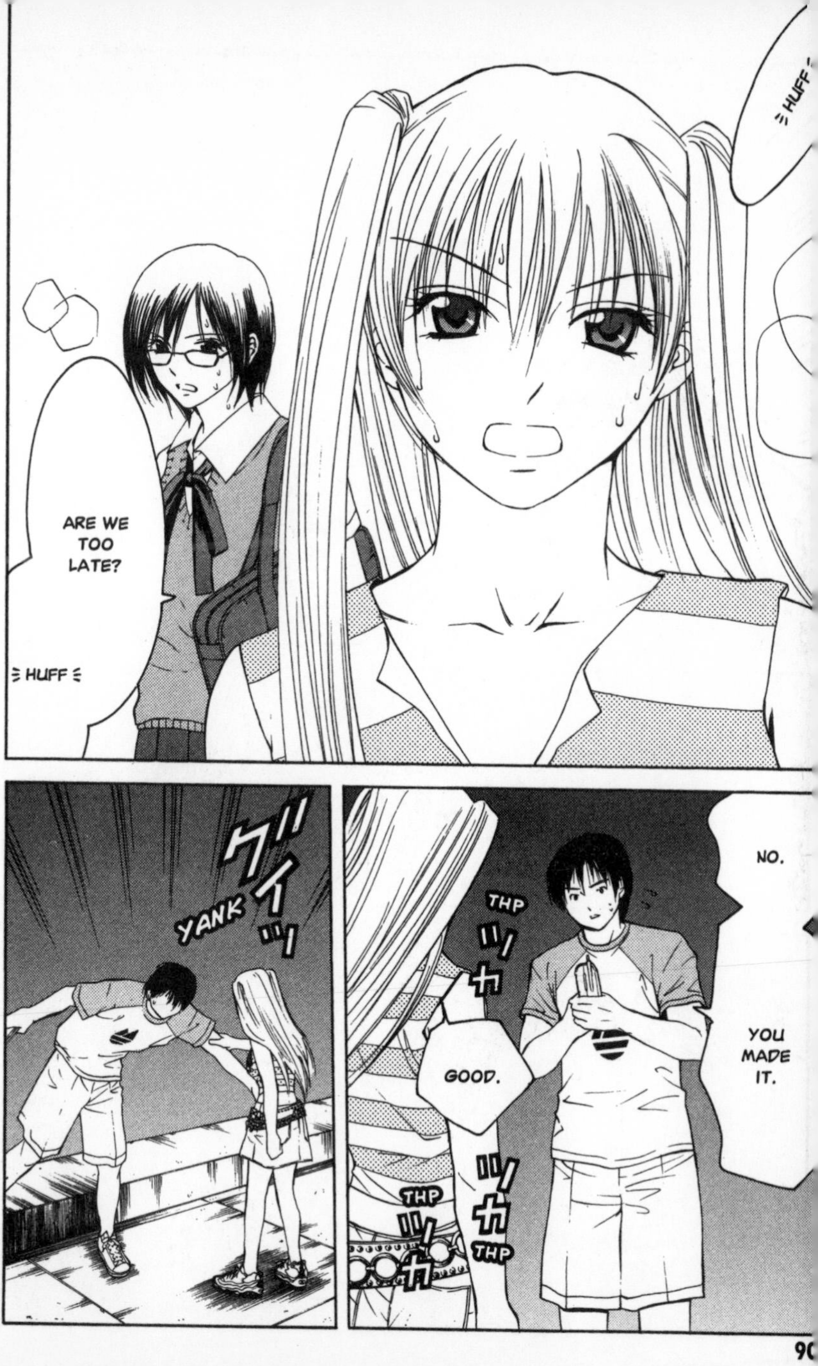
HUFF
ARE WE TOO LATE?
HUFF
NO.
YOU MADE IT.
THP
GOOD.
THP
THP
YANK

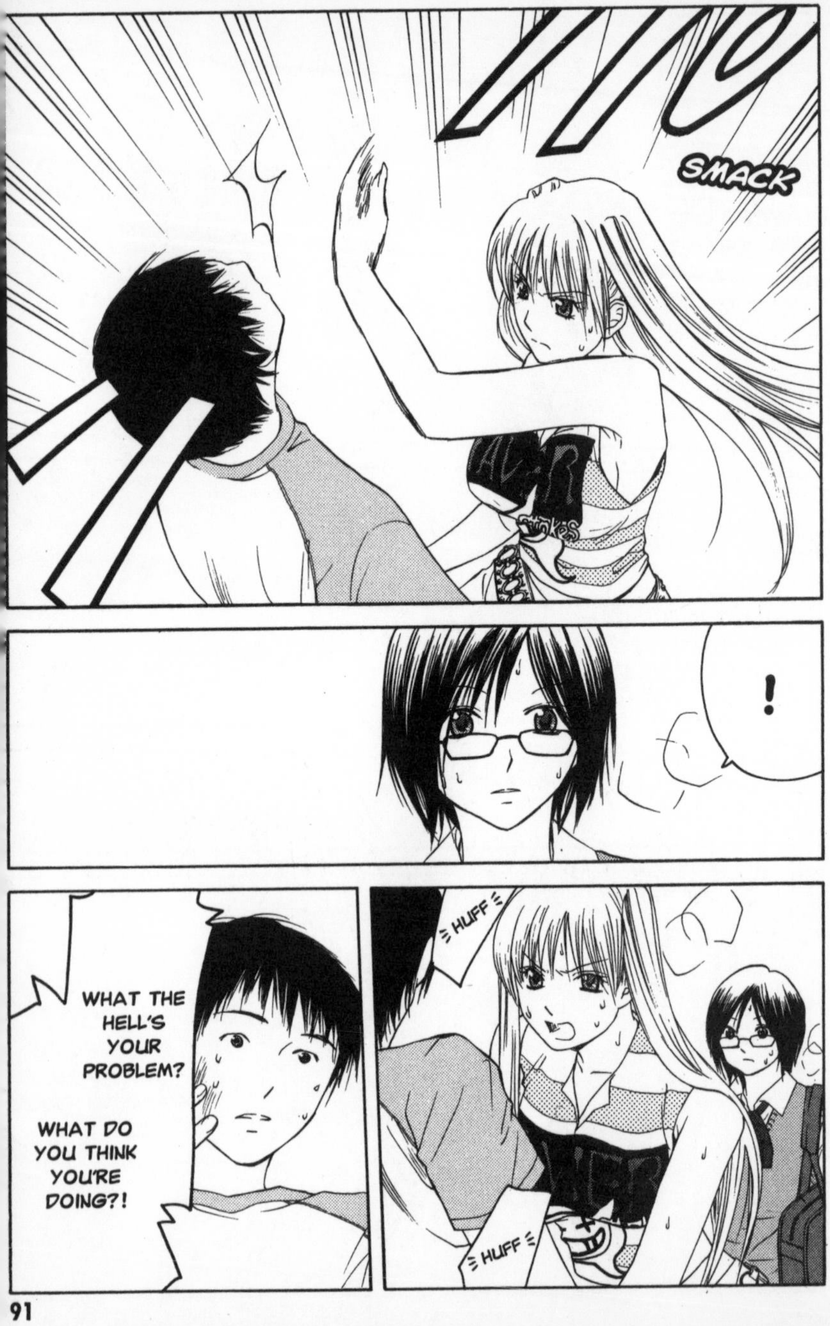
SMACK
!
HUFF
HUFF
WHAT THE HELL'S YOUR PROBLEM?
WHAT DO YOU THINK YOU'RE DOING?!

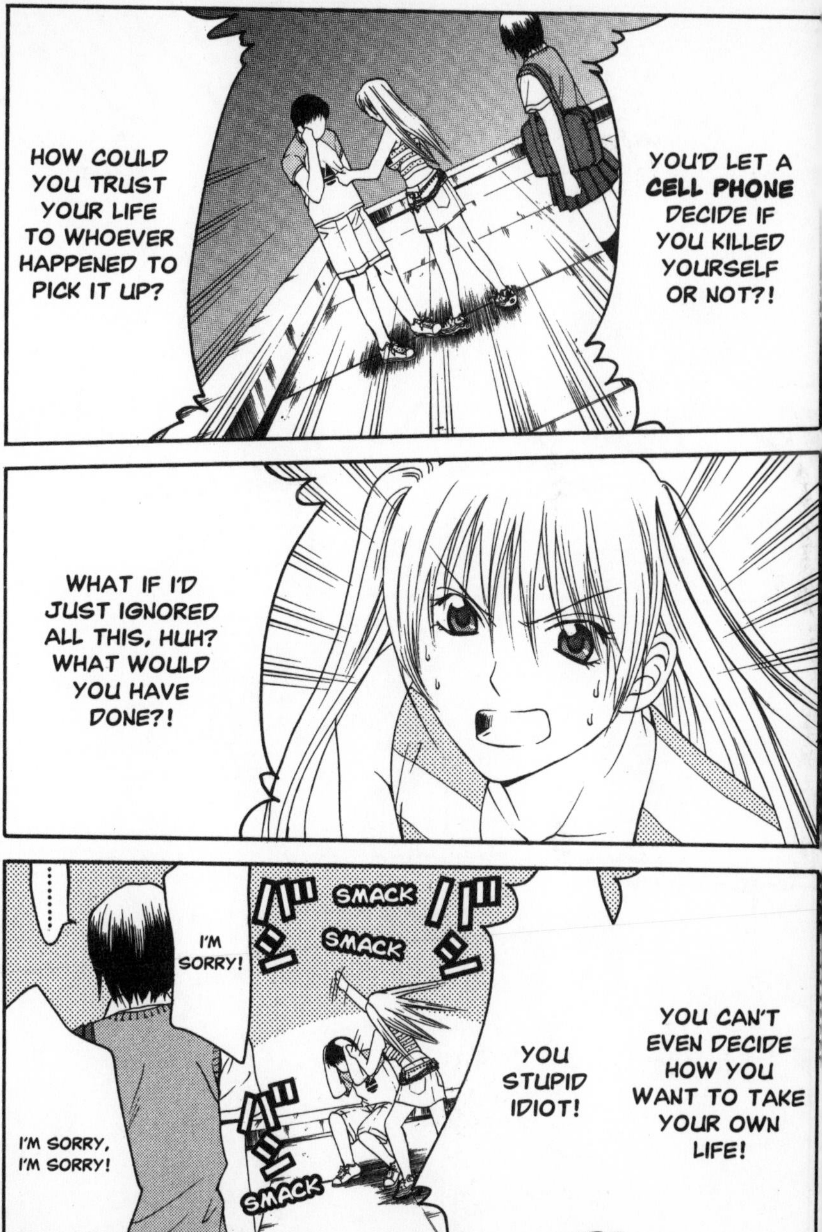
YOU'D LET A CELL PHONE DECIDE IF YOU KILLED YOURSELF OR NOT?!
HOW COULD YOU TRUST YOUR LIFE TO WHOEVER HAPPENED TO PICK IT UP?
WHAT IF I'D JUST IGNORED ALL THIS, HUH? WHAT WOULD YOU HAVE DONE?!
YOU CAN'T EVEN DECIDE HOW YOU WANT TO TAKE YOUR OWN LIFE!
YOU STUPID IDIOT!
SMACK
SMACK
I'M SORRY!
......
SMACK
I'M SORRY, I'M SORRY!

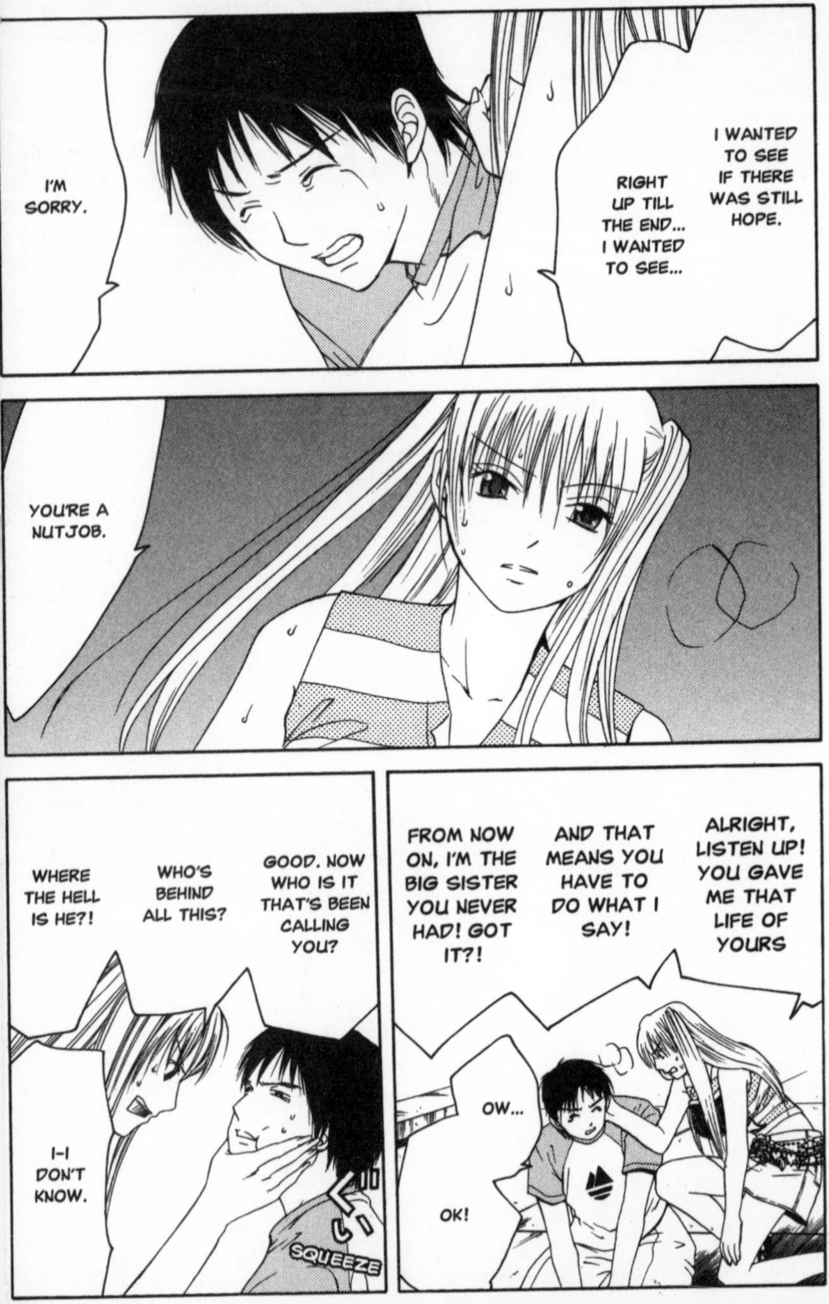
I WANTED TO SEE IF THERE WAS STILL HOPE.
RIGHT UP TILL THE END... I WANTED TO SEE...
I'M SORRY.
YOU'RE A NUTJOB.
ALRIGHT, LISTEN UP! YOU GAVE ME THAT LIFE OF YOURS
AND THAT MEANS YOU HAVE TO DO WHAT I SAY!
FROM NOW ON, I'M THE BIG SISTER YOU NEVER HAD! GOT IT?!
OW...
OK!
GOOD. NOW WHO IS IT THAT'S BEEN CALLING YOU?
WHO'S BEHIND ALL THIS?
WHERE THE HELL IS HE?!
I-I DON'T KNOW.
SQUEEZE

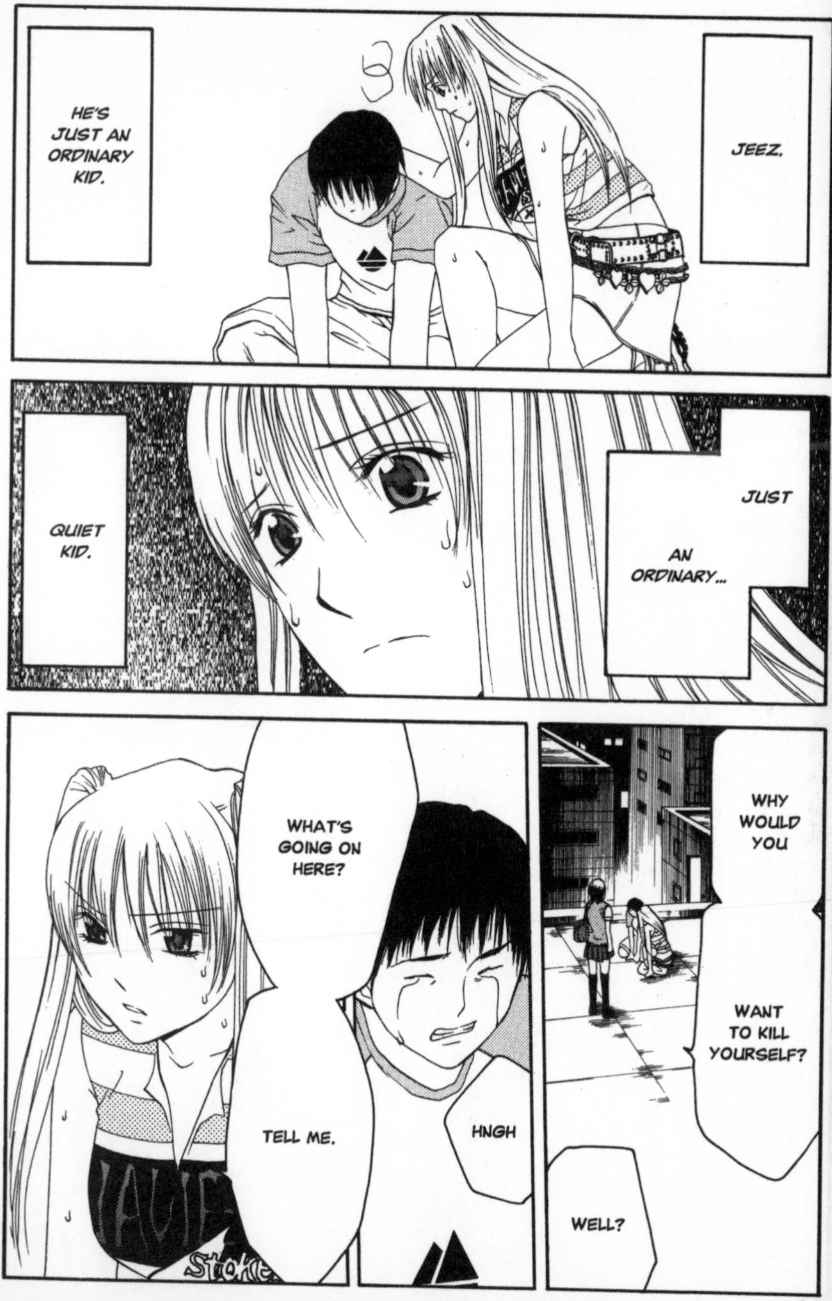
JEEZ.
HE'S JUST AN ORDINARY KID.
JUST AN ORDINARY...
QUIET KID.
WHY WOULD YOU WANT TO KILL YOURSELF?
WELL?
WHAT'S GOING ON HERE?
HNGH
TELL ME.

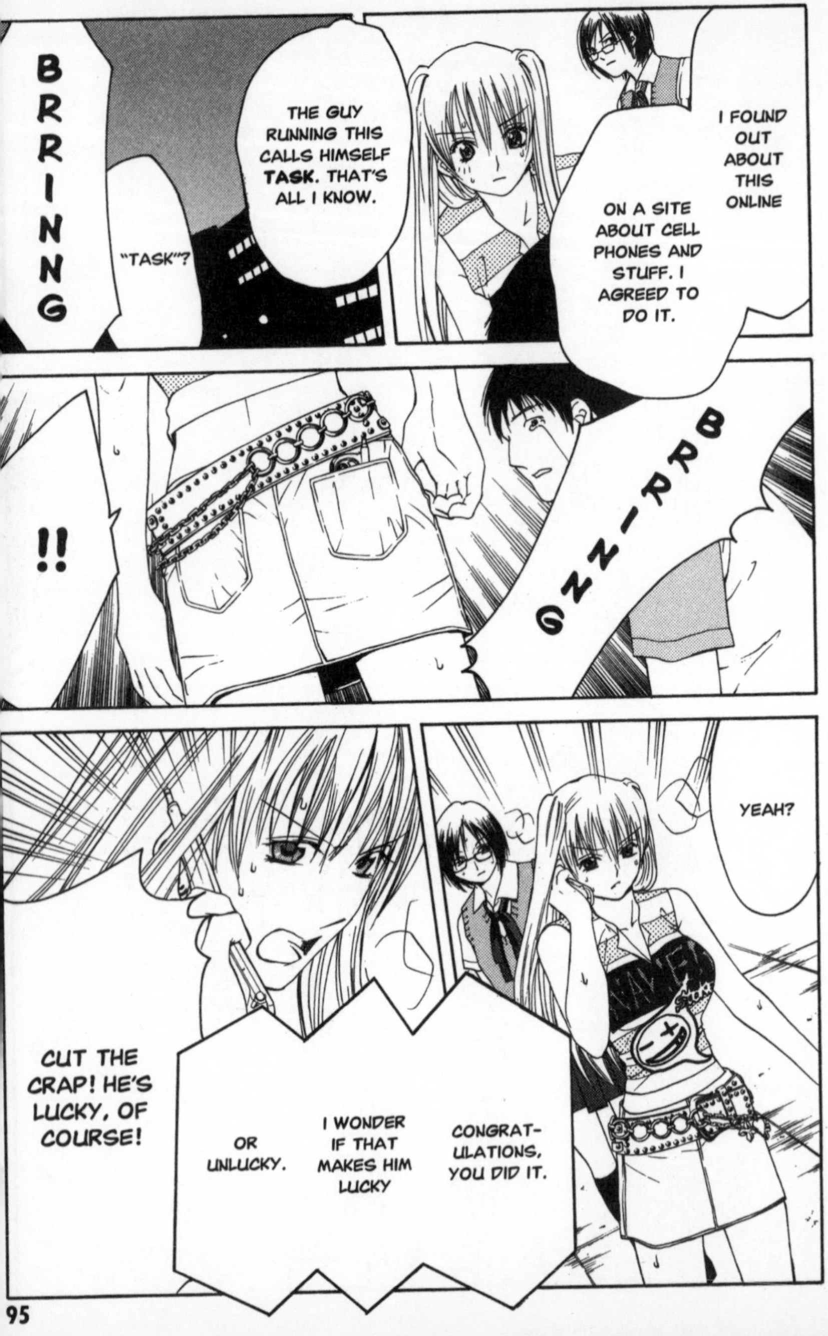
I FOUND OUT ABOUT THIS ONLINE
ON A SITE ABOUT CELL PHONES AND STUFF. I AGREED TO DO IT.
THE GUY RUNNING THIS CALLS HIMSELF **TASK**. THAT'S ALL I KNOW.
BRRINNG
"TASK"?
BRRINNG
!!
YEAH?
CONGRAT-ULATIONS, YOU DID IT.
I WONDER IF THAT MAKES HIM LUCKY
OR UNLUCKY.
CUT THE CRAP! HE'S LUCKY, OF COURSE!

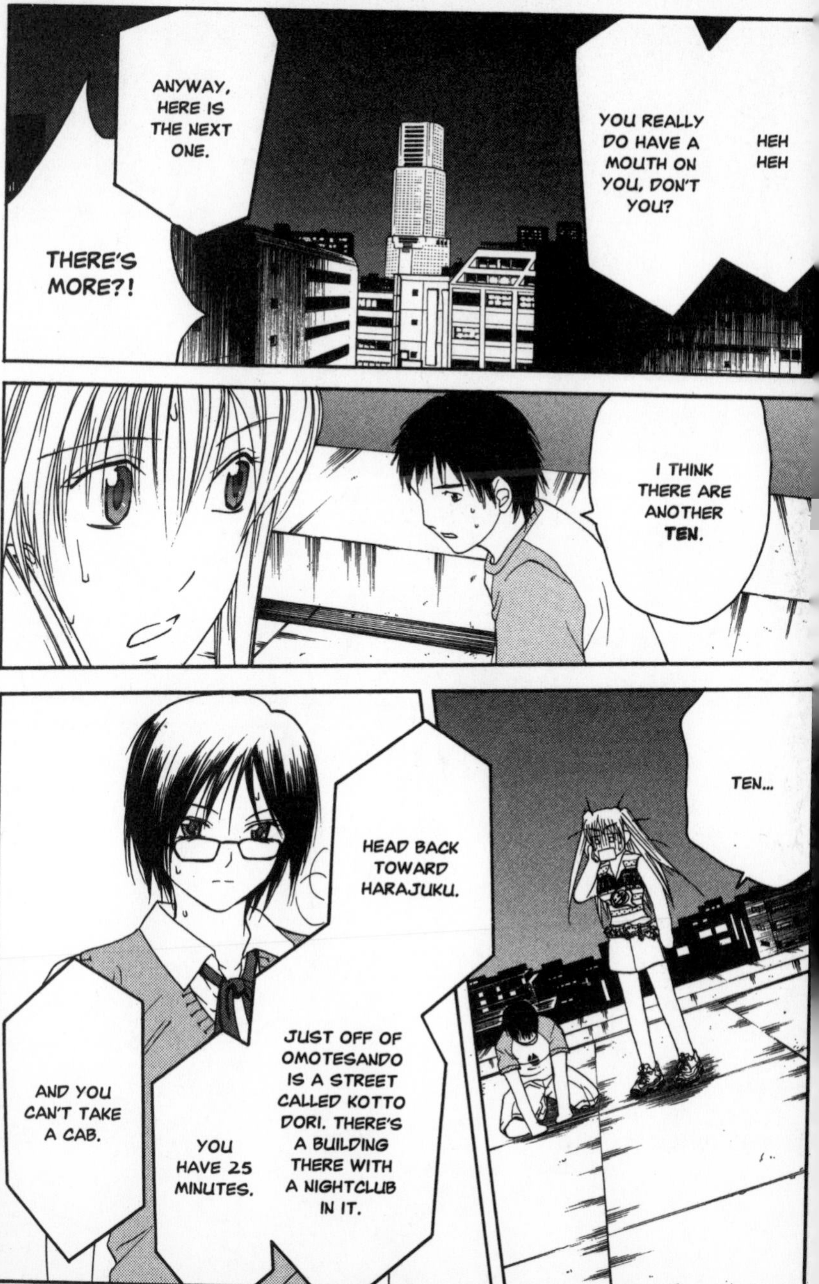
YOU REALLY DO HAVE A MOUTH ON YOU, DON'T YOU?
HEH HEH
ANYWAY, HERE IS THE NEXT ONE.
THERE'S MORE?!
I THINK THERE ARE ANOTHER **TEN.**
TEN...
HEAD BACK TOWARD HARAJUKU.
JUST OFF OF OMOTESANDO IS A STREET CALLED KOTTO DORI. THERE'S A BUILDING THERE WITH A NIGHTCLUB IN IT.
YOU HAVE 25 MINUTES.
AND YOU CAN'T TAKE A CAB.

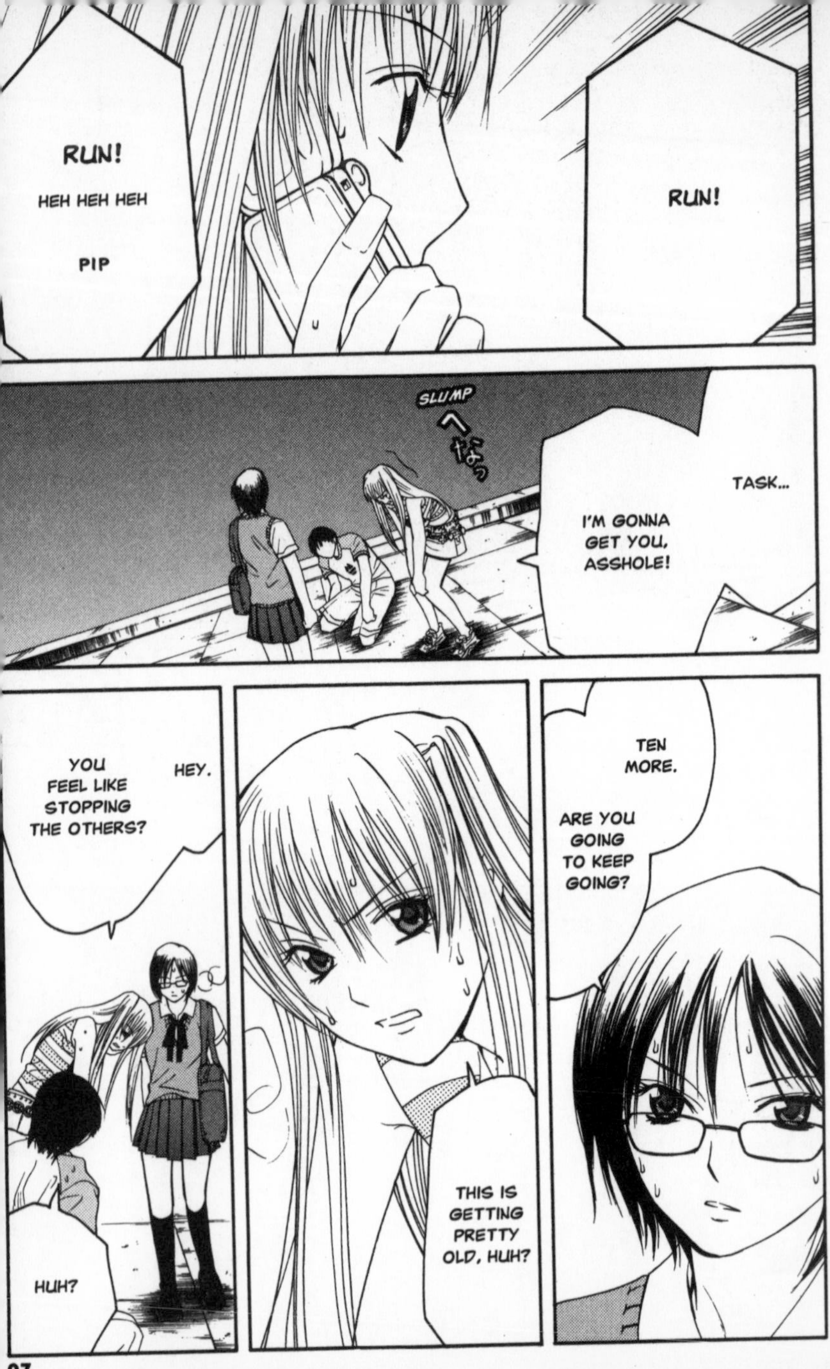
RUN!
RUN!
HEH HEH HEH
PIP
TASK...
I'M GONNA GET YOU, ASSHOLE!
SLUMP
へなっ
TEN MORE.
ARE YOU GOING TO KEEP GOING?
THIS IS GETTING PRETTY OLD, HUH?
HEY.
YOU FEEL LIKE STOPPING THE OTHERS?
HUH?

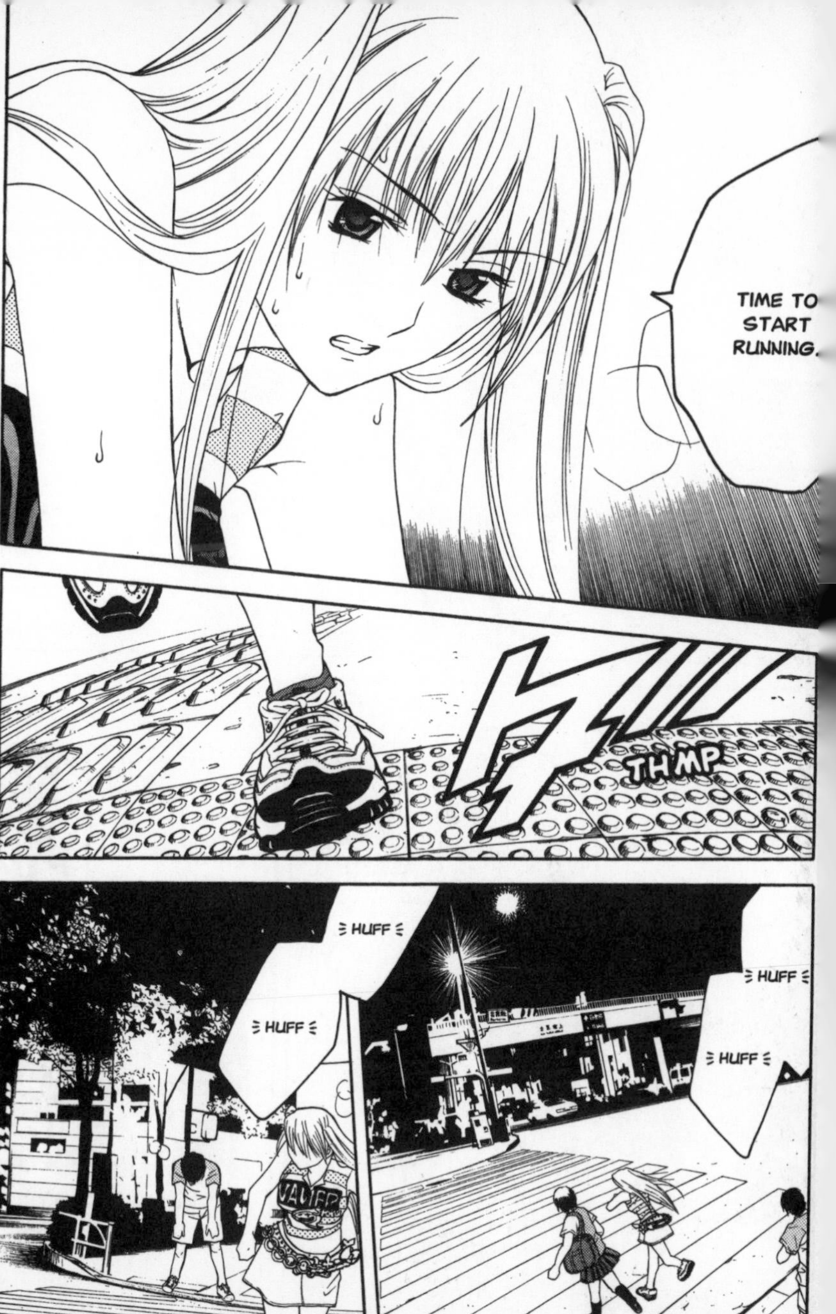
TIME TO START RUNNING.
THMP
HUFF
HUFF
HUFF
HUFF

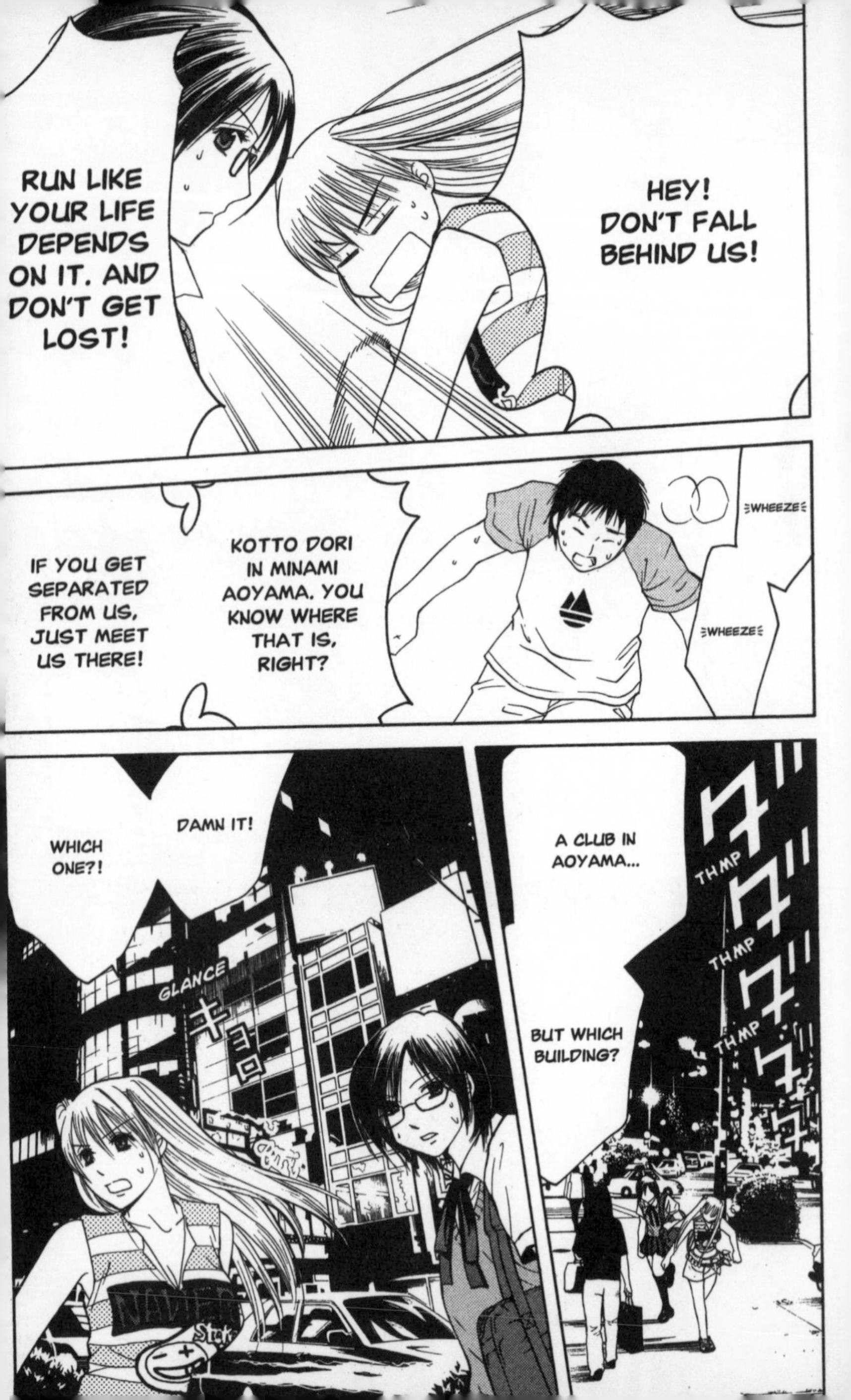
HEY! DON'T FALL BEHIND US!
RUN LIKE YOUR LIFE DEPENDS ON IT. AND DON'T GET LOST!
WHEEZE
WHEEZE
KOTTO DORI IN MINAMI AOYAMA. YOU KNOW WHERE THAT IS, RIGHT?
IF YOU GET SEPARATED FROM US, JUST MEET US THERE!
A CLUB IN AOYAMA...
THMP
THMP
THMP
BUT WHICH BUILDING?
DAMN IT!
WHICH ONE?!
GLANCE

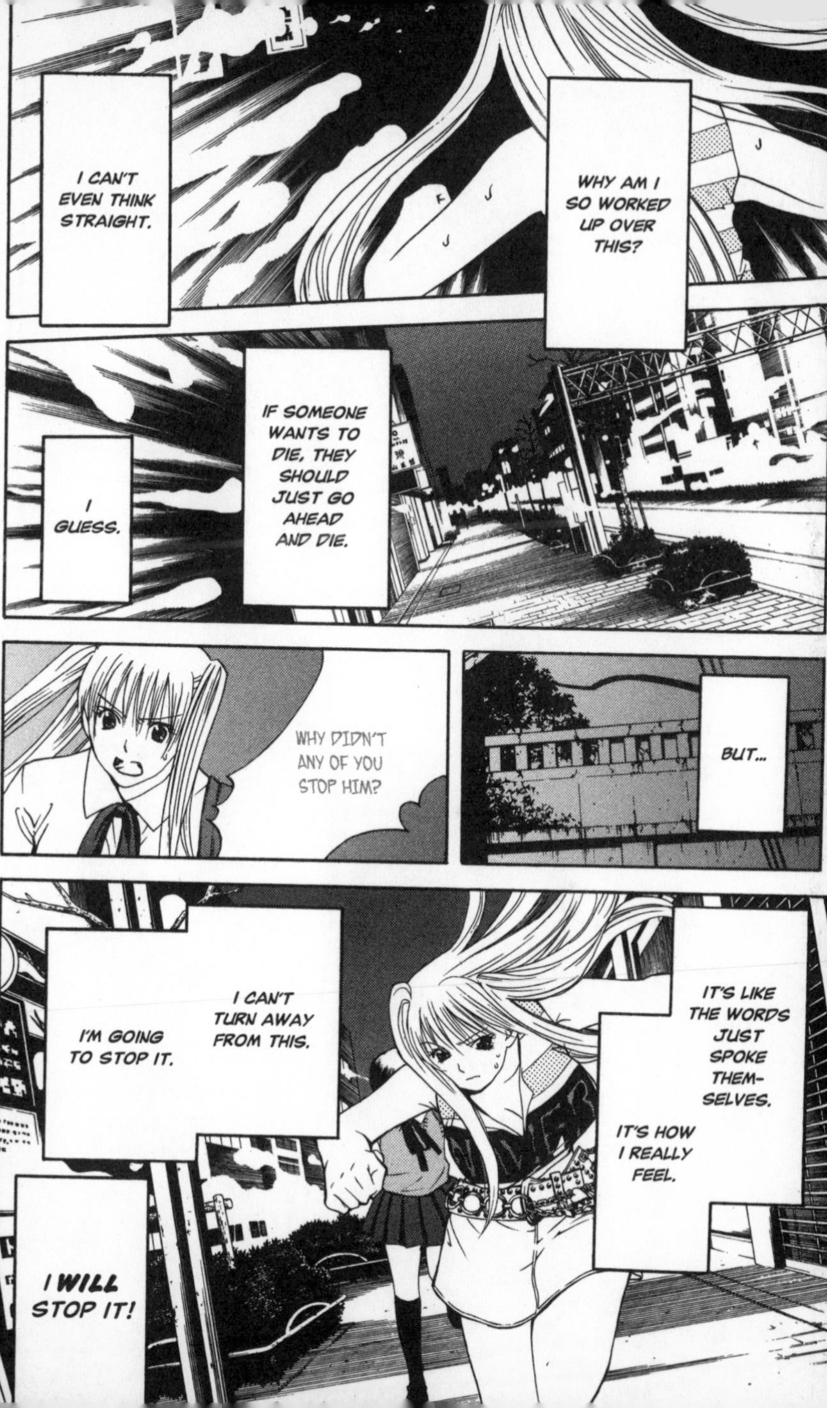
WHY AM I SO WORKED UP OVER THIS?
I CAN'T EVEN THINK STRAIGHT.
IF SOMEONE WANTS TO DIE, THEY SHOULD JUST GO AHEAD AND DIE.
I GUESS.
BUT...
WHY DIDN'T ANY OF YOU STOP HIM?
IT'S LIKE THE WORDS JUST SPOKE THEMSELVES.
IT'S HOW I REALLY FEEL.
I CAN'T TURN AWAY FROM THIS.
I'M GOING TO STOP IT.
I **WILL** STOP IT!

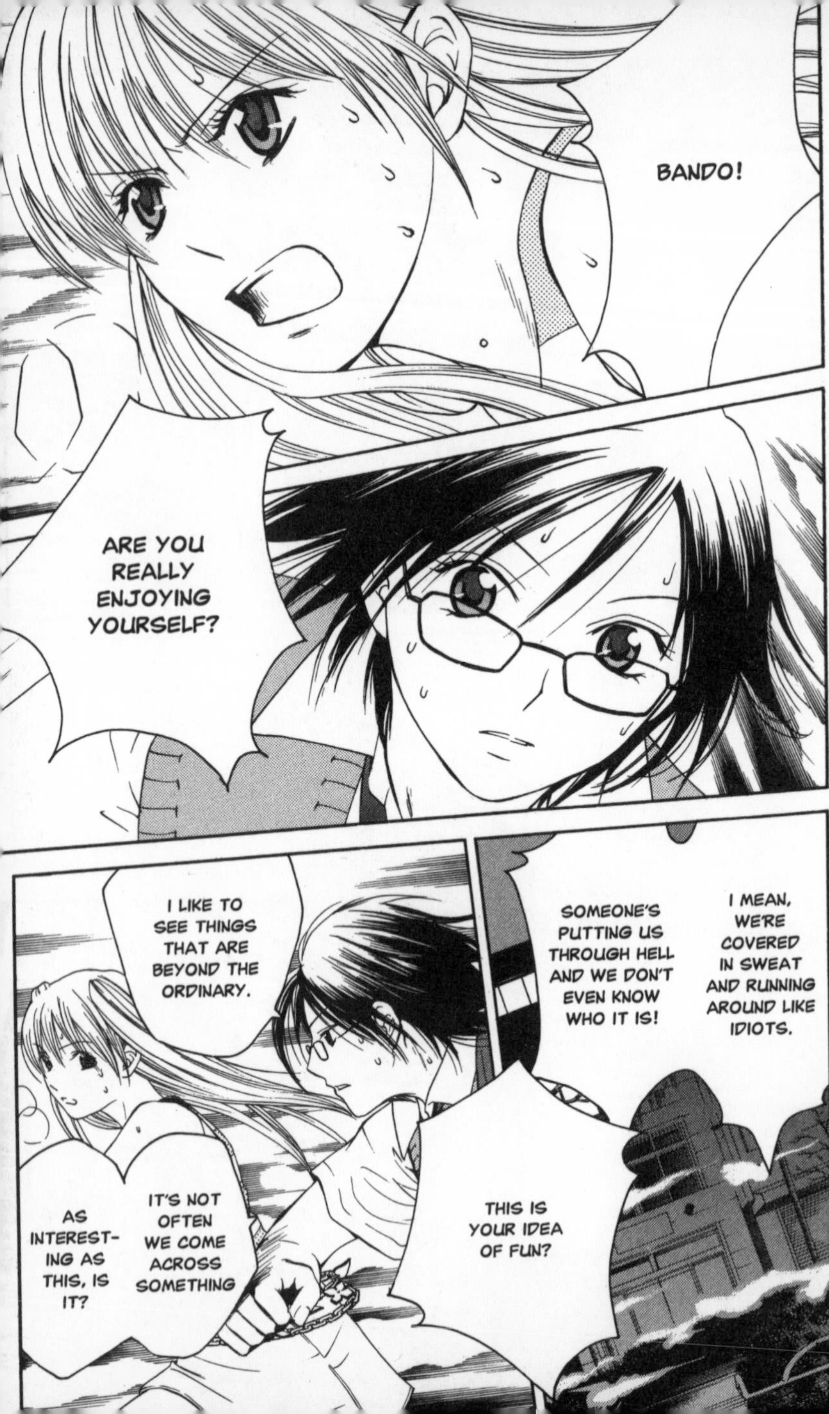
BANDO!
ARE YOU REALLY ENJOYING YOURSELF?
I MEAN, WE'RE COVERED IN SWEAT AND RUNNING AROUND LIKE IDIOTS.
SOMEONE'S PUTTING US THROUGH HELL AND WE DON'T EVEN KNOW WHO IT IS!
THIS IS YOUR IDEA OF FUN?
I LIKE TO SEE THINGS THAT ARE BEYOND THE ORDINARY.
IT'S NOT OFTEN WE COME ACROSS SOMETHING
AS INTERESTING-ING AS THIS, IS IT?

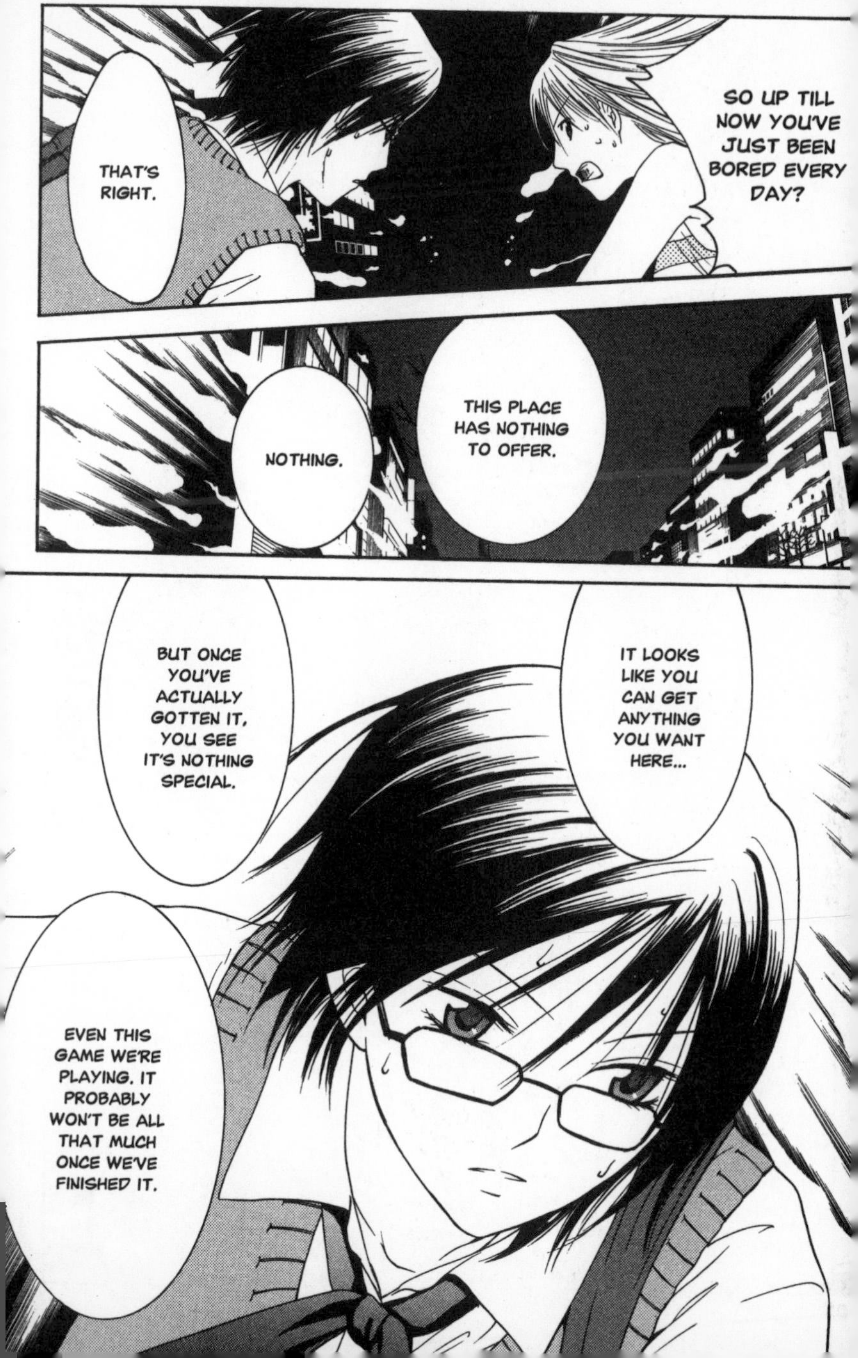
SO UP TILL NOW YOU'VE JUST BEEN BORED EVERY DAY?
THAT'S RIGHT.
THIS PLACE HAS NOTHING TO OFFER.
NOTHING.
IT LOOKS LIKE YOU CAN GET ANYTHING YOU WANT HERE...
BUT ONCE YOU'VE ACTUALLY GOTTEN IT, YOU SEE IT'S NOTHING SPECIAL.
EVEN THIS GAME WE'RE PLAYING. IT PROBABLY WON'T BE ALL THAT MUCH ONCE WE'VE FINISHED IT.

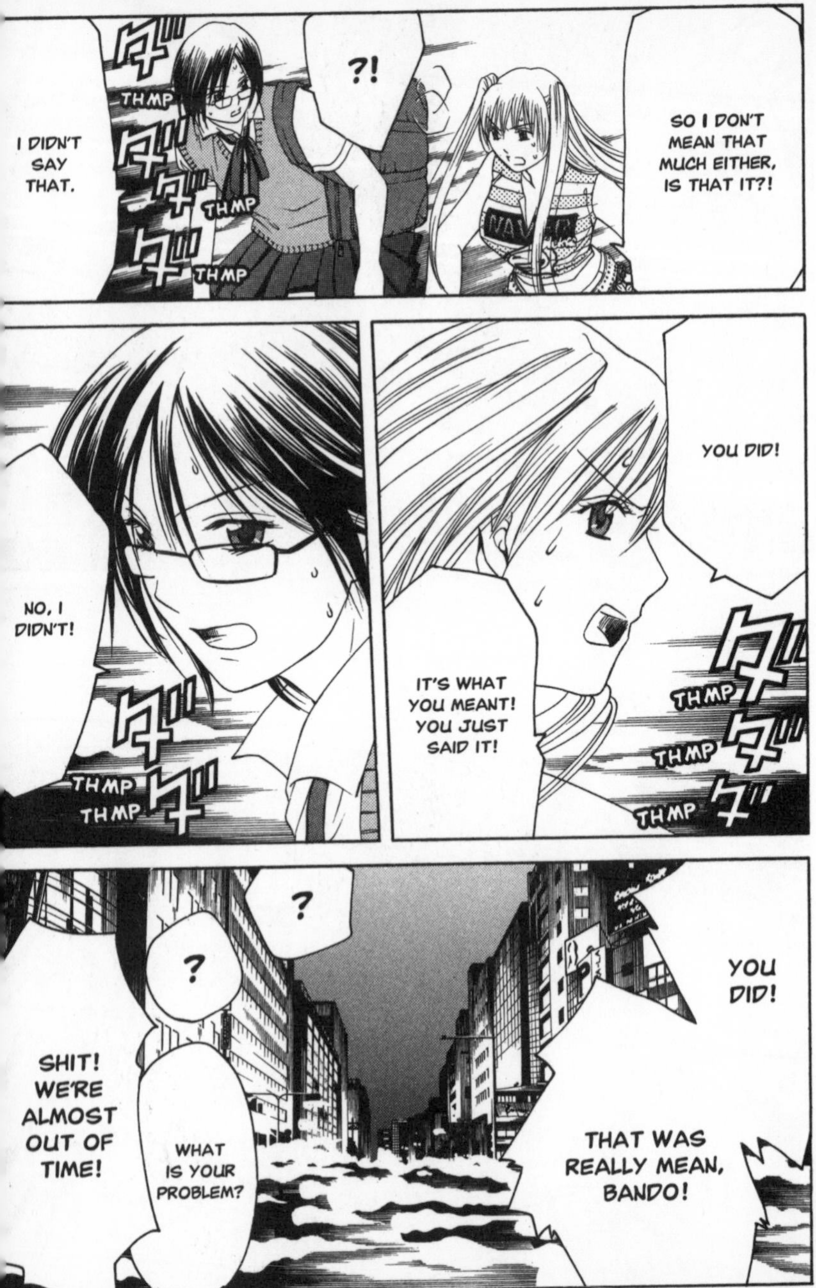
SO I DON'T MEAN THAT MUCH EITHER, IS THAT IT?!
?!
THMP
THMP
THMP
I DIDN'T SAY THAT.
YOU DID!
THMP
THMP
THMP
IT'S WHAT YOU MEANT! YOU JUST SAID IT!
NO, I DIDN'T!
THMP
THMP
YOU DID!
THAT WAS REALLY MEAN, BANDO!
?
?
WHAT IS YOUR PROBLEM?
SHIT! WE'RE ALMOST OUT OF TIME!

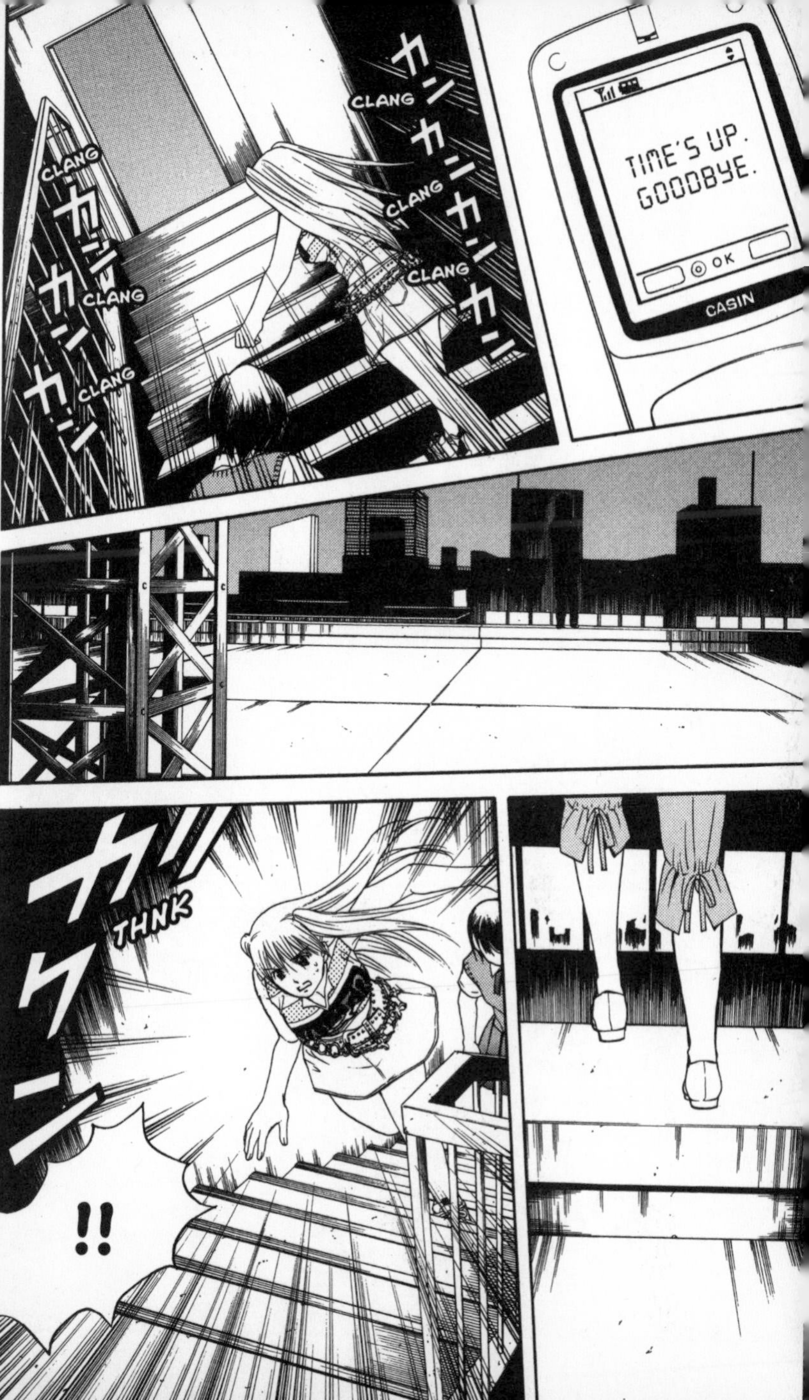
TIME'S UP.
GOODBYE.
OK
CASIN
CLANG
CLANG
CLANG
CLANG
CLANG
CLANG
THNK
!!

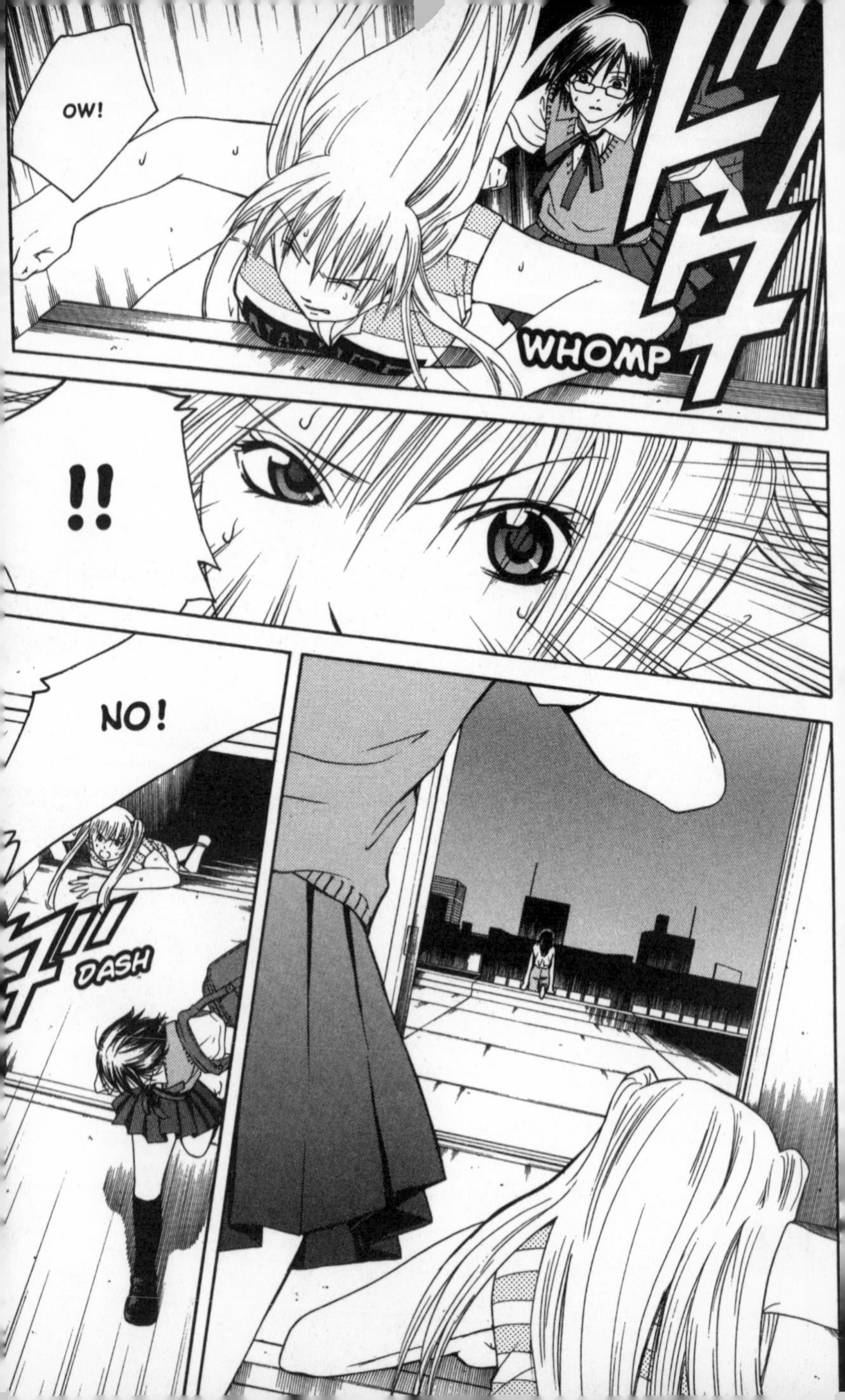

WHOMP
OW!
!!
NO!
DASH

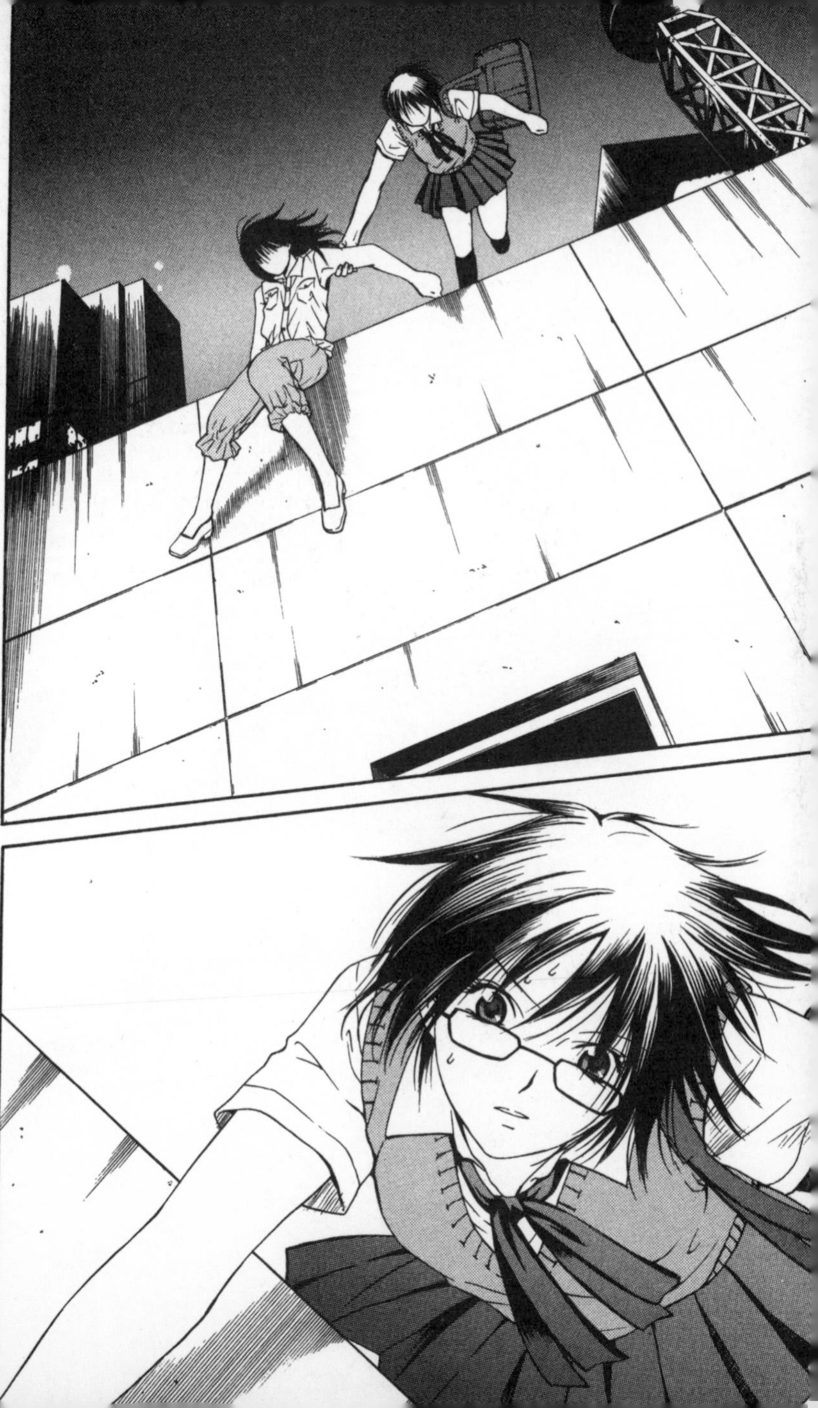

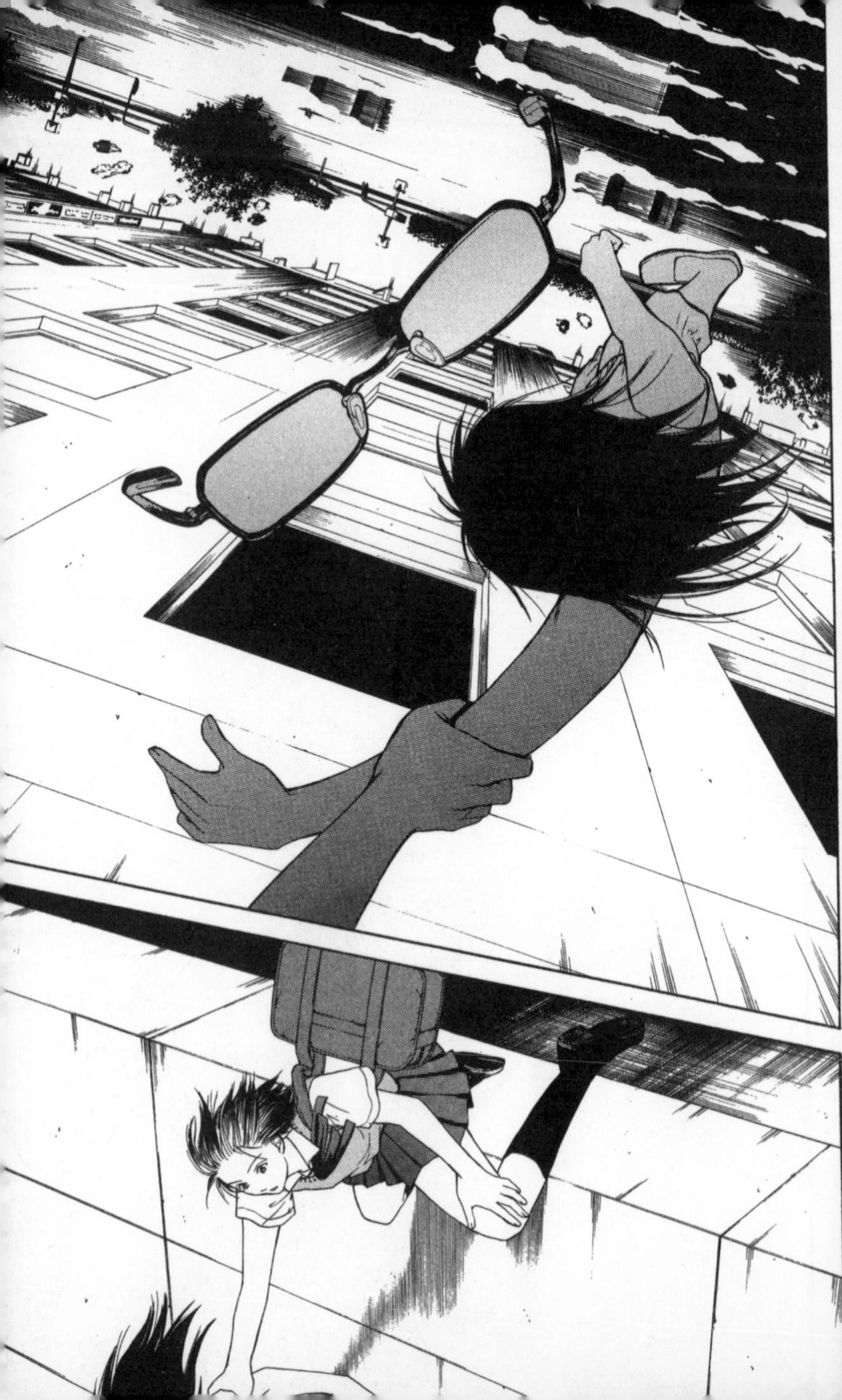

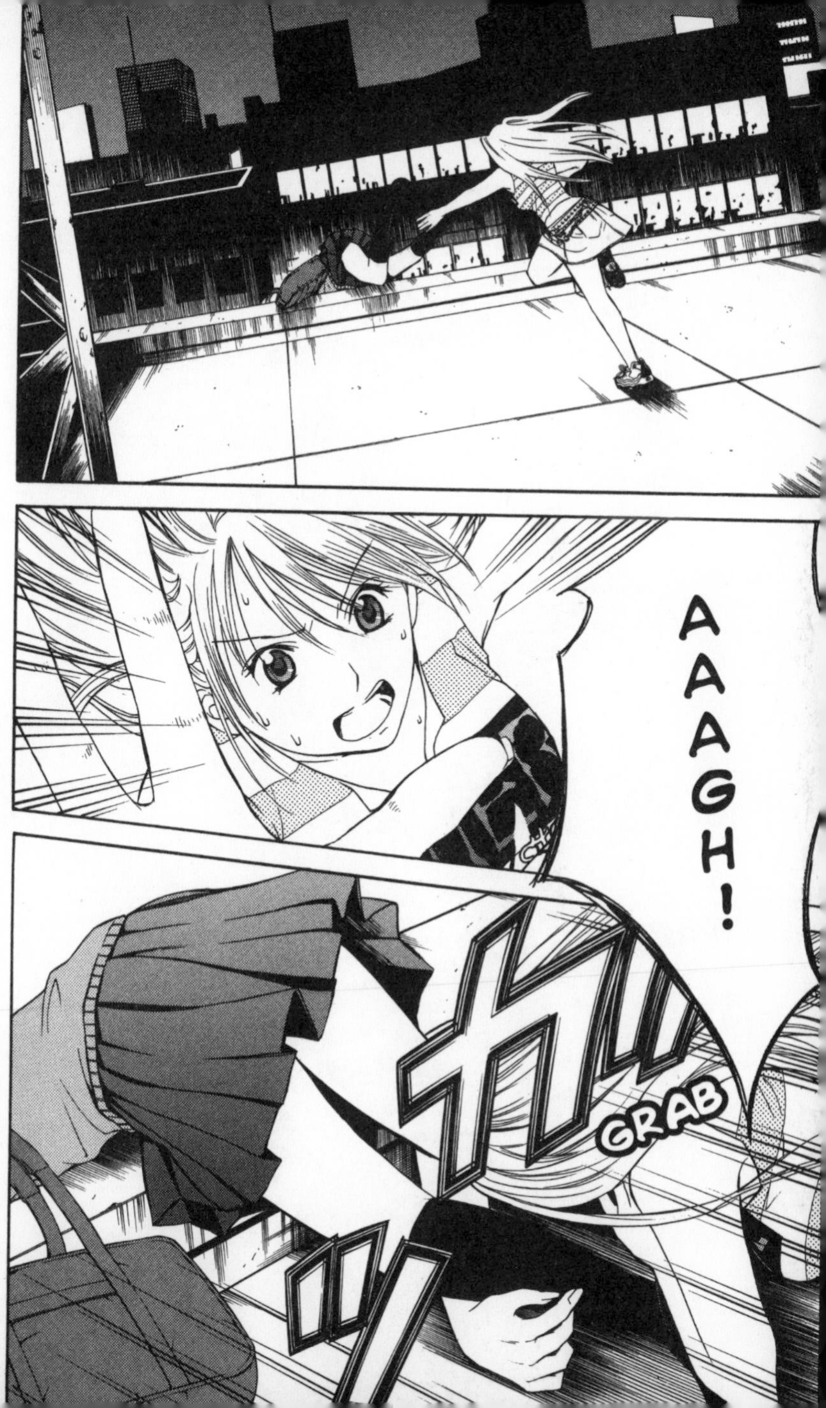
AAAGH!
GRAB

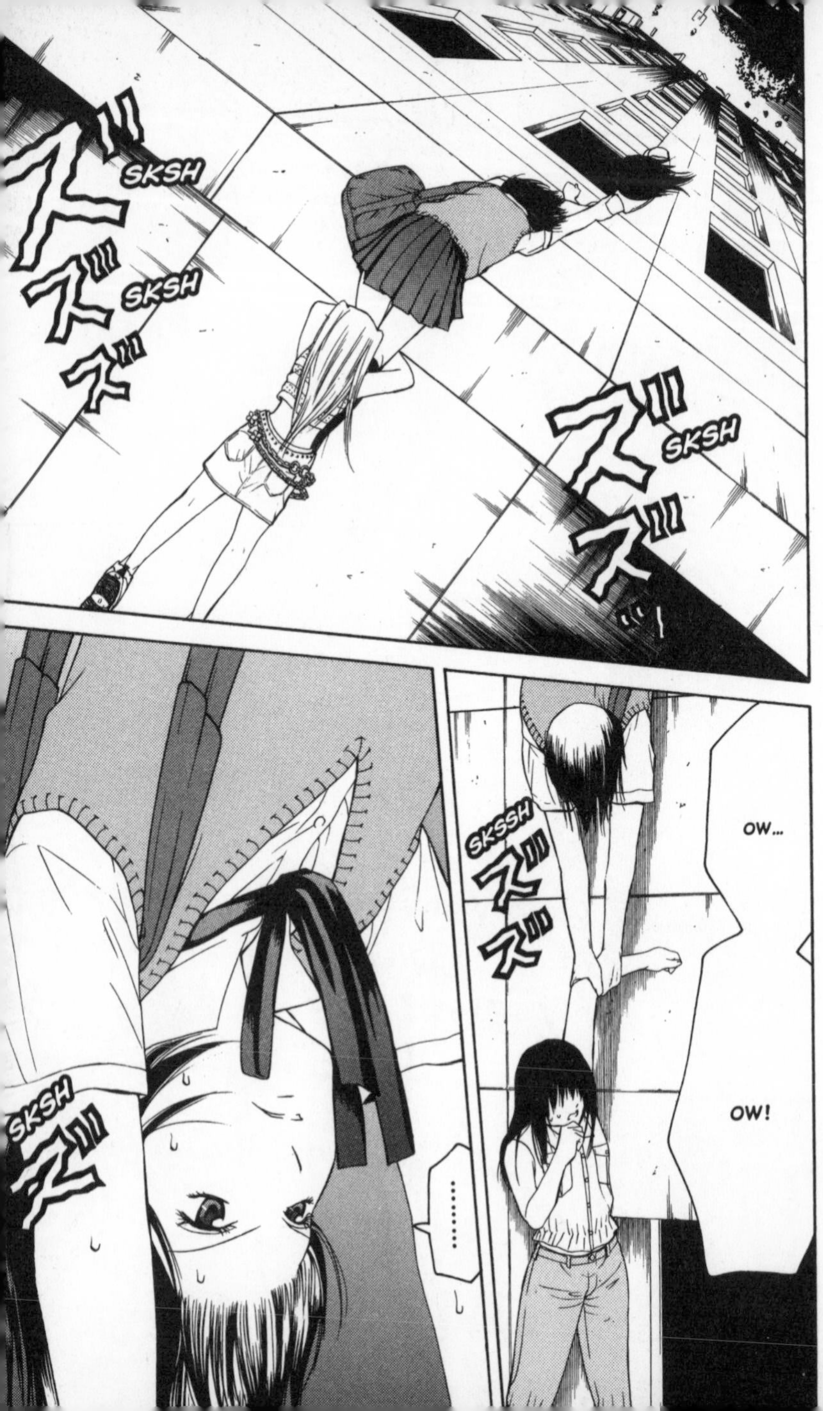

ズズズ
SKSH
SKSH
ズズズ
SKSH
OW...
OW!
ズズ
SKSSH
......
ズ
SKSH

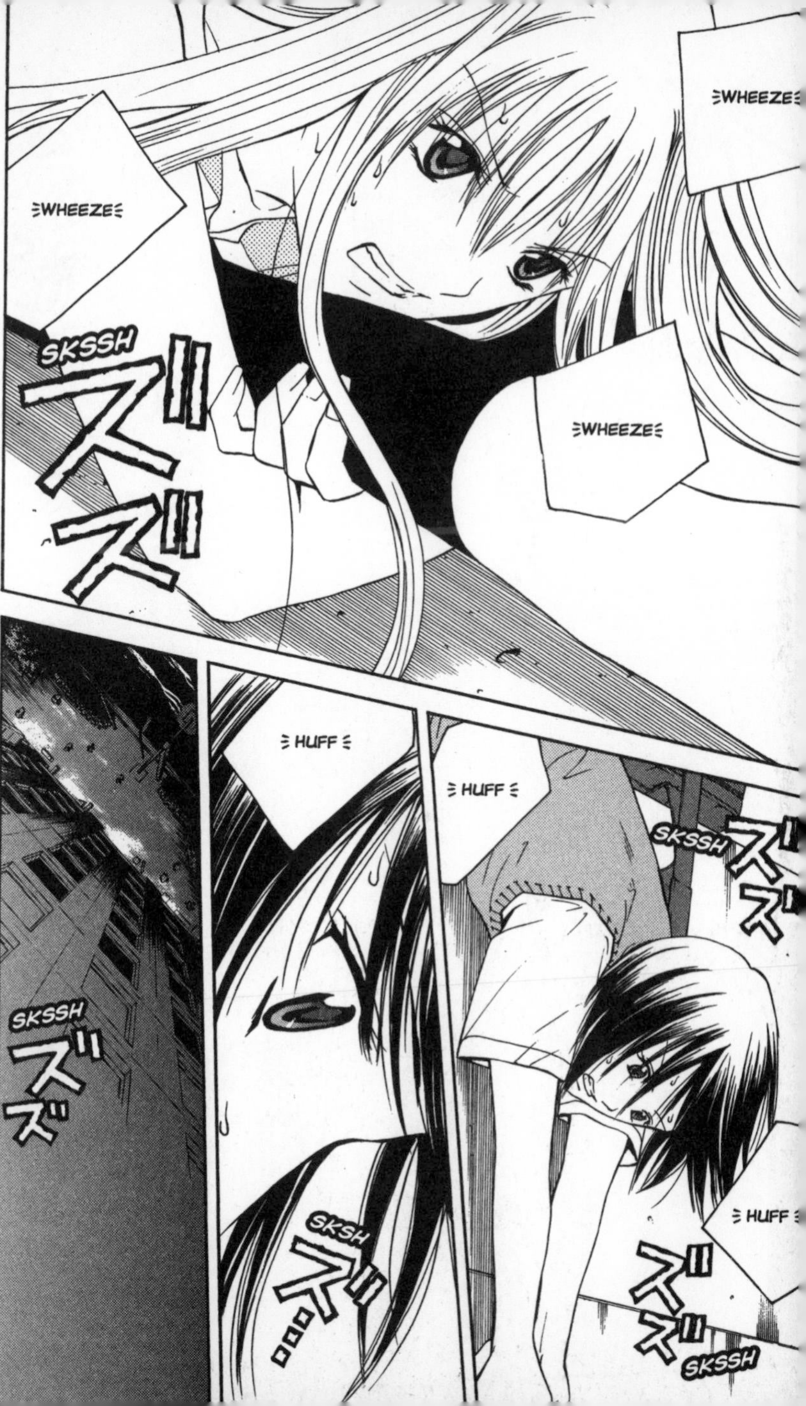
WHEEZE
WHEEZE
WHEEZE
SKSSH
ズズ
HUFF
SKSSH
ズズ
HUFF
ズズ
SKSSH
HUFF
SKSH
ズ...
SKSSH
ズズ

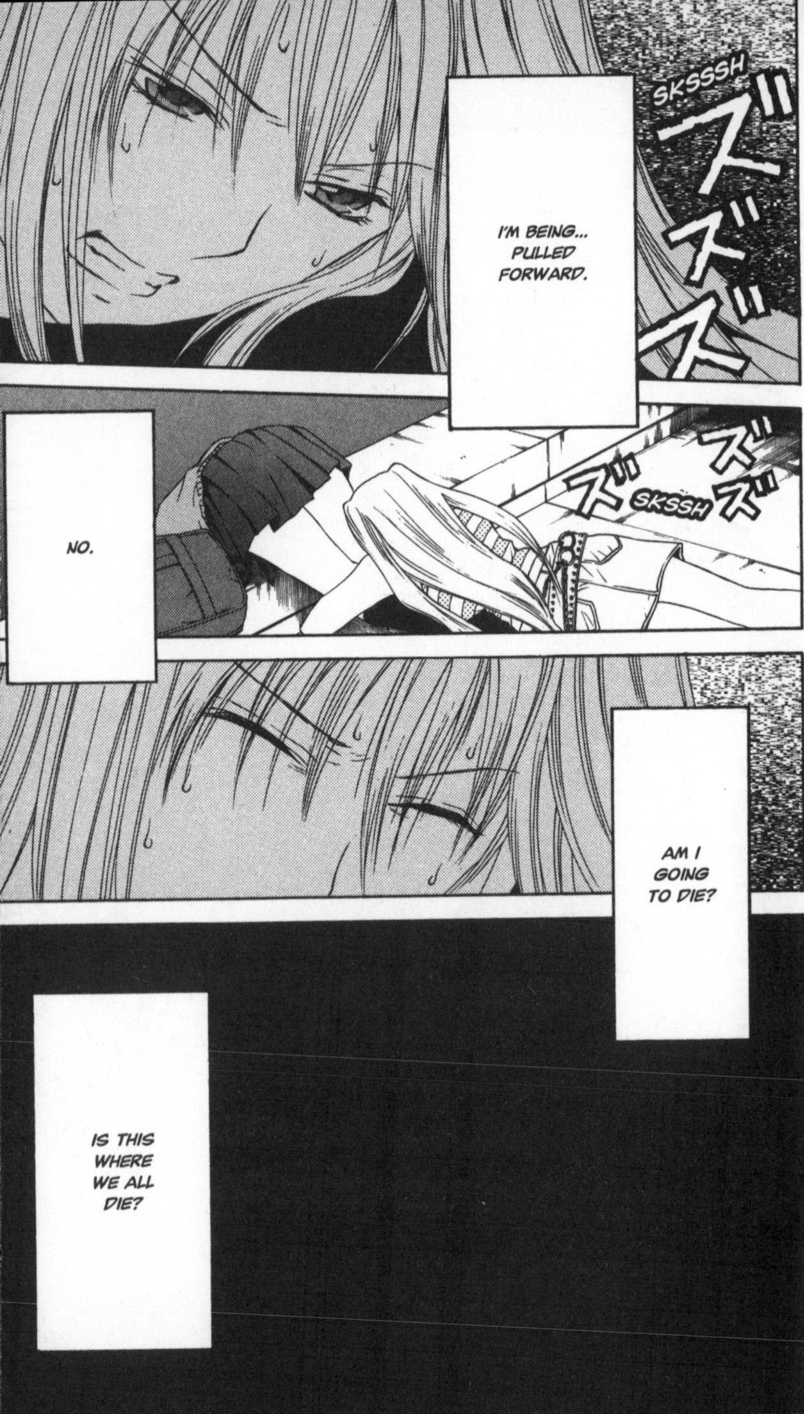
SKSSSH
I'M BEING... PULLED FORWARD.
SKSSH
NO.
AM I GOING TO DIE?
IS THIS WHERE WE ALL DIE?

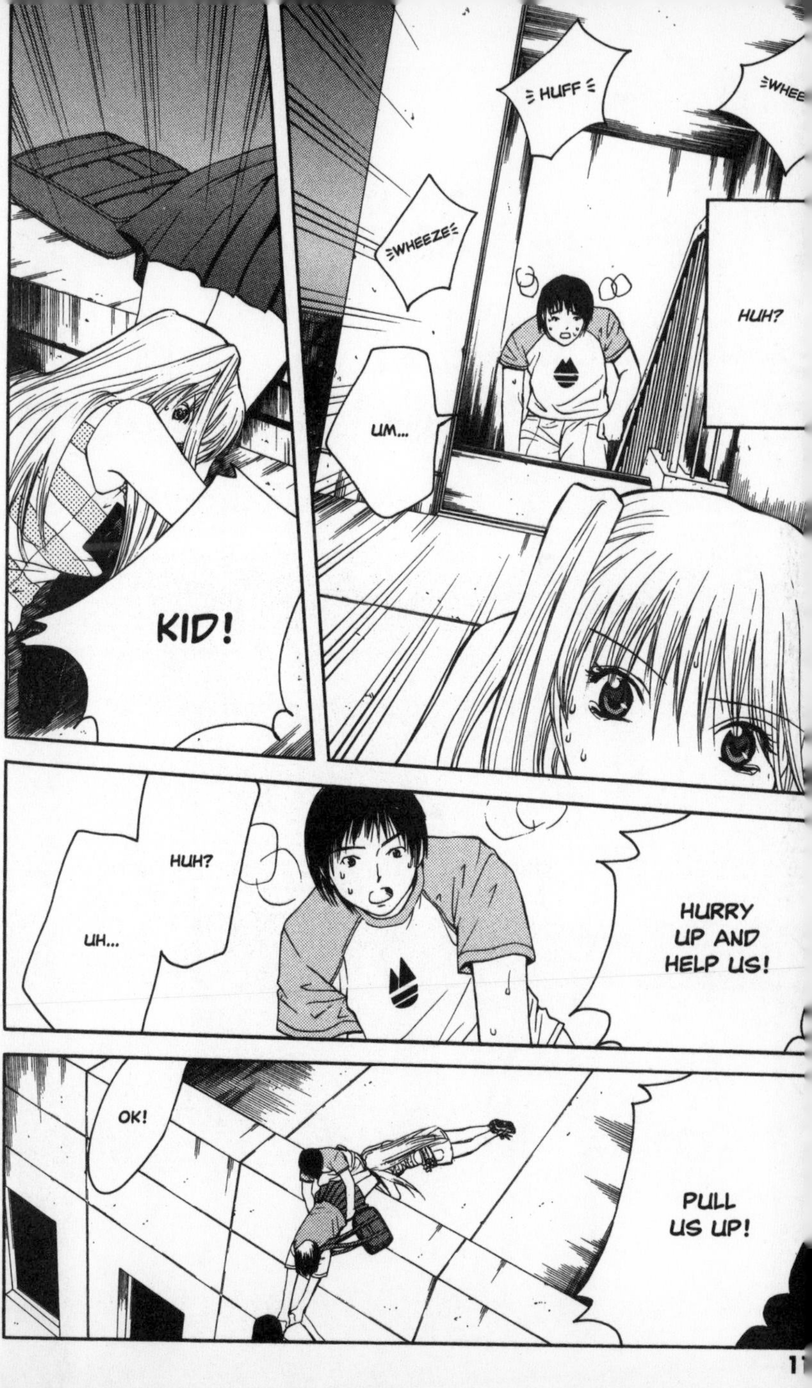

WHEE
HUFF
HUH?
WHEEZE
UM...
KID!
HURRY UP AND HELP US!
HUH?
UH...
PULL US UP!
OK!

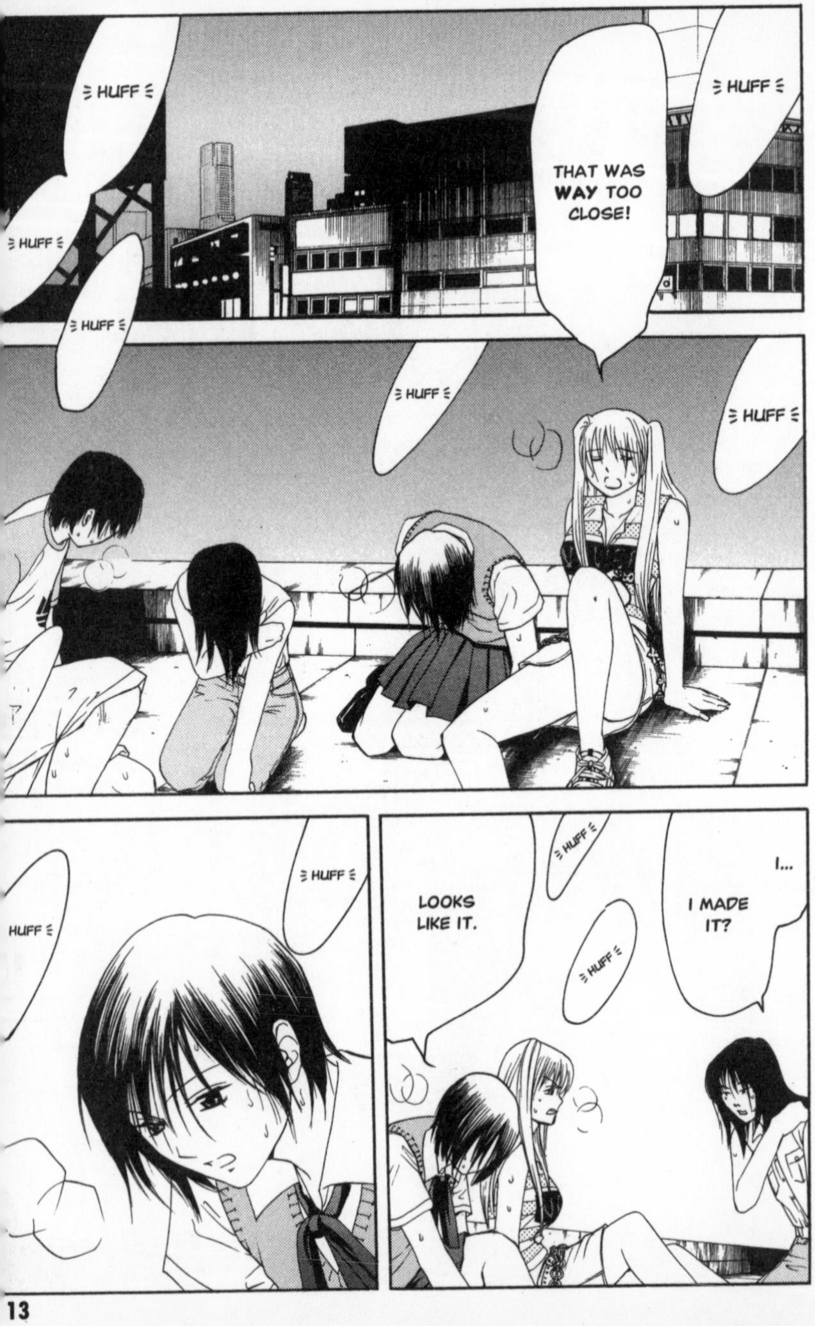
HUFF
THAT WAS WAY TOO CLOSE!
HUFF
HUFF
HUFF
HUFF
HUFF
I... I MADE IT?
HUFF
HUFF
LOOKS LIKE IT.
HUFF
HUFF

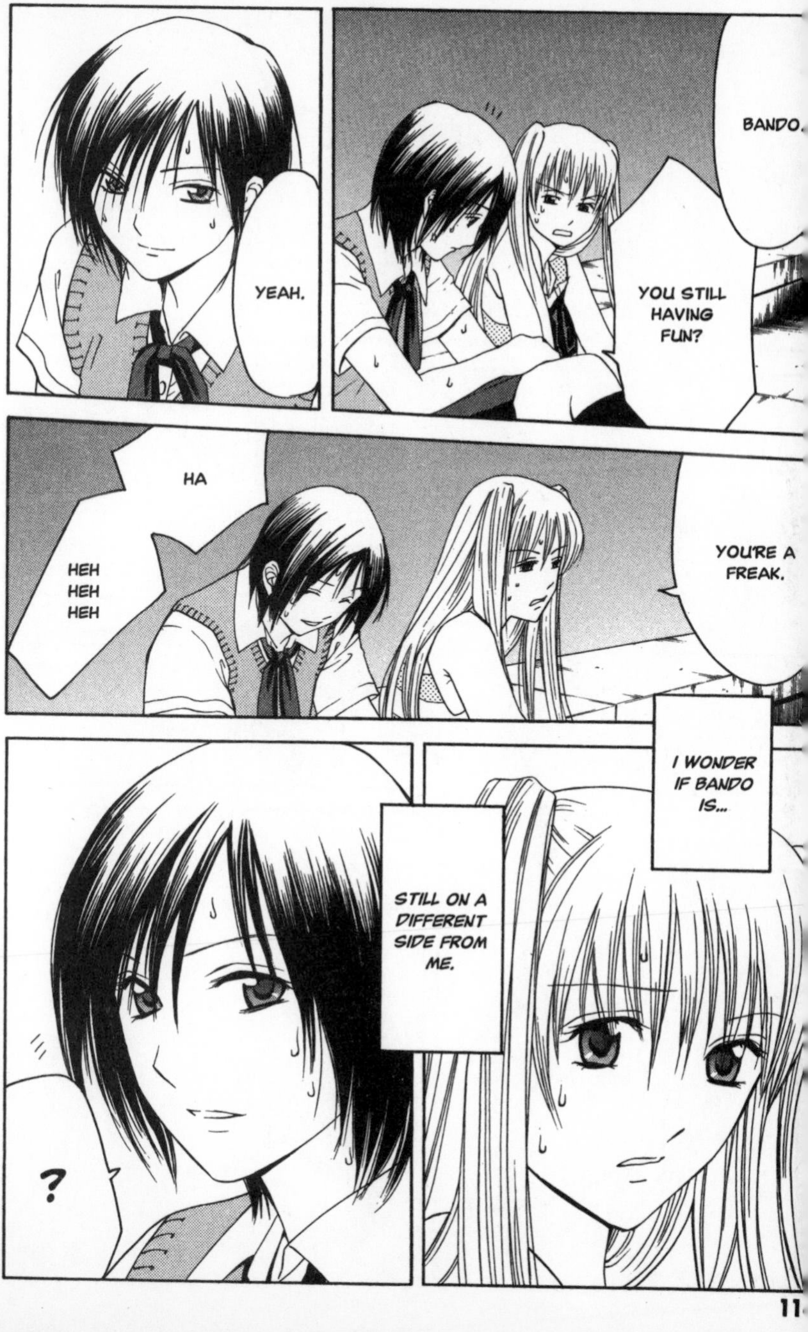
BANDO.
YOU STILL HAVING FUN?
YEAH.
YOU'RE A FREAK.
HA
HEH HEH HEH
I WONDER IF BANDO IS...
STILL ON A DIFFERENT SIDE FROM ME.
?

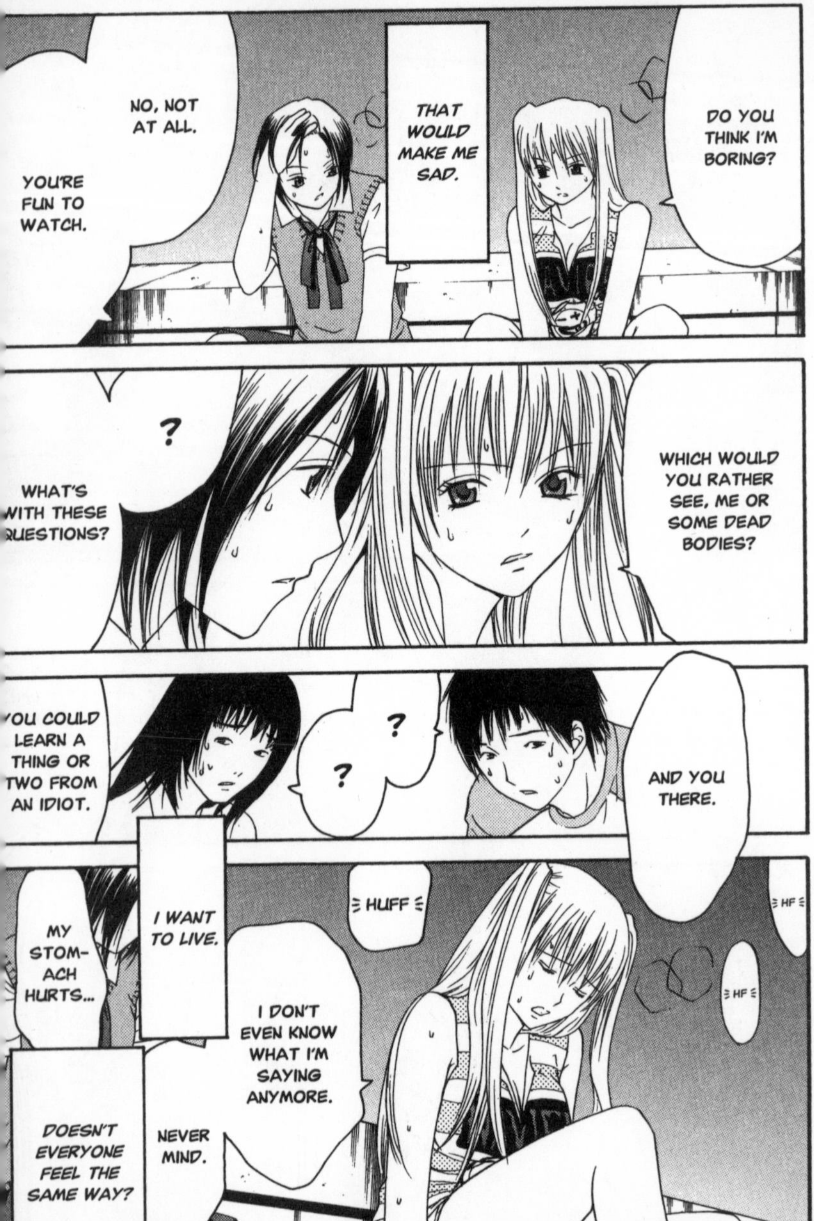
DO YOU THINK I'M BORING?
THAT WOULD MAKE ME SAD.
NO, NOT AT ALL.
YOU'RE FUN TO WATCH.
WHICH WOULD YOU RATHER SEE, ME OR SOME DEAD BODIES?
?
WHAT'S WITH THESE QUESTIONS?
AND YOU THERE.
?
?
YOU COULD LEARN A THING OR TWO FROM AN IDIOT.
HF
HF
HUFF
I DON'T EVEN KNOW WHAT I'M SAYING ANYMORE.
NEVER MIND.
I WANT TO LIVE.
MY STOM-ACH HURTS...
DOESN'T EVERYONE FEEL THE SAME WAY?

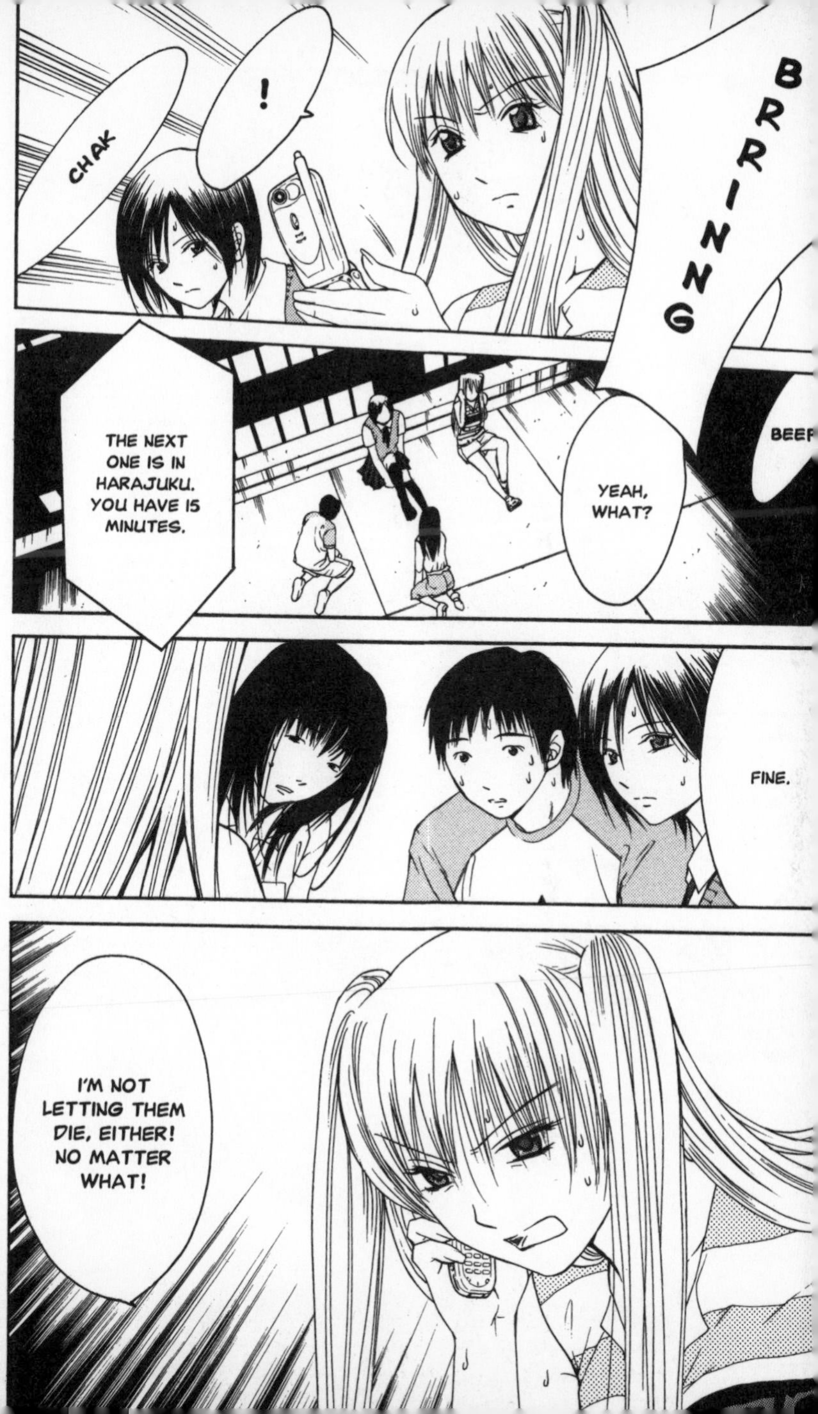
BRRING
!
CHAK
BEEP
YEAH, WHAT?
THE NEXT ONE IS IN HARAJUKU. YOU HAVE 15 MINUTES.
FINE.
I'M NOT LETTING THEM DIE, EITHER! NO MATTER WHAT!

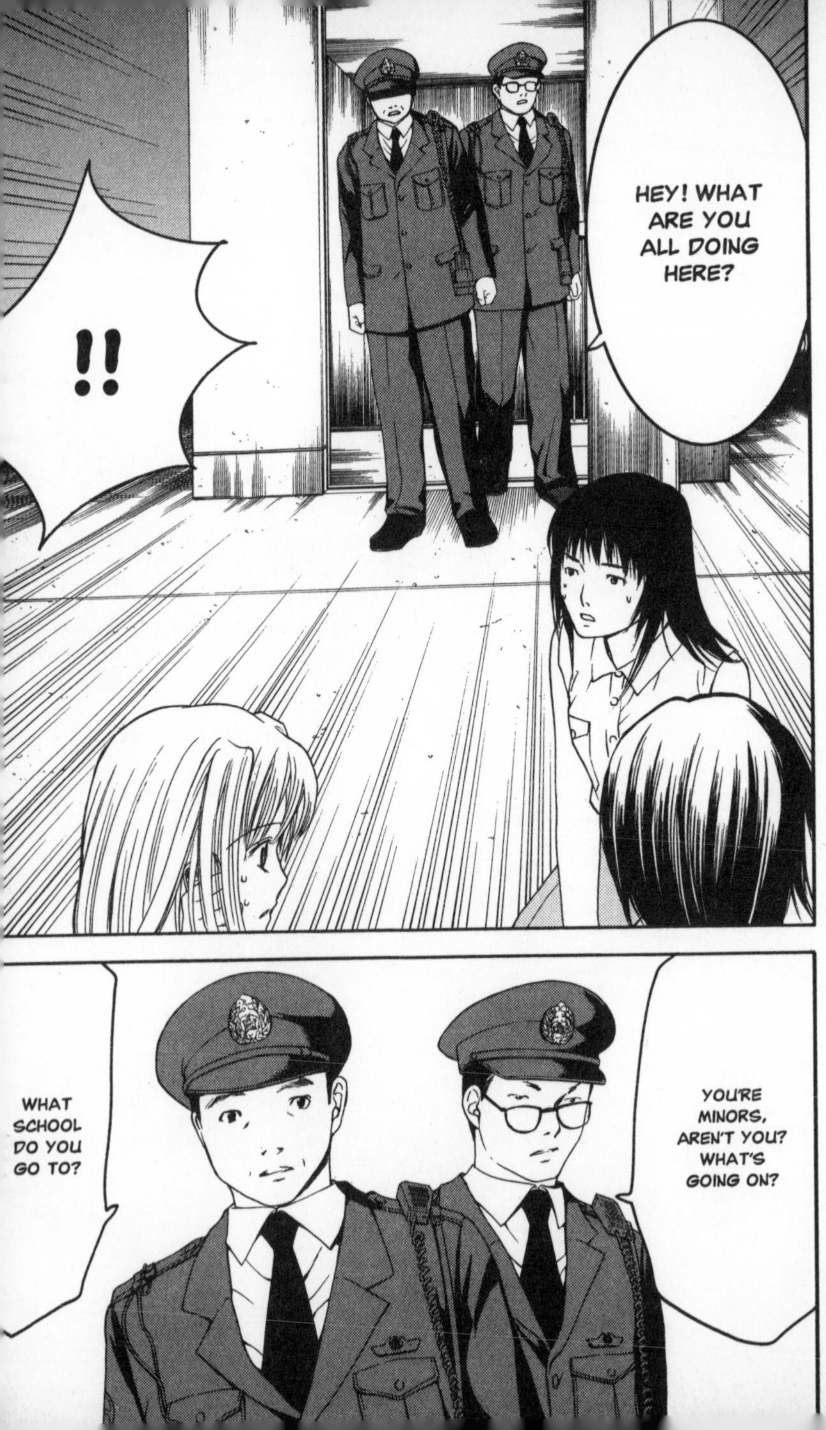
HEY! WHAT ARE YOU ALL DOING HERE?
!!
YOU'RE MINORS, AREN'T YOU? WHAT'S GOING ON?
WHAT SCHOOL DO YOU GO TO?

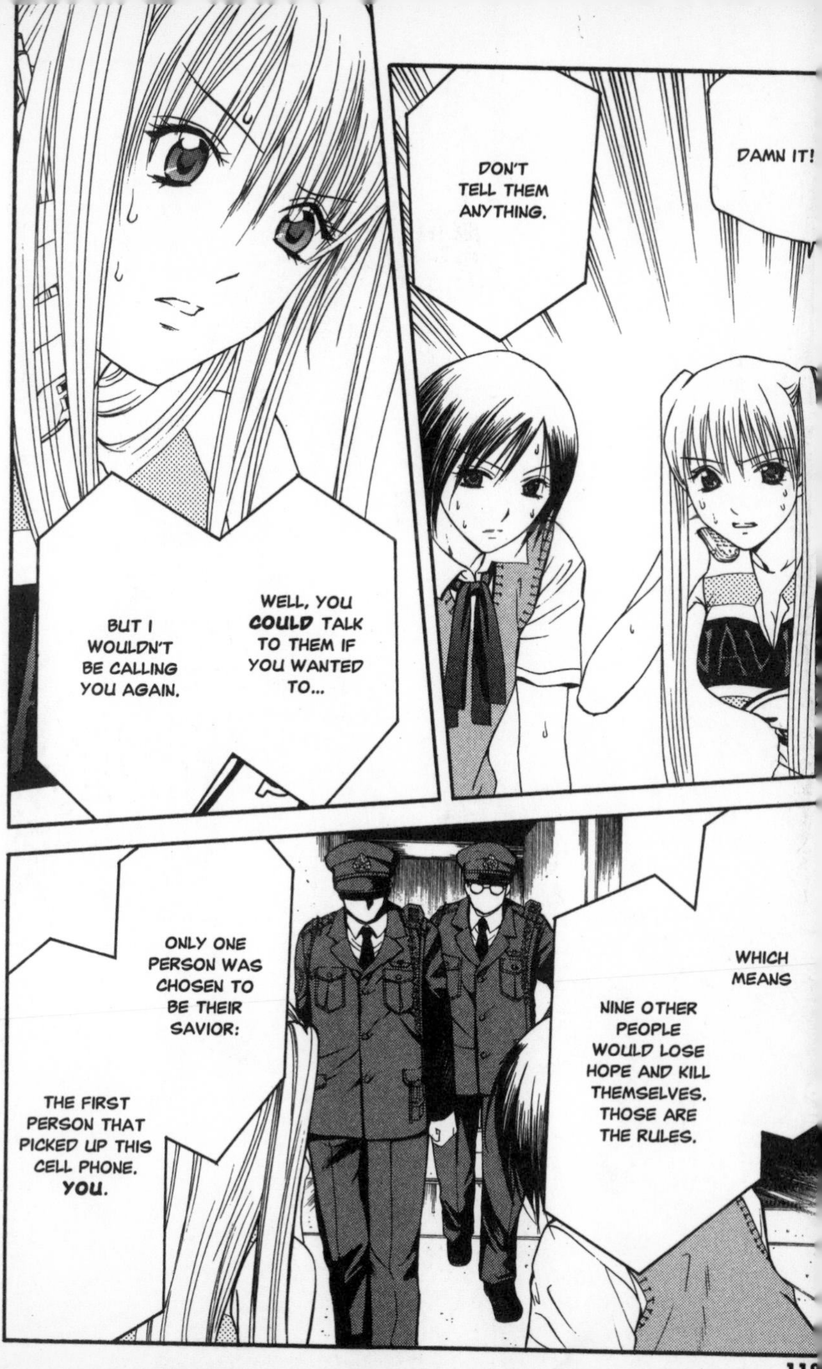
DAMN IT!
DON'T TELL THEM ANYTHING.
WELL, YOU **COULD** TALK TO THEM IF YOU WANTED TO...
BUT I WOULDN'T BE CALLING YOU AGAIN.
ONLY ONE PERSON WAS CHOSEN TO BE THEIR SAVIOR:
THE FIRST PERSON THAT PICKED UP THIS CELL PHONE. **YOU**.
WHICH MEANS
NINE OTHER PEOPLE WOULD LOSE HOPE AND KILL THEMSELVES. THOSE ARE THE RULES.

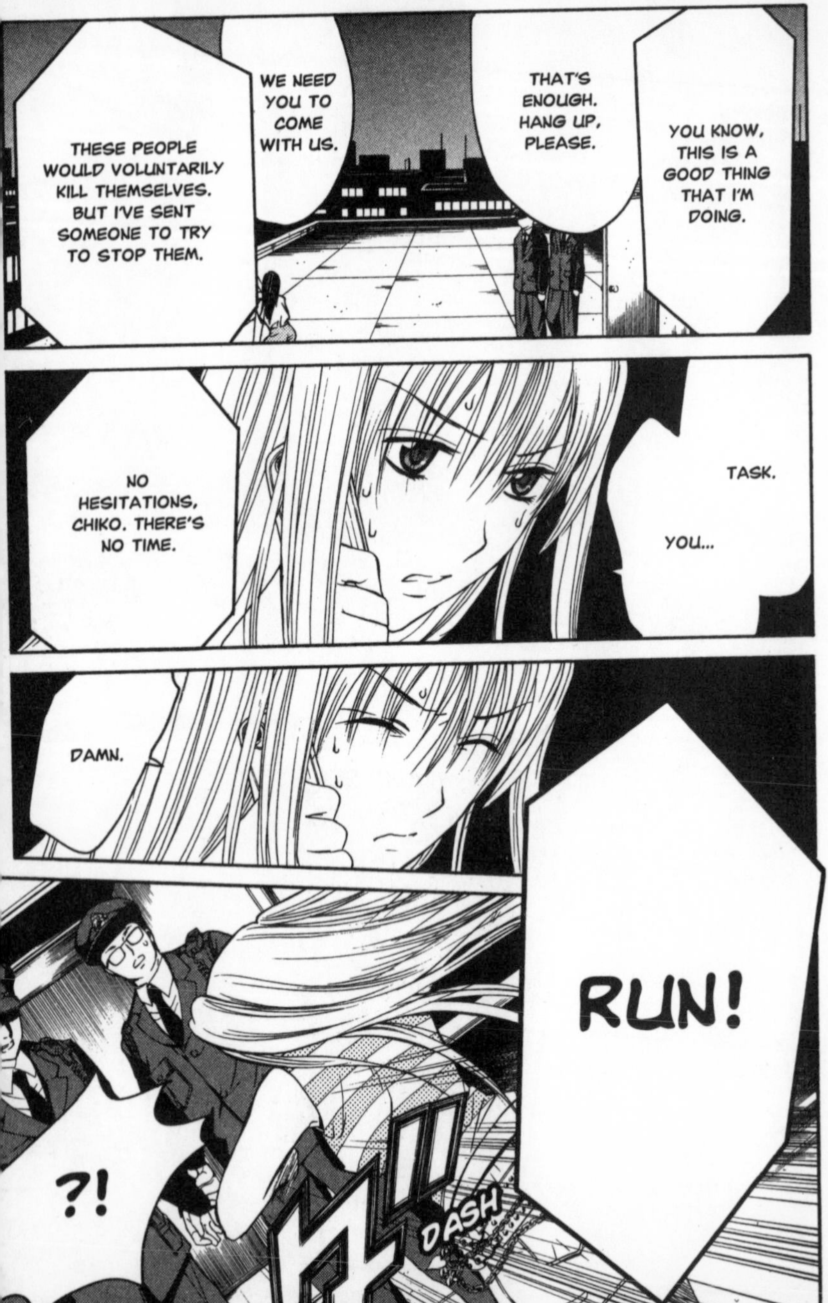

YOU KNOW, THIS IS A GOOD THING THAT I'M DOING.
THAT'S ENOUGH. HANG UP, PLEASE.
WE NEED YOU TO COME WITH US.
THESE PEOPLE WOULD VOLUNTARILY KILL THEMSELVES. BUT I'VE SENT SOMEONE TO TRY TO STOP THEM.
TASK.
YOU...
NO HESITATIONS, CHIKO. THERE'S NO TIME.
DAMN.
RUN!
DASH
?!

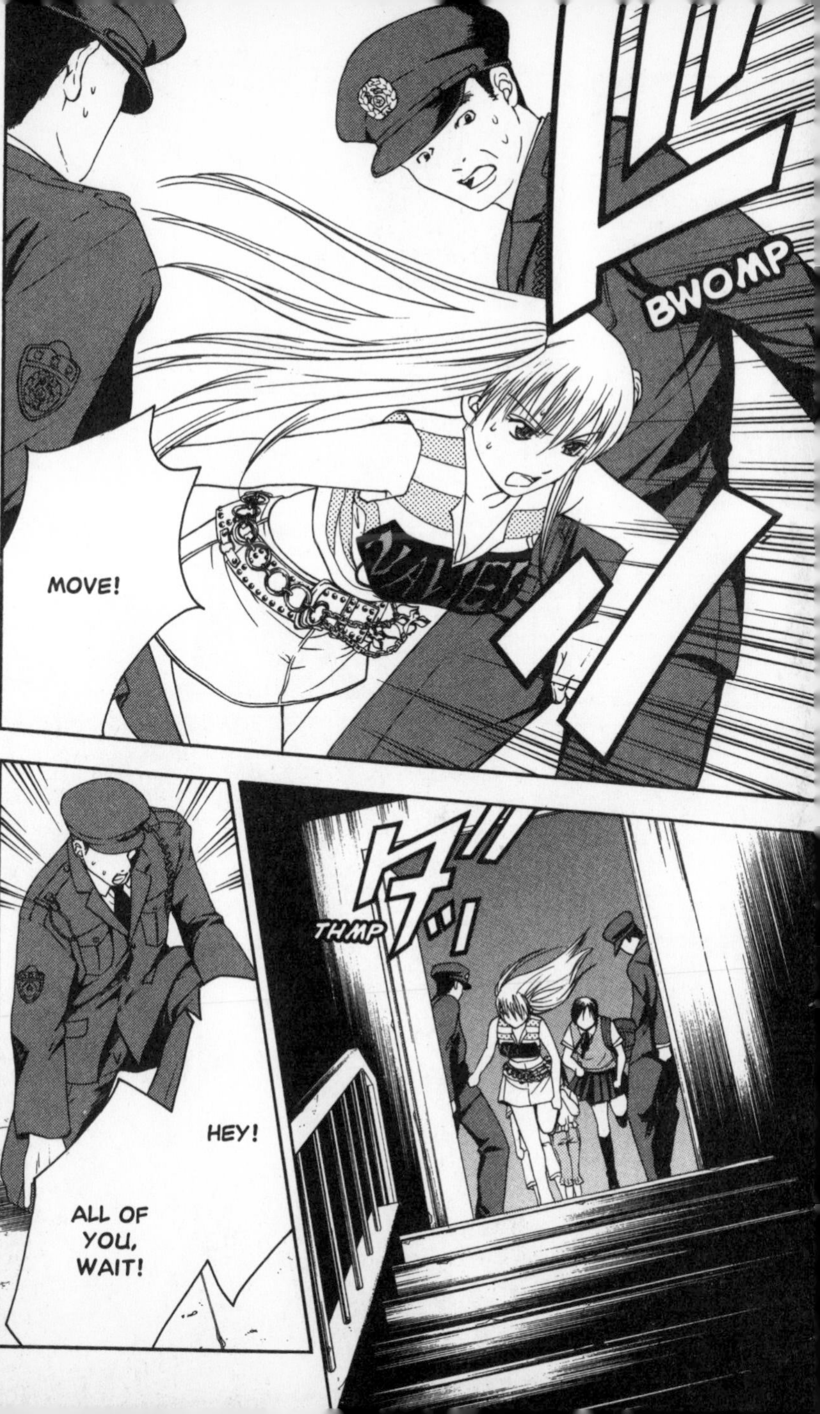
BWOMP
MOVE!
THMP
HEY!
ALL OF YOU, WAIT!

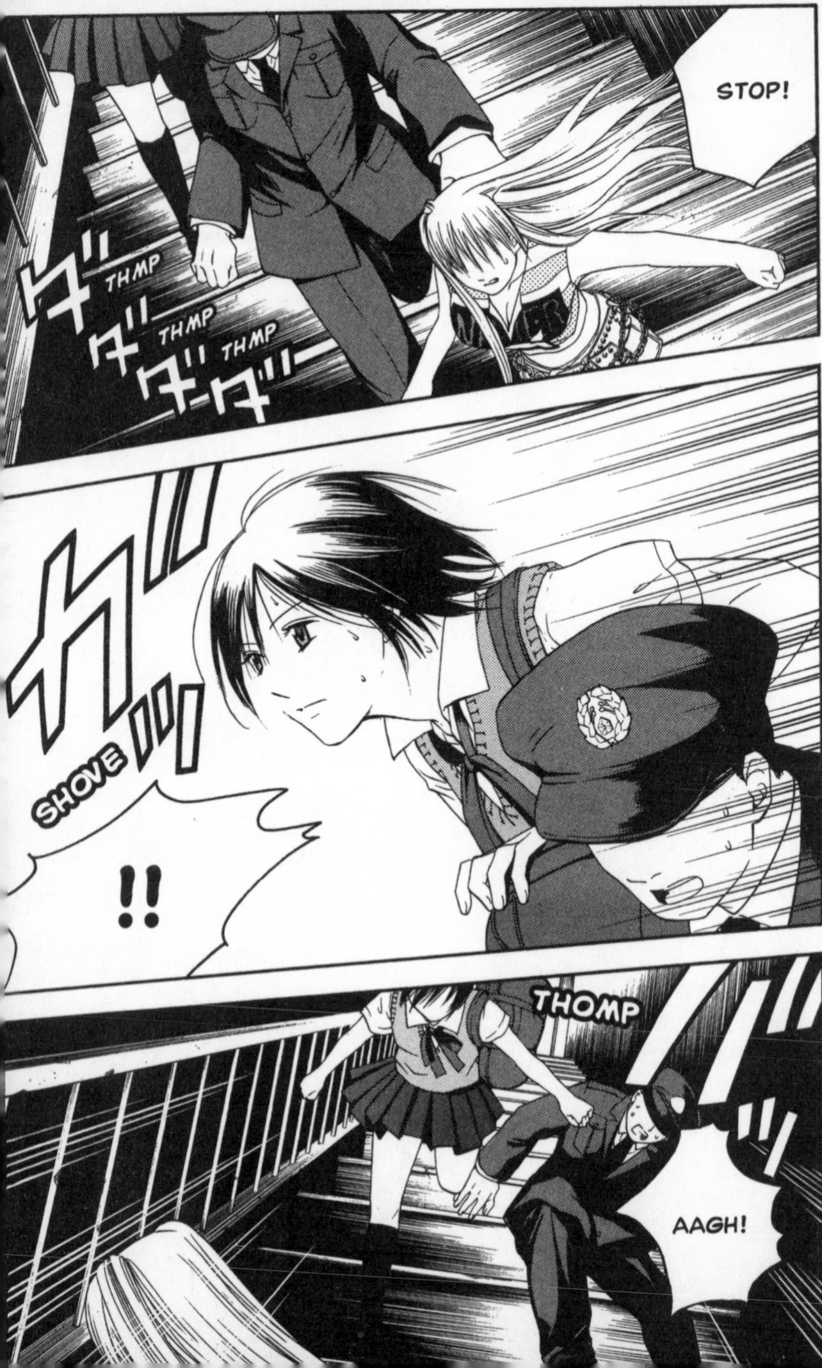
STOP!
THMP
THMP
THMP
SHOVE
!!
THOMP
AAGH!

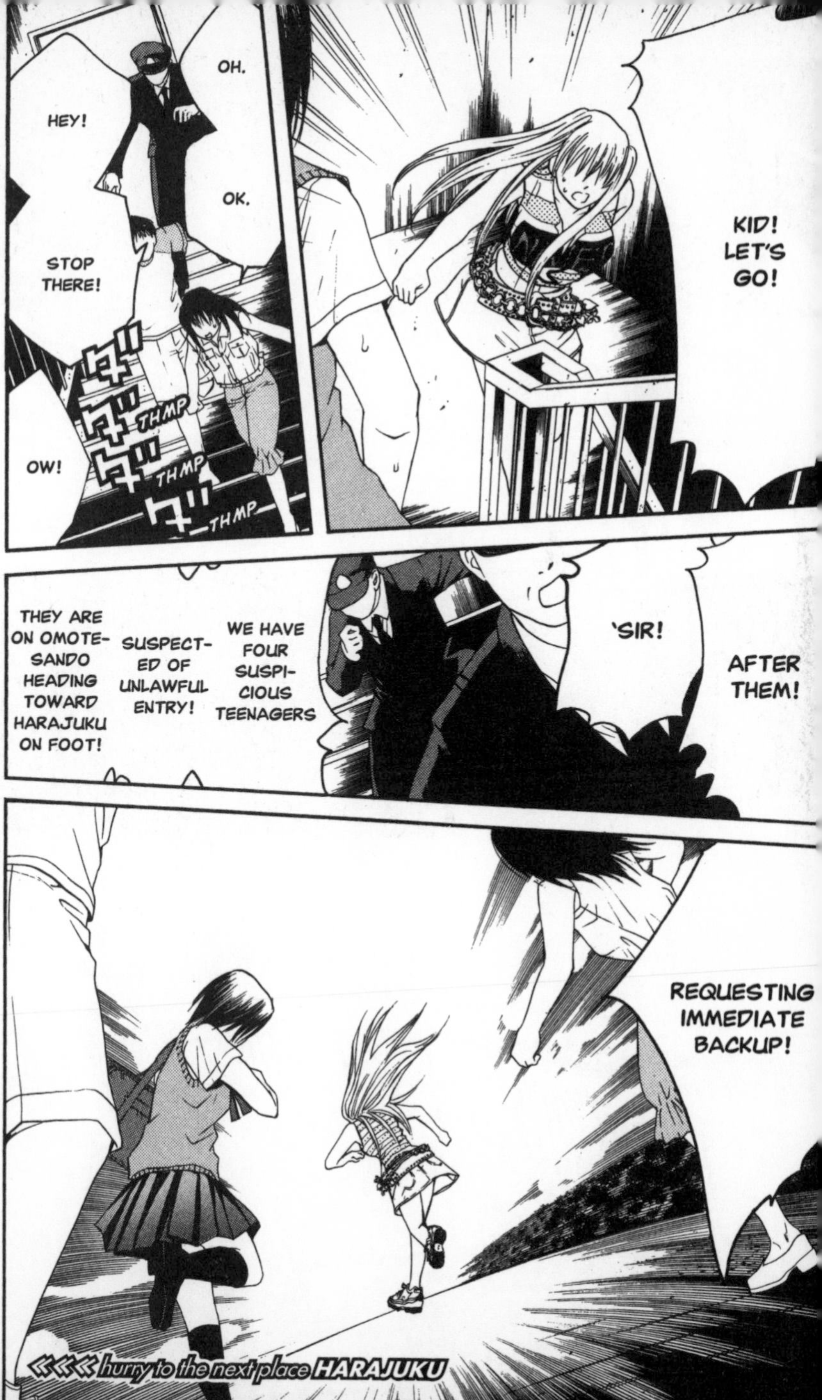
KID! LET'S GO!
OH.
HEY!
OK.
STOP THERE!
THMP
THMP
THMP
OW!
AFTER THEM!
'SIR!
WE HAVE FOUR SUSPICIOUS TEENAGERS
SUSPECTED OF UNLAWFUL ENTRY!
THEY ARE ON OMOTE-SANDO HEADING TOWARD HARAJUKU ON FOOT!
REQUESTING IMMEDIATE BACKUP!
hurry to the next place HARAJUKU

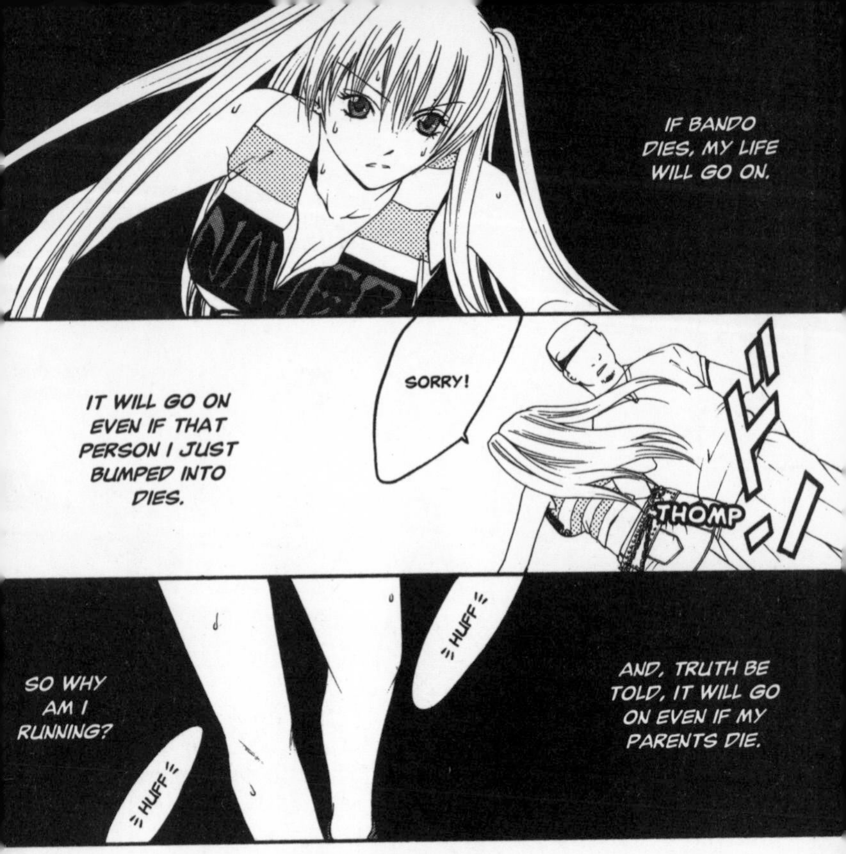
IF BANDO DIES, MY LIFE WILL GO ON.
THOMP
SORRY!
IT WILL GO ON EVEN IF THAT PERSON I JUST BUMPED INTO DIES.
AND, TRUTH BE TOLD, IT WILL GO ON EVEN IF MY PARENTS DIE.
HUFF
HUFF
SO WHY AM I RUNNING?

IT FEELS LIKE I'VE BEEN DRAGGED INTO SOME DARK HOLE THAT'S OPENED UP IN MY OTHERWISE NORMAL LIFE.

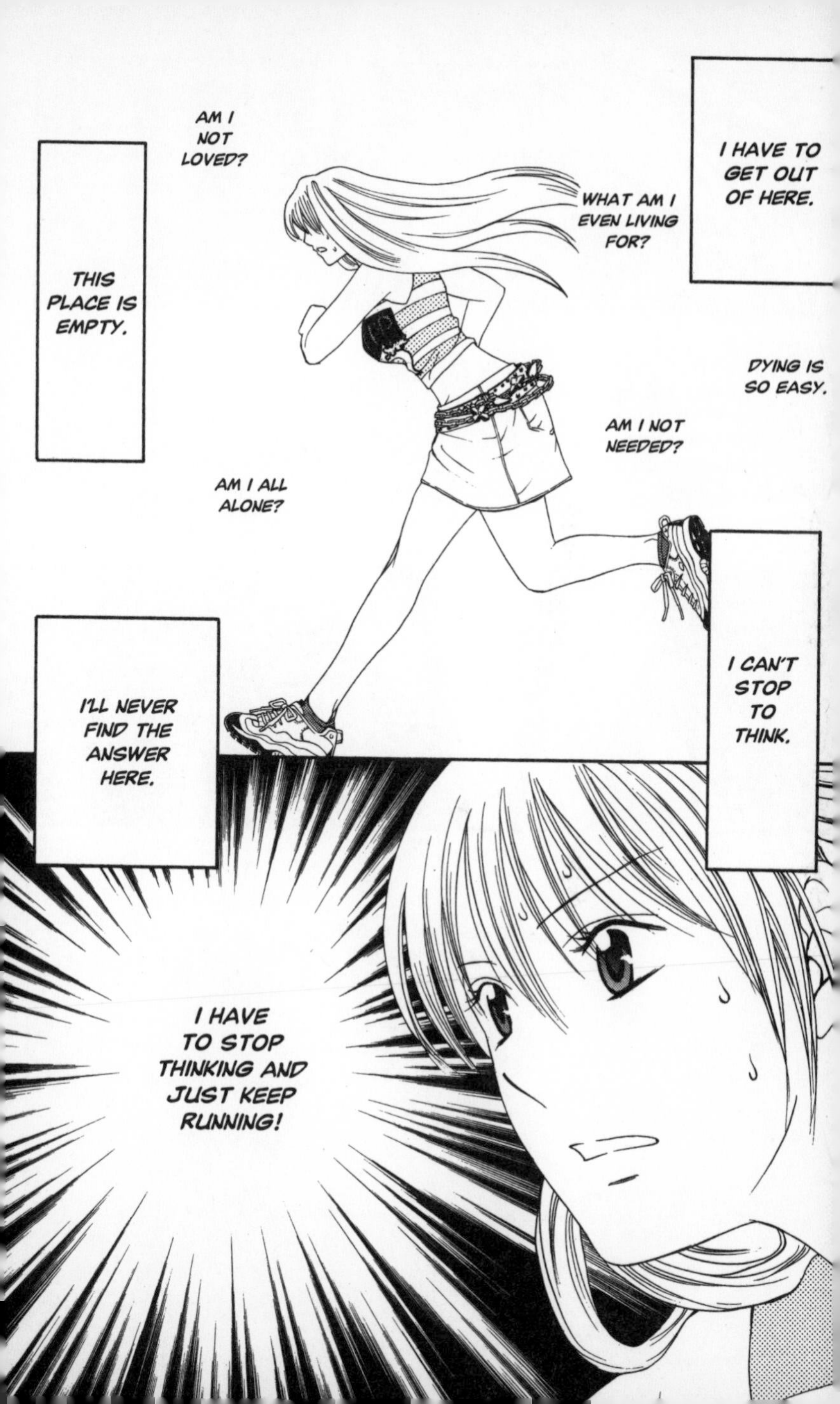
I HAVE TO GET OUT OF HERE.
WHAT AM I EVEN LIVING FOR?
AM I NOT LOVED?
THIS PLACE IS EMPTY.
DYING IS SO EASY.
AM I NOT NEEDED?
AM I ALL ALONE?
I CAN'T STOP TO THINK.
I'LL NEVER FIND THE ANSWER HERE.
I HAVE TO STOP THINKING AND JUST KEEP RUNNING!

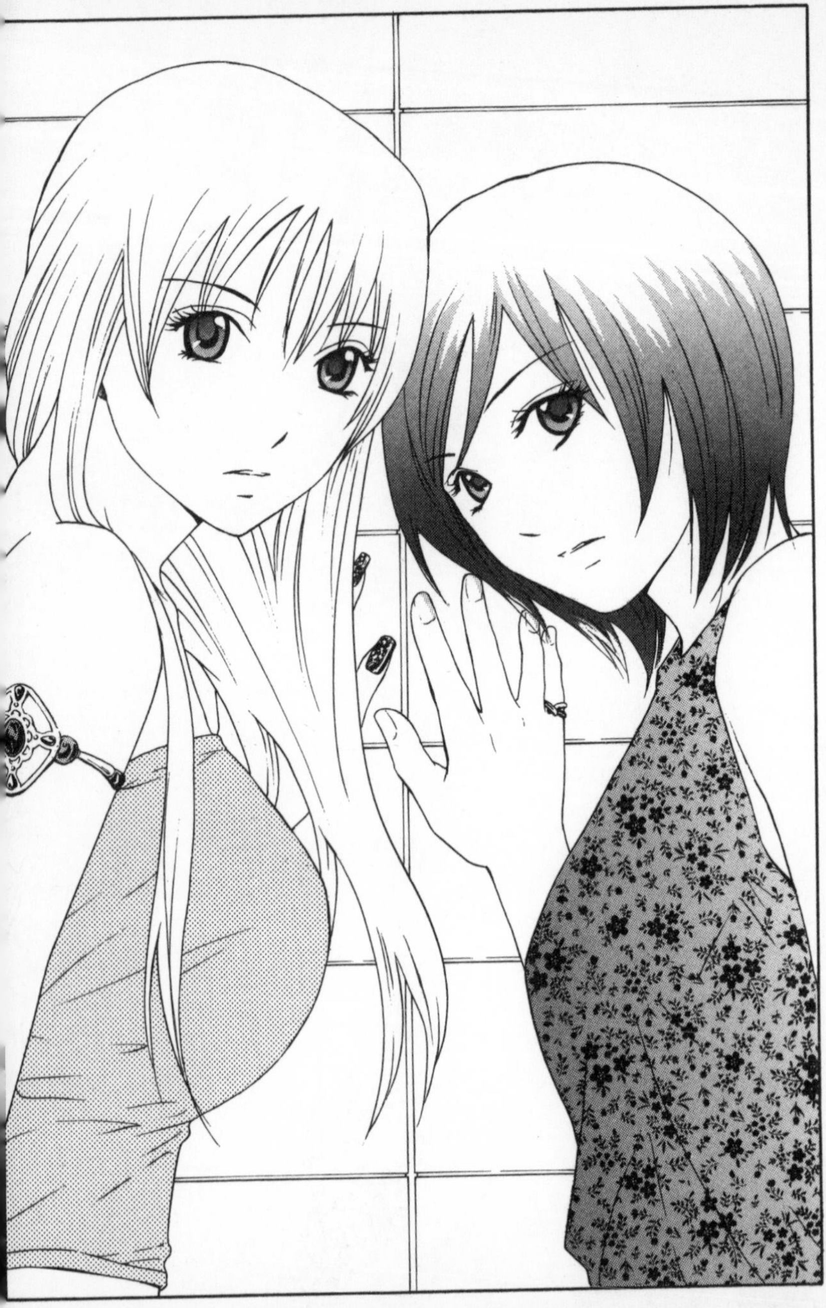

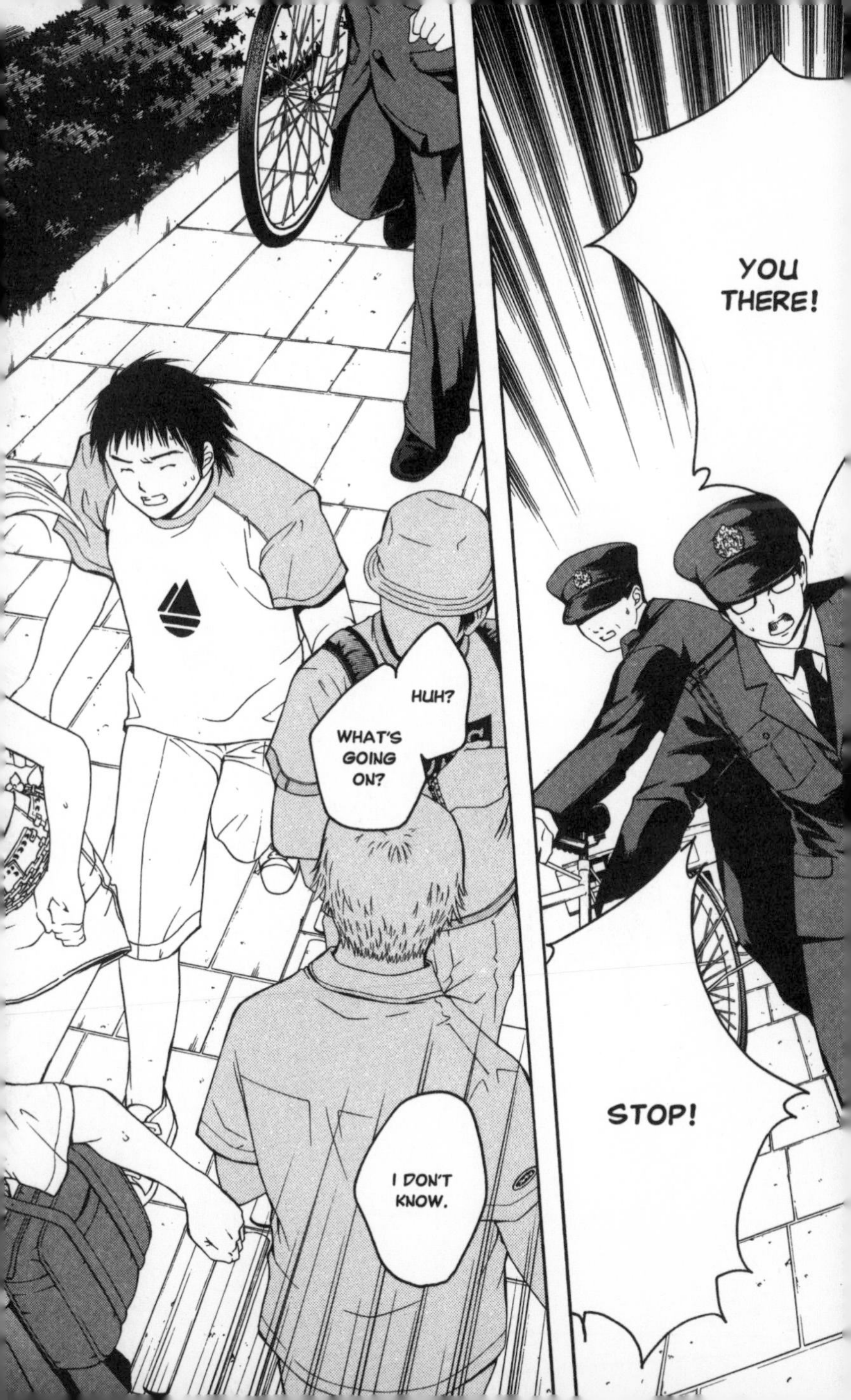
YOU THERE!
STOP!
HUH? WHAT'S GOING ON?
I DON'T KNOW.

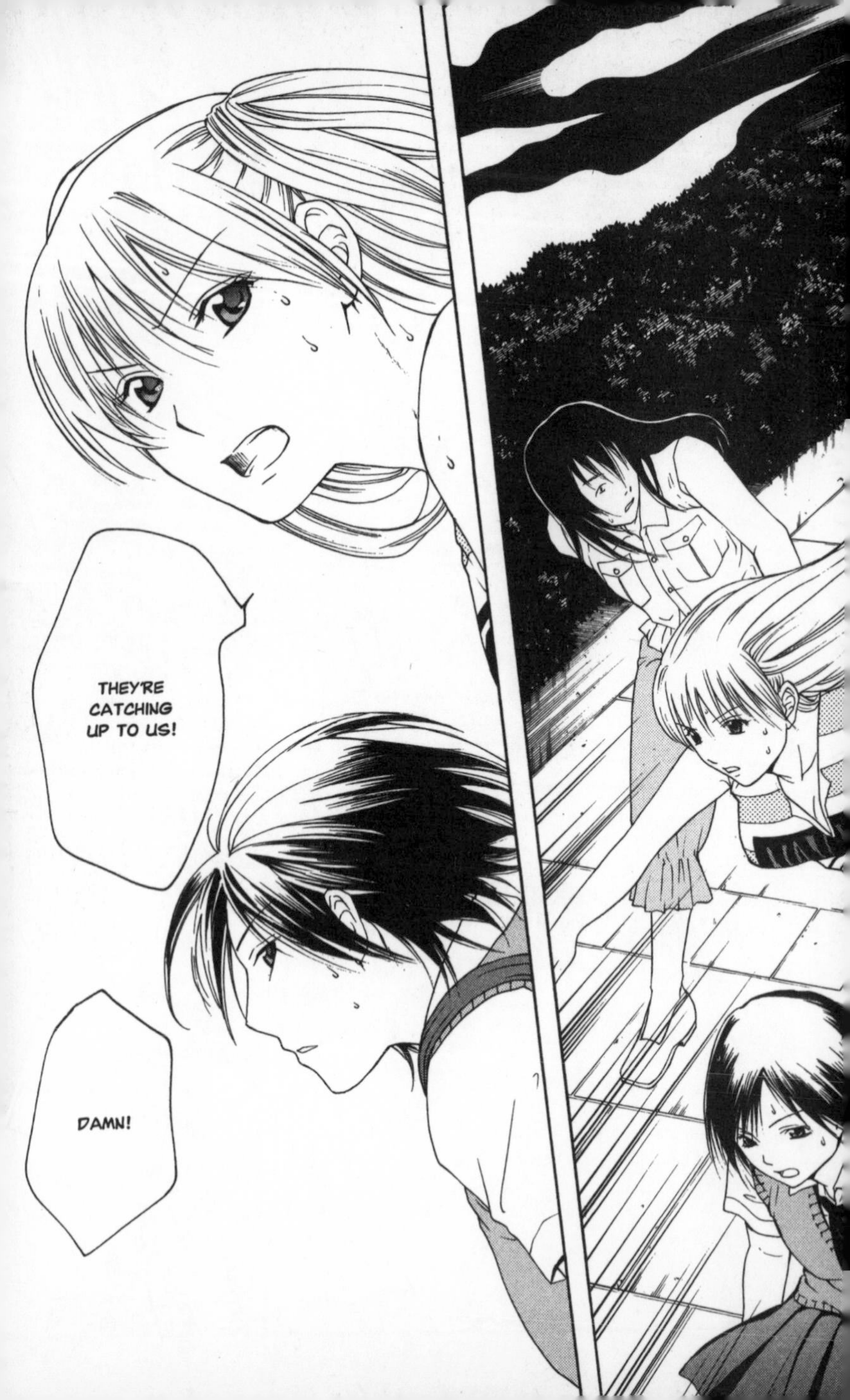
THEY'RE CATCHING UP TO US!
DAMN!

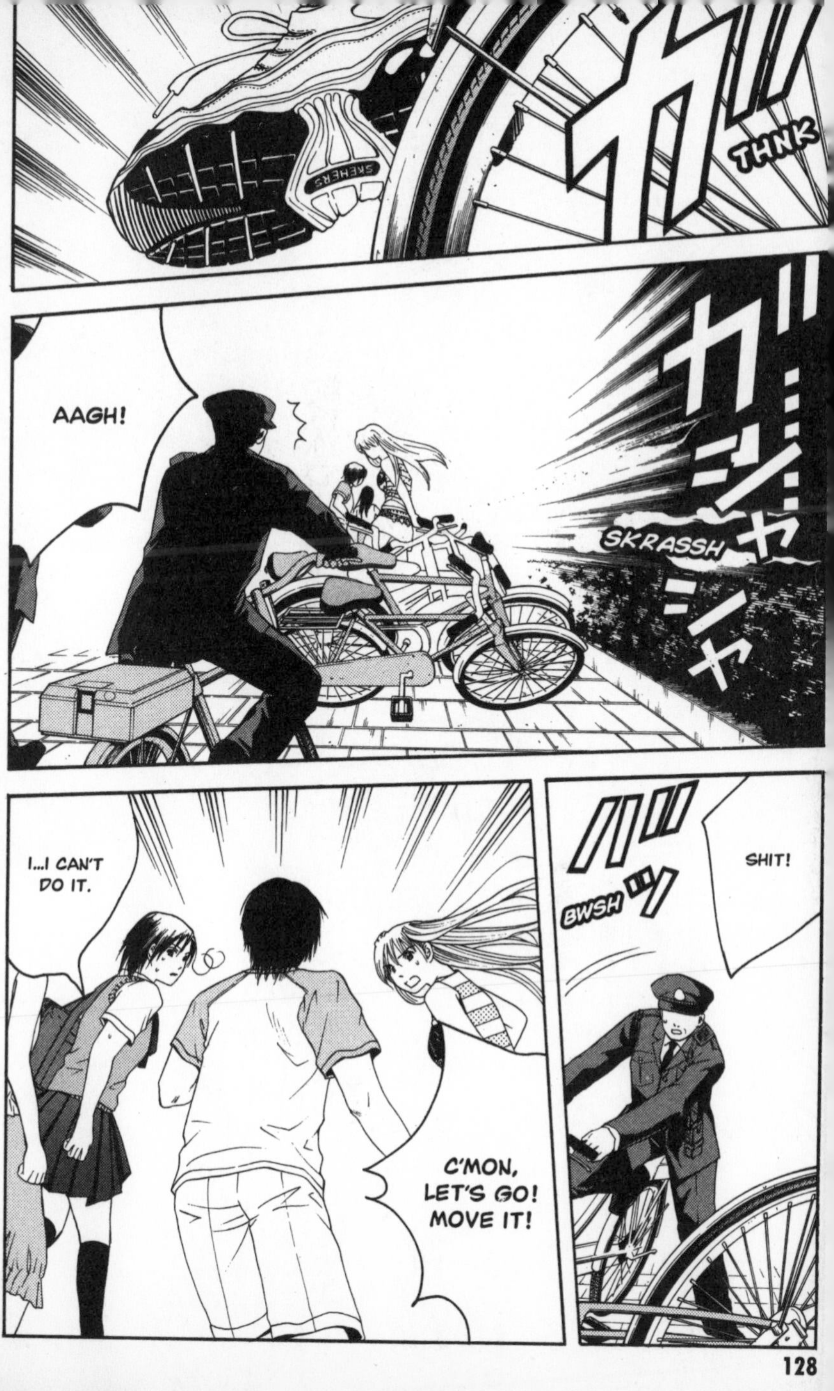
THNK
SKRASSH
AAGH!
BWSH
SHIT!
I...I CAN'T DO IT.
C'MON, LET'S GO! MOVE IT!

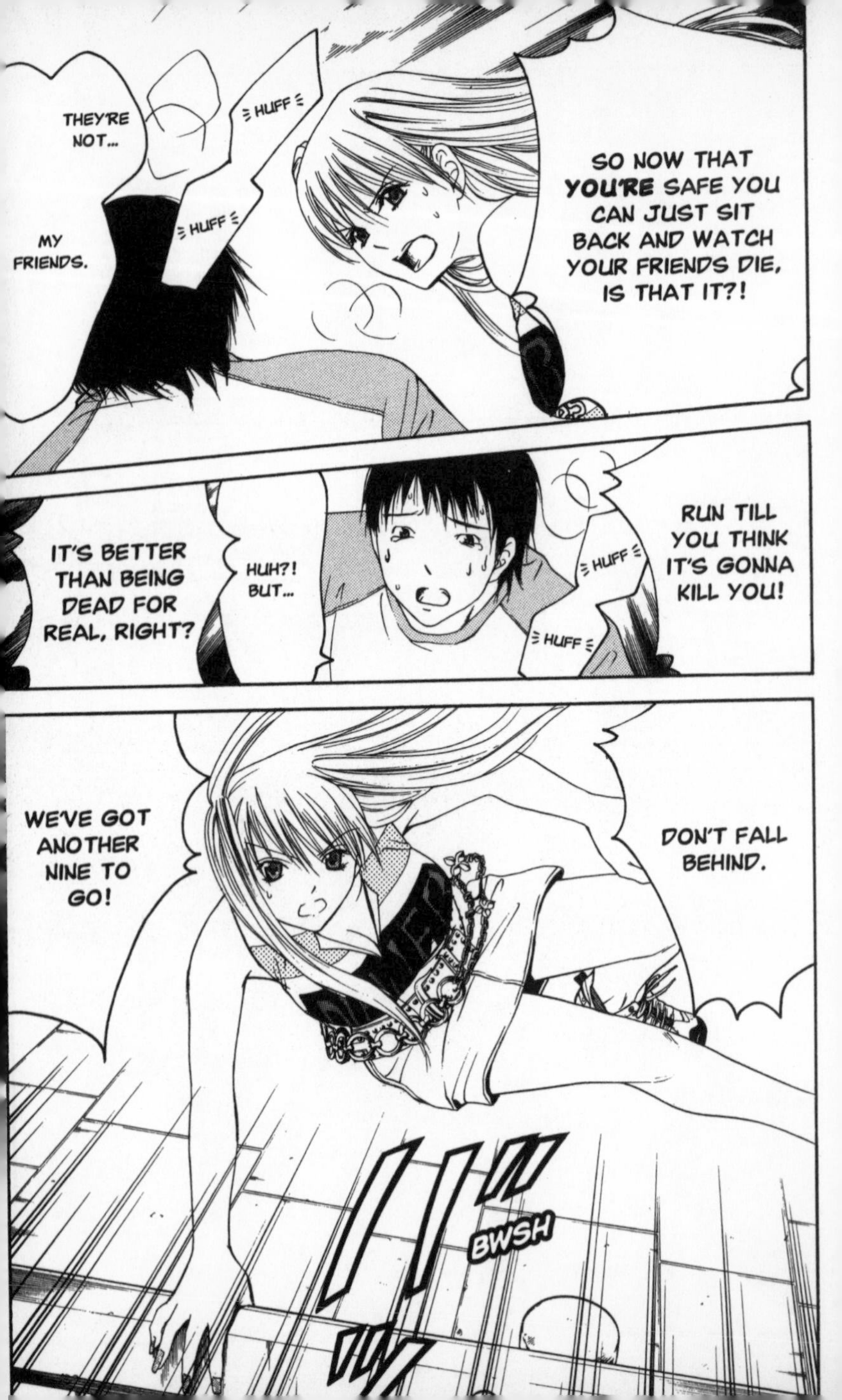

SO NOW THAT YOU'RE SAFE YOU CAN JUST SIT BACK AND WATCH YOUR FRIENDS DIE, IS THAT IT?!
HUFF
HUFF
THEY'RE NOT...
MY FRIENDS.
RUN TILL YOU THINK IT'S GONNA KILL YOU!
HUFF
HUFF
HUH?! BUT...
IT'S BETTER THAN BEING DEAD FOR REAL, RIGHT?
DON'T FALL BEHIND.
WE'VE GOT ANOTHER NINE TO GO!
BWSH

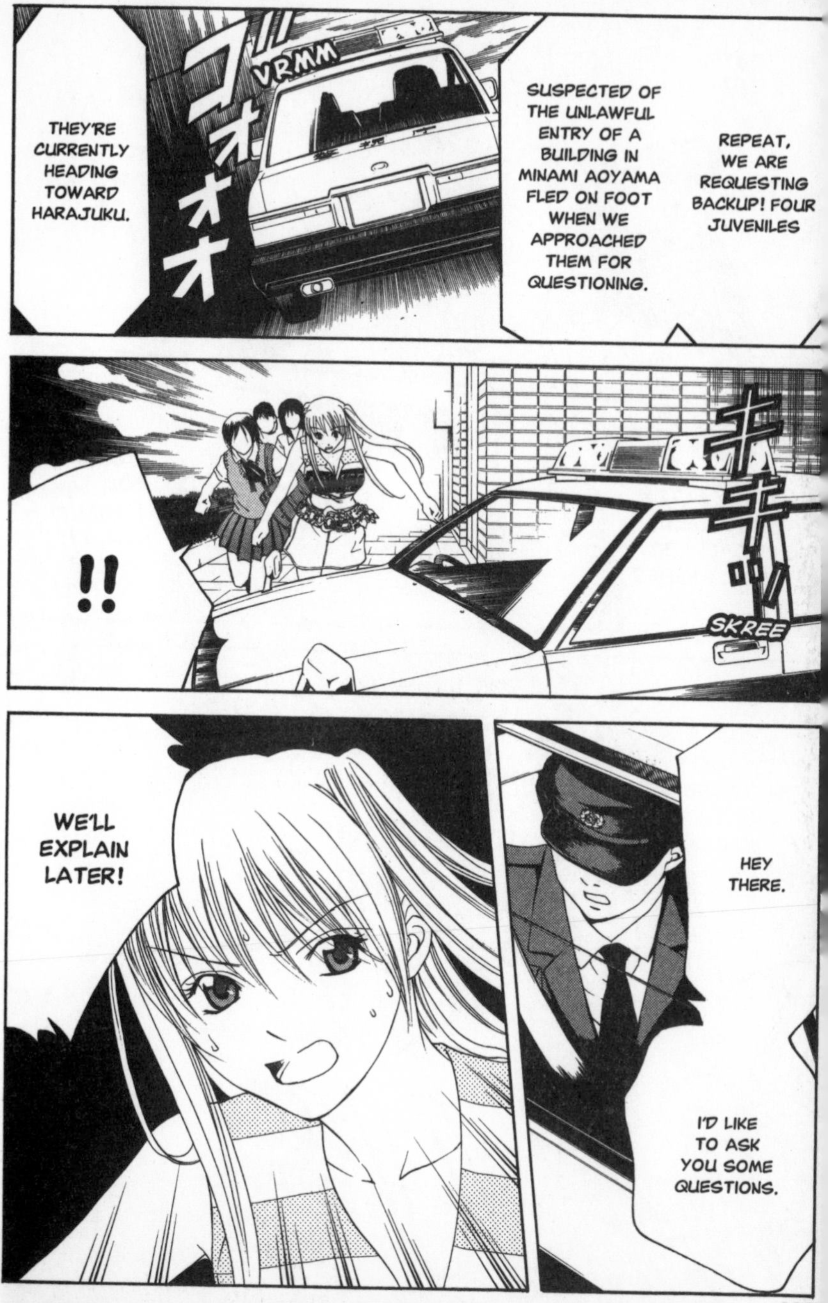

REPEAT, WE ARE REQUESTING BACKUP! FOUR JUVENILES
SUSPECTED OF THE UNLAWFUL ENTRY OF A BUILDING IN MINAMI AOYAMA FLED ON FOOT WHEN WE APPROACHED THEM FOR QUESTIONING.
VRMM
THEY'RE CURRENTLY HEADING TOWARD HARAJUKU.
SKREE
!!
HEY THERE.
I'D LIKE TO ASK YOU SOME QUESTIONS.
WE'LL EXPLAIN LATER!

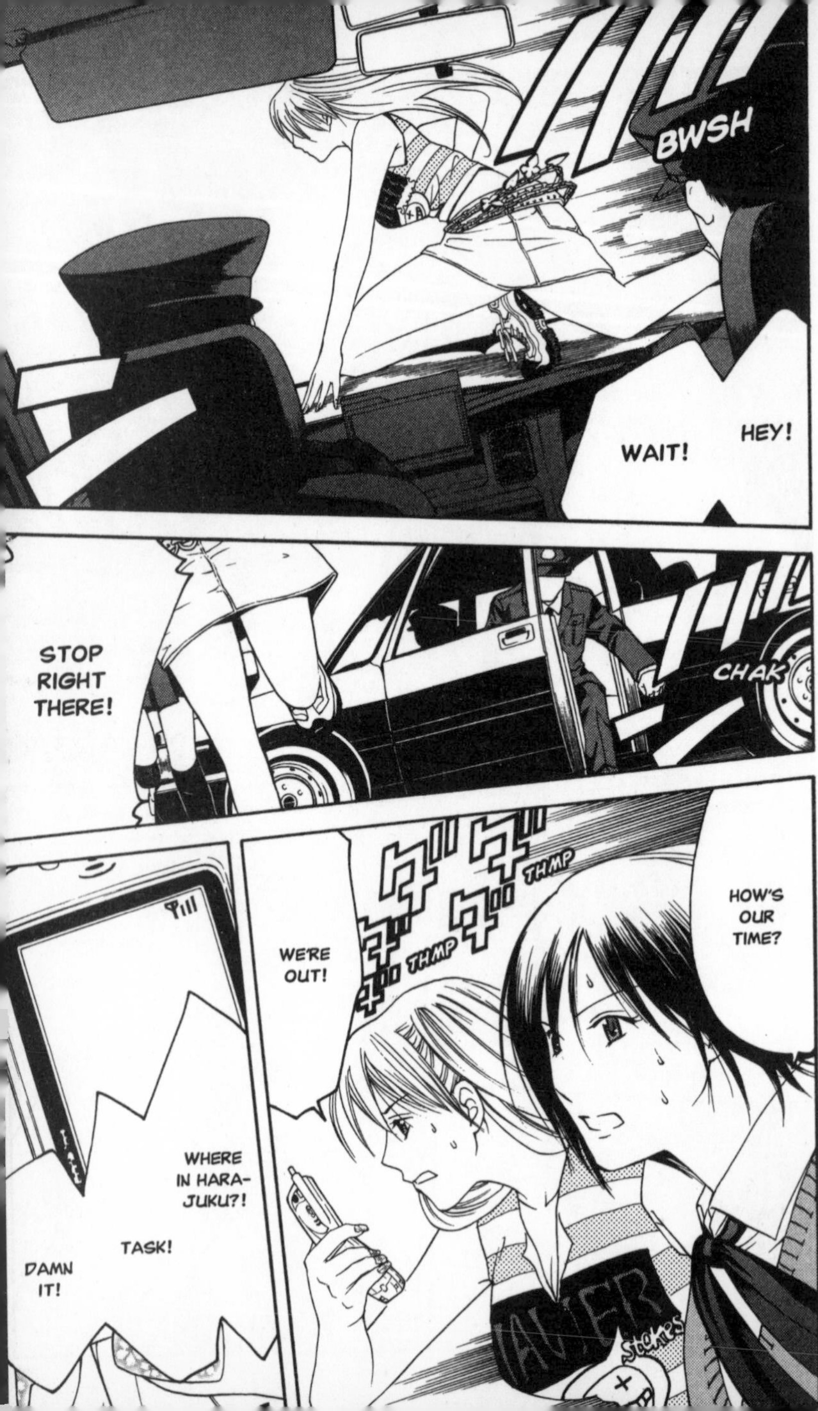
BWSH
HEY!
WAIT!
CHAK
STOP RIGHT THERE!
THMP
THMP
HOW'S OUR TIME?
WE'RE OUT!
WHERE IN HARA-JUKU?!
TASK!
DAMN IT!

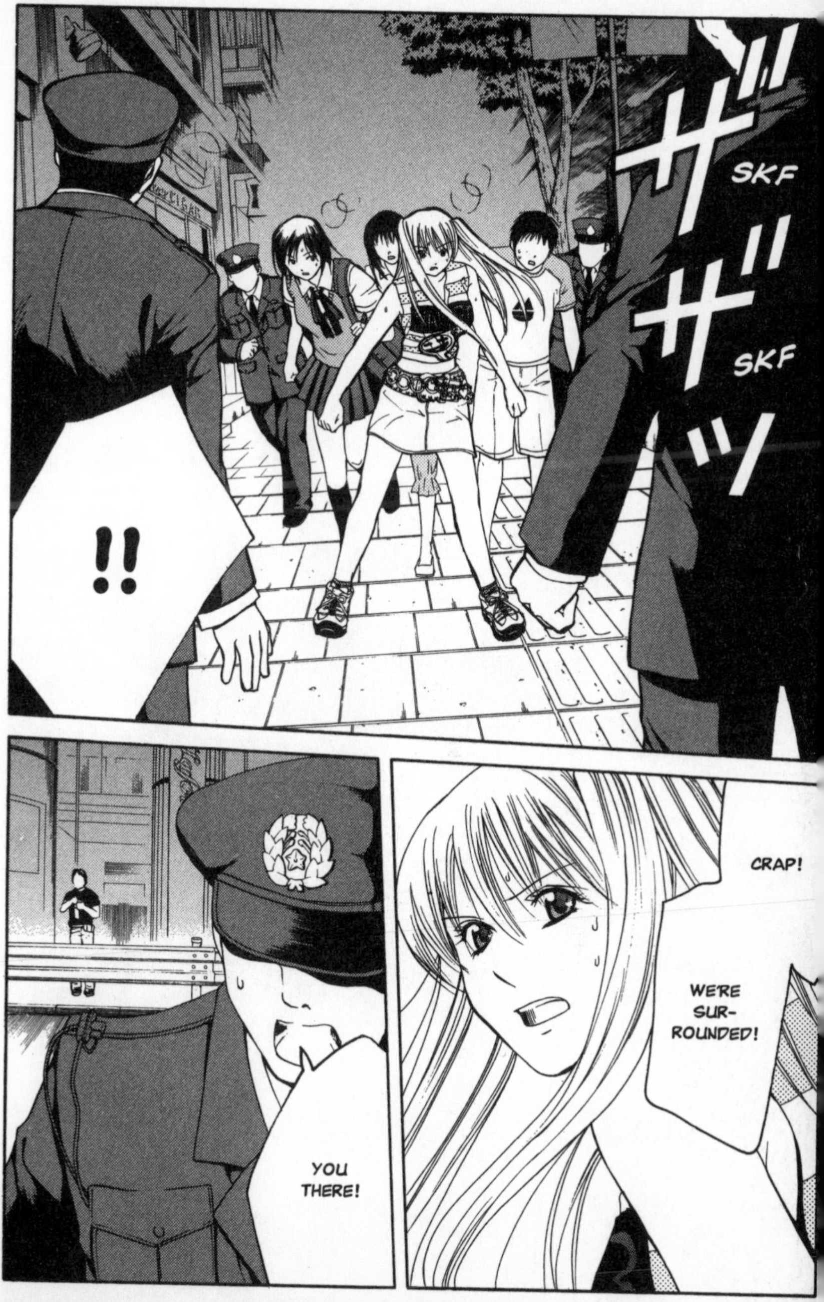
ザザッ
SKF
SKF
!!
CRAP!
WE'RE SUR-ROUNDED!
YOU THERE!

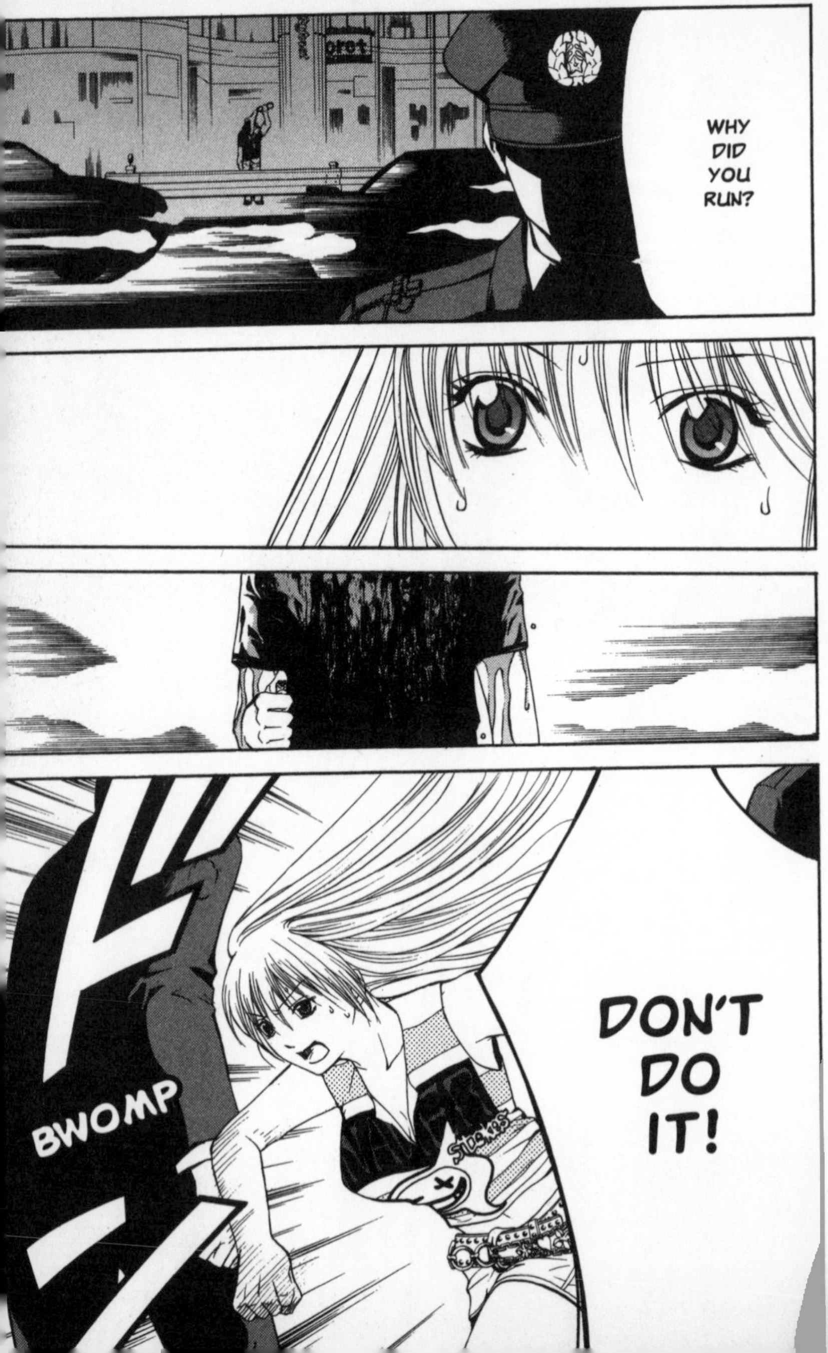
WHY DID YOU RUN?
DON'T DO IT!
BWOMP

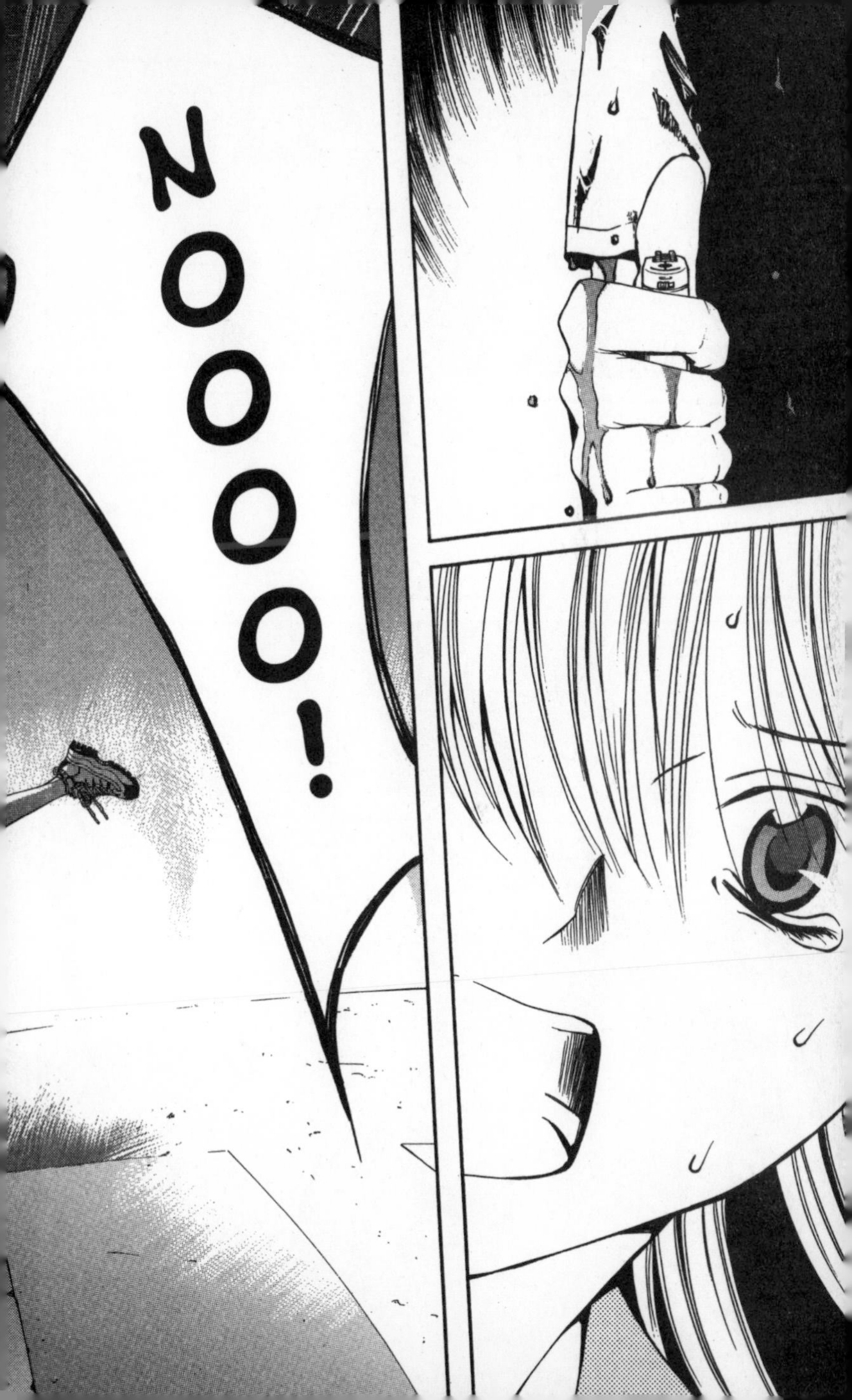
NOOOO!

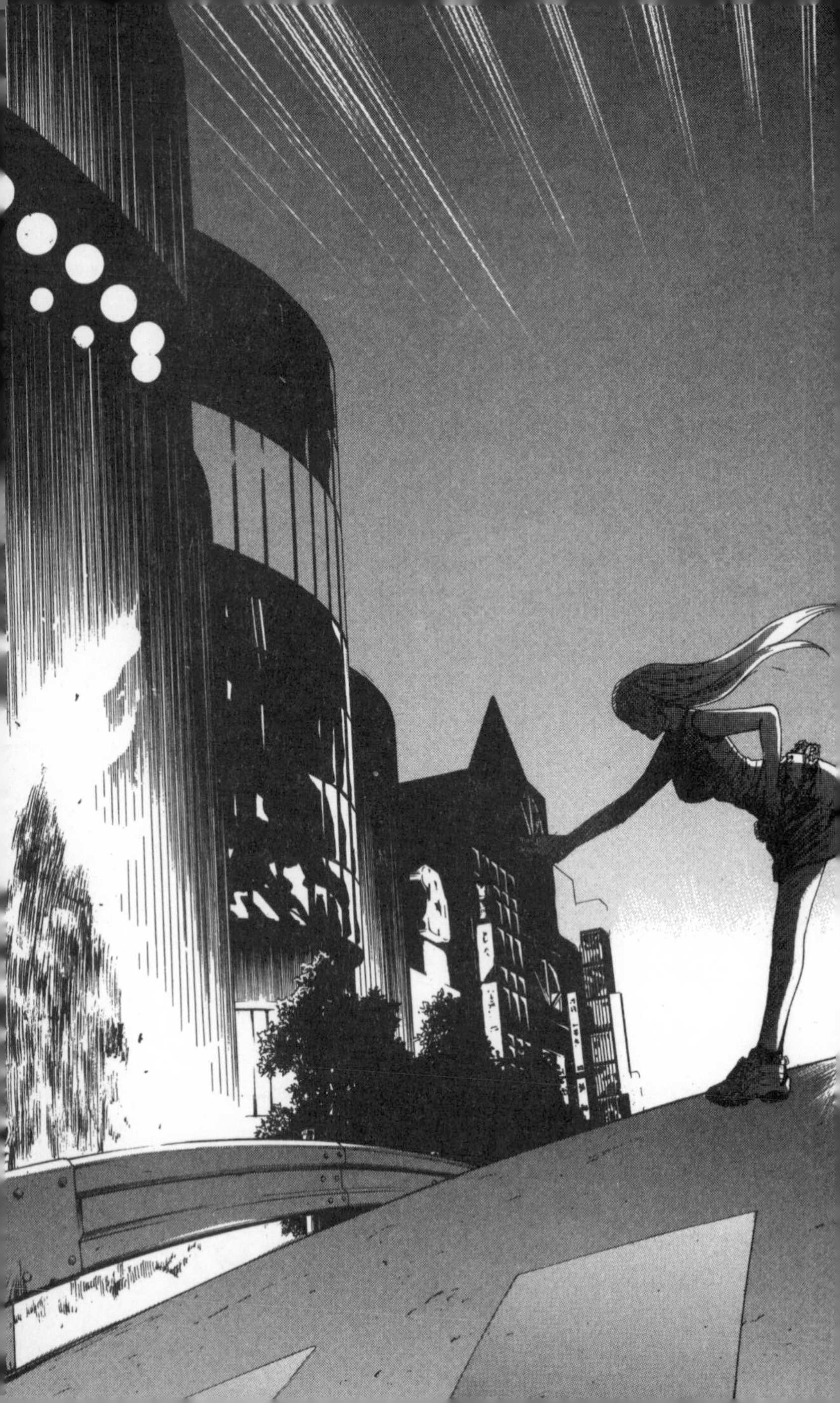

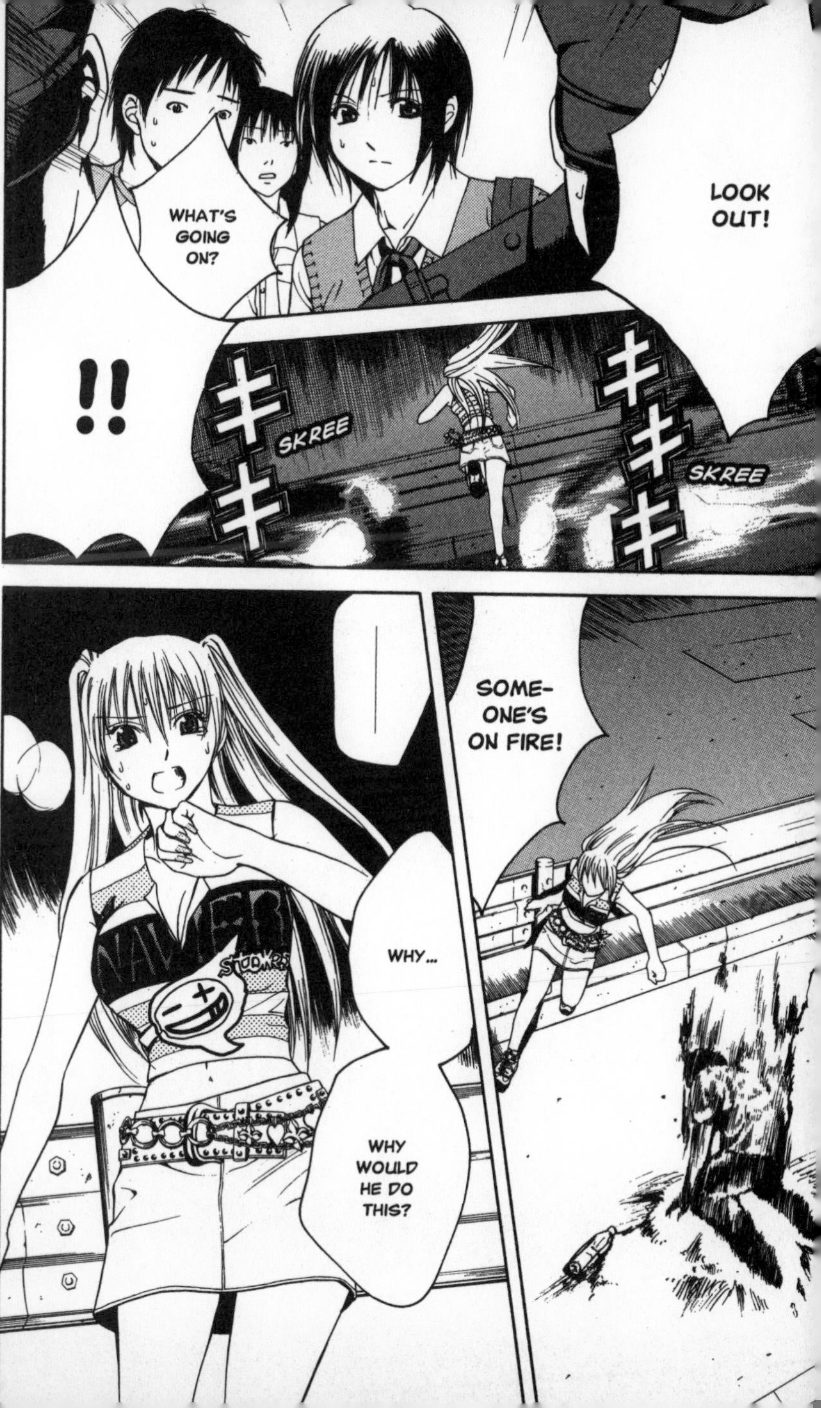
LOOK OUT!
WHAT'S GOING ON?
キキキ
SKREE
キキキ
SKREE
!!
SOME-ONE'S ON FIRE!
—
WHY...
WHY WOULD HE DO THIS?

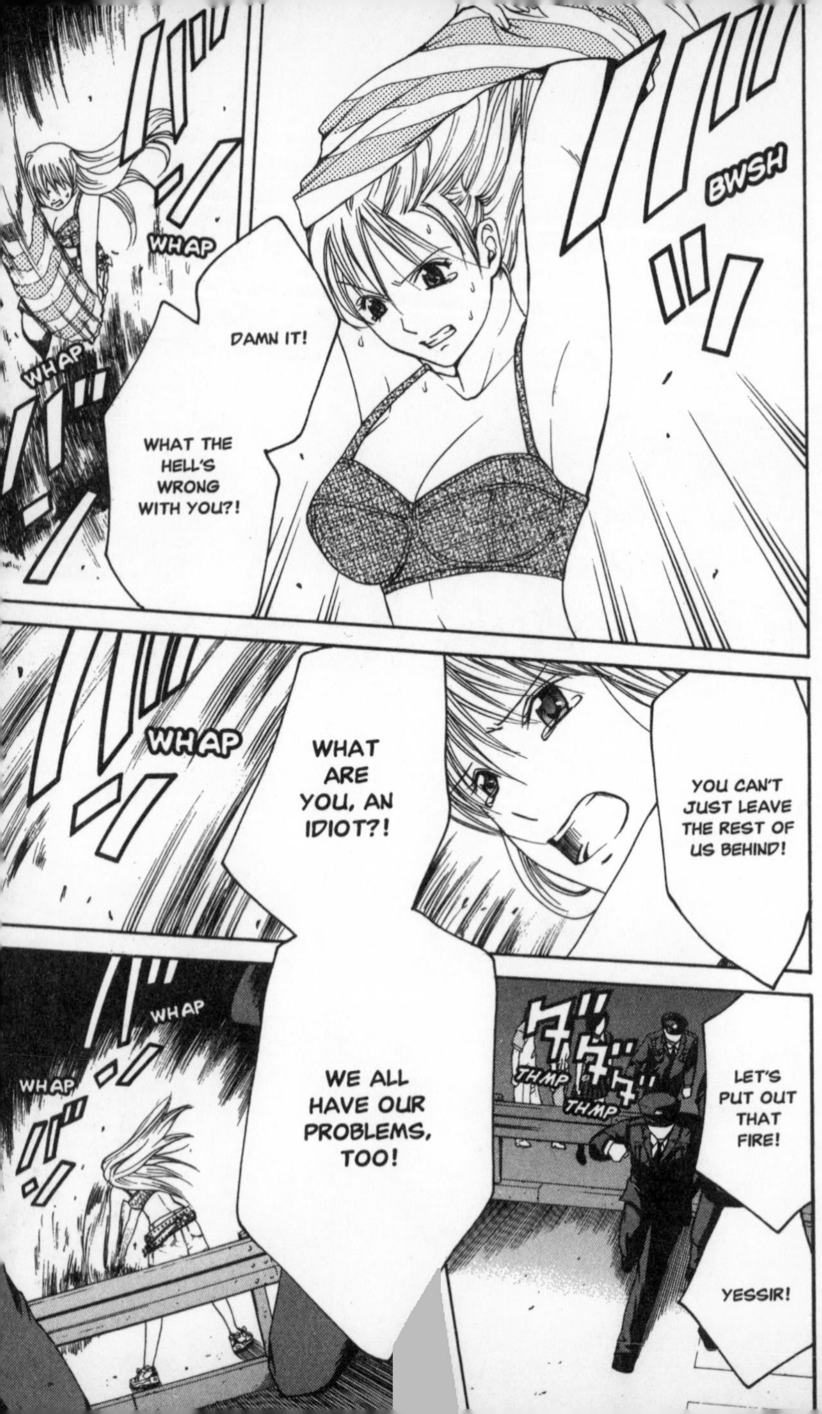
BWSH
DAMN IT!
WHAT THE HELL'S WRONG WITH YOU?!
WHAP
WHAP
YOU CAN'T JUST LEAVE THE REST OF US BEHIND!
WHAT ARE YOU, AN IDIOT?!
WHAP
LET'S PUT OUT THAT FIRE!
THMP
THMP
YESSIR!
WE ALL HAVE OUR PROBLEMS, TOO!
WHAP
WHAP

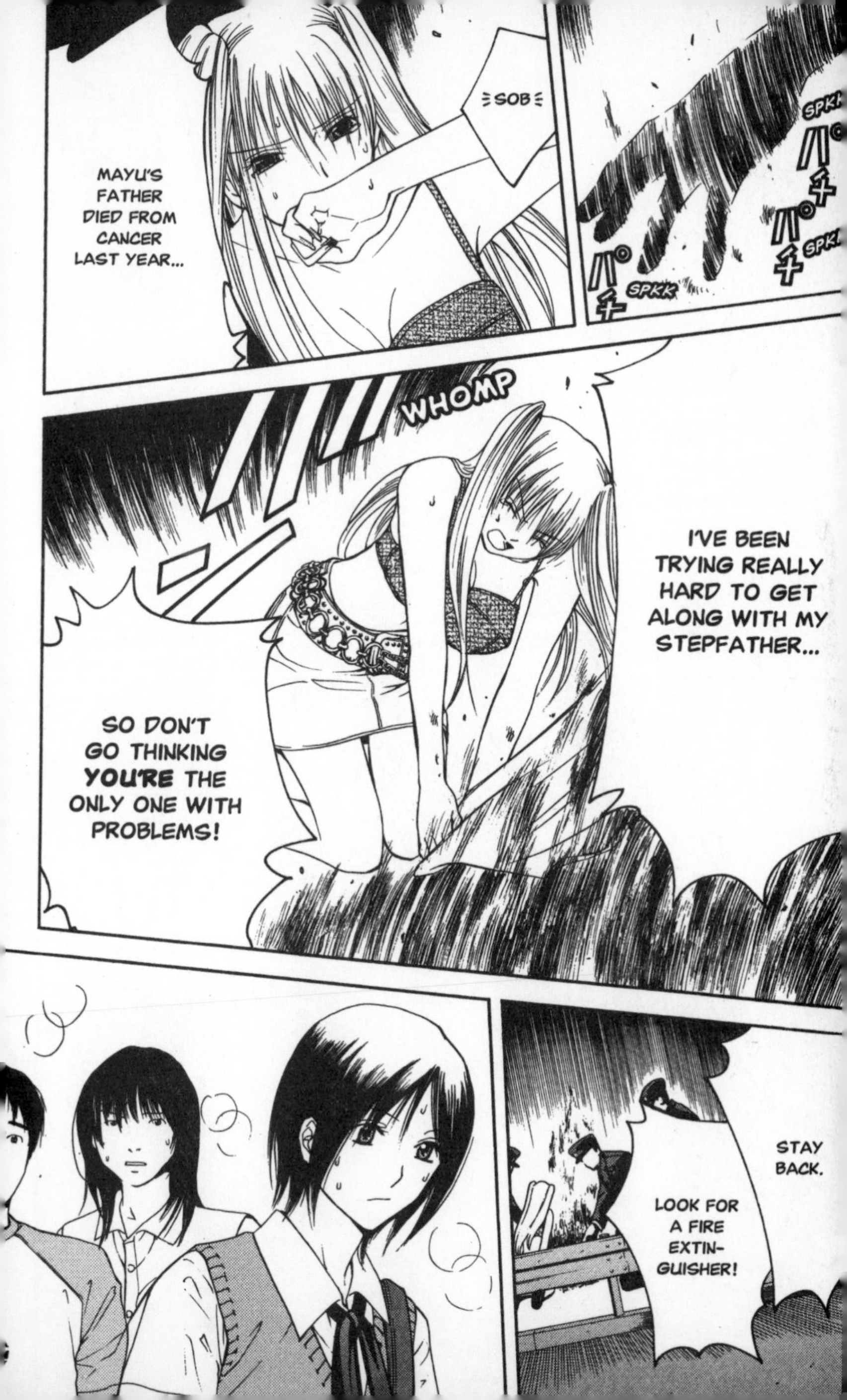
SPKK
パチ
SPKK
パチ
SPKK
パチ
SOB
MAYU'S FATHER DIED FROM CANCER LAST YEAR...
WHOMP
I'VE BEEN TRYING REALLY HARD TO GET ALONG WITH MY STEPFATHER...
SO DON'T GO THINKING **YOU'RE** THE ONLY ONE WITH PROBLEMS!
STAY BACK.
LOOK FOR A FIRE EXTIN-GUISHER!

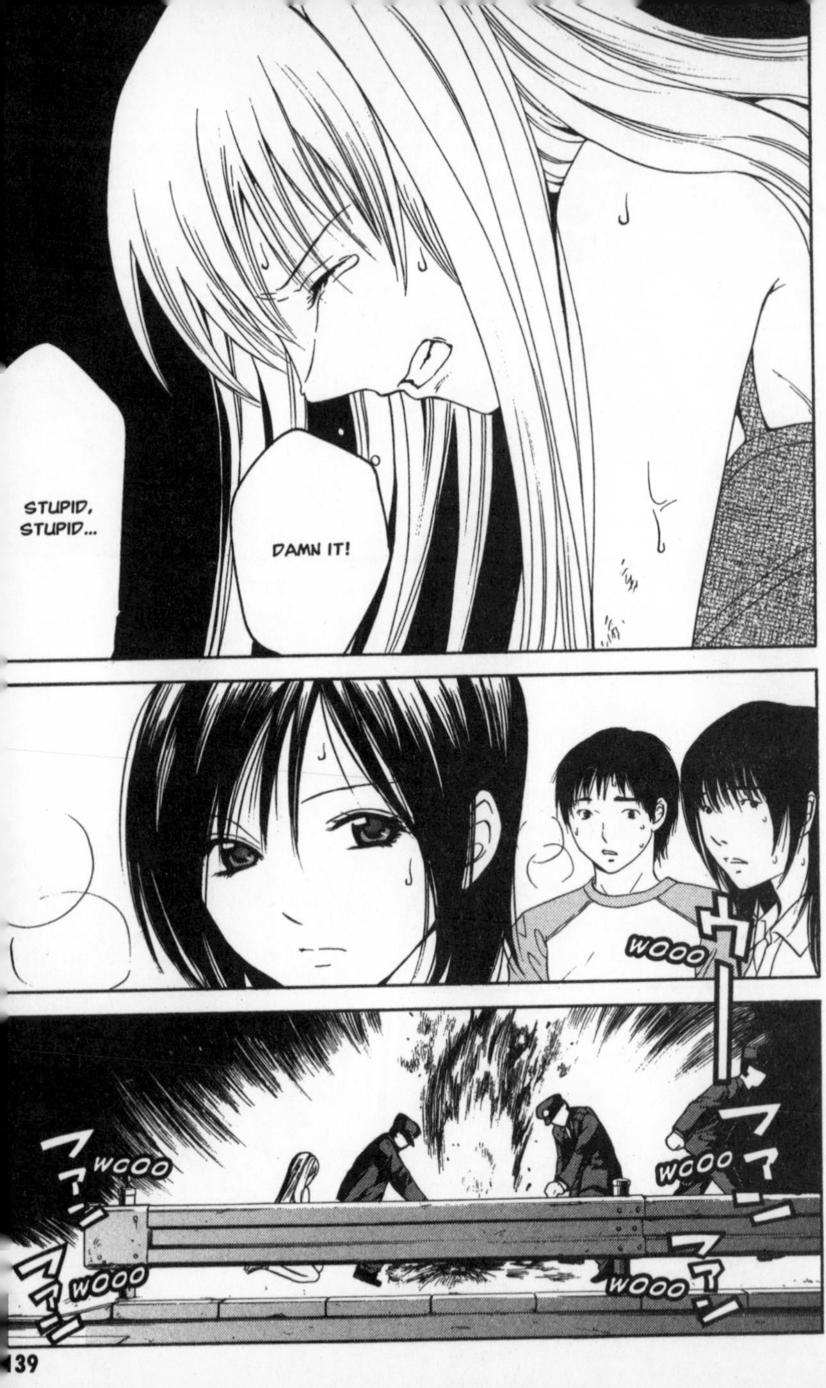
DAMN IT!
STUPID, STUPID...
WOOO
WOOO
WOOO
WOOO
WOOO

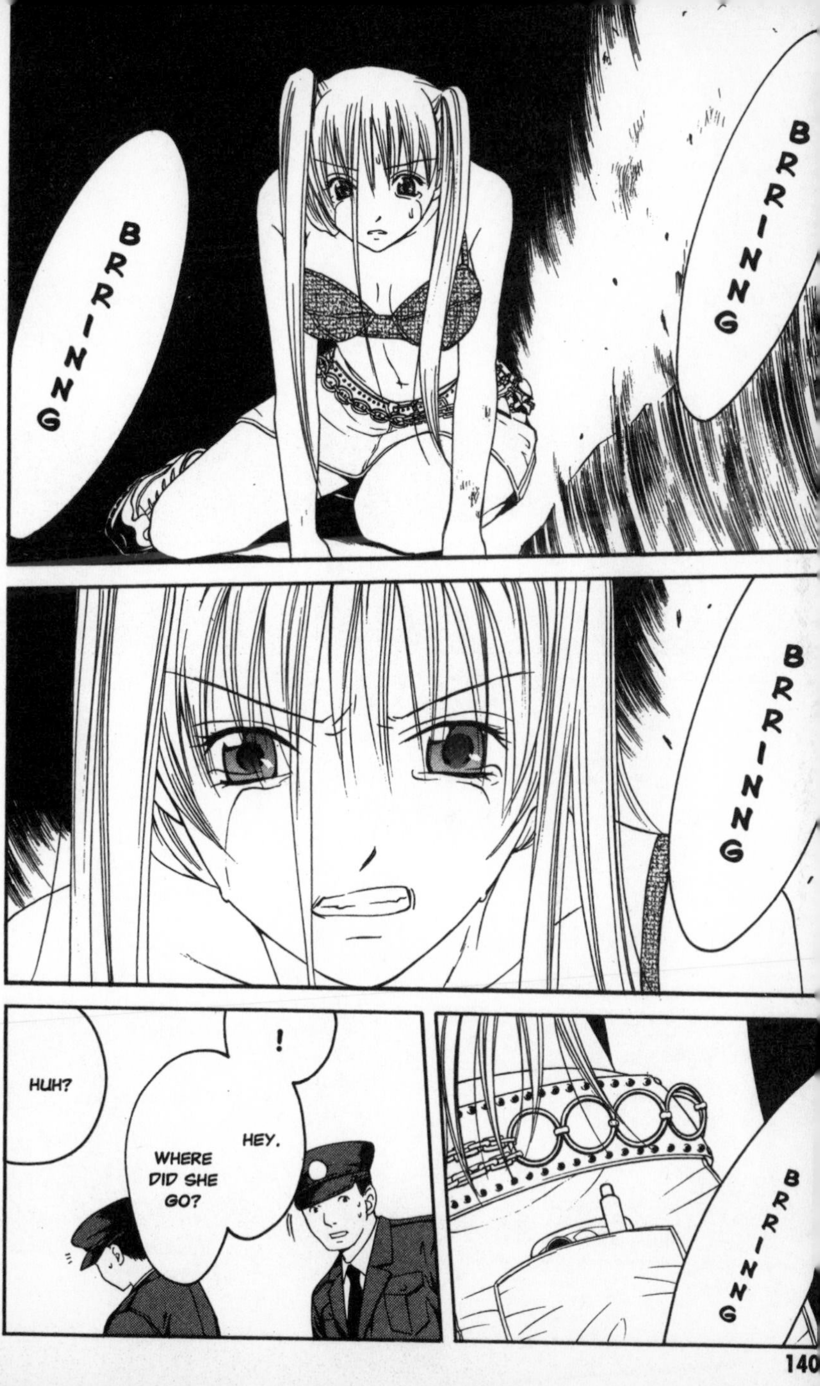
BRRINNG
BRRINNG
BRRINNG
BRRINNG
!
HEY.
WHERE DID SHE GO?
HUH?

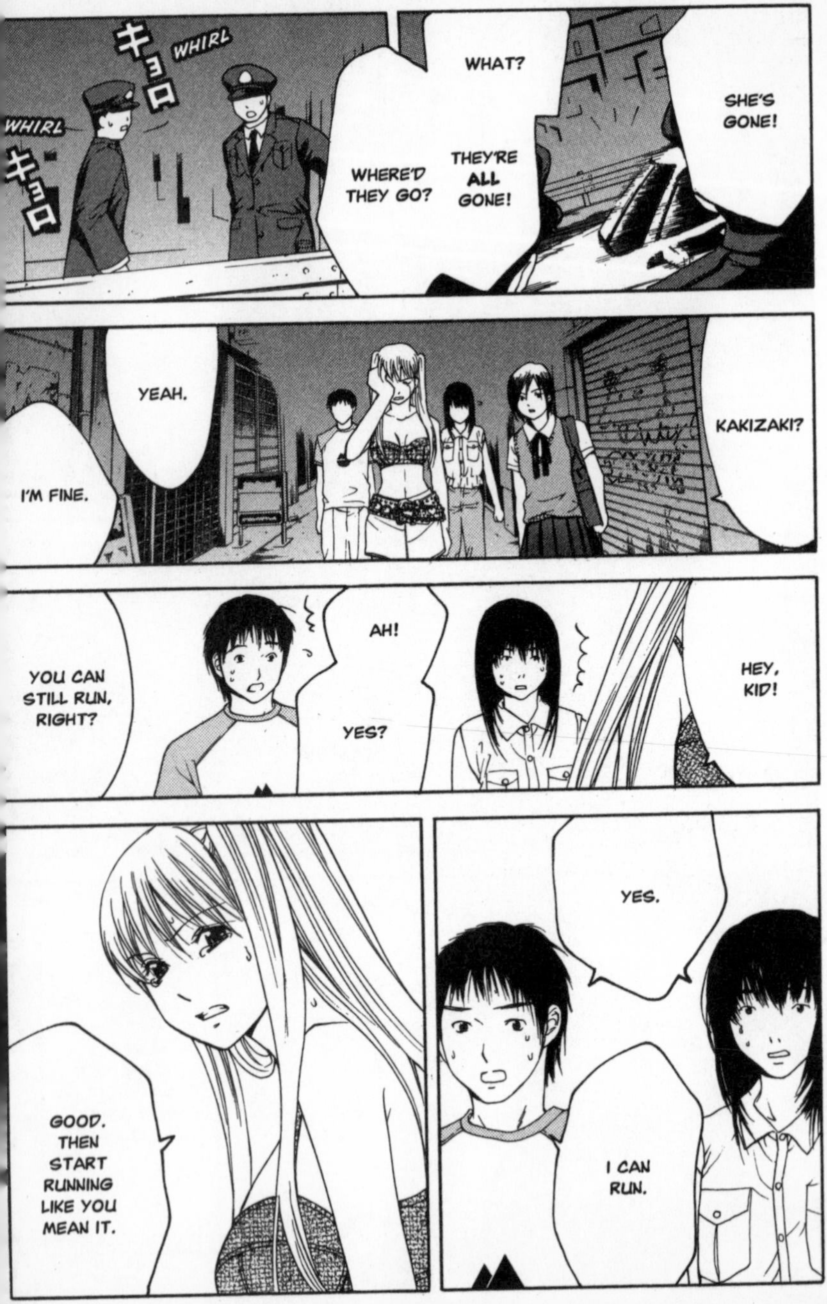
SHE'S GONE!
WHAT?
THEY'RE ALL GONE!
WHERE'D THEY GO?
キョロ WHIRL
WHIRL キョロ
KAKIZAKI?
YEAH.
I'M FINE.
HEY, KID!
AH!
YES?
YOU CAN STILL RUN, RIGHT?
YES.
I CAN RUN.
GOOD. THEN START RUNNING LIKE YOU MEAN IT.

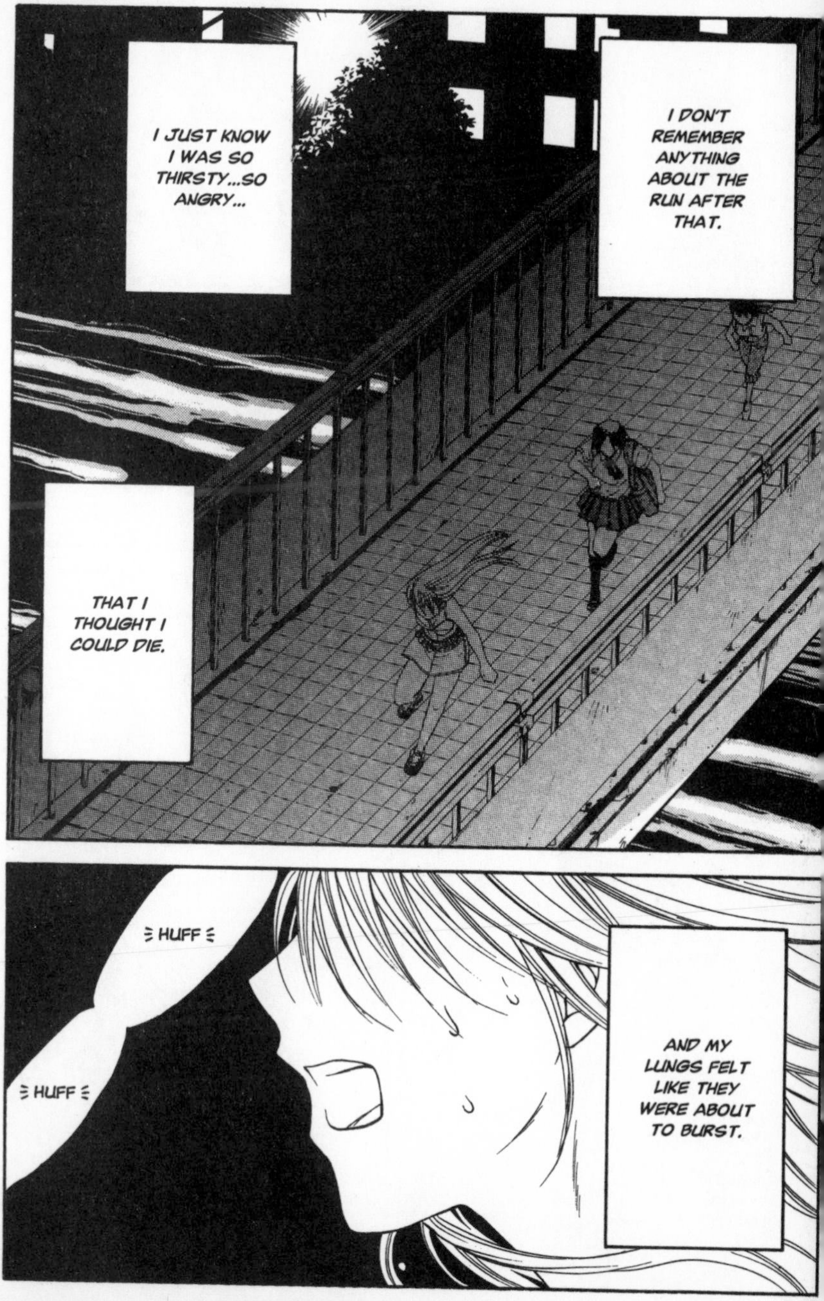
I DON'T REMEMBER ANYTHING ABOUT THE RUN AFTER THAT.
I JUST KNOW I WAS SO THIRSTY...SO ANGRY...
THAT I THOUGHT I COULD DIE.
AND MY LUNGS FELT LIKE THEY WERE ABOUT TO BURST.
HUFF
HUFF

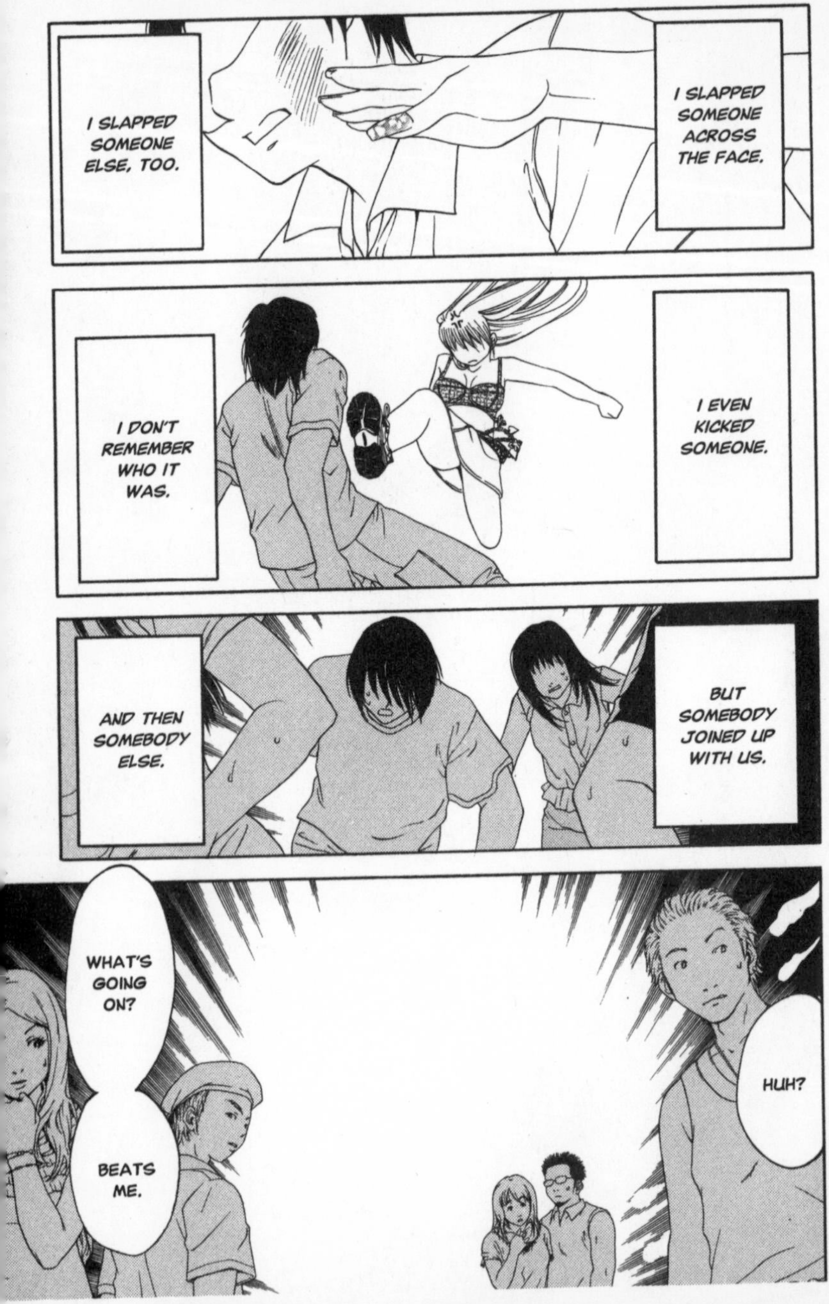
I SLAPPED SOMEONE ACROSS THE FACE.
I SLAPPED SOMEONE ELSE, TOO.
I EVEN KICKED SOMEONE.
I DON'T REMEMBER WHO IT WAS.
BUT SOMEBODY JOINED UP WITH US.
AND THEN SOMEBODY ELSE.
HUH?
WHAT'S GOING ON?
BEATS ME.

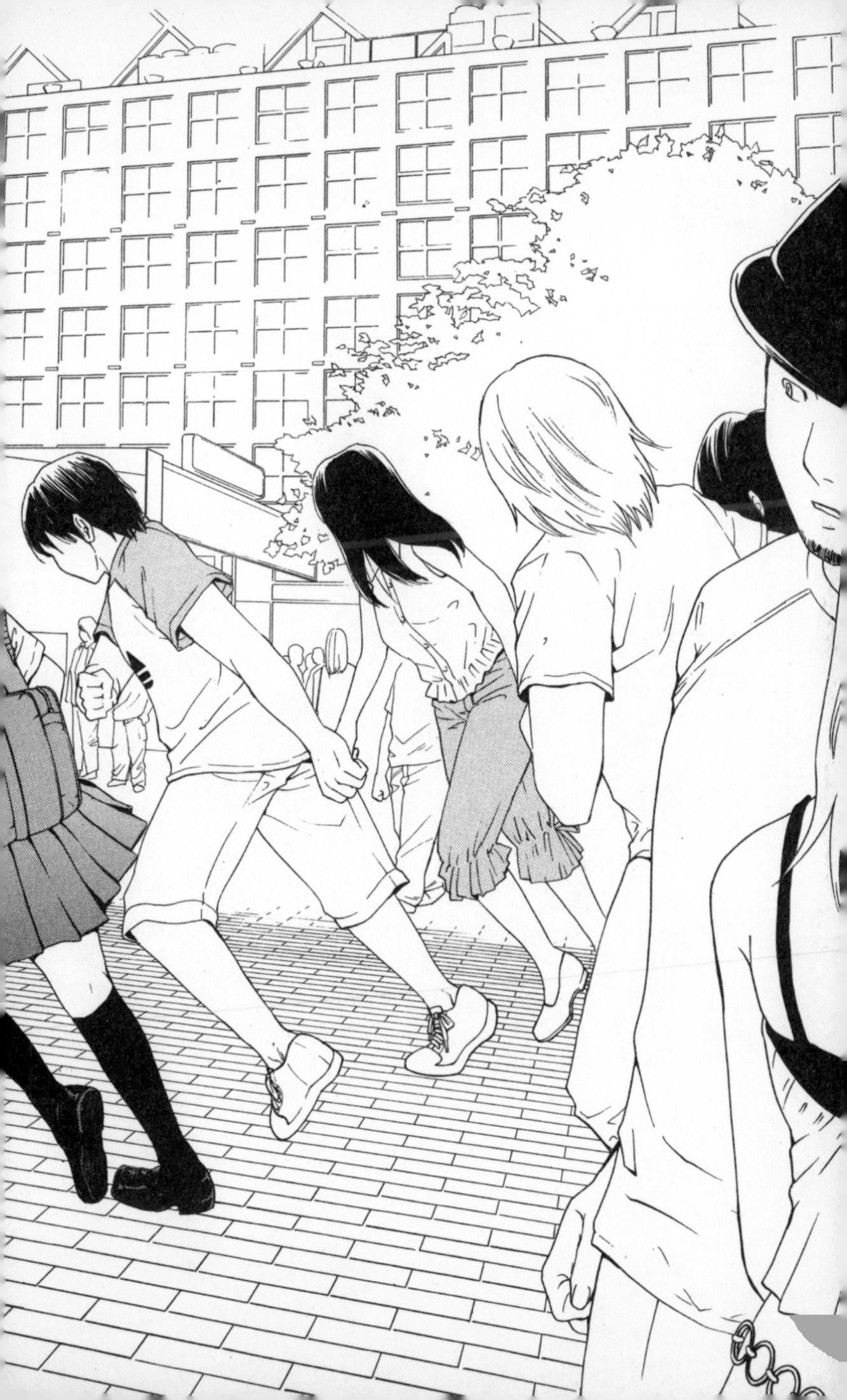

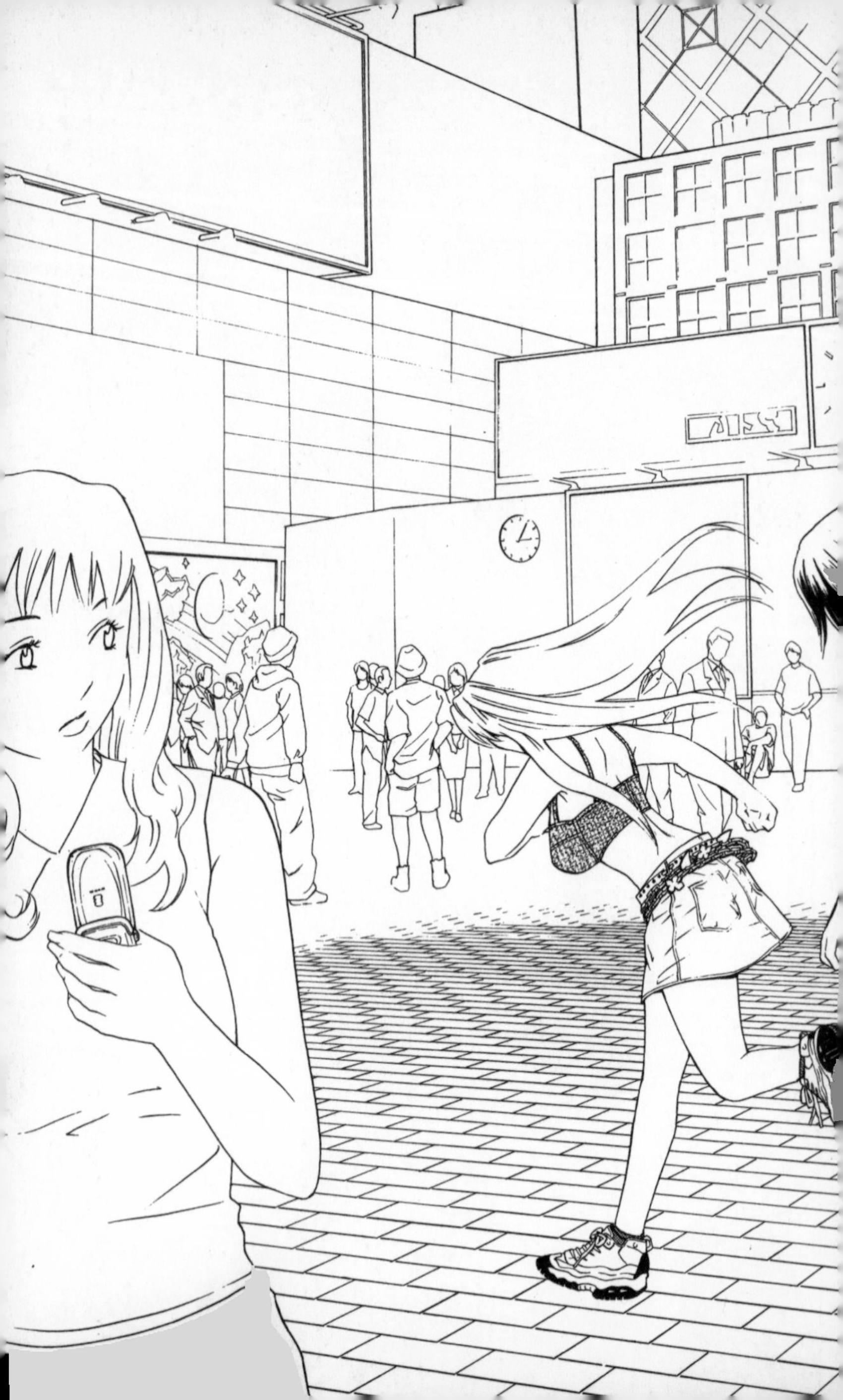

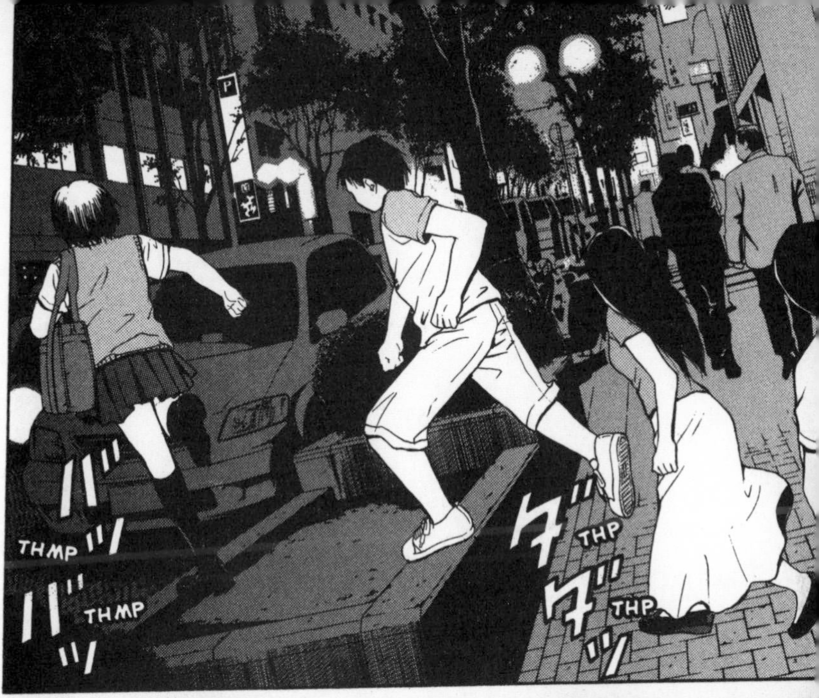
THP
THP
THMP
THMP
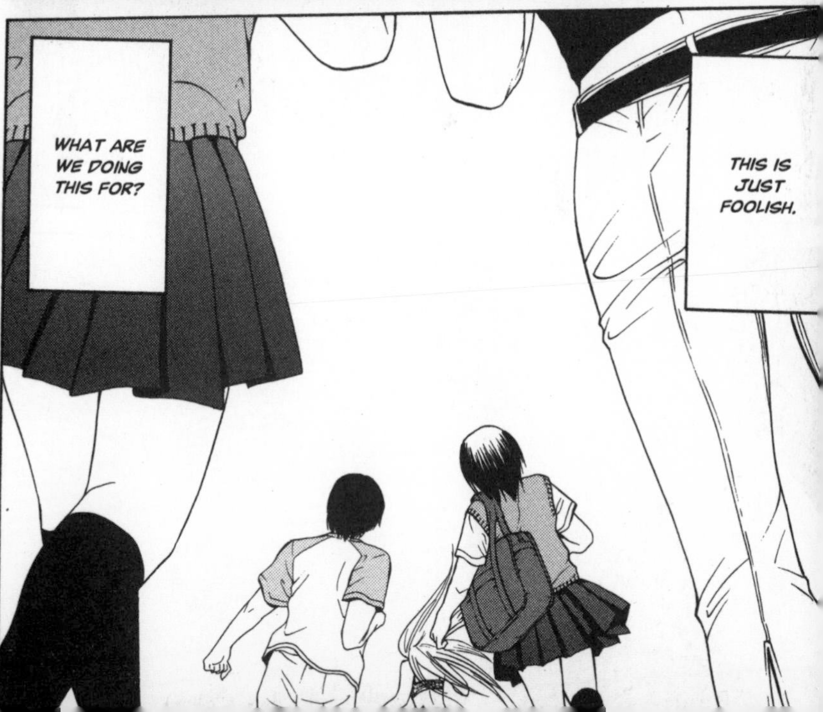
THIS IS JUST FOOLISH.
WHAT ARE WE DOING THIS FOR?

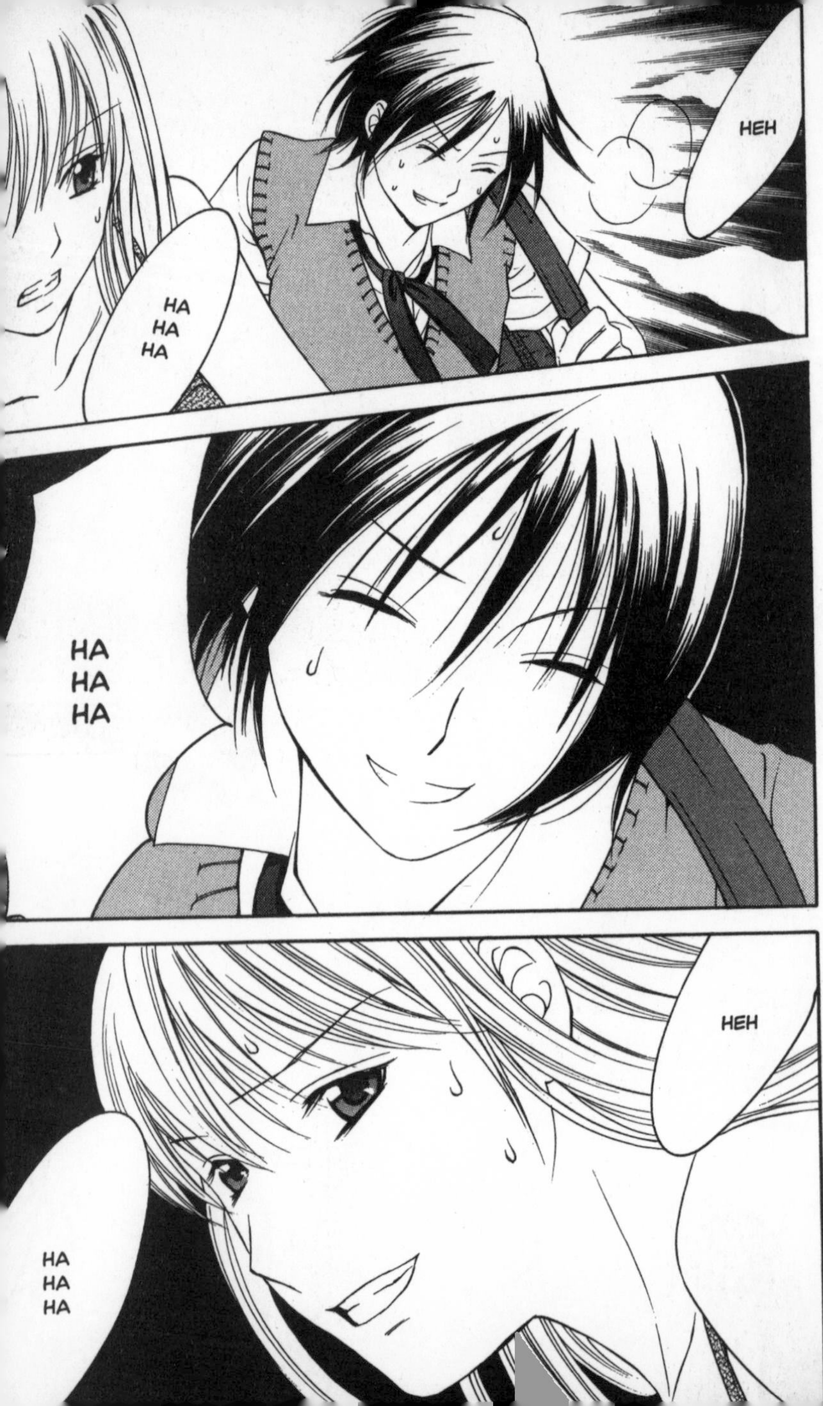
HEH
HA HA HA
HA HA HA
HEH
HA HA HA

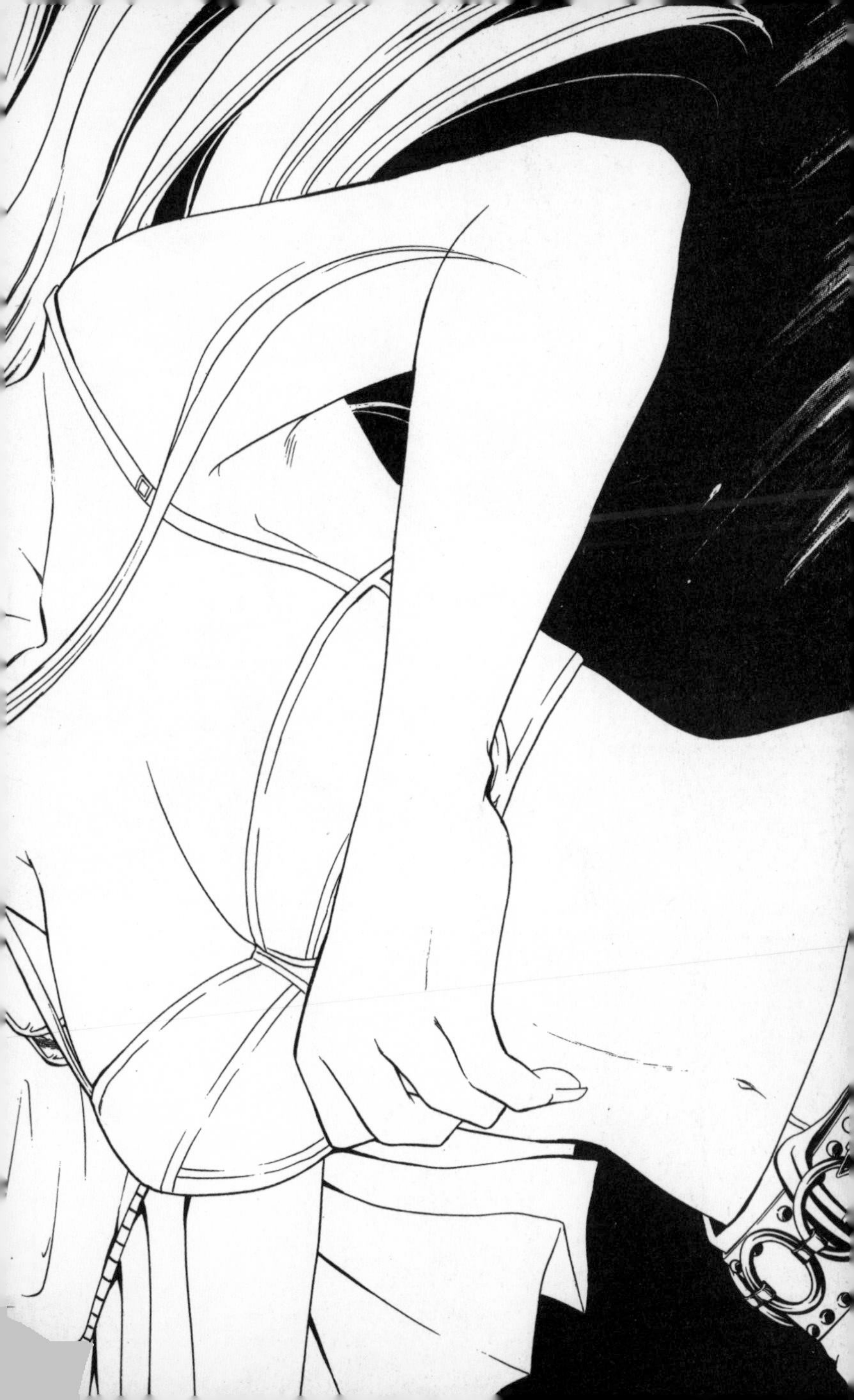

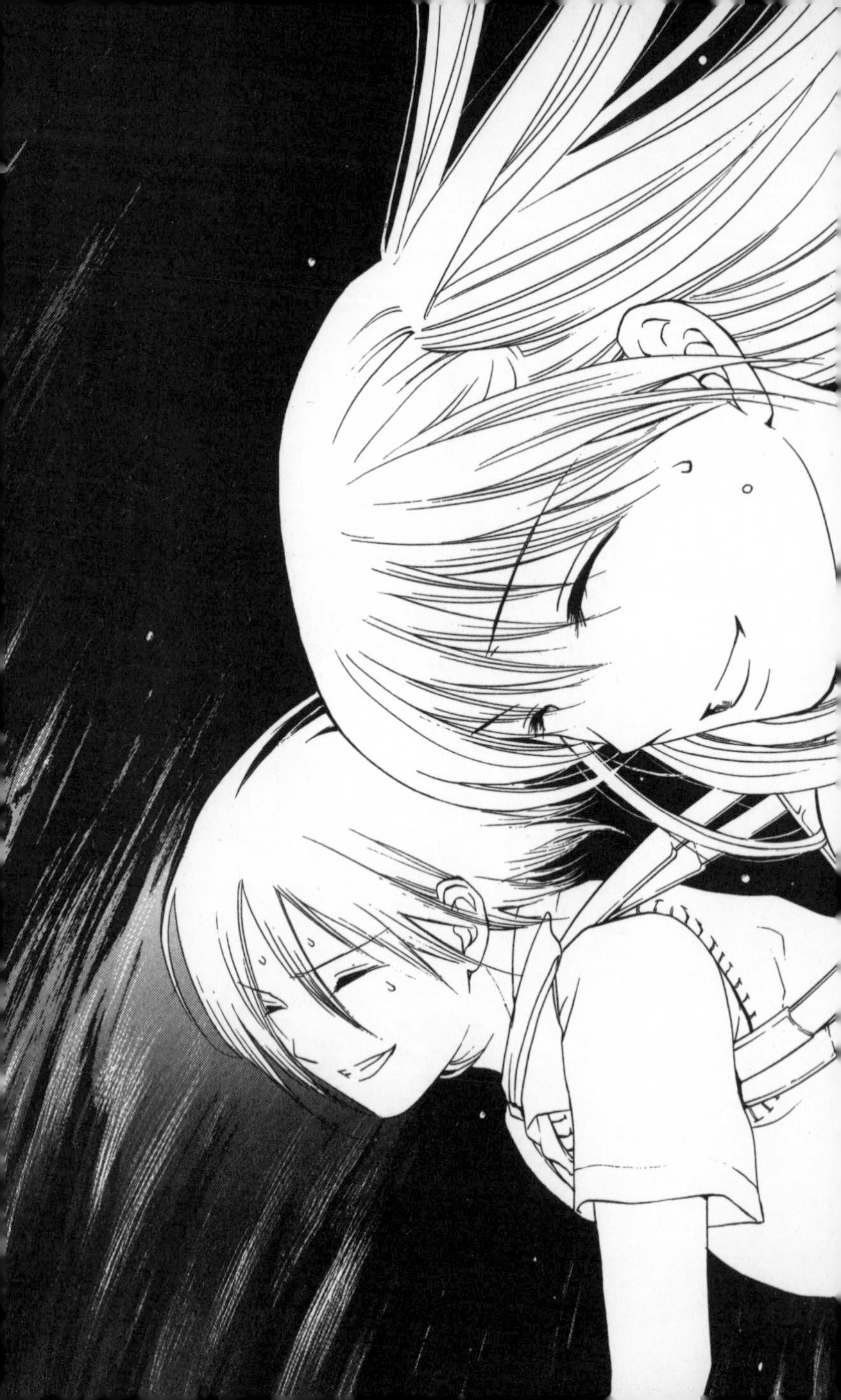

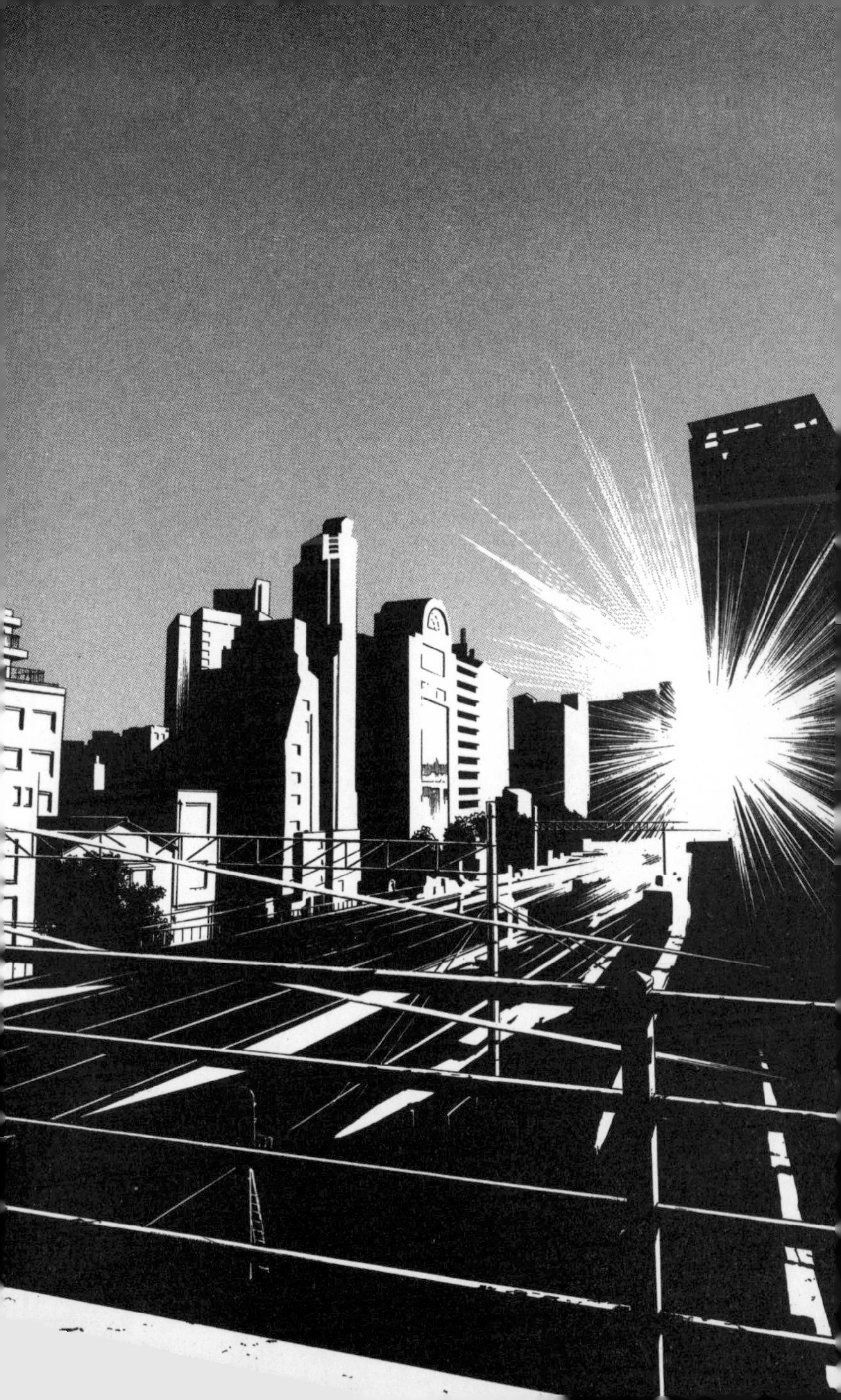

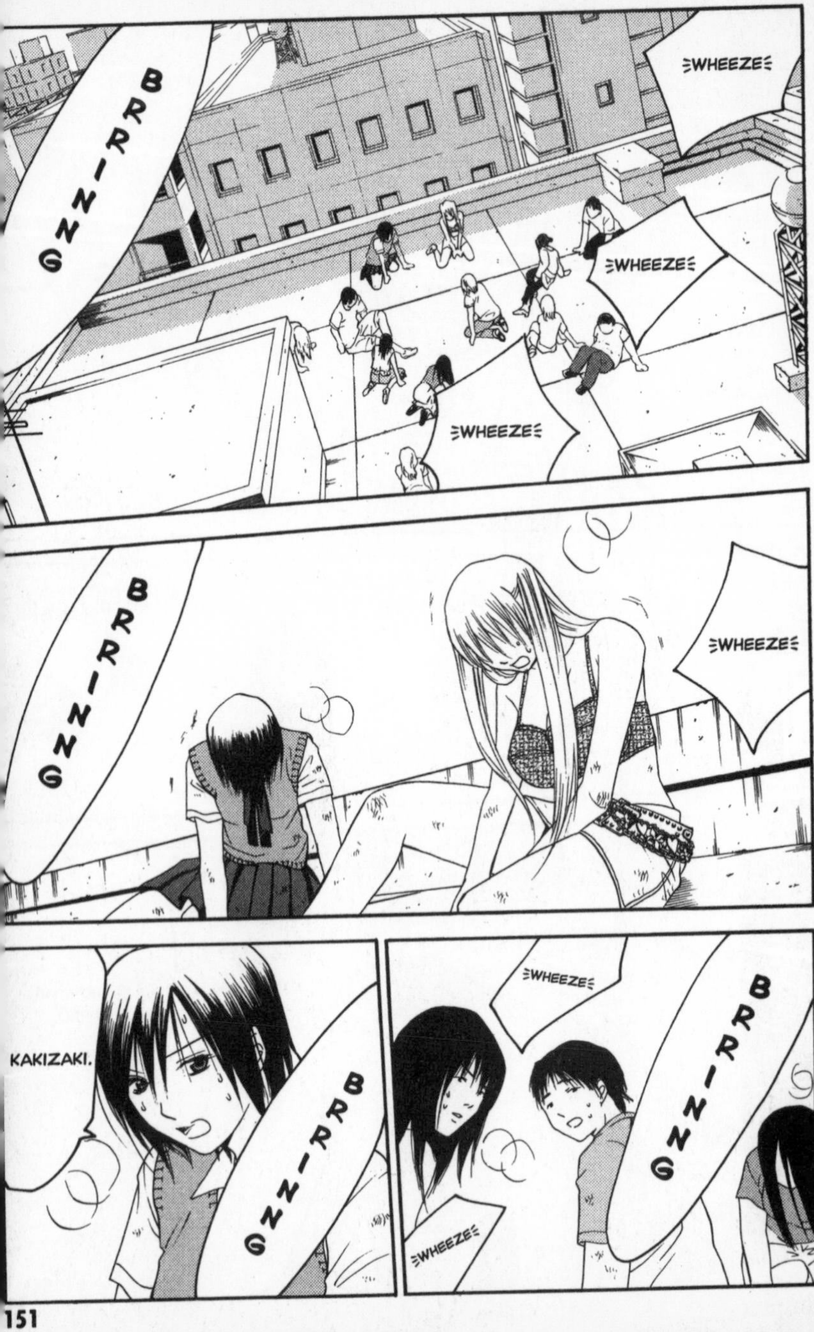
WHEEZE
BRRINNG
WHEEZE
WHEEZE
WHEEZE
BRRINNG
WHEEZE
BRRINNG
WHEEZE
KAKIZAKI.
BRRINNG

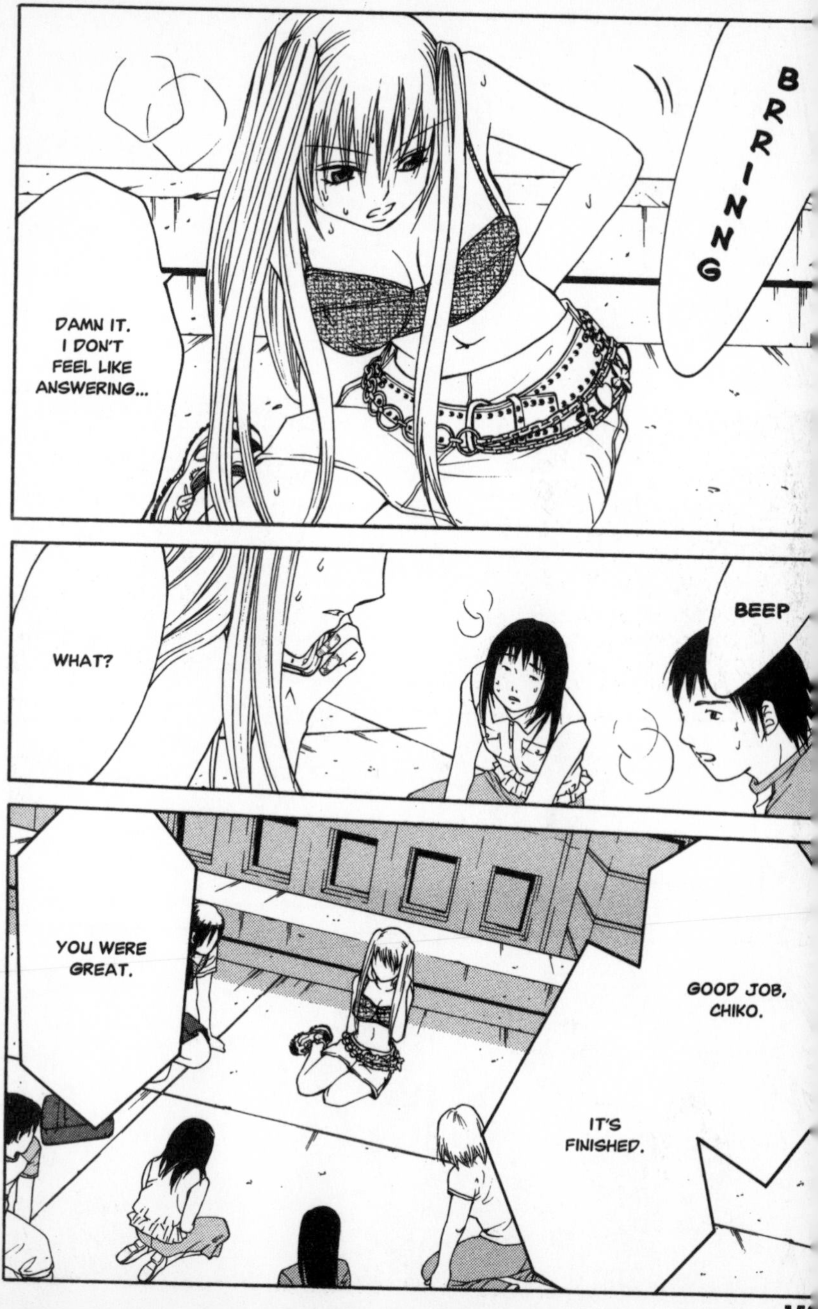
BRRINNG
DAMN IT. I DON'T FEEL LIKE ANSWERING...
BEEP
WHAT?
GOOD JOB, CHIKO.
IT'S FINISHED.
YOU WERE GREAT.

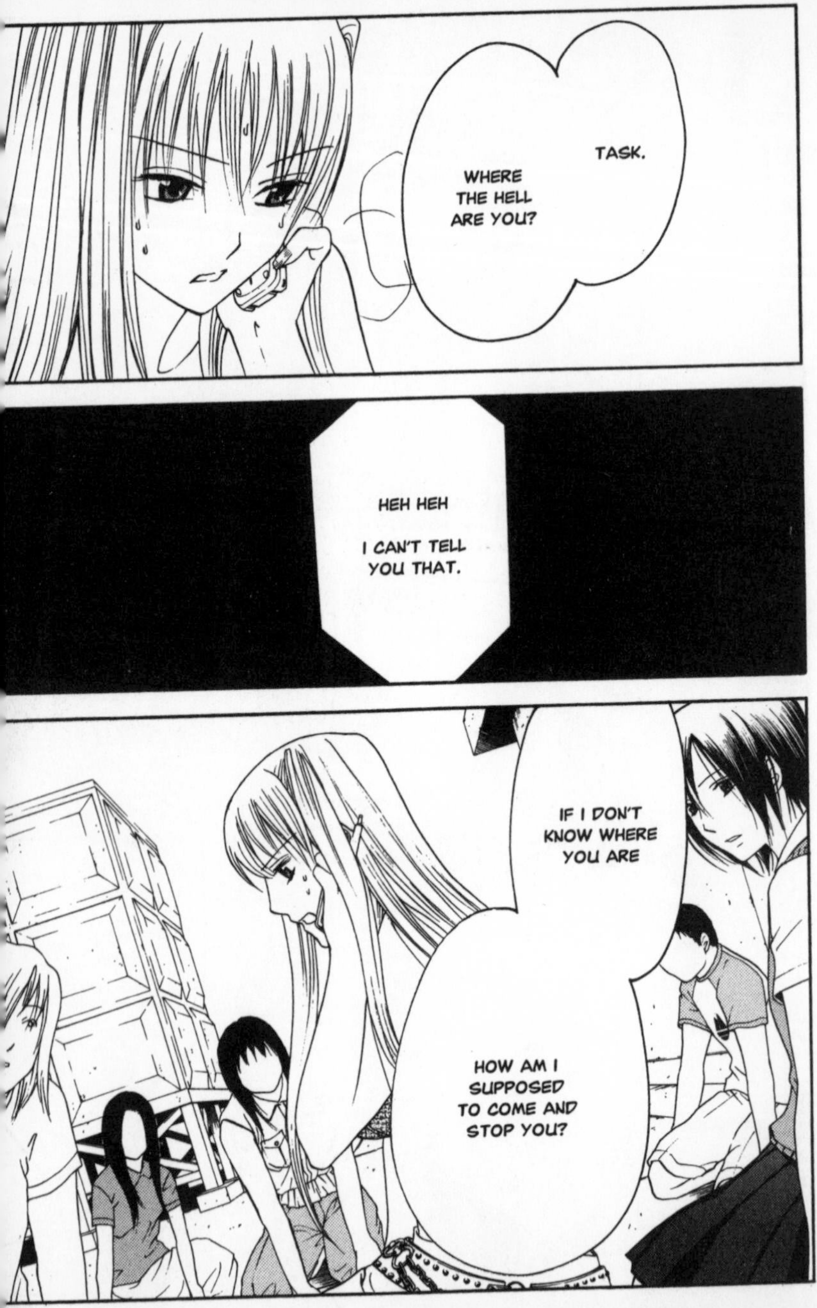
TASK.
WHERE THE HELL ARE YOU?
HEH HEH
I CAN'T TELL YOU THAT.
IF I DON'T KNOW WHERE YOU ARE
HOW AM I SUPPOSED TO COME AND STOP YOU?

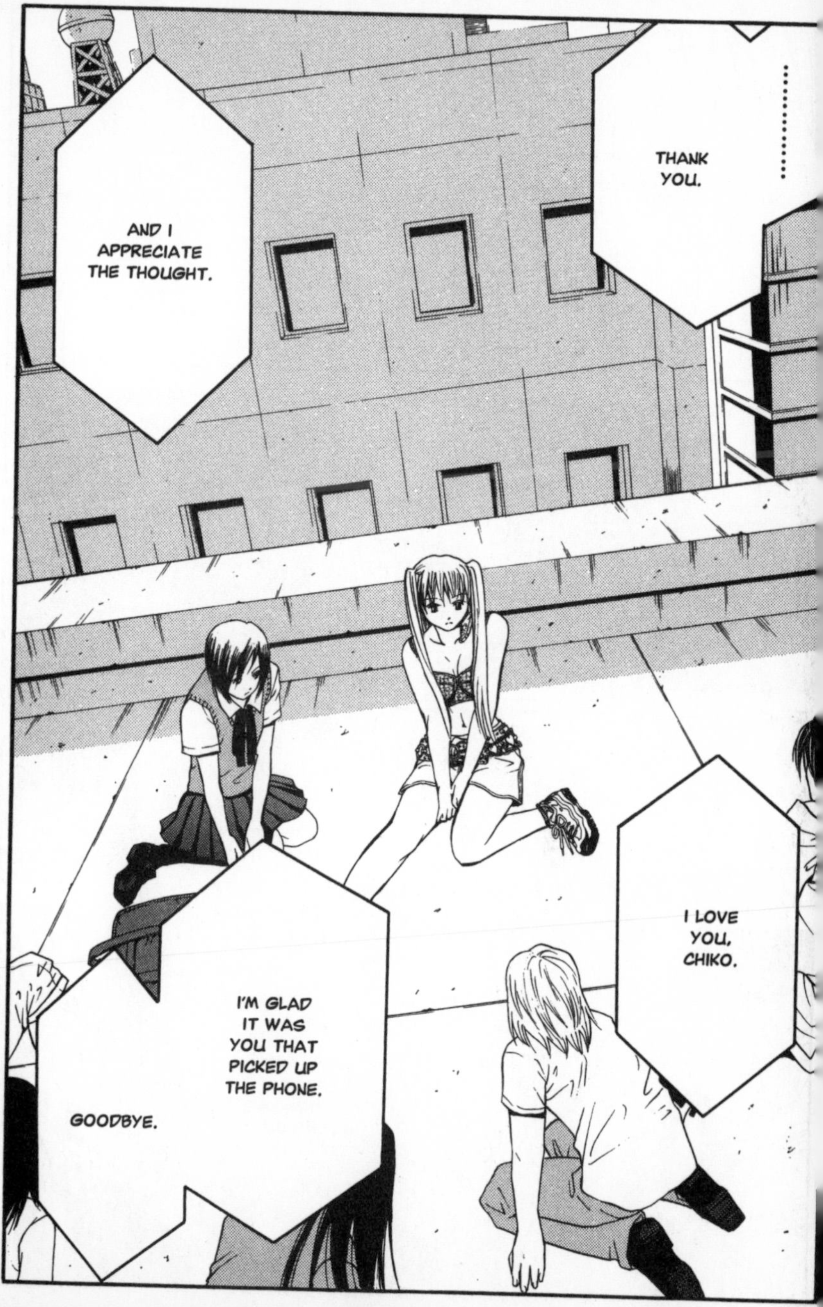
......
THANK YOU.
AND I APPRECIATE THE THOUGHT.
I LOVE YOU, CHIKO.
I'M GLAD IT WAS YOU THAT PICKED UP THE PHONE.
GOODBYE.

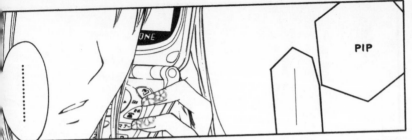

PIP

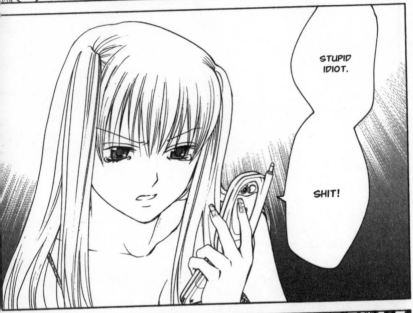

STUPID IDIOT.

SHIT!

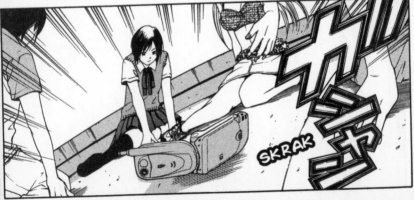

SKRAK

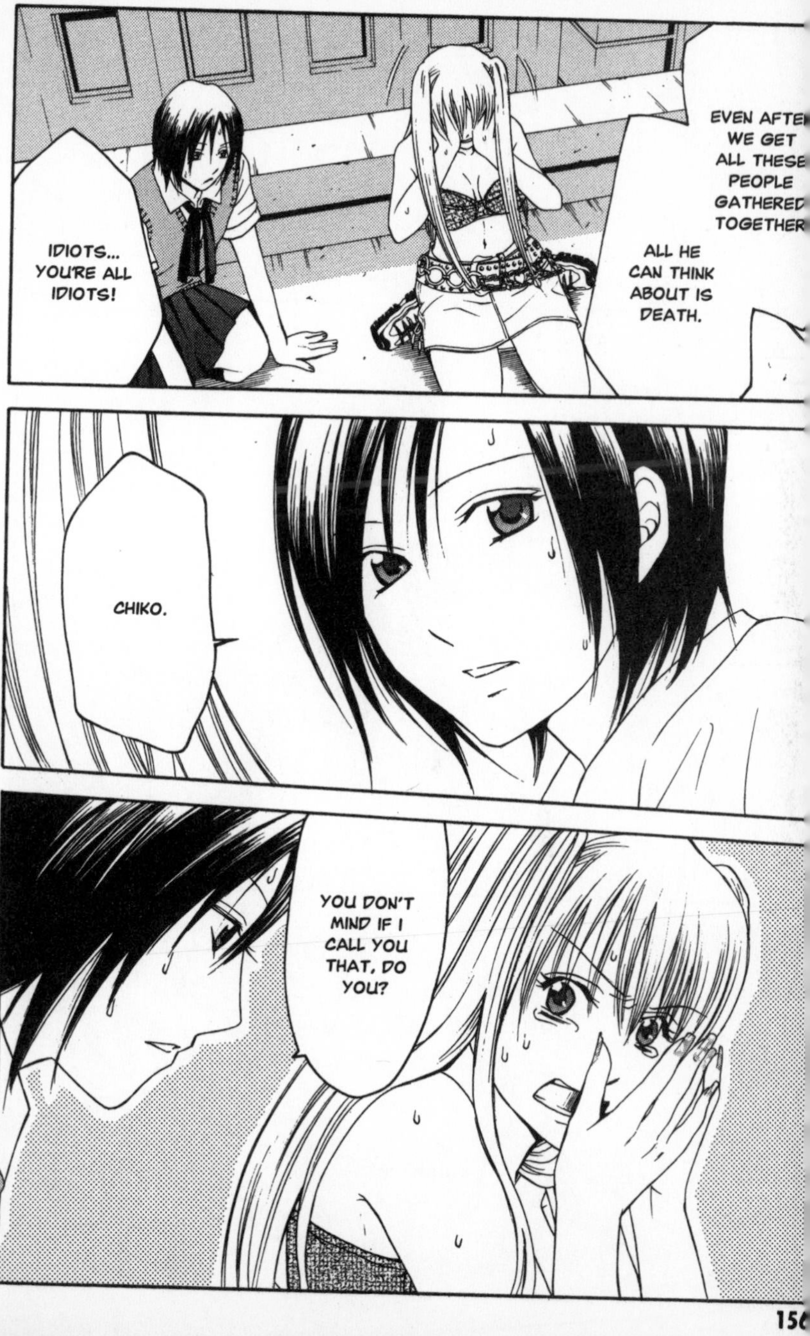
EVEN AFTE WE GET ALL THESE PEOPLE GATHERED TOGETHER
ALL HE CAN THINK ABOUT IS DEATH.
IDIOTS... YOU'RE ALL IDIOTS!
CHIKO.
YOU DON'T MIND IF I CALL YOU THAT, DO YOU?

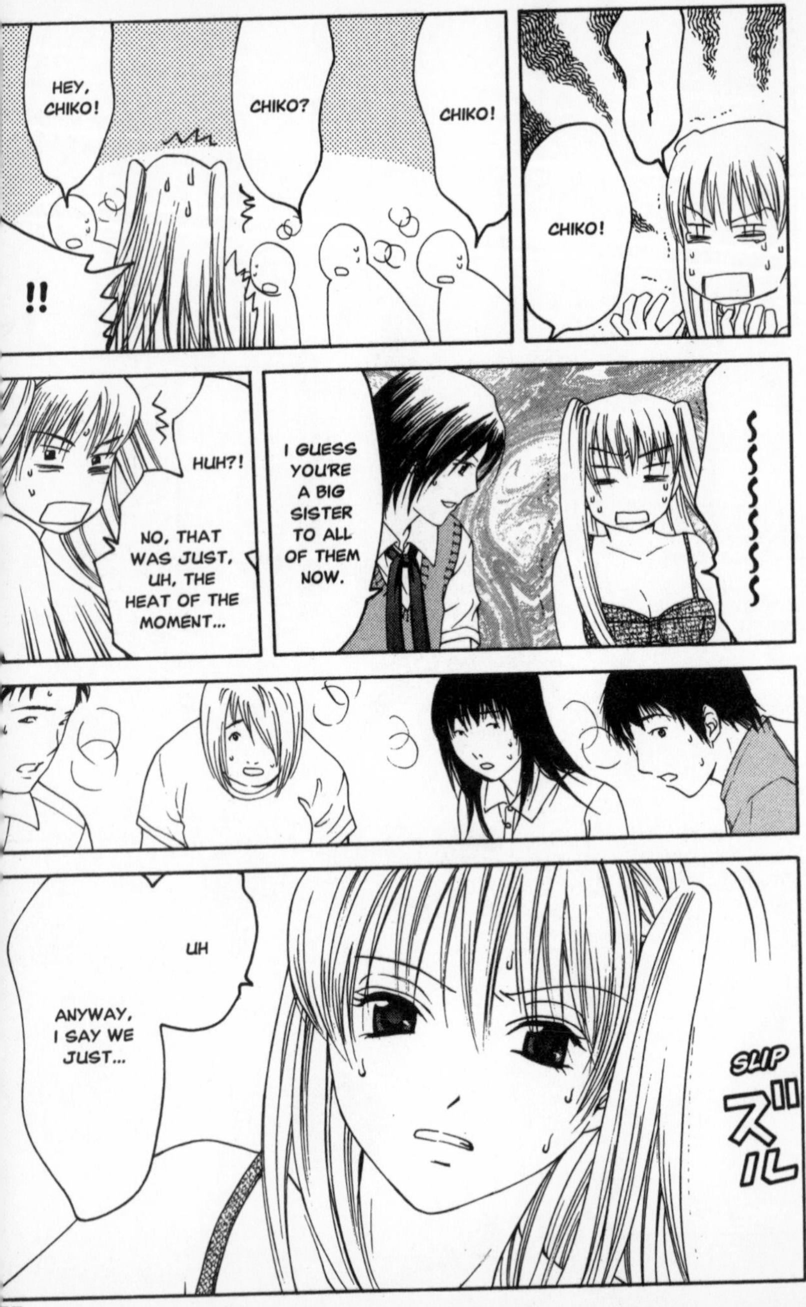
......
CHIKO!
CHIKO!
CHIKO?
HEY, CHIKO!
!!
I GUESS YOU'RE A BIG SISTER TO ALL OF THEM NOW.
HUH?!
NO, THAT WAS JUST, UH, THE HEAT OF THE MOMENT...
SLIP
ズル
UH
ANYWAY, I SAY WE JUST...

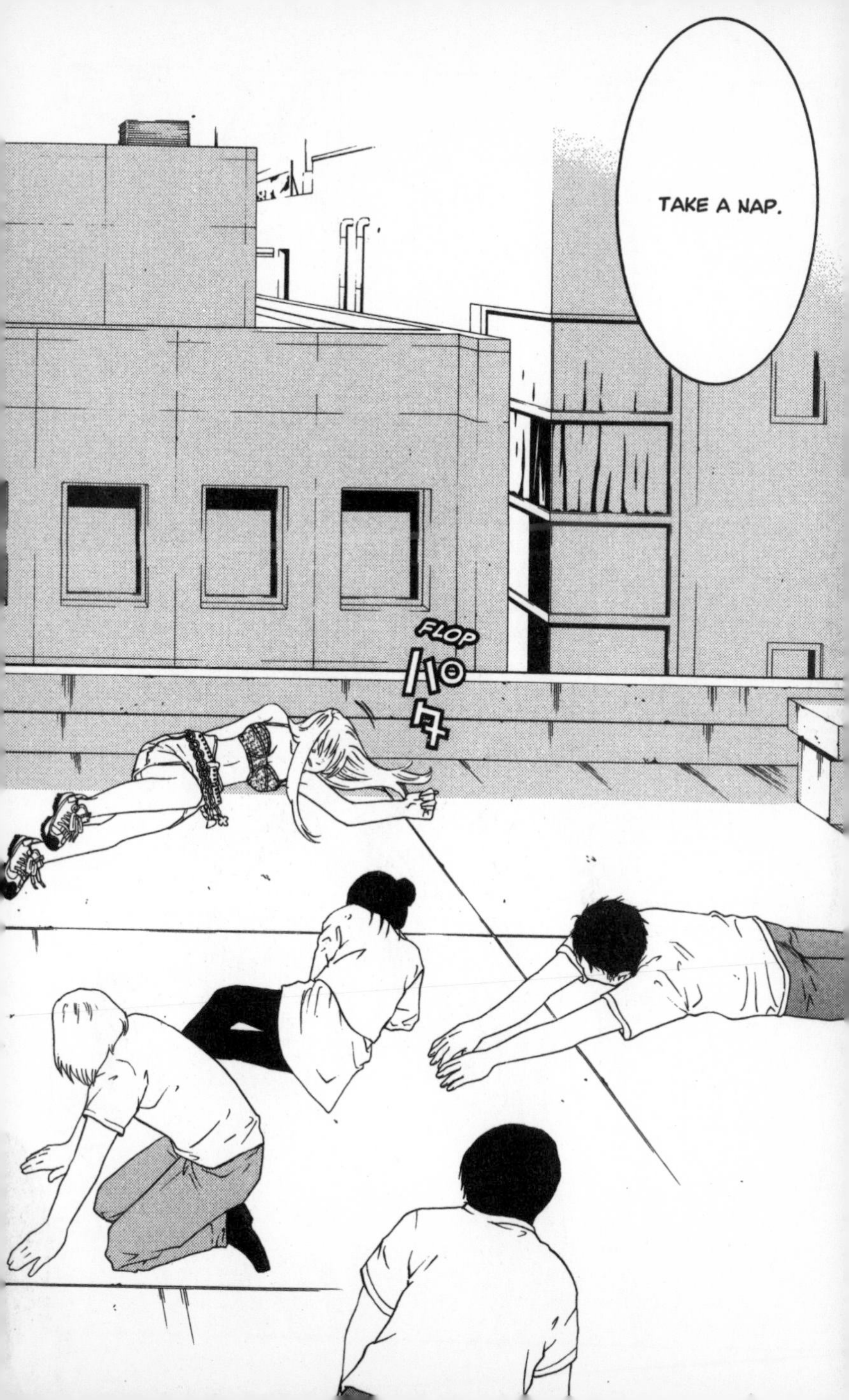
TAKE A NAP.
FLOP

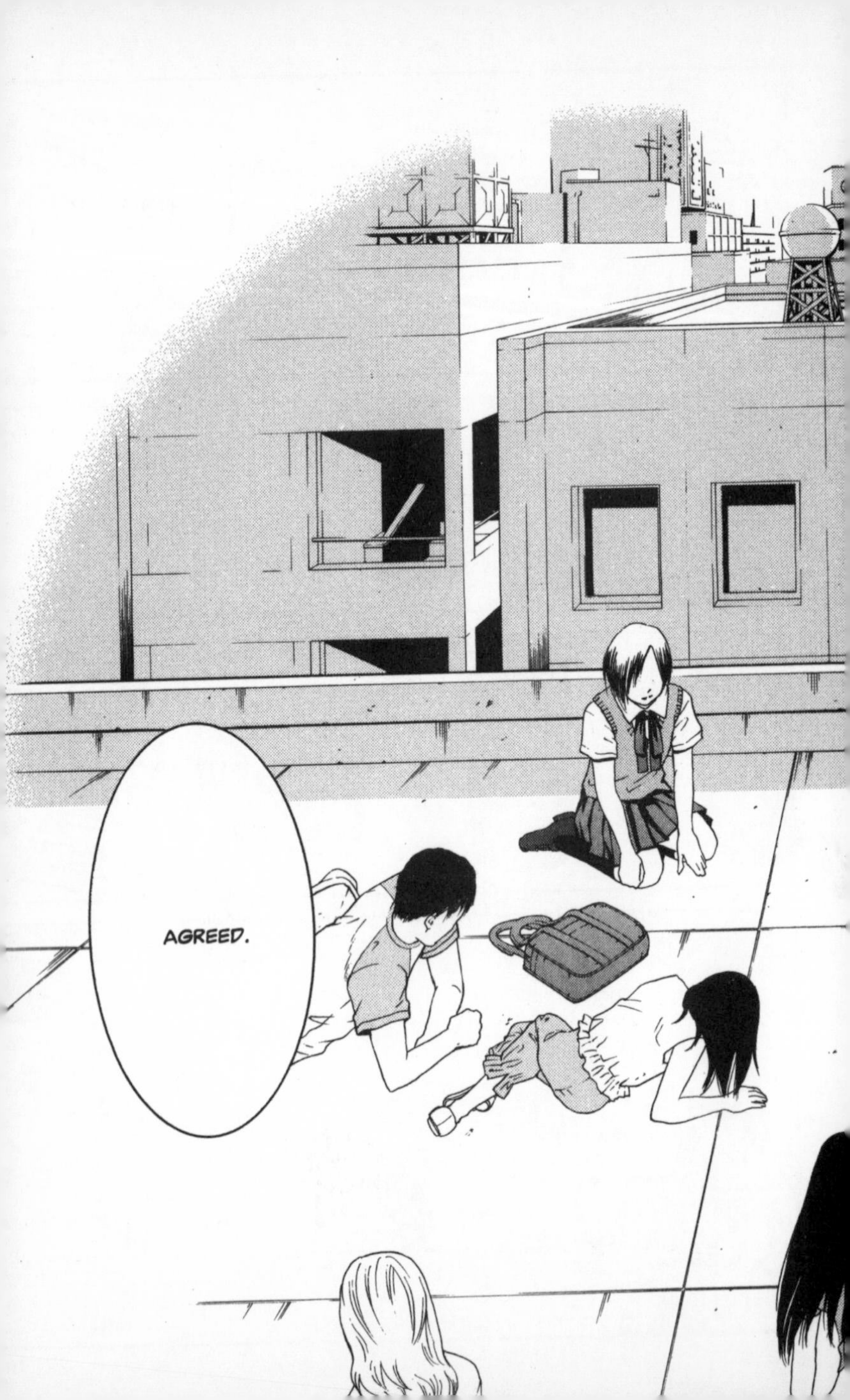
AGREED.

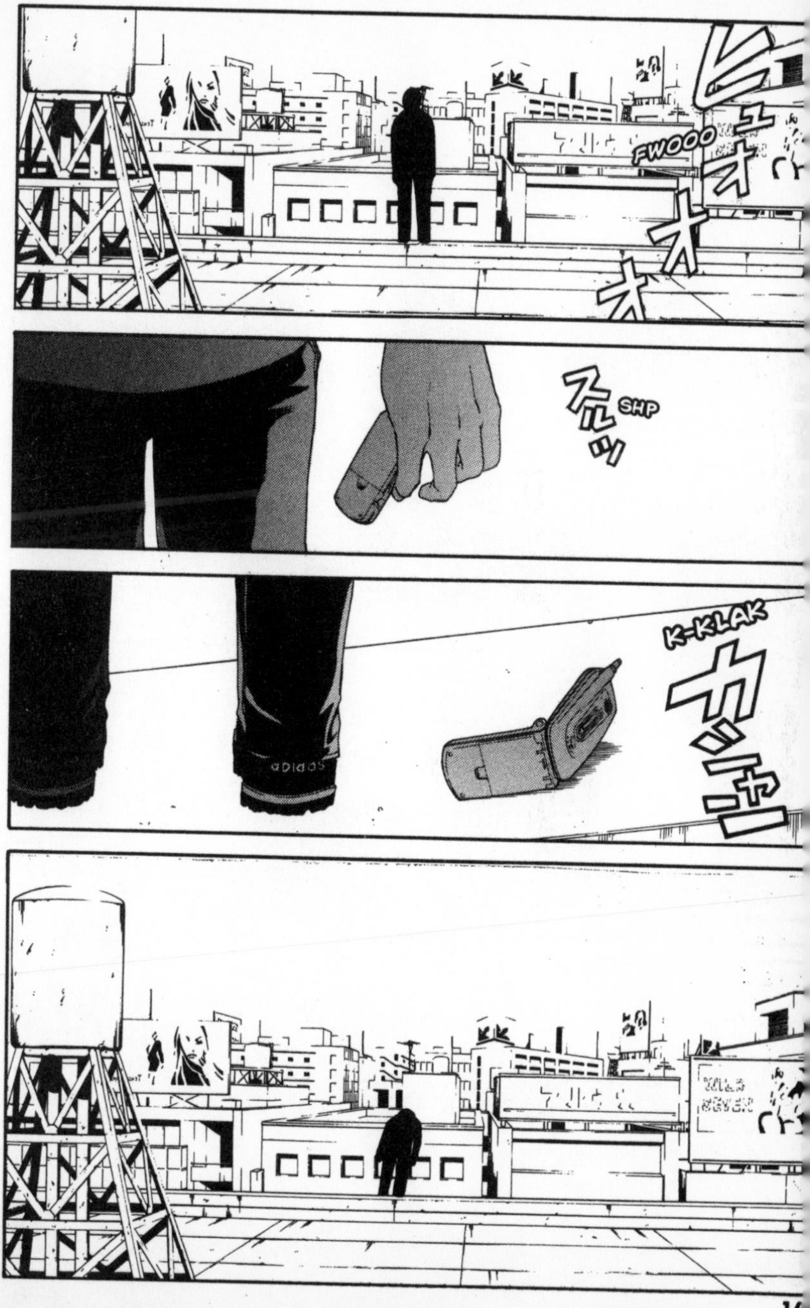
ヒュオオオ
FWOOO
スルッ
SHP
K-KLAK
カシャン

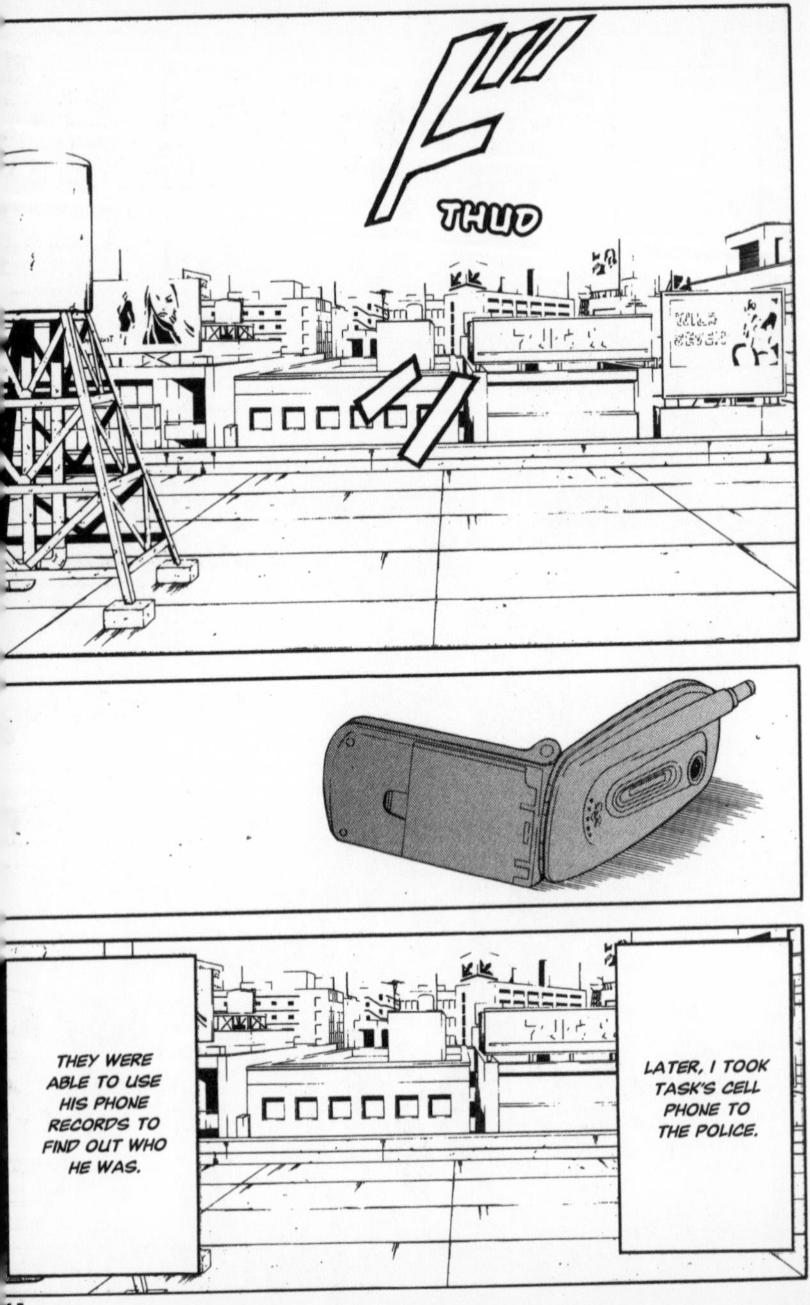
ド
THUD
LATER, I TOOK TASK'S CELL PHONE TO THE POLICE.
THEY WERE ABLE TO USE HIS PHONE RECORDS TO FIND OUT WHO HE WAS.

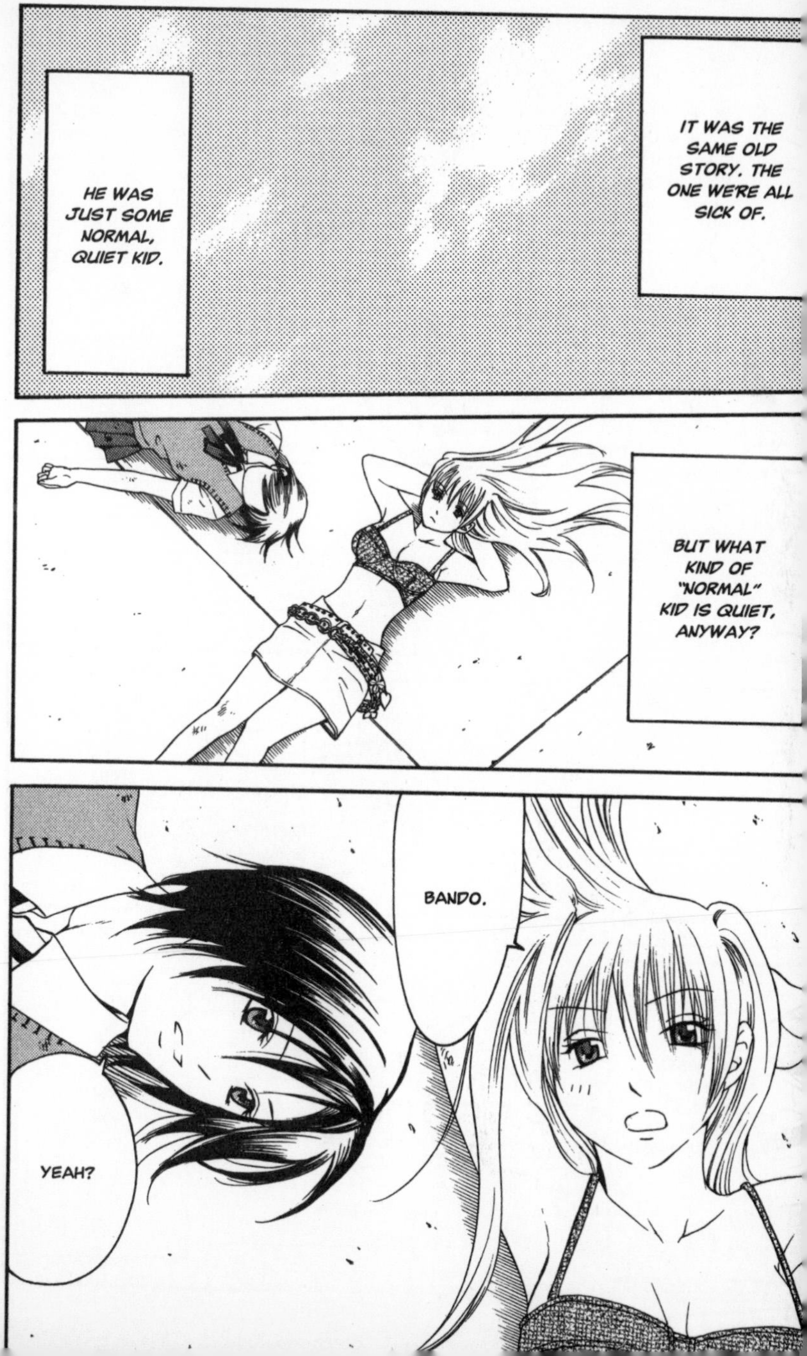
IT WAS THE SAME OLD STORY. THE ONE WE'RE ALL SICK OF.
HE WAS JUST SOME NORMAL, QUIET KID.
BUT WHAT KIND OF "NORMAL" KID IS QUIET, ANYWAY?
BANDO.
YEAH?

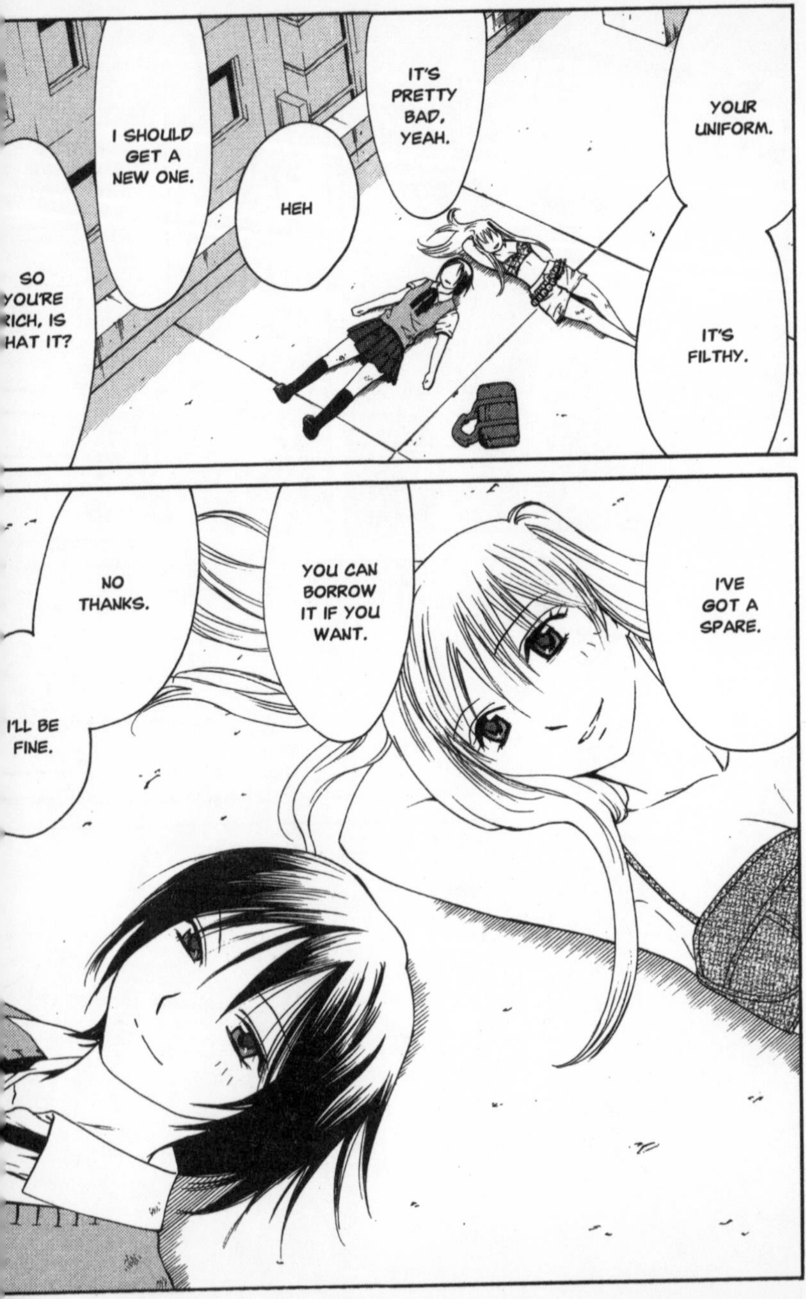
YOUR UNIFORM.
IT'S FILTHY.
IT'S PRETTY BAD, YEAH.
HEH
I SHOULD GET A NEW ONE.
SO YOU'RE RICH, IS HAT IT?
I'VE GOT A SPARE.
YOU CAN BORROW IT IF YOU WANT.
NO THANKS.
I'LL BE FINE.

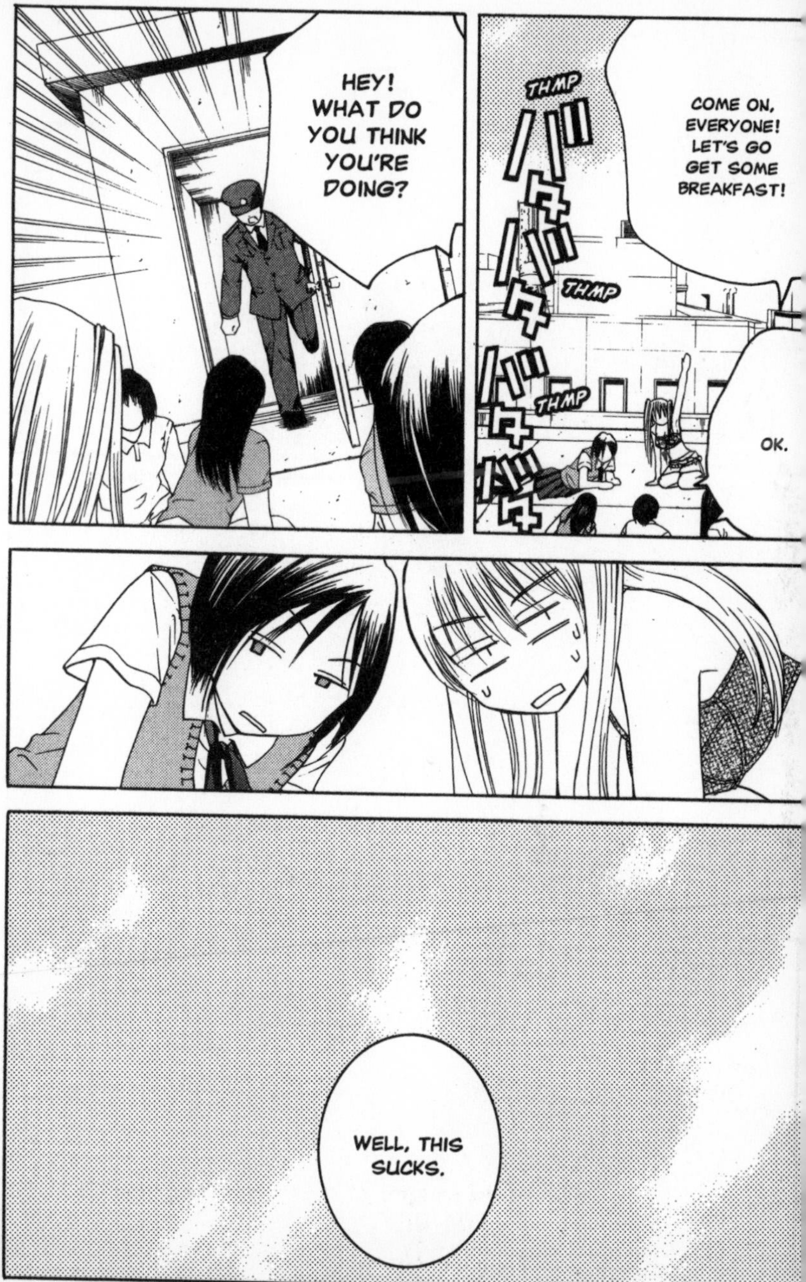
COME ON, EVERYONE! LET'S GO GET SOME BREAKFAST!
THMP
THMP
THMP
OK.
HEY! WHAT DO YOU THINK YOU'RE DOING?
WELL, THIS SUCKS.

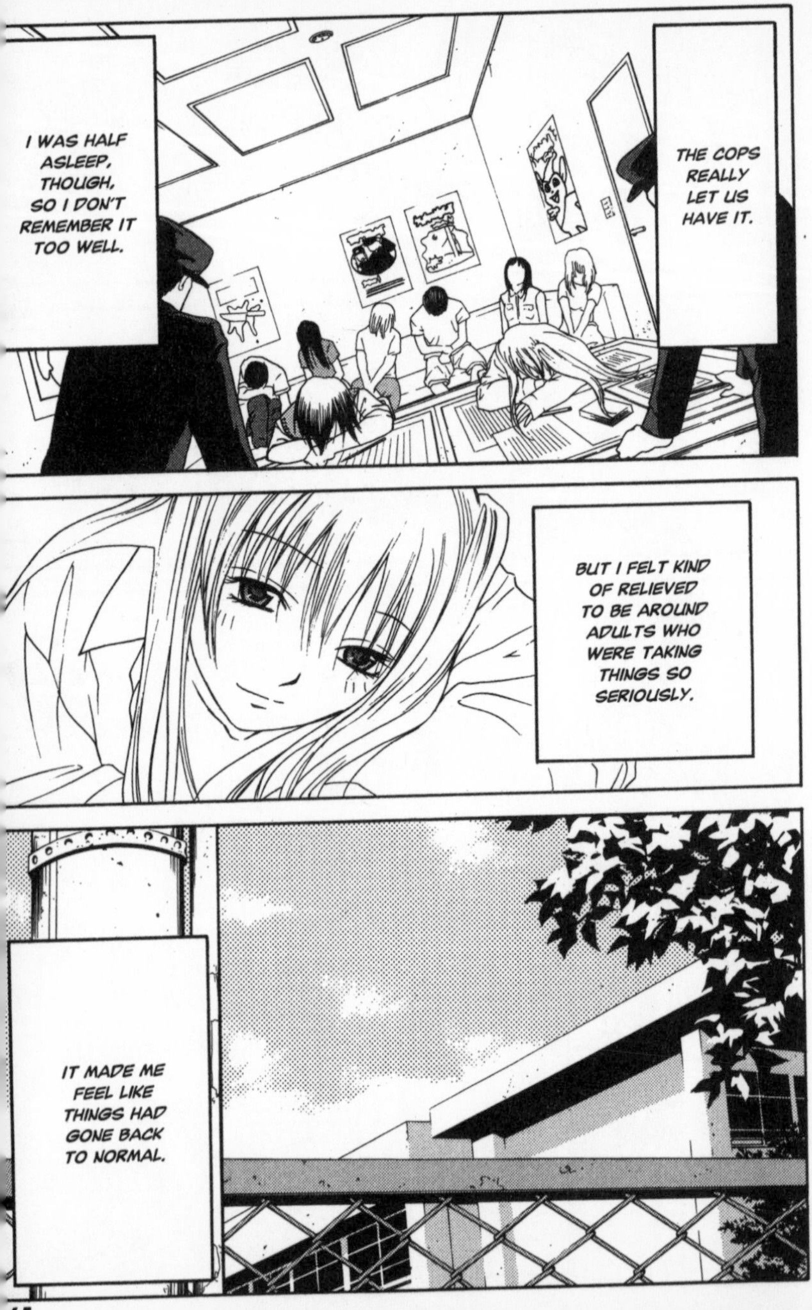
THE COPS REALLY LET US HAVE IT.
I WAS HALF ASLEEP, THOUGH, SO I DON'T REMEMBER IT TOO WELL.
BUT I FELT KIND OF RELIEVED TO BE AROUND ADULTS WHO WERE TAKING THINGS SO SERIOUSLY.
IT MADE ME FEEL LIKE THINGS HAD GONE BACK TO NORMAL.

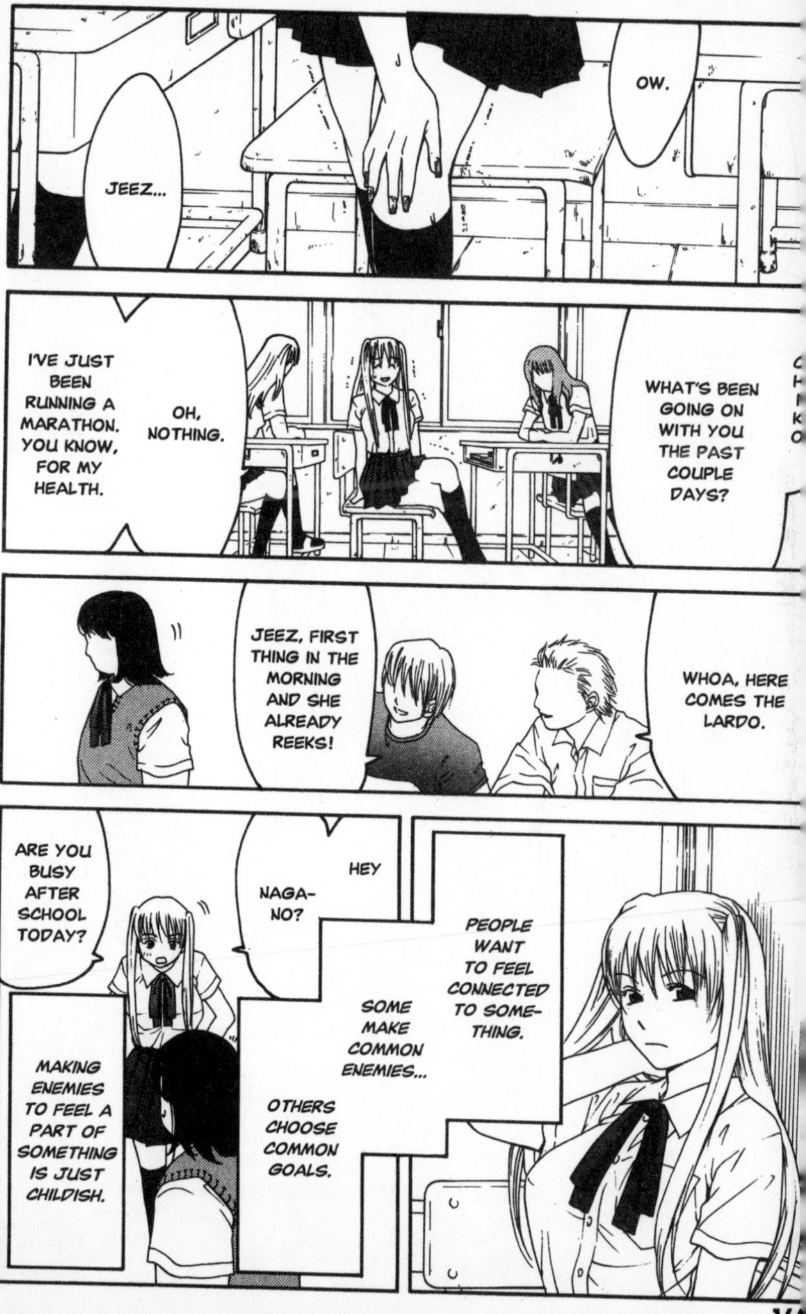
OW.
JEEZ...
WHAT'S BEEN GOING ON WITH YOU THE PAST COUPLE DAYS?
OH, NOTHING.
I'VE JUST BEEN RUNNING A MARATHON. YOU KNOW, FOR MY HEALTH.
WHOA, HERE COMES THE LARDO.
JEEZ, FIRST THING IN THE MORNING AND SHE ALREADY REEKS!
PEOPLE WANT TO FEEL CONNECTED TO SOME-THING.
SOME MAKE COMMON ENEMIES...
OTHERS CHOOSE COMMON GOALS.
HEY NAGA-NO?
ARE YOU BUSY AFTER SCHOOL TODAY?
MAKING ENEMIES TO FEEL A PART OF SOMETHING IS JUST CHILDISH.

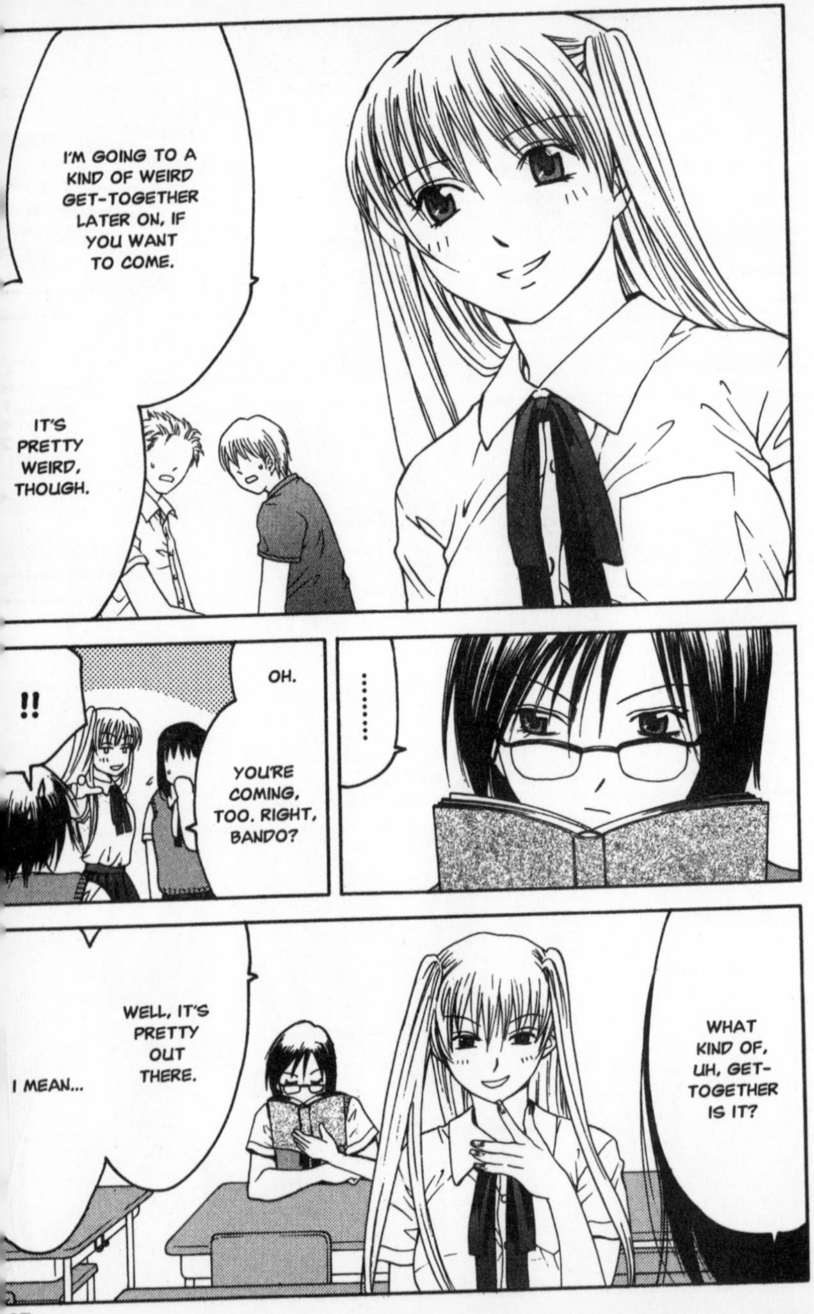

I'M GOING TO A KIND OF WEIRD GET-TOGETHER LATER ON, IF YOU WANT TO COME.
IT'S PRETTY WEIRD, THOUGH.
....
OH.
YOU'RE COMING, TOO. RIGHT, BANDO?
!!
WHAT KIND OF, UH, GET-TOGETHER IS IT?
WELL, IT'S PRETTY OUT THERE.
I MEAN...

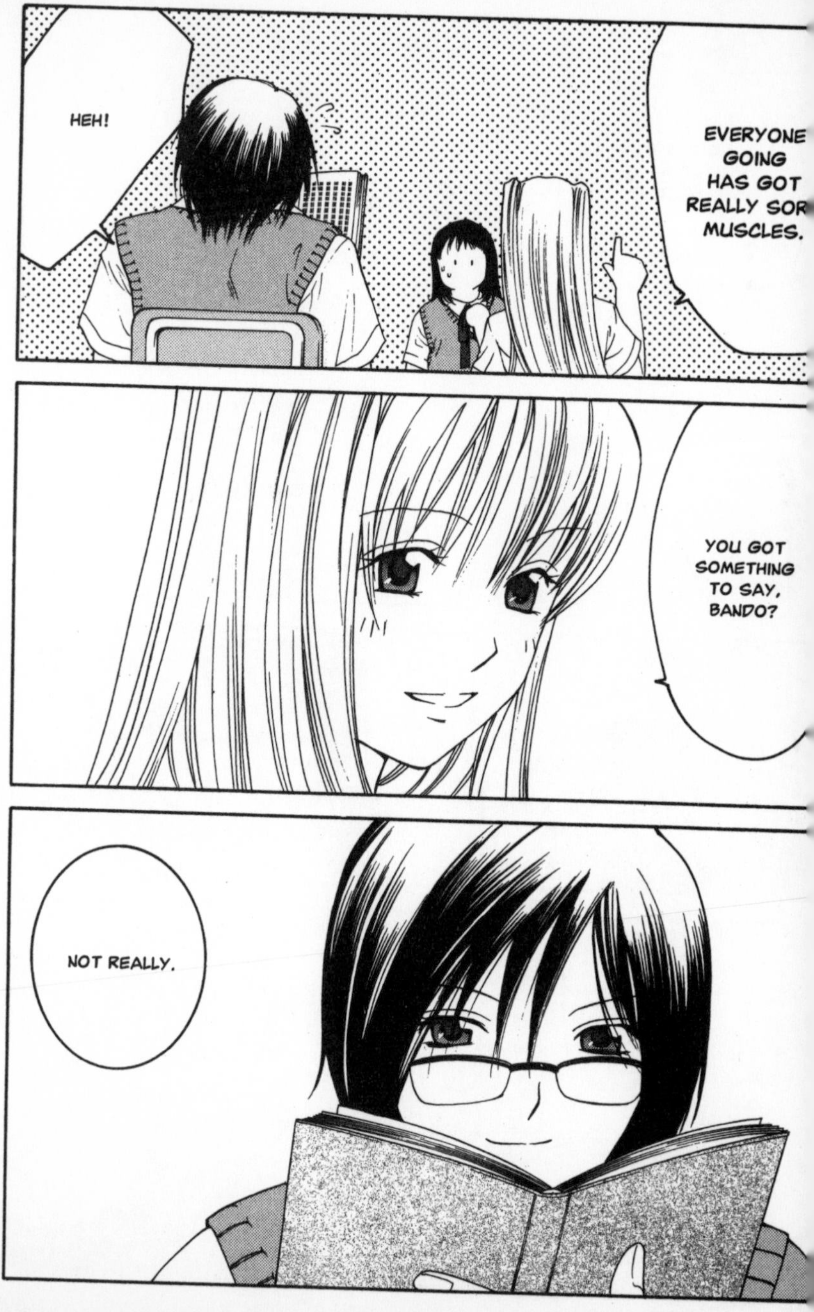
EVERYONE GOING HAS GOT REALLY SOR MUSCLES.
HEH!
YOU GOT SOMETHING TO SAY, BANDO?
NOT REALLY.

E N D

SPECIAL THANKS
Katsuki Soma
Ryo Yamane
Noriko Takahashi
Masashi Motegi
Kame ♡ Kiyo

LINE

© YUA KOTEGAWA 2003
Originally published in Japan in 2003 by
KADOKAWA SHOTEN PUBLISHING CO., LTD., Tokyo.
English translation rights arranged with
KADOKAWA SHOTEN PUBLISHING CO., LTD., Tokyo.

Editor **JAVIER LOPEZ**
Graphic Artist **SCOTT HOWARD**
Translator **KAORU BERTRAND**

Editorial Director **GARY STEINMAN**
Print Production Manager **BRIDGETT JANOTA**
Production Coordinator **MARISA KREITZ**

International Coordinators **TORU IWAKAMI & MIYUKI KAMIYA**

President, CEO & Publisher **JOHN LEDFORD**

Email: editor@adv-manga.com
www.adv-manga.com

www.advfilms.com

For sales and distribution inquiries please call 1.800.282.7202

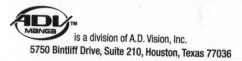

is a division of A.D. Vision, Inc.
5750 Bintliff Drive, Suite 210, Houston, Texas 77036

English text © 2006 published by A.D. Vision, Inc. under exclusive license.
ADV MANGA is a trademark of A.D. Vision, Inc.

ISBN: 1-4139-0249-9
First printing, October 2006
10 9 8 7 6 5 4 3 2 1
Printed in Canada

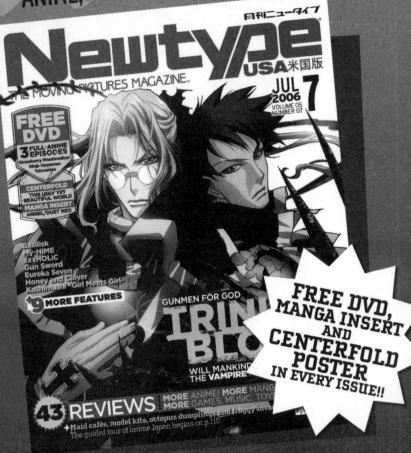

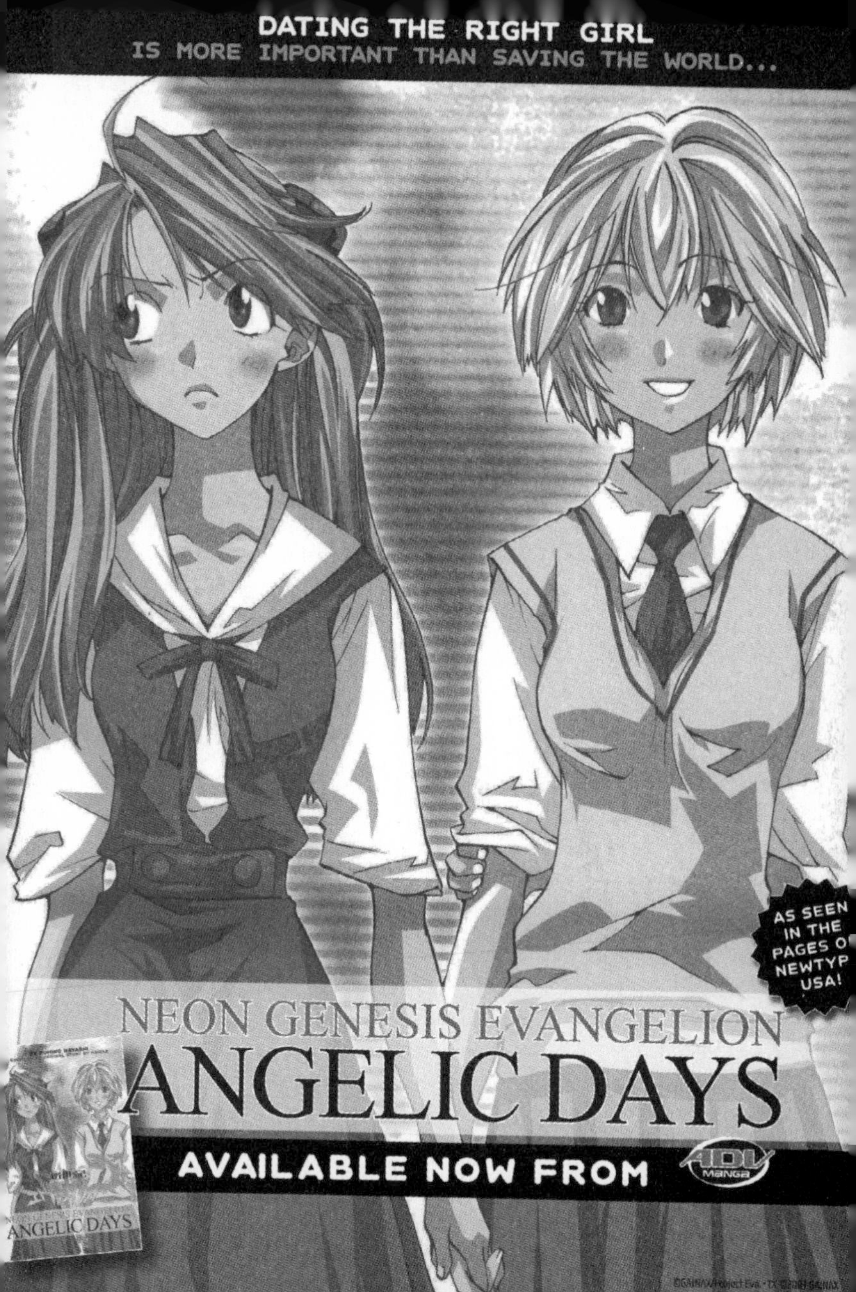
DATING THE RIGHT GIRL
IS MORE IMPORTANT THAN SAVING THE WORLD...
AS SEEN IN THE PAGES OF NEWTYPE USA!
NEON GENESIS EVANGELION
ANGELIC DAYS
AVAILABLE NOW FROM
ADV Manga

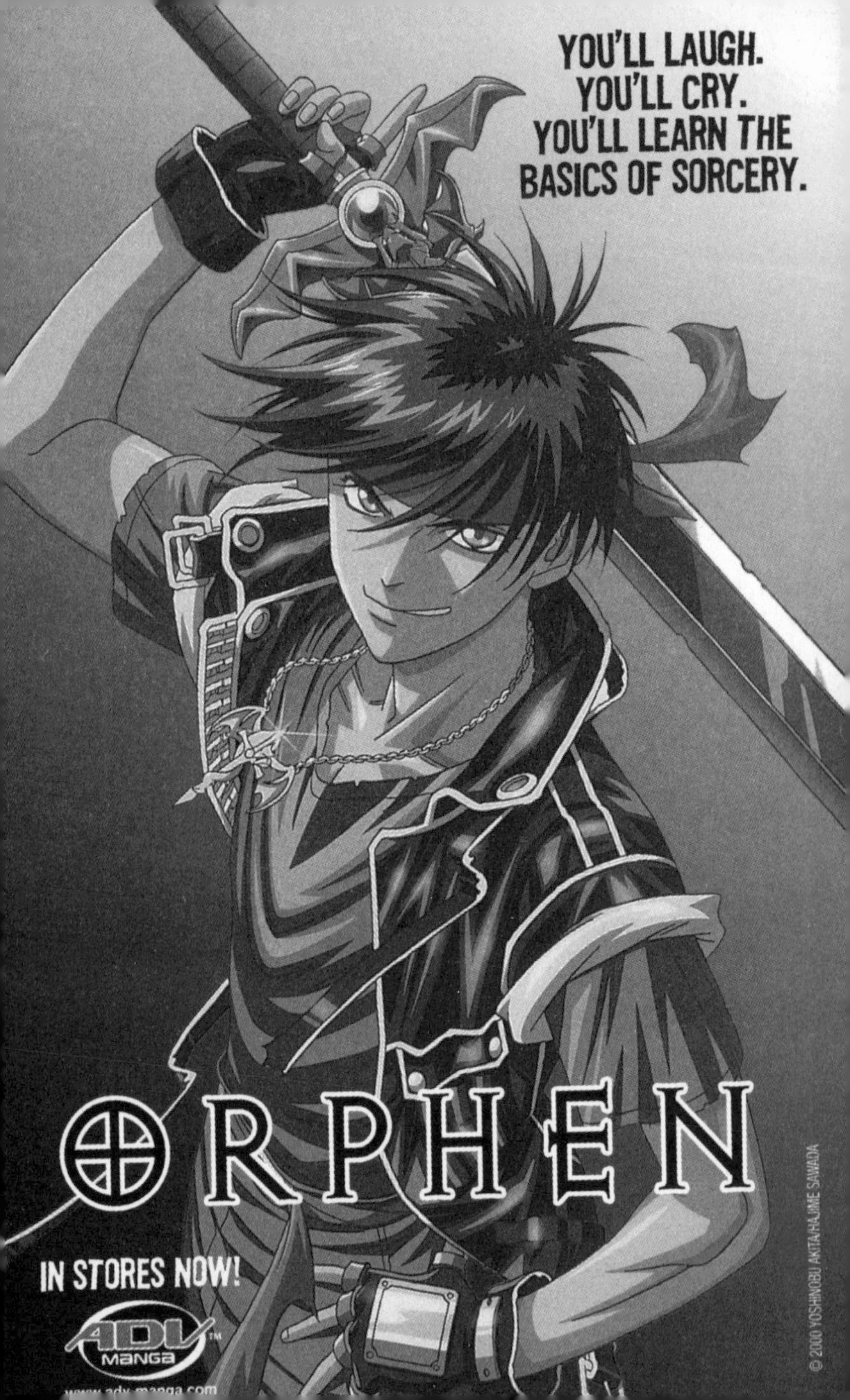
YOU'LL LAUGH.
YOU'LL CRY.
YOU'LL LEARN THE
BASICS OF SORCERY.
ORPHEN
IN STORES NOW!
ADV Manga
www.adv-manga.com
© 2000 YOSHINOBU AKITA/HAJIME SAWADA

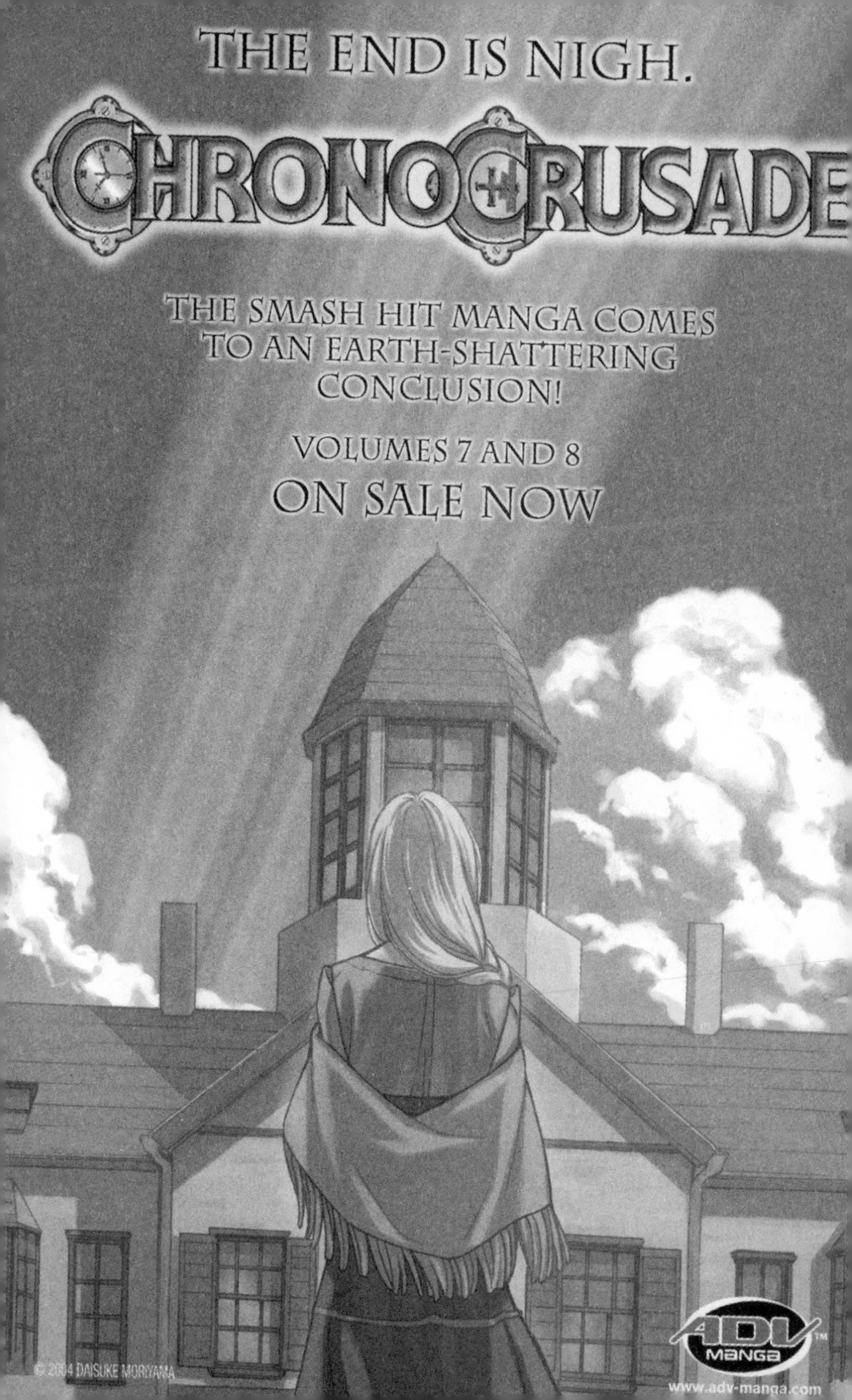
THE END IS NIGH.
CHRONO CRUSADE
THE SMASH HIT MANGA COMES TO AN EARTH-SHATTERING CONCLUSION!
VOLUMES 7 AND 8
ON SALE NOW
© 2004 DAISUKE MORIYAMA
ADV Manga
www.adv-manga.com

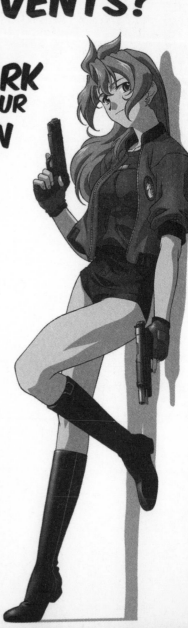

Three people united by
a terrifying secret.

Yuri, a young man who
killed his own mother.

Mitsuba, who will gladly
murder to avenge the
sister that was taken
from him.

Anna, the mysterious
assassin with a
chilling beauty.

Together, they'll
stop at nothing
to bring down
a terrorist
organization...

And along the
way, they'll come
closer to the
truth that binds
them together.

D0954299

www.adv-manga.com

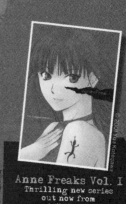

© 2001 Yua Kotegawa

Anne Freaks Vol. I
Thrilling new series
out now from
ADV Manga